Mary Ambrose Birdsall
Mother's Day, 1986
from Pat & Sunil Creegan

THE FIRST CHOUTEAUS

The First Chouteaus

RIVER BARONS
OF EARLY ST. LOUIS

William E. Foley and C. David Rice

UNIVERSITY OF ILLINOIS PRESS

URBANA AND CHICAGO

Library of Congress Cataloging in Publication Data

Foley, William E., 1938-
The first Chouteaus, river barons of early St. Louis.

Bibliography: p.
Includes index.
1. Saint Louis (Mo.)—Biography.   2. Chouteau
family.   3. Saint Louis (Mo.)—Commerce.   4. Fur trade
—West (U.S.)—History.   I. Rice, C. David (Charles
David), 1941———.   II. Title.
F474.S253A24   1983   977.8'66   83-1325
ISBN 0-252-01022-1

for Martha, Laura and David

and Judy and Maggie

CONTENTS

PREFACE

HEROES AND HEROINES abound in the annals of the American West, but few of the celebrities and mythic figures popularly associated with the region can match the Chouteaus of St. Louis in their contributions to westward expansion. Described variously as the "Royal Family of the Wilderness," the "First Citizens of Upper Louisiana," and the "Founding Family of St. Louis," this distinguished clan of merchant-capitalists assumed an active and vital role in opening the trans-Mississippi West. Its members pioneered in developing the western fur trade, in establishing commercial relations with key Missouri and Mississippi river Indian tribes, and in initiating a variety of business and financial enterprises west of the Mississippi. They also participated directly in the growth of St. Louis and Upper Louisiana as governmental advisers, officeholders, public benefactors, and social and cultural leaders.

Never far from the centers of power and authority, the Chouteaus, led by René Auguste and his half-brother Jean Pierre,[1] managed to retain substantial influence during an era which saw the Louisiana Territory pass from the control of France to Spain, momentarily back to France, and finally to the United States. When international developments beyond their control dictated sudden and unexpected changes, they displayed a remarkable facility for adaptation. Though linguistically and culturally Frenchmen, the first Chouteaus won the confidence and trust of Spanish colonial officials in the latter decades of the eighteenth century. Maturing in a political and economic order grounded in the Spanish traits of elitism and hierarchical authority, they flourished under a system which recognized and encouraged monopoly and inequality. Nonetheless, when the Louisiana Purchase threatened to erode their accustomed way of life, the Chouteau brothers quickly adjusted to the requirements of an alien culture, government, and language and enjoyed long and productive lives under the American regime. That genius for practical accommodation served them well on the rapidly changing frontier they inhabited and, as much as anything, contributed to their ultimate success.

1. Because of the confusion surrounding Auguste's birth (see Chap. 1 below), considerable doubt remains concerning his given name. Occasionally the records refer to him as René Auguste Chouteau, which was also his father's name, but he always used only Auguste. Likewise although Auguste's younger half-brother was christened Jean Pierre Chouteau, he seldom used his full name. Instead he normally chose to refer to himself only as Pierre Chouteau. Throughout this study, in conformity with those usages, the Chouteau brothers will be called Auguste and Pierre.

This study represents an attempt to provide a comprehensive account of Auguste and Pierre Chouteau, who, along with their mother, Marie Thérèse Bourgeois Chouteau, founded the family dynasty. To a remarkable degree the biographies of Auguste and Pierre provide a prospect of Upper Louisiana's early history. Among other things, their careers offer ample evidence of the relationship between the fur trade and the initial advance of white settlement west of the Mississippi. Beyond that, the diversity of the family's wide-ranging mercantile activities and the multinational character of its commercial transactions demonstrate the complexity of early frontier trading patterns and business practices. Moreover, by reaffirming the merchant-trader's crucial role, the Chouteau story reiterates the importance of entrepreneurial forces in the frontier process.

The first Chouteaus' careers also provide a special opportunity to gauge Indian-white relations under French, Spanish, and American regimes. As Howard Lamar has noted, the trader's world served as the focal point of Indian-white relations in North America between 1600 and 1850. Because successful traders had to function in both Indian and white society, they became the major link between the two worlds, and the Chouteau brothers epitomized that connection. A lifetime of close and intimate association with the Osages and other western tribes gave them a unique understanding of Indian cultures, which they capitalized upon in developing their highly profitable and successful trade with those tribes. Not surprisingly, government officials frequently called upon the Chouteaus to assist in handling Indian matters. Auguste's agreement to establish Fort Carondelet for the Spaniards in the 1790s and Pierre's appointment as the first U.S. Indian agent west of the Mississippi in 1804 are but two examples of their active roles in supervising day-to-day relations with Upper Louisiana's Indian inhabitants. Although their attitudes toward the Indians were paternalistic and their policies were shaped by self-interest, it seems doubtful that the respect and allegiance they consistently enjoyed among the Indians could have existed for so many years in the absence of genuine affection and goodwill.

Because of their intimate involvement in the growth and development of St. Louis from a tiny frontier trading post to a major metropolitan center, their careers also make it possible to assess the impact of the urban frontier. Not only were the Chouteaus active as business and community leaders, but their homes also served as social and cultural centers in Upper Louisiana. Whether they were hosting the Spanish inspector-general of Natchez, Manuel Gayoso de Lemos, the American explorers Meriwether Lewis and William Clark, or the renowned French "Hero of Two Worlds," the Marquis de Lafayette, the Chouteaus rarely failed to impress their guests with their lavish hospitality. Sure of the amenities and social graces of the times, the Chouteaus were as comfortable with the rich and powerful as they were with the French *coureurs de bois* or the Indian tribesmen whose lodges they sometimes shared. By combining a facility for dealing with people from differing social and cultural backgrounds with shrewd judgment, sound business practices, and a unique understanding of frontier mercantile operations, the Chouteau brothers earned for themselves personal fortunes as well as lasting places in the history of disparate societies experiencing a fateful rendezvous in the heartland of the North American wilderness at the turn of the nineteenth century.

Many individuals and organizations facilitated the research and writing of this study. We wish to acknowledge the National Endowment for the Humanities for a summer stipend, Central Missouri State University for a summer study leave, and the Central Missouri State University Graduate School for assisting with reproduction costs. We also appreciate the assistance provided by the directors and staffs of the various libraries, historical societies, and archives that we visited during the course of our research. We are especially indebted to the Missouri Historical Society, without whose valuable collections this study would not have been possible. Francis H. Stadler, the longtime archivist at that venerable institution, was particularly helpful, as were current director Raymond F. Pisney and staff members Anthony R. Crawford, Beverly D. Bishop, Gary N. Smith, and Marie L. Schmitz. Special thanks also go to Richard S. Brownlee, James W. Goodrich, and Mary K. Dains at the State Historical Society of Missouri, John Neal Hoover at the Lovejoy Library at Southern Illinois University at Edwardsville, Gary Beahan at the Missouri State Archives, Eula J. Kidd, circuit clerk of Jefferson County, Missouri, and the Ward Edwards Library staff at Central Missouri State University.

The late John Francis McDermott, dean of the Mississippi valley scholars and a Chouteau descendant himself, generously advised us at the outset of this project, and his unpublished research regarding the paternity of the younger Chouteau children enabled us to complete that important story. Mrs. Max Myer's translations of many of the documents in the Chouteau Collections made our task easier. We owe much to Donald Jackson for his perceptive comments, his wise counsel, and his thoughtful encouragement. A. P. Nasatir, who pioneered in the study of the Chouteaus over a half-century ago, also read a draft of the manuscript and provided helpful suggestions, as did Savoie Lottinville. Martha Ellenburg Foley and Perry McCandless offered welcome editorial advice. Any errors, of course, are the authors' alone. David Daniels, cartographer and member of the Central Missouri State University geography department, deserves special thanks for his assistance in producing the maps. Janis Russell typed the original manuscript with skill and patience, and Ruth Hirner generously assisted with the final revisions. Parts of Chapters 4, 5, 6, 7, and 8 appeared in different versions in the *Missouri Historical Review* 72 (July 1978), 365–87, and 77 (Jan. 1983), 131–46, the *Bulletin of the Missouri His-*

torical Society 34 (Apr. 1978), 131–39, and *Montana, the Magazine of Western History* 29 (Summer 1979), 2–15. Finally, to Martha, Laura, and David Foley and to Judy and Maggie Rice, who had to endure the long hours during which we secluded ourselves in our studies, goes the most special thank-you of all. The dedication is an inadequate expression of our love and gratitude.

WARRENSBURG, MO.   *William E. Foley*
SEPTEMBER, 1982   *C. David Rice*

THE FIRST CHOUTEAUS

A DYNASTY IS BORN

AUGUSTE CHOUTEAU stood atop a limestone bluff overlooking the Mississippi River a short distance below the Missouri junction in mid-February 1764. From his vantage point on the site of present-day St. Louis, he could observe the rapidly flowing Mississippi as it rushed downstream toward its inevitable rendezvous with the Gulf of Mexico. To the west, the grass- and tree-covered landscape stretched as far as the eye could see. Chouteau, who was no more than fourteen, probably did not realize it then, but his future was destined to be inextricably linked to that majestic river and its vast western hinterland. For the moment, however, he was a virtual stranger in the unfamiliar wilderness whose broad vistas he surveyed. Chouteau's stepfather and employer, Pierre de Laclède Liguest,[1] had sent him to this location to begin work on a settlement and trading headquarters for his New Orleans–based firm, Maxent, Laclède and Company.[2]

Despite his youth and inexperience, Chouteau quickly proved his worth in this untamed land. He helped Laclède found a new city, and in the years that followed, he and his younger half-brother, Pierre, established themselves as its leading citizens. For more than a half-century, the Chouteau brothers assumed active and vital roles as merchants, Indian traders, bankers, land speculators, governmental advisers, public officials, and community leaders. Not only did their family become one of the region's wealthiest and most powerful, but the Chouteau name came to be synonymous with much of the early history of the trans-Mississippi West.

Only the sketchiest details are available concerning Auguste Chouteau's life before he traveled to Upper Louisiana with Laclède in 1763. His father, René Auguste Chouteau, was a New Orleans inn- and tavern-keeper who had immigrated to the New World from his native France sometime prior to his marriage to Marie Thérèse Bourgeois on September 20, 1748. The son of a *notarie* or solicitor, René Chouteau had been born in the village of L'Hermenault in the western province of Poitou on September 2, 1723.[3] Marie Thérèse Bourgeois, who was nearly ten years René Chouteau's junior, had been born in New Orleans on January 14, 1733, the daughter of Nicolas Charles Bourgeois and Marie Joseph Tarare. Shortly before Marie Thérèse's sixth birthday, her father unexpectedly died and left his wife with three small children and another on the way. The next year Bourgeois's widow wed Nicolas Pierre Carco, at which time Marie Thérèse presumably joined her new stepfather's household, where in all likelihood she remained until her marriage to René Chouteau.[4]

If René Chouteau's last will and testament is to be believed, he and Marie Thérèse had two legitimate children—René and Auguste. Since the couple separated long before Pierre Chouteau's birth in 1758, Auguste's brother René remains an enigma. The extant records are strangely silent about him, as are all family accounts. In fact, aside from the will, which stated that both sons were living when it was prepared in 1776, there is not a single additional known reference to the boy or his subsequent fate.[5]

The confusion caused by the possibility that there were two sons makes it virtually impossible to determine Auguste's precise birthdate. The baptismal register in St. Louis Cathedral in New Orleans contains only one entry for a Chouteau child born during the years that René Chouteau and Marie Thérèse Bourgeois lived together as husband and wife. According to the parish records, both parents were present on September 9, 1749, when the priest baptized their two-day-old infant René.[6] After discovering that information, members of later Chouteau generations in St. Louis assumed that René Chouteau was in fact Auguste, since as an adult, Auguste, like his father, was sometimes called René Auguste. The September 7, 1749, date they accepted for Auguste's birth was at variance with the September 26, 1750, date engraved on his original tombstone in St. Louis's Calvary Cemetery, but it did conform with statements published in St. Louis newspapers giving Auguste's age as eighty at the time of his death in February 1829. Barring the discovery of new documents, Auguste's exact date of birth seems destined to remain a matter of conjecture, as does the issue of a second Chouteau child named René.[7]

Within a few years after Auguste's birth, whatever the date, René Chouteau, Sr., abandoned his wife and young son and returned to France. His reasons for leaving and the date of his departure remain a mystery. Court documents in the New Orleans cabildo place him in that city in 1752, but after that his name is conspicuously missing from all public and private provincial records until 1767.[8] René Chouteau was not mentioned in the 1763 Louisiana census, but the New Orleans enumeration for that year did include a woman identified as *Veuve* or Widow Chouteau. Inasmuch as Marie Thérèse Bourgeois Chouteau was not listed elsewhere, and the number, ages, and sexes of her children matched those given for Widow Chouteau, it seems likely that she was calling herself *veuve*—one further sign that René Chouteau was missing and not expected to return.[9]

Four years after the 1763 census René Chouteau resurfaced almost as suddenly as he had vanished. On July 29, 1767, he was listed as a passenger departing from La Rochelle, France, on board the *Parthosa,* a ship destined for

Louisiana.[10] By the time Chouteau arrived back in New Orleans, his wife had moved upriver to St. Louis, where she had made a new life for herself with Pierre de Laclède Liguest. From every indication, Chouteau had left Marie Thérèse and Auguste to fend for themselves in New Orleans as best they could. Demonstrating the same fortitude and resourcefulness that in later years made her a respected businesswoman and esteemed member of the St. Louis community, Madame Chouteau somehow managed to provide for herself and her young son even though at the time René Chouteau deserted them she was barely out of her teens. Within a few years of her husband's departure she met Laclède. Born in Bedous in the French Pyrenees on November 22, 1729, Laclède came from a prominent family whose members had achieved recognition in their native province as attorneys, officeholders, and scholars. The dashing young Frenchman arrived in New Orleans in 1755 and quickly established himself as a successful wholesaler who regularly dealt with many of the city's leading businessmen. Like so many younger sons of successful European families, Laclède had taken his part of the family inheritance and come to North America with plans for building his own fortune. By all accounts he was capable and well educated. When contrasted with her churlish, truant husband, it is little wonder that the polished and self-assured Laclède favorably impressed Marie Thérèse Bourgeois Chouteau.[11]

Under the circumstances, the ambitious French merchant and the determined young mother became close friends who in the words of early St. Louis historian Frederic Billon formed "a mutual attachment . . . they chose to consider their legal union."[12] Although the arrangement was contrary to the teachings of the Roman Catholic Church, Laclède and Madame Chouteau remained together until the death of the former in 1778, notwithstanding René Chouteau's attempts to assert his marital rights following his return to Louisiana. The Laclède-Chouteau union produced four children: Jean Pierre, born on October 10, 1758, Marie Pelagie, born on October 6, 1760, Marie Louise, born on December 4, 1762, and Victoire, born on March 3, 1764.[13] The children were all born in New Orleans, and since neither French statutes nor church law sanctioned divorce and remarriage, the circumstances dictated that Marie Thérèse retain the name Chouteau. Likewise, each of her four children by Laclède was christened Chouteau, and the absent René Chouteau's name was entered in the church baptismal register as their legitimate father.[14]

Along with looking after his own children, Laclède also assumed a personal interest in his stepson Auguste. Almost certainly the well-educated Frenchman served as the lad's principal mentor. Although nothing is known about young Chouteau's schooling, it seems obvious that by the time he left New Orleans in 1763 he had acquired a solid educational foundation and a healthy respect for learning. He already had demonstrated sufficient promise for Laclède to employ him as his clerk—a decision neither ever had cause to regret. From every indication, even at his young age Chouteau thrived among the account books and ledgers at his stepfather's place of business, where he took full advantage of the opportunities afforded him. Auguste's early introduction to the commercial world provided him with valuable experience and important connections that helped facilitate his subsequent rise within the Mississippi valley mercantile community, and in the meantime Laclède had gained an able and trusted employee.[15]

Laclède was well qualified to instruct his youthful charge about the vagaries of the New World marketplace. He had arrived in New Orleans in 1755 not long after the outbreak of the French and Indian War in North America. Conditions worsened the next year when that conflict spread to Europe, but despite the vicissitudes of a wartime economy the enterprising Frenchman pressed ahead with his merchandising operations. The ensuing struggle between Britain and France took a heavy toll on all forms of commercial activity in Louisiana, as wartime conditions produced rampant inflation, an unstable monetary system, and chronic shortages of goods.[16] Conducting business under such adverse circumstances was a trying ordeal for even the most skilled merchants, and like many others Laclède probably sustained heavy losses,[17] but new opportunities in the fur trade afforded him a welcome chance to recover financially.

Hoping to lift Louisiana's sagging economy from the doldrums, Jean Jacques D'Abbadie, the province's newly appointed governor, introduced changes in economic policy immediately following his arrival in New Orleans in June 1763.[18] As a part of his program to stimulate the languishing fur trade and to improve relations with the Indians in Upper Louisiana, he granted Gilbert Antoine Maxent, a prominent and successful merchant in the seaport town, exclusive trading rights for six years with tribes along the Missouri and the west bank of the upper Mississippi.[19]

D'Abbadie's decision to abandon free trade in favor of a monopoly system for the fur trade was not popular with most members of the New Orleans mercantile community. Twenty-two merchants in that town signed a petition charging the governor with violating the king's free-trade policy, but Laclède was not one of them and for good reason.[20] He had agreed to establish and supervise a trading post in Upper Louisiana in partnership with Maxent and Jean François Le Dée.[21]

The new partners hastily organized a trading expedition, which set out from New Orleans under Laclède's command in August 1763.[22] Auguste Chouteau joined his stepfather for the trip up the Mississippi, but for the time being his mother remained with her younger children in New Orleans, where the following March she gave birth to Victoire, her fourth child by Laclède.[23] For Laclède and young Chouteau the 700-mile journey to the Illinois country must at times have seemed endless as day after day the rugged boatmen struggled to propel the merchandise-laden barges upstream against the strong Mississippi currents. Although the crewmen hoisted the sails on their cumbersome river crafts to take advantage of favorable winds whenever possible, the average speed for such trips remained no more than ten to twelve miles per day.

On November 3, after nearly three months on the river, the expedition arrived in Ste. Genevieve, a small French village on the stream's west bank. When Laclède failed to find a building in Ste. Genevieve large enough to house the supplies and equipment he had brought with him, he readily accepted an offer from the commandant of nearby Fort Chartres to store his merchandise there until a better place could be located.[24]

Once his goods were safely under cover, Laclède established a temporary trading camp in the adjacent village of St. Anne de Fort Chartres. As news of the French trader's presence reached nearby Indian tribes, their delegations began arriving with furs, which they offered to exchange for his merchandise. Encouraged by their eagerness to trade, Laclède set out in early December to look for a more accessible spot for a permanent company headquarters. He confined his search to the region west of the Mississippi, because shortly before he left New Orleans officials there had informed him that France had agreed to cede all of its territory east of the river to Great Britain. According to Chouteau, who accompanied his stepfather on the reconnaissance mission, Laclède examined all the lands along the western bank between Fort Chartres and the mouth of the Missouri before finally selecting the St. Louis site.[25]

The location seemed ideal. Its elevation afforded natural protection against the dangers of flooding, yet it also offered easy access to the Mississippi, Missouri, and Illinois rivers. After choosing the place for his headquarters, Laclède returned to Fort Chartres boasting that this new settlement might hereafter become "one of the finest cities in America."[26]

As soon as the late winter thaws made it possible to navigate the Mississippi, he dispatched Chouteau and a party of thirty laborers to begin work on the new settlement. On February 14 they reached the site Laclède had designated, and the next day, under Chouteau's direction, the workers began clearing the land. By the time Laclède arrived on the scene in early April to inspect the project, Chouteau's crews had already constructed a storage shed and several cabins.[27] During his visit Laclède directed that the town be laid out in a grid-iron pattern similar to the one in New Orleans. His plan called for three streets paralleling the Mississippi, intersected by shorter cross streets, and for a public plaza along the waterfront.[28] After unveiling the city's design, the enterprising Frenchman announced that to honor his nation's reigning monarch Louis XV, he intended to call the settlement St. Louis after the king's patron saint, Louis IX.[29]

With the new city now beginning to take shape, Laclède departed for Fort Chartres in order to finalize arrangements for transferring his goods and supplies to St. Louis. He knew that the British might arrive at any time to take possession of the French settlements east of the Mississippi. Pierre Joseph Ne-yon de Villiers, the French commandant at Fort Chartres, had already begun making preparations for evacuating the region. Captain Louis St. Ange de Bellerive, the commanding officer at Post Vincennes on the Wabash River, brought his forces to Fort Chartres in June 1764, and shortly thereafter Captain de Villiers departed for New Orleans with all but forty of the French troops stationed in the Illinois country. Before leaving, de Villiers placed St. Ange in charge of the small remaining garrison and directed him to oversee operations at Fort Chartres until British officers arrived on the scene.[30]

The prospect of British rule on the eastern bank triggered a mass exodus of the predominantly French-speaking inhabitants. Some accompanied de Villiers to New Orleans, but others accepted Laclède's invitation and moved across the river to his new settlement. When they began arriving in St. Louis during the summer of 1764, the youthful and energetic Chouteau extended every effort to make them welcome.[31]

Chouteau was considerably less cordial to the 150 Missouri Indian warriors who descended upon St. Louis with their families and announced their intention to take up residence nearby. The visiting Indians did not exhibit any signs of hostility, but their sudden appearance threatened to untrack Laclède's well-laid plans. Finding themselves outnumbered, some of the village's uneasy white settlers hastily retreated across the Mississippi to the safety of their former homes. Auguste immediately sent to Fort Chartres for Laclède, who came to St. Louis and met in council with the Missouri tribal leaders.[32] After observing the way his stepfather adroitly combined threats of force with promises of gifts in persuading the tribesmen to withdraw to their former villages, the young apprentice undoubtedly made a quick mental note of the technique for future use in Indian negotiations. The Indians' departure had the desired effect. Tensions in St. Louis rapidly subsided, and the panicky residents who had temporarily fled to Cahokia began coming back.

Although Chouteau had looked to his more experienced mentor for guidance, he had remained calm under obviously trying circumstances. While awaiting Laclède's arrival, the lad was sufficiently in control of the situation to take advantage of the Indians' otherwise unwelcome presence to accelerate the pace of construction on the trading headquarters Laclède had directed him to build. In exchange for small amounts of verdigris, vermilion, and a few awls, Chouteau hired the Missouri women and children to dig a cellar for the building. Under his watchful eye, they scooped away the earth and carried it off in baskets and wooden platters borne on their heads.[33]

When the Indian laborers completed the excavation, Chouteau put his men to work laying stones for the impressive new trading edifice, located on Main Street between Market and Walnut.[34] The building was ready for occupancy in September, when Auguste's mother reached St. Louis with her younger children. Her unimpeded departure from New Orleans the previous June provides yet another indication that René Chouteau was not in Louisiana at the time, for had he applied to the authorities he could easily have prevented her from leaving to join Laclède. Following their arrival in the Illinois country, she and the children probably stayed for a short time at Laclède's residence at Ste. Anne de Fort Chartres while they awaited the completion of their new home in St. Louis. Pierre Chouteau was not quite six when he, his mother, and three younger sisters traveled by cart from Fort Chartres to Cahokia on their way to the burgeoning river community founded by his father and half-brother.[35]

They joined a growing number of other newcomers who had decided to make St. Louis their home. The town was already well established when word reached there in December 1764 that two years previously France had secretly agreed to surrender New Orleans and all the territories west of the Mississippi to Spain in the Treaty of Fontainebleau.[36] The news surprised Laclède and could scarcely have been welcomed by St. Louis's French-speaking inhabitants, who suddenly found themselves about to become Spanish subjects. Although they could only speculate about the long-range effects of these sudden and unexpected developments, neither Laclède nor the other settlers were disposed to leave their growing community. For the present they intended to remain where they were.

The uncertain conditions prevailing throughout the upper Mississippi valley at this time actually favored St. Louis. For when British officials finally arrived at Fort Chartres in October 1765 and took possession of the lands east of the Mississippi, many of that region's remaining French subjects moved across the river, joining those who had previously taken up residence on the opposite shore. Some of the fleeing French inhabitants literally dismantled their abandoned homes and hauled door frames, windows, boards, and anything else they could carry to the west bank. They also brought along livestock, grain, and miscellaneous personal belongings. Shortly after he replaced Captain St. Ange as commandant at Fort Chartres, Captain Thomas Stirling informed his British superiors that fear of English rule, combined with the absence of troops to provide protection against the Indians, had prompted many French families in Prairie du Rocher, Fort Chartres, and Ste. Philippe to follow the former French commandant to St. Louis. Stirling's efforts to dissuade them had proven futile, and he doubted that much could be done to prevent their departure.[37]

In accordance with his instructions from New Orleans, St. Ange established a new headquarters in St. Louis. The Canadian-born French commandant was no stranger to the problems of administering a frontier outpost. After more than four decades of serving his king in the North American wilderness, St. Ange had been placed in charge of governmental operations in Upper Louisiana until such time as Spain might assume control. As the ranking French official west of the Mississippi, he exercised both civil and military authority in St.

Louis, which he now made the seat of government. St. Ange spent much of his time issuing and confirming land grants for the region's inhabitants. Although his administration was only temporary, the aging French soldier quickly won the respect and confidence of St. Louis's citizens.[38]

With the French still in control in St. Louis, British authorities in Illinois eyed the growing settlement across the river with suspicion. Captain Harry Gordon visited the town in 1766, and his report did little to allay British concerns: "At This Place Mr Le Clef [Laclède] the principal Indian Trader resides, who takes so good Measures, that the whole Trade of the Missouri, That of the Mississippi Northwards, and that of the Nations near la Baye, Lake Michigan, and St. Joseph's, by the Illinois River, is entirely brought to him. He appears to be sensible, clever, and has been very well educated; is very active, and will give us some Trouble before we get the Parts of this Trade that belong to us out of his hands."[39] Gordon's account made clear that under Laclède's guidance, St. Louis was quickly emerging as the focal point of the region's fur-trading operations. Its location made it easily accessible to Indians on both sides of the river, and many of them were obviously coming there to trade and to receive presents from the French.

Not all Indians had to travel to St. Louis. Laclède hired and outfitted agents who went to the villages of tribes in the surrounding territory to purchase their furs, but he failed in his efforts to retain absolute control over the commerce in furs for Maxent, Laclède and Company. Claiming that the firm had exclusive trading rights in Upper Louisiana, Laclède demanded the seizure of a boatload of merchandise belonging to Ste. Genevieve merchant Jean Datchurut when he attempted to enter the lower Missouri to trade in April 1765. Officials in St. Louis complied with the request, but their superiors in New Orleans subsequently overruled the action and ordered Maxent and Laclède to pay Datchurut and his associates for the confiscated goods and for damages.[40] The king's ministers at Versailles had canceled D'Abbadie's exclusive grants on the grounds that they were detrimental to commerce.[41] The loss of the trading monopoly was a setback for Laclède, but he continued to be St. Louis's principal merchant.

As Laclède's chief clerk, Chouteau became a familiar figure to the traders and Indian tribesmen who dealt with his stepfather. For young Chouteau and for most early St. Louisans, the traffic in furs consumed a substantial portion of their time and energies. In Laclède's town, the preoccupation with the Indian trade was universal. Even agriculture had to take a back seat to the pursuit of hides and peltries, and as a result the village's inhabitants sometimes found it necessary to purchase foodstuffs from the neighboring settlement of Ste. Genevieve to supplement local production. These occasional shortages prompted onlookers to dub the town Paincourt—French for short of bread. Yet despite its unflattering nickname, St. Louis prospered as its newly established traders collected precious furs from throughout the region for shipment to New Orleans. Not only was St. Louis becoming the commercial center for the surrounding area, but it also served as Upper Louisiana's administrative headquarters as well.[42] With a population in excess of 300 when the first Spanish officials belatedly arrived in 1767, the village seemed assured of a promising future, and in that Auguste Chouteau could justifiably take pride.[43]

NOTES

1. Because Pierre de Laclède was a second son, he frequently added the name Liguest to his signature in order to distinguish himself from his elder brother.

2. Unlike many American cities, St. Louis has an eyewitness description of its founding. Although it was written long after the actual event, Auguste Chouteau's "Narrative of the Settlement of St. Louis" is an important document. Unfortunately, this brief account is the only remaining portion of Auguste's more extensive "Memoirs," which were destroyed by fire in the 1840s while on loan to the French topographer Joseph N. Nicollet. See Gabriel Chouteau to Sylvester Waterhouse, Jan. 16, 1882, in J. Thomas Scharf, *History of St. Louis City and County, from Its Earliest Periods to the Present Day* (Philadelphia, 1883), I, 66–67. The surviving fragment was found among Auguste's papers in St. Louis and is now in the collections of the St. Louis Mercantile Library. Hereafter cited as "Chouteau's Narrative," an exact translation can be found in John Francis McDermott, ed., *The Early Histories of St. Louis* (St. Louis, 1952), 47–49. James Neal Primm's *Lion of the Valley: St. Louis, Missouri* (Boulder, Colo., 1981) provides the most comprehensive treatment of the city's history.

3. Mary B. Cunningham and Jeanne C. Blythe, *The Founding Family of St. Louis* (St. Louis, 1977), 2. This work stands as the definitive genealogy of the Chouteau family.

4. John Francis McDermott, "Laclède and the Chouteaus: Fantasies and Facts" (unpublished ms in the John Francis McDermott Mississippi Valley Research Collection, Lovejoy Library, Southern Illinois University at Edwardsville), 47–51. With regard to the widely held supposition that Marie Thérèse Bourgeois spent her childhood at the Ursuline convent in New Orleans, McDermott concluded, "There is no scrap of record that she ever lived at the Ursuline convent or that she was under the tuition of those nuns. This claim was apparently one more of those bids for 'elegance' of background for which some of the descendants were looking." *Ibid.* 50.

5. Will of René Chouteau, Apr. 10, 1776, photostatic copy in Chouteau Collections, Missouri Historical Society, St. Louis.

6. Second Register of Baptisms, fol. 165, Bureau of Archives, St. Louis Cathedral, New Orleans, photostatic copy in Chouteau Collections.

7. It is of course possible that there were two sons, the elder one, René, born on Sept. 7, 1749, and the second boy, Auguste, born on Sept. 26, 1750. The original inscription on Auguste Chouteau's tombstone read:

Auguste Chouteau
born in New Orleans
September 26, 1750
sent by

M. L. de Laclède
he was the first to arrive
in this savage land
and founded
the town of St. Louis
February 13, 1764.
His life has been a model
of civic and social virtues
He died February 24, 1829, and
rests in this tomb

In 1921 Henri Chouteau, Auguste's great-great-grandson, added to the confusion when he had the original inscription altered as a part of his campaign to prove that Chouteau was the real founder of St. Louis and that Laclède was merely his assistant. At Henri's instigation the references to Laclède were removed and the date of Auguste's birth was changed to 1740. A full account of these misguided efforts can be found in the miscellaneous correspondence and documents in the Chouteau Collections. For example, see Nettie Harney Beauregard to Archivist, St. Louis Cathedral, New Orleans, Aug. 1, 1921. Obituaries for Auguste Chouteau were published in the St. Louis *Missouri Republican,* Feb. 24, 1829, and the St. Louis *Beacon,* Mar. 2, 1829.

8. Credit for discovering Chouteau's return to France belongs to the late John Francis McDermott. His detailed evidence on that subject is presented in "Laclède and the Chouteaus: Fantasies and Facts."

9. Photostatic copies of the 1763 New Orleans census can be found in the McDermott Mississippi Valley Research Collection.

10. Etat nominatif des passagères embarqués pour les colonies pendant l'année 1767, Arch. Nat., Col. F⁵ B 57, cited in McDermott, "Laclède and the Chouteaus: Fantasies and Facts," 43.

11. John Francis McDermott, "Myths and Realities Concerning the Founding of St. Louis," in John Francis McDermott, ed., *The French in the Mississippi Valley* (Urbana, Ill., 1965), 11–13. At the time of his death Laclède owned a library containing more than 200 volumes. See John Francis McDermott, *Private Libraries in Creole St. Louis* (Baltimore, 1938), 26–43.

12. Frederic L. Billon, *Annals of St. Louis in Its Early Days under the French and Spanish Dominations, 1765–1804* (St. Louis, 1886), 412.

13. For years a controversy raged in St. Louis concerning the paternity of Madame Chouteau's four youngest children. Alexander De Menil's *Madame Chouteau Vindicated* (St. Louis, 1921) attempted to make the case that René Chouteau was their father. He and the others who sought to disprove the Chouteau-Laclède connection argued that any such relationship would have been illegal, immoral, and therefore unthinkable, but thanks to the methodical research of John Francis McDermott, Laclède's paternity of the four younger Chouteau children is no longer in doubt. In addition to showing that René Chouteau was in all probability in France during the years when they were born, McDermott discovered previously undisclosed documents in the Spanish Archives involving René Chouteau's efforts in 1774 to assert his marital rights that make the nature of the relationship between Laclède and Madame Chouteau abundantly clear. All of the evidence is contained in McDermott, "Laclède and the Chouteaus: Fantasies and Facts."

14. Photostatic copies of the baptismal records for each of the Laclède-Chouteau children can be found in the Chouteau Collections and in the McDermott Mississippi

Valley Research Collection. Although he was listed as the father, René Chouteau was not present at any of the four baptisms in question, and business associates of Laclède acted as sponsors for the two eldest daughters.

15. Although specific information about Auguste's schooling is lacking, he was a literate and educated individual. See McDermott, *Private Libraries,* 128–66.

16. For a summary of economic conditions in New Orleans, see John G. Clark, *New Orleans, 1718–1812: An Economic History* (Baton Rouge, 1970), 123–24, 151.

17. Primm, *Lion of the Valley,* 14.

18. Abraham P. Nasatir, *Before Lewis and Clark: Documents Illustrating the History of Missouri, 1785–1804* (St. Louis, 1952), 60–63.

19. John Francis McDermott, "The Exclusive Trade Privileges of Maxent, Laclède and Company," *Missouri Historical Review* 29 (July 1935), 272–78.

20. Nasatir, *Before Lewis and Clark,* 60–61.

21. McDermott, "Myths and Realities Concerning the Founding of St. Louis," 9.

22. "Chouteau's Narrative," 47.

23. Baptismal record of Victoire Chouteau, May 9, 1764, St. Louis Cathedral Archives, New Orleans, photostatic copy in Chouteau Collections.

24. "Chouteau's Narrative," 47–48.

25. *Ibid.*

26. *Ibid.*

27. *Ibid.,* 48–49.

28. Richard C. Wade, *The Urban Frontier* (Chicago, 1964), 3–4.

29. "Chouteau's Narrative," 52–54.

30. Clarence W. Alvord, *The Illinois Country* (Springfield, Ill., 1920), 262.

31. "Chouteau's Narrative," 52–54.

32. *Ibid.,* 49–52.

33. *Ibid.*

34. Not only was this building one of the most important structures in early St. Louis, but it also occupied a special place in the lives of the Chouteau family through the years. Following their arrival in St. Louis in 1764, Madame Chouteau and her children resided in it until 1768. In 1789 Auguste purchased the dwelling from Antoine Maxent and had it rebuilt and refurbished for use as his personal residence. See Billon, *Annals under the French and Spanish,* 148–50.

35. *Testimony before the Recorder of Land Titles* (St. Louis, 1825), compiled by Theodore Hunt, hereafter referred to as *Hunt's Minutes,* III, 100. The originals are located in the Missouri State Archives in Jefferson City, but the Missouri Historical Society has a typescript of those documents prepared by Idress Head. An entry in Governor D'Abbadie's Journal dated June 1764 indicates that the Illinois and Missouri traders had dispatched an expedition up the Mississippi consisting of three royal barges carrying three commanders, four patrons, sixty-five rowers, and five passengers. Although those passengers are not identified, they could well have been Madame Chouteau and her four children. Clarence W. Alvord and Clarence E. Carter, *The Critical Period, 1763–1765* (Springfield, Ill., 1915), 188.

36. McDermott, "Myths and Realities Concerning the Founding of St. Louis," 10.

37. Aubry to the Minister, Mar. 12, 1766, in Clarence W. Alvord and Clarence E. Carter, *The New Regime, 1765–1767* (Springfield, Ill., 1915), 185; Captain Thomas Stirling to General Thomas Gage, Dec. 15, 1765, in *ibid.,* 125–26.

38. Carter and Alvord, *The Critical Period,* 289n1; Billon, *Annals under the French and Spanish,* 27–29; Land grant to Laclède, Aug. 11, 1766, Chouteau Collections.

39. Journal of Captain Harry Gordon, Aug. 1766, in Carter and Alvord, *The New Regime,* 300.

40. Billon, *Annals under the French and Spanish,* 50–51.

41. Nasatir, *Before Lewis and Clark,* I, 62.

42. John Francis McDermott, "Paincourt and Poverty," *Mid-America* 5 (Apr. 1934), 210–12.

43. Glen E. Holt, "The Shaping of St. Louis, 1763–1860" (Ph.D. diss., University of Chicago, 1975), 27.

Chapter 2

LIFE IN A FRONTIER OUTPOST

AN AURA of uneasiness gripped Laclède's town as its inhabitants observed the approach of two royal Spanish barges carrying soldiers up the Mississippi in the summer of 1767. For more than two years the residents of the frontier outpost overlooking the Mississippi had been expecting their new rulers to arrive, but until that moment no Spaniards had come to their village. A treasury depleted by heavy wartime expenditures and a shortage of royal troops in America had caused Spain to postpone taking possession of her new territories.[1] When it became apparent, however, that further delays might undermine Spanish jurisdiction in the region, Don Antonio de Ulloa, Spain's new governor in New Orleans, dispatched a military expedition upriver under the command of Captain Don Francisco Ríu. Alarmed by reports of increasing British activity throughout the Mississippi valley, Ulloa instructed Ríu to establish fortifications at the mouth of the Missouri River. The governor hoped this show of force would discourage additional British intrusions west of the Mississippi and aid in controlling Indian tribes.[2]

Ríu's arrival in western Illinois marked the beginning of a new era for Upper Louisiana and for the members of the Laclède-Chouteau family. If their French heritage caused them to have misgivings about the changeover, their fears gradually subsided, and like most other St. Louisans they willingly embraced Charles III as their new sovereign. Although Spain's mercantilist policies and bureaucratic political system spawned strong resistance in New Orleans, opposition to the incoming Spanish regime remained considerably more subdued in St. Louis.[3] No doubt the isolation of that city's inhabitants predisposed them to be cautious in responding to the transfer of power.

To be sure, there were problems in Upper Louisiana. Immediately following the Spanish occupation of that region, the inept Captain Ríu managed to get things off to a bad start. The trouble began when serious bickering and quarreling erupted among the men stationed at Fort Don Carlos, the military installation Ríu established on the Missouri River near the strategic Mississippi junction. Tensions were so great that an inconsequential disagreement between a Spanish officer and a stonemason working at the fort concerning the disposal of a piece of fresh fish provoked the commandant to order the hapless worker hauled before a St. Louis judge in chains. Attempts to calm the explosive situation failed as resentment festered and tempers flared. At one point the angry men refused to allow Ríu to enter the fortification, and a short time later the fort's storekeeper and twenty soldiers deserted their posts and headed down the Mississippi.[4]

Since, in accordance with his instructions, Ríu had not supplanted St. Ange's authority in St. Louis, the village's residents initially remained aloof from the turbulent proceedings at the nearby fort. But when Ríu announced some highly restrictive policies governing the issuance of licenses for trading, they added their voices to the clamor against the military commandant. The most objectionable proviso reserved the Missouri River trade exclusively for Spanish officials. That decision also angered the Indians, who feared it would reduce the availability of merchandise. Auguste Chouteau's stepfather and employer, Pierre de Laclède Liguest, joined several other St. Louis traders in lodging a strong protest against the new regulations in May 1768. Ríu had been following Ulloa's directives regarding the trade, but he prudently acquiesced to the traders' demands and rescinded the controversial restrictions.[5]

The resulting diminution of local discontent did not come in time, however, to save the embattled Ríu. Upon learning of the troubles in Upper Louisiana, Ulloa had named Captain Don Pedro Piernas to replace him as commandant at Fort Don Carlos. Piernas took charge of the Missouri River installation in March 1769, but two weeks later he received orders to evacuate the fort and return immediately with his troops to New Orleans to assist in quelling an insurrection that had broken out there shortly after his departure. Meanwhile, in St. Louis, the Spaniards continued to employ the former French commandant, Captain St. Ange, as the province's chief administrator.[6]

The New Orleans rebellion that prompted Piernas's sudden recall from Upper Louisiana had erupted in the fall of 1768, when a group of conspirators ousted Ulloa in a bold attempt to reestablish French rule in the province. Spanish authorities subsequently moved to subdue the rebels and to restore order by dispatching General Alejandro O'Reilly and 2,000 royal troops to the gulf port city. O'Reilly made it clear following his arrival there the next year that he intended to brook no opposition. After ordering the arrest of the conspirators, including five who later were executed, he directed all Louisianans to swear allegiance to the Spanish monarch.[7]

There were no arrests in St. Louis, where, in compliance with O'Reilly's directives, the residents dutifully assembled on November 19, 1769, and proclaimed their loyalty to Charles III under the supervision, paradoxically, of the Frenchman St. Ange.[8] In publicly acknowledging their new sovereign, Laclède and his nineteen-year-old stepson signaled their willingness to cooperate with the Spaniards. As he would on so many occasions in the future, the pragmatic

Auguste Chouteau demonstrated his remarkable ability for adapting to changing circumstances.

Improved conditions in New Orleans enabled Piernas to return to St. Louis the next year. On June 18, 1770, he supplanted St. Ange's authority and officially assumed the duties of the newly created office of lieutenant governor and commandant for Upper Louisiana. The installation of a Spanish lieutenant governor in St. Louis brought only minor changes to the remote French community. Although Piernas had not made a favorable impression during his brief earlier visit to St. Louis, he quickly won over local leaders following his return as lieutenant governor. Among other things, he wisely solicited their advice and hired the well-liked St. Ange as a paid consultant. A decision to confirm all land grants made during the previous regime added to his growing popularity. As a further sign of good faith, Piernas employed a local merchant, Martin Duralde, to complete a survey of all lots in St. Louis. Pierre Chouteau, who was barely in his teens at the time, assisted Duralde with the project and in the process acquired a rudimentary knowledge of surveying.[9]

Although Piernas was the first in a succession of Spanish lieutenant governors at St. Louis, few of his countrymen followed him to Upper Louisiana. Aside from the soldiers and administrators stationed there on official duty, not many Spaniards ever took up residence in the region. In fact, more than three decades of Spanish occupation would do little to alter St. Louis's distinctive French character. French-style buildings, with their steep hip roofs and wide porches, still dotted the landscape along the bluff overlooking the Mississippi, and on Sunday afternoons following the Catholic mass, the town's residents continued to gather in true Gallic fashion for dancing and general merriment. French also remained the universal language in oral communication and in private correspondence. Official letters and reports to New Orleans were in Spanish, but occasionally even that posed a problem for the understaffed Spanish administrators and civil servants in St. Louis. Such was the case in 1778 when Lt. Governor Fernando de Leyba apologized to Governor General Bernardo de Gálvez for sending certain documents to the capital in French rather than Spanish because, as he explained it, "there is not at this post anyone who can write Spanish even moderately well unless it is a soldier, of whose services I have not availed myself because of the many errors which he makes."[10]

A few months after the Spanish dons came to St. Louis, Laclède moved his family from the quarters they had been occupying in his firm's trading headquarters to a new stone dwelling he had constructed for them down the street at the corner of Main and Chestnut. The building, which measured fifty by thirty-four feet, had a shingled roof and was divided into several apartments with wooden flooring and ceilings. Laclède shared the new lodging with Madame Chouteau and her family until his death, but residents of the close-knit frontier community appear never to have seriously questioned the unmarried couple's living arrangements. The nature of that relationship remained a matter so private that even the pair's four children could never bring themselves to acknowledge Laclède publicly as their father.[11]

Since conventional rules were inapplicable to their situation, Laclède found it necessary to provide for his family in other ways. Following the completion of the family's new residence in 1768, he deeded it, along with a piece of property on the Grand Prairie and several slaves, jointly to Auguste in consideration for his good services as a clerk, and to the four Laclède-Chouteau children, Pierre, Pelagie, Marie Louise, and Victoire, as proof of his affection for them. The agreement allowed their mother, Madame Chouteau, to retain use of all the properties during her lifetime, but it stipulated that if at any time prior to her death she decided to dispose of them, all proceeds were to go to the children.[12]

Once Laclède and his family had settled in their new home, he leased the stone trading headquarters building they had been occupying to Lieutenant Governor Piernas, who used it as an official residence and government house. For several years afterward, the Spanish lieutenant governors in St. Louis resided and maintained offices in the upper level while a detachment of soldiers occupied the quarters below them.[13]

The Laclède-Chouteau residence was only one of many new buildings in St. Louis. Although it was not yet four years old, the town boasted more than seventy-five houses and cabins scattered in the narrow strip of land along the river's edge. The gristmill and adjoining pond that Laclède had purchased from Joseph Tayon in 1767 bounded the village on the south. Naturally, not all of the dwellings were as elaborate as those Laclède built to house his business and family. Many were simply small cabins made of posts driven into the ground and hastily thrown up to accommodate the influx of newcomers crowding into the city. Open spaces separated the structures, and some of the larger ones were enclosed with cedar pickets designed to keep out the stray livestock and wild animals that often wandered into the village. There was no separate commercial district. Merchants such as Laclède and Chouteau transacted business from quarters located in their homes. The town's several common fields, where habitants and slaves cultivated most of the local crops, encircled the city. During the rainy season the village streets turned to mud, and stagnant water collected in the deep ruts and sinkholes. When a series of spring downpours created swamp-like conditions in some of the town's back lots in 1778, Auguste Chouteau joined his fellow residents in backing measures to improve drainage in the settlement.[14]

As with most boom towns, St. Louis attracted a conglomeration of persons of widely varying backgrounds, cultures, and lifestyles. In addition to well-educated and successful merchant-traders and professionals like Laclède, Sylvestre Labbadie, Louis Perrault, Dr. André Condé, Jean Baptiste Martigny, and the Chouteaus, and the less affluent but still successful artisans and smaller traders like Amable Guion, a stonemason, and Joseph Tayon, who built the first mill, a motley and more numerous assortment of boatmen, rowers, trappers, farmers, and common laborers also called St. Louis home.[15] Considerably less prosperous than either the principal merchants or the smaller businessmen, they had to settle for a more modest standard of living dictated by their low wages and seasonal unemployment. Below them on the social scale were the slaves, who in 1772 constituted 33 percent of Upper Louisiana's population. Most slaves were blacks, but a few cases of Indian slavery persisted long after Spanish authorities attempted to eliminate the practice. The Indian slaves were the only Native Americans residing permanently in the city, but delegations of visiting tribesmen regularly came there to trade and to receive presents.

Maintaining order in a community composed of such disparate elements required local officials to keep constant vigilance. The authoritarian Spanish system of justice gave the local commandant broad powers for handling disturbances. For example, in August 1770, after Amable Litoureau openly ridiculed new Spanish regulations before a gathering outside the village church, Lieutenant Governor Piernas found him guilty of treating authorities with contempt, disturbing the peace, being seditious, and giving a bad impression to the public, and ordered him banished from the territory for ten years. The next month, the commandant pronounced a similar sentence upon one Jeanot, "a good-for-nothing" whose crimes included destruction of property, stealing, and illicit sexual relations with a slave woman. To assist him in coping with the on-going problems of lawlessness, Piernas contracted with Laclède in 1774 to construct a small jail attached to the government house which, according to Auguste Chouteau's reckoning, cost 841 livres to build.[16]

If the Spanish authorities occasionally worried about controlling local rowdies, an intensifying Anglo-Spanish rivalry in the Mississippi valley presented them with a more serious challenge. After taking control of Canada and the region east of the Mississippi at the conclusion of the French and Indian War, the British stepped up efforts to extend their influence on both sides of the upper Mississippi. The growing number of British traders operating from northern outposts such as Michilimackinac, in the Straits of Mackinac between Lakes Michigan and Huron, Prairie du Chien, on the upper Mississippi, and Detroit, on the Detroit River a short distance above Lake Erie, provided the St. Louis merchants with stiff competition and siphoned off to Montreal many of the furs formerly sent to New Orleans.[17]

Traders seldom paid much attention to international boundaries in the wilderness, and when the new fortifications at the mouth of the Missouri failed to halt British incursions into their territory, Spanish officials took steps to end forcibly the illicit traffic. In 1773 a group of volunteers organized under Laclède's command pursued and captured a British party trading illegally with the Little Osages along the Missouri River. Although the band's British-licensed leader, Jean Marie Ducharme, managed to escape and flee to Canada, Laclède seized his furs and merchandise and took the other expedition members to St. Louis for Piernas to interrogate.[18]

The British countered with protests alleging Spanish encroachment east of the Mississippi. Indeed, one Michilimackinac trader complained in 1768 that business there was "very dull," because French and Spanish competitors supplied from New Orleans had undersold them.[19] Likewise, General Thomas Gage, the commander of British forces in North America, objected to the activities of Spanish traders and called upon Governor Ulloa to prevent their violations of British soil.[20]

As a part of the continuing contest, both powers actively courted the Indians. Following the practices of their French predecessors, the Spaniards distributed gifts to friendly Indian nations in the hope of retaining their allegiance. They were particularly eager to keep the northern tribes from casting their lot with the English and French-Canadian traders now threatening to overrun the upper Missouri and Mississippi valleys. Every year during May and June when Indian delegations descended upon St. Louis to receive their presents, Spanish authorities drew upon the royal treasury to entertain the visiting sachems, who departed following the festivities loaded down with an assortment of merchandise. An inventory of the Indian presents on hand in St. Louis in 1787 included brandy, despite a prohibition against its use, tobacco, guns, powder, shot, musket flints, blankets, Limbourg cloth, shirts, fancy garments for the chiefs, hats, plumes, hawks' bells, jewelry, medals, ribbons, vermilion, mirrors, sewing needles, thread, scissors, awls, hoes, axes, hatchets, knives, steels for striking fires, kettles, and wire. Especially important were the *collars*—medals suspended on grosgrain ribbons that the Spaniards gave to influential chiefs and headmen.

The annual ritual was costly—officials in New Orleans and Havana repeatedly urged their subordinates in Upper Louisiana to exercise restraint in making distributions. Nonetheless, gift-giving and feasting were the most effective methods available for retaining influence among the Indians, and as such they remained crucial ingredients in Spanish Indian diplomacy.[21]

When intoxicated, the visiting Indians quickly wore out their welcome; consequently, officials in St. Louis adopted an ordinance prohibiting the sale of liquor to them.[22] Yet Spanish laws notwithstanding, the temptation to ply Indians with strong drink was simply too great to overcome. Indian traders often dispensed liquor, and on occasion even Spanish officials succumbed and offered them alcoholic spirits in order to win their favor. Likewise, Spanish attempts to restrict Indian slavery proved equally difficult to enforce. In 1770, Lieutenant Governor Piernas posted at the door of St. Louis's newly con-

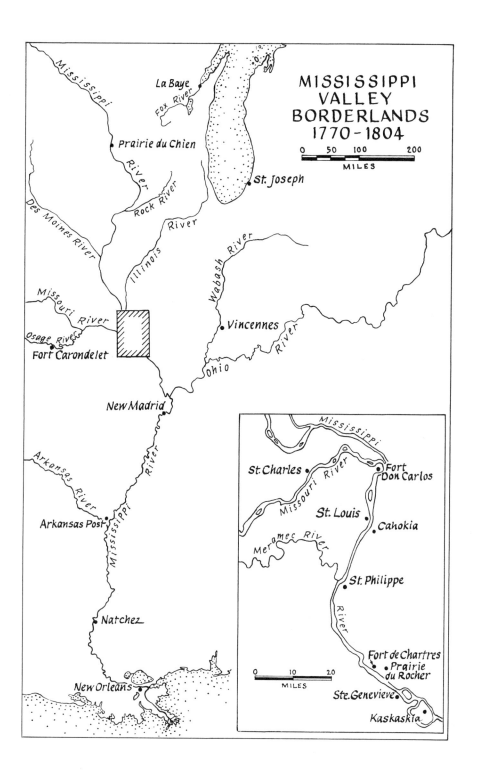

MISSISSIPPI
VALLEY
BORDERLANDS
1770–1804

0 50 100   200
MILES

Mississippi

La Baye

Fox River

Prairie du Chien

St. Joseph

River

Des Moines River

Rock River

River

Illinois River

Missouri River

Osage River

Fort Carondelet

Wabash River

Vincennes

River

Ohio

New Madrid

Arkansas River

Mississippi River

Arkansas Post

Natchez

New Orleans

Mississippi

St. Charles

Fort
Don Carlos

Missouri River

St. Louis

Cahokia

Meramec River

St. Philippe

River

Fort de Chartres
Prairie
du Rocher

Ste. Genevieve

Kaskaskia

0   10   20
MILES

structed log church Governor General Alejandro O'Reilly's 1769 proclamation outlawing the acquisition and sale of Indian slaves in Louisiana. Although the ordinance permitted owners to retain their current Indian slaves, it required them to give a strict accounting of all such slaves to the local commandant.[23] Auguste Chouteau apparently did not own any Indian slaves at the time, but his mother informed Piernas that she had two "savage girls," aged sixteen and thirteen, whose combined value she estimated to be 2,000 livres in silver, and his stepfather declared that he owned six Indians worth more than 7,350 livres in silver.[24]

As did their European rivals, the Spaniards viewed trade as a key to continued good relations with the Indians. Officials in St. Louis attempted to reward friendly tribes by keeping them well supplied with merchandise and to punish errant tribes by withholding goods until they mended their ways. In practice, the negative sanctions seldom worked, because the Indians simply turned to traders from competing nations to secure the merchandise they needed. Even so, all aspects of the Indian trade were subject to Spanish regulations. The government licensed its traders, who in effect became ex officio agents to the tribes with whom they were authorized to trade. For the Spaniards, the combination of public business and private enterprise seemed to provide a sensible way for managing Indian affairs, but as the Chouteaus would later discover, much to their chagrin, that approach was not universally accepted.

Theoretically the trade was open to all Spanish subjects, but in reality the requirement for a license, issued by the lieutenant governor in St. Louis, limited actual participation. Routinely, licenses for the most lucrative posts went to the highest bidders. In addition, the lieutenant governor normally reserved a portion of the trade for himself. Despite occasional attempts by some officials to liberalize trading policies, the closed system generally prevailed during the Spanish regime.

When the annual issuance of licenses unleashed a barrage of protests from unhappy traders who failed to secure permission to trade, beleaguered officials defended themselves by noting that the demand for trading licenses greatly exceeded the number of available posts. Lieutenant Governor Leyba observed in 1778 that the inhabitants of St. Louis are "interested only in trading with the Indians, and neglect their farming. All are, or wish to be, merchants."[25] Although the restrictive Spanish system displeased many would-be traders, the Chouteaus found it to their liking. The elitist and hierarchical principles upon which it was founded appealed to the aristocratically inclined young Frenchmen, who managed not only to survive but to flourish under Spanish monopolistic and anti-egalitarian policies.

Until his death in 1778, Laclède, Auguste Chouteau's stepfather and employer, remained one of St. Louis's leading merchants, even though the volume of his business declined sharply when he and partner Antoine Maxent lost their exclusive trading privileges in Upper Louisiana. Maxent protested to Louisiana's incoming Spanish officials in 1769 that he and Laclède had been "extremely wronged," and urged them to grant them sole trading rights with the Big Osages and the Otos as indemnification. But since neither merchant apparently held out much hope for a favorable response, they terminated their partnership on the same day. For a sum of 80,000 livres, Maxent sold Laclède his three-fourths interest in their joint venture, including his share of all the firm's assets in St. Louis—merchandise, furs, slaves, livestock, implements, tools, furniture, utensils, silverware, trading headquarters, mill, and other buildings and property. Since he did not have sufficient cash on hand to pay for his purchase, Laclède gave Maxent a series of notes payable between June 1771 and 1774.[26]

Once Laclède was on his own, he made Auguste Chouteau a partner in his reorganized business operations.[27] From the moment he first arrived in Upper Louisiana, Laclède had relied heavily upon his young clerk, most notably in establishing his new St. Louis trading headquarters. Chouteau subsequently spent much of his time among the Indians overseeing the exchange of goods for his employer. As Laclède's principal field agent and troubleshooter, Auguste always stood ready for special assignments. For example, when a shortage of *engagés* in St. Louis made it impossible to complete a crew for one of the firm's boats in 1770, Auguste hurried off to Ste. Genevieve and hired one or more rowers.[28] During Laclède's numerous absences from St. Louis, necessitated by his frequent journeys to the Maxent-Laclède warehouse in New Orleans, young Chouteau looked after his stepfather's affairs. In elevating his former clerk to the status of partner sometime during the early 1770s, Laclède rewarded Auguste's dedicated service and at the same time publicly acknowledged the young man's emergence as a trader in his own right. Indeed, Laclède's confident endorsement suggests that by the time he was in his early twenties, Auguste had acquired the business acumen and managerial skills that would soon make him Upper Louisiana's wealthiest merchant.

The confident young trader established a strong rapport with the Osages and certain other Indian tribes, who considered him an ambitious but fair-minded person whose word they could trust. The Osages asked him to accompany them to St. Louis when they conferred with officials there sometime around 1770, and his role as intermediary between the warlike tribesmen and the Spaniards, whom they constantly bedeviled, soon became a familiar one.[29] In the years that followed, Indian and European alike turned to Auguste whenever trouble developed between their two peoples.

Pierre Chouteau quickly followed in his elder brother's steps and also became a vital link between the disparate Indian and white societies. As a boy growing up in a frontier trading outpost in the heart of the North American wilderness,

Pierre had been around Indians for as long as he could remember. Indian delegations frequently came to St. Louis to trade at his father's establishment or to confer with local officials, and it seems likely that the boy occasionally accompanied his father and his brother when they visited nearby tribes.

By the time he was seventeen, Pierre had taken up residence in one of the Osage villages.[30] When Laclède's declining health and subsequent death in 1778 forced Auguste to spend more of his time in St. Louis overseeing operations there, Pierre replaced him as the family's resident Osage agent. The Osages took an immediate liking to Pierre. Less reserved and aloof than his elder brother, Cadet, as family members called him, was spontaneous and outgoing. His occasional unpredictable and passionate outbursts stood in stark contrast with Auguste's cold, calculating demeanor. Yet by working as a team, those temperamental opposites proved a winning combination among the Osages. The businesslike Auguste gained their trust and confidence while the volatile Pierre won their hearts.

Their prolonged and intimate contact with the Osages enabled the Chouteau brothers to master the Osage tongue and to understand the tribe's ways almost as well as their own. They knew and respected the major Osage tribal divisions, the Tzi-Sho (Sky People) and the Hunkah (Land People), and their respective headmen. Similarly, they were well acquainted with the various clans or subdivisions and their particular roles in tribal life.[31] Possessed with that kind of information, the Chouteaus were able to maximize their influence within the tribe. Familiarity with Osage culture soon taught them that success in trading operations depended as much upon respect for Indian customs and ceremonies as upon a knowledge of the demands of the marketplace. By bestowing appropriate gifts and honors upon the proud Indians, and by dealing fairly with them, Auguste and Pierre earned their respect and their goodwill.

The brothers took advantage of their ascendancy among the Osages to build a thriving trade. Auguste first shipped furs to New Orleans in his own name in 1775, and only two years later Spanish officials assigned him the largest share of the lucrative Osage trade. According to the 1777 records, Chouteau sent merchandise valued at 10,000 livres in deer skins to the Osages for trading, and his trading partner, Sylvestre Labbadie, dispatched goods worth another 6,000 livres to the same tribe.[32]

Chouteau and Laclède had joined forces with Labbadie, who in 1776 married Pelagie, eldest of the Chouteau-Laclède daughters. A Frenchman by birth, Labbadie had come to St. Louis via Canada several years previously and had established himself as one of the town's more successful traders. One of Labbadie's partners, the Canadian-born and French-educated Joseph Marie Papin, married Marie Louise Chouteau in 1779.[33] Extended family enterprises became a familiar characteristic of Auguste and Pierre Chouteau's business empire. To them, working with trusted relatives and keeping business in the family was simply a good way to minimize risks.

The Chouteaus were well on their way to becoming the first family of the wilderness when an unwelcome figure from the past threatened to compromise the family matriarch. In 1774 René Chouteau took legal steps to assert his marital rights and have Marie Thérèse Bourgeois Chouteau returned to his domicile in New Orleans. After coming back from France, he had purchased in 1769 a dwelling on Conti Street where he operated a bakery. Never particularly successful in any of his ventures, the elder Chouteau seems not to have been highly regarded in his new vocation. In 1771 Bernando Schiloc, a rival baker, charged him with falsely circulating the rumor that Schiloc put poison in his pastries. When Schiloc filed suit accusing him of slander, local authorities arrested and temporarily imprisoned Chouteau. After hearing the evidence in the case, a New Orleans judge found Chouteau guilty as charged and ordered him to desist from making further derogatory statements against his competitors. Because Chouteau had already spent time in jail while awaiting the dispute to be resolved, the judge released him, but only after compelling him to pay the court costs.[34]

Despite his poor reputation, René Chouteau remained Marie Thérèse Bourgeois's lawful husband, and apparently at his request Governor Luis de Unzaga directed Lieutenant Governor Piernas in St. Louis to send her to the capital "so that she shall be under the authority of her husband René Chouteaux." Piernas informed the governor he would dispatch Madame Chouteau and Chouteau's children to New Orleans but allow the others to remain with their corresponding father. While promising to respect the husband's rights, the St. Louis official did note "that for a long time the said woman has been established in her separate house, owning land in this post and her own slaves that work for her, and two adult sons that earn their own living, the one employed in dealings with Indian nations, and the other as an active resident."[35]

Even in a time when women had few rights under the law, the prospect of compelling the mother of the city's founding family to leave St. Louis and rejoin her long-estranged husband must have seemed unthinkable to everyone who knew her. The family's response to the crisis remains unknown, but Piernas's assurances notwithstanding, Madame Chouteau remained in St. Louis. Officials there and in New Orleans seemed disinclined to press the issue. René Chouteau may have persisted, but the inconsequential pastry cook was no match for Laclède or the St. Louis Chouteaus. In a letter to Piernas's successor, Francisco Cruzat, Unzaga instructed the new lieutenant governor of Spanish Illinois to give Madame Chouteau sufficient time to settle her affairs and not to force her return to New Orleans because of the harm that would follow. To forestall further criticism, Cruzat did promise to keep Madame Chouteau and Laclède apart, but he acknowledged that would not be easy. In response to his importuning, Madame Chouteau consented to move to the family's farm located about a league outside of town. There was no further mention of the matter in the official records, but when Laclède died nearly two and a half years later he still occupied a room in Madame Chouteau's home, where she also continued to reside.[36]

René Chouteau's death on April 21, 1776, brought the unseemly affair to a formal close. Bitterness generated by this latest episode did not prevent family members in St. Louis from attempting to claim their rightful share of René Chouteau's estate. Auguste, his half-brother Pierre, who in the eyes of the law was Chouteau's son, and his mother took steps to collect their inheritance. The irony must have been evident to all concerned when the Chouteau brothers granted Laclède their power of attorney and authorized him to represent them in the matter. Unrelated complications apparently prevented Laclède from making the trip to New Orleans, and Auguste and Pierre then asked another St. Louisan, Martin Duralde, to take charge of any sum due them. Their mother also assigned Duralde to look after her interests. A squabble over the senior Chouteau's attempts to emancipate some slaves at the time of his death delayed the final settlement and increased court costs as a consequence of an appeal to authorities in Havana. However, by the end of the year the meager estate had been closed, with the 792 pesos in remaining assets divided between Chouteau's estranged widow and her sons.[37]

If Laclède in fact postponed his trip to New Orleans during the winter of 1776, he probably did so because of his growing pecuniary embarrassment. Through the years he had accumulated many uncollectible notes which now threatened to drive him into bankruptcy. Since his mounting debts included the 80,000 livres he still owed Antoine Maxent, Laclède may have delayed going downriver as long as possible in order to avoid a meeting with his former partner. Not only did he lack funds to repay Maxent, but he also had to borrow money in St. Louis to meet current expenses. When Laclède finally did go to New Orleans late the next year, Maxent foreclosed on him. On December 13, 1777, the founder of St. Louis had to relinquish ownership of his buildings and land in that city to the New Orleans merchant. Despite his misfortunes, Laclède apparently bore no ill will against his former partner, whom he described as "clear and pure" in his uprightness. Indeed, Laclède's acute financial problems notwithstanding, Maxent consented to sell Laclède and his current partners, Chouteau and Labbadie, a large shipment of merchandise on consignment for the coming year's trade.[38]

Writing to Auguste from New Orleans on the final day of 1777, the ailing Laclède noted the sad state of his affairs and acknowledged that he had been forced to borrow in order to continue earning a living in the fur trade. Although that news certainly came as no surprise to Auguste, the letter's somber tone could only have worried him and the other family members. Laclède's mood was melancholy, and he seemed to sense that he was nearing death. After instructing Auguste on the steps he should follow in that event, he concluded with what would prove to be his final words to his faithful friend and stepson: "Goodbye, my dear sir, I desire to see you again, and to be able myself to settle my affairs, because it is very hard and painful as I see, to have to die in debt. One bequeaths nothing but pain and trouble to friends when one dies poor. Such is my situation. One must suffer and not murmur."[39]

Those observations were ominously prophetic. While en route back to St. Louis, the city's founder died on board his boat on May 27, 1778, about two leagues below the Arkansas Post. Officials at that place determined that he had died of natural causes and ordered him buried at a site long since forgotten.[40] Many in St. Louis mourned his passing, but the loss of their father and friend affected the Chouteau family most of all. For Auguste, there must have been a special sadness in the knowledge that his mentor had so little to show for a lifetime of labor, but the tragic lesson would not be lost on him. The cautious and conservative approach that characterized Auguste's later business operations was no accident. Laclède's misfortunes made it clear that the fur trade was a risky enterprise in which shrewd judgment and sound business practices were essential for success, and Chouteau did not intend to suffer the same fate as his stepfather.

In accordance with Laclède's instructions, Auguste undertook to put his late partner's affairs in final order. After completing an inventory of Laclède's personal property in St. Louis, Chouteau headed for New Orleans during the winter of 1778–79 to make a preliminary report concerning the estate's tangled finances. At the behest of Laclède's principal creditor, Antoine Maxent, Louisiana's Governor Bernardo de Gálvez named Chouteau to supervise the liquidation of all remaining assets.[41]

Back in St. Louis the following spring, Chouteau petitioned Lieutenant Governor Leyba for permission to sell Laclède's mill and his farm before they deteriorated further. Leyba approved Auguste's request, and, in accordance with local custom, they were offered for sale at public auction on three successive Sundays at the main door of the village church immediately following mass. At the third and final auction day on July 4, 1779, Auguste outbid three competitors and purchased the mill, all equipment, and more than 800 arpents of land that went with it for a price of 2,000 livres in peltries.[42]

Chouteau knew it was a bargain, and he had the capital to acquire it. Laclède had raised the dam and made other improvements at the flour mill. Because it was the only mill in the region, its value had steadily appreciated with the increase in local agricultural output. Auguste's mother also expanded her holdings. With a bid of 750 livres, Madame Chouteau acquired Laclède's former farm on Grand Prairie. The property, which adjoined land already belonging to her, contained a house and other improvements. Although Maxent had approved of the sale of his late partner's other St. Louis properties, he kept the stone headquarters building and square which Spanish officials still leased for use as a government house and barracks.[43]

Laclède's estate also included a 200-volume library, and when it was offered for sale, Auguste Chouteau seized upon the opportunity to begin his own collection. He purchased eight items from the estate, including Rousseau's *La Nouvelle Heloise* and Bacon's *Essays;* later that year he added a seventeen-volume *Ecclesiastical History* to his holdings. The habit of buying books was another of Laclède's legacies to Chouteau—at the time of his death fifty-one years later, Auguste's personal library had grown to more than 600 volumes.[44]

Once all remaining property had been disposed of and Laclède's debts in St. Louis had been paid, Chouteau returned to New Orleans in the summer of 1780 to give Maxent a final accounting.[45] Auguste delivered assets valued at 41,148 livres to the New Orleans merchant, but they included nearly 28,000 livres in worthless notes. Although Maxent still retained ownership of the government house and square in St. Louis, the final settlement fell far short of the 80,000 livres Laclède owed him.[46]

Since as partners their financial affairs had been closely entwined, Auguste Chouteau undoubtedly did all he could to protect his personal assets against claims from Laclède's creditors. He and his brother Pierre did have to relinquish to Maxent some slaves Laclède had given them, but aside from short-term cash-flow problems which caused him to borrow 3,960 livres from Louis Marcheteau in October 1778, Auguste Chouteau appears not to have experienced any serious financial setbacks in the wake of his stepfather's death.[47] On January 10, 1779, he had delivered to Maxent on his own account an assortment of skins and bills of exchange whose combined value amounted to 41,806 livres—considerably more than the 21,360 livres he owed the New Orleans merchant for the supplies Laclède had purchased the previous year. After he had settled his accounts in New Orleans, there was more than enough left for Chouteau to repay Marcheteau as soon as he returned to St. Louis and to purchase Laclède's mill later that summer. All in all, 1779 appears to have been a good year for the fur trade in general and for the Chouteau brothers in particular. Records in the Spanish Archives indicate that in that year various St. Louis merchants, including the Chouteaus, shipped furs valued at 161,227 livres to New Orleans.[48]

Just when the business fortunes of Auguste Chouteau and his fellow St. Louis traders appeared to be on the rise, unforeseen developments far removed from the Upper Louisiana frontier threatened to curtail their fur-trading operations. What began as a revolt by thirteen of England's seaboard colonies seeking their independence suddenly became an international struggle involving most of Europe's major powers. As the widening conflict disrupted commerce on the high seas, severe shortages developed in various parts of Spain's far-flung empire.

Auguste Chouteau first experienced these war-related economic dislocations during his 1779 visit to New Orleans, when he was unable to purchase scarce Indian trade goods. He also found the merchants there reluctant to accept American bills of credit drawn on the state of Virginia which had begun to circulate in St. Louis. This state of affairs prompted Charles Gratiot, a trader at Cahokia and future Chouteau brother-in-law, to complain that "our paper currency . . . won't buy a cat at Paincourt."[49] Failing to secure the desired Indian merchandise, Chouteau had to settle for a boatload of "drinkables, coffee, and sugar," which he brought back to St. Louis with him.[50]

In response to the failure of Chouteau and other merchants to acquire trading supplies, Lieutenant Governor Leyba warned his superiors in New Orleans that the shortage of goods in St. Louis would cause the Indians to turn to the British. To prevent this from happening, Leyba allowed five merchants, including Auguste Chouteau, to make purchases from suppliers across the Mississippi in contravention of Spanish restrictions against foreign trade. Because they had to pay higher prices for the merchandise, which had been imported from Canada, Leyba attempted to compensate them by granting fewer trading licenses and allowing them to trade directly with the Indians. Leyba defended his decision on the grounds that it had been necessary to retain the loyalty of the Missouri tribes, but the traders who found themselves left out of the arrangement hardly agreed.[51] One such trader, Jean Baptiste Martigny, angrily protested that the lieutenant governor had granted licenses to those "who could afford to pay," and charged that all of the posts on the Missouri had gone to Chouteau, Labbadie, and Gabriel Cerré "for a considerable sum."[52]

Although conditions in St. Louis caused by the scarcity of goods probably justified Leyba's actions, the resentment they provoked was understandable. Chouteau, Labbadie, and Cerré were unquestionably the town's richest inhabitants. Moreover, Cerré was a newcomer. The wealthy Kaskaskia merchant and future father-in-law of Auguste Chouteau had just moved across the river to take up residence in St. Louis.[53] Whether Leyba personally profited from this arrangement is unclear, but since he retained at least a portion of the trade for himself, it seems probable that he did.

As the American Revolution crept ever closer to the Spanish frontier, the long-simmering Anglo-Spanish rivalry intensified. Both nations sought to protect their vital interests in the Mississippi valley, thus creating a highly volatile and unpredictable situation which further strained Spanish Louisiana's limited resources and threatened to ruin its traders.[54] In St. Louis, Leyba reported being inundated by Indian delegations from both sides of the river seeking presents. So many came to the wilderness capital on the Mississippi that he quickly expended the food, merchandise, and medals his government had provided for diplomacy. With the stockpile in His Majesty's storehouse exhausted, the commandant had to turn to hard-pressed local merchants for the scarce commodities to satisfy the demands of the visiting tribesmen.[55]

Although Spain technically remained neutral until 1779, Leyba secretly cast his lot with the Americans across the river well before his government made it official. As Spain's ranking officer in Upper Louisiana, he regularly conferred with George Rogers Clark following the American's successful western campaign and provided whatever aid he could.[56] On several occasions Clark visited St. Louis, where he purchased badly needed supplies from Auguste Chouteau and other merchants.[57] Without this assistance it seems unlikely that the American soldier could have maintained his positions in British Illinois.

Upon his return to St. Louis from New Orleans in February 1780, Auguste brought word that the preceding July, Spain had joined the Americans and their French allies in the war against the British.[58] After hearing Chouteau's news, residents of the exposed village anxiously took stock of their generally defenseless situation. Surrounded on all sides by vast empty spaces, St. Louis stood nearly alone in the great North American heartland. The old fort that Ríu had constructed at the mouth of the Missouri was so dilapidated that it was useless, and Leyba's pleas for the construction of new military installations had fallen on deaf ears.[59] As rumors of a possible British attack against St. Louis began to circulate, Leyba attempted to upgrade the town's defenses. Having already exceeded the amount he was authorized to spend for protection, the lieutenant governor turned to the local community for funds to construct the needed fortifications. He gave 400 piastres from his own pocket and raised an additional 600 piastres from the town's inhabitants. How much the Chouteaus contributed is not a matter of record, but since they were, by that time, among the village's principal merchants, Leyba must have looked to them for a substantial donation.[60]

Once the money had been collected, workers immediately began building a stone tower on the west edge of the village. Although the tower's roof and parapet remained unfinished when St. Louis was attacked a few weeks later, the longtime St. Louis landmark, known as Fort San Carlos, played a key role in repelling the enemy assault. Leyba's original plan had called for the construction of three additional towers, but insufficient funds forced him to scale down the project. In lieu of the other towers, he ordered trenches dug around the city's outskirts.[61]

The hasty preparations came none too soon. On May 9 Leyba learned that a sizable military force consisting of British soldiers, Canadian traders, and Indians was heading down the Mississippi for St. Louis. To augment the handful of regular Spanish troops and the St. Louis militia, Leyba summoned the militia from neighboring Ste. Genevieve to assist in defending the provincial capital. He also called in all hunters and trappers within twenty leagues of the city. These reinforcements brought the city's total fighting force to slightly more than 300 men.[62]

On May 23 a reconnaissance expedition returned to St. Louis with reports that the approaching enemy force had been spotted only twenty-six leagues away. Three days later a British party under the command of Emmanuel Hesse swooped down upon the city from the northwest. Estimates of the number of attackers varied considerably, but the entire force, composed mostly of Indians, did not exceed 950 and may have been somewhat smaller. As the screaming band boldly advanced into the unprotected common fields beyond the city, a guard on duty at Fort San Carlos sounded the alarm. All women and children in the village took refuge in Laclède's former trading headquarters, which now served as the governor's residence. The precise activities of the Chouteau brothers during the battle are unknown. They were in St. Louis at the time, however, and since both were members of the infantry company of the local militia, they undoubtedly seized their arms and reported to their assigned stations.

St. Louis's defenders repulsed the raid on their town. Before the battle began, Leyba had ordered five cannons, retrieved from the abandoned fort on the Missouri, placed on the platform atop the stone tower. The volleys fired from those guns surprised the attacking forces, who had not expected to find the city fortified. When they discovered that St. Louis could not be taken easily the undisciplined enemy retreated, but not before inflicting heavy casualties among the farmers and slaves, who failed to heed warnings of the impending attack and chose to remain outside the fortified areas.

With assistance from the Americans, who turned back a simultaneous assault against Cahokia, St. Louisans had momentarily checked Britain's ambitious plans to capture their town and take control of the valuable region and its lucrative fur trade. But the triumph had been costly. More than ninety persons were killed, wounded, or captured during the Battle of St. Louis. Although most of the casualties had occurred in the unprotected areas beyond the city limits, the toll was a heavy one for a village of only 700 persons. Auguste and Pierre Chouteau, their mother, and their sisters all managed to escape harm during the onslaught, but one of Madame Chouteau's slaves was killed and another five were taken away as prisoners.[63]

The victory did not blind St. Louisans to the continuing dangers threatening them. Fears that the city might soon again be besieged spawned new demands for better protection. Although he had successfully engineered the defense of their town, criticism mounted against the seriously ill Leyba, who died on June 28.[64] Following the lieutenant governor's death, Auguste affixed his signature to a petition asking St. Louis's acting commandant, Lieutenant Don Silvio Francisco de Cartabona, to seek immediate relief from Spanish officials in New Orleans. Noting their limited resources and dwindling supplies, the petitioners requested additional munitions and men for their town.[65] Cartabona designated Chouteau, who was at the time preparing to go to New Orleans to wrap up Laclède's estate, to present their demands to Governor General Gálvez.

Even before Chouteau reached the capital city, Gálvez had dispatched Francisco Cruzat to Upper Louisiana with all the supplies he could spare from his dwindling stocks.[66] Cruzat's appointment to succeed Leyba was well received in St. Louis, where the popular official had previously served as commandant between 1775 and 1778. Following his arrival in St. Louis on September 24, Cruzat immediately attempted to reassure the city's unhappy residents. Still angry with the Spanish government's failure to provide for their defense, a local delegation appeared before him in the stone governmental headquarters to demand compensation for services they had rendered in constructing fortifications for their town.[67] Since his brother had not yet come back from New Orleans, Pierre represented the Chouteau family at the proceedings, but on this occasion even the pleas of the city's chosen few failed to move the economy-minded Spaniards.

When Auguste did return a short time later, he found his friend Cruzat making plans for regaining the allegiance of former Indian allies through diplomacy and gift-giving. To secure the merchandise he needed for the negotiations, Cruzat drew upon the royal treasury to purchase supplies from local merchants, probably including Chouteau. The efficacy of this strategy became readily apparent, as representatives of the influential Sac tribe surrendered British flags and medals to Auguste in return for promises of Spanish replacements. Likewise, several Missouri River tribes turned over similar symbols of British authority.[68]

Cruzat also tried to improve local defenses and issued instructions to be followed in case of another surprise attack. His initial plans listed Auguste Chouteau as a lieutenant in one of the town's two militia companies.[69] By December the Spanish commandant's growing estimation of Chouteau's abilities prompted him to promote the French merchant to the rank of captain and to place him in command of the first militia company, "since in him are found the qualities of honor, activity, and zeal necessary for the position."[70]

Cruzat also ordered the construction of a new line of fortifications around St. Louis as a further precaution against a rumored spring offensive against the city. After carefully assessing the situation, he ruled out building a fort, digging trenches, or constructing additional towers and chose instead to surround the village with a ten-foot-high stockade. Once that decision had been made, Auguste sketched a plan for Cruzat depicting a suggested location for the proposed pickets. Although Cruzat initially asked Chouteau to oversee construction of the palisade, he decided to assign that task to someone else when it became apparent that the young merchant's talents could be put to better use in New Orleans.[71]

For the second time in less than six months, Chouteau again headed down the Mississippi, this time carrying a copy of his drawing of Cruzat's proposed fortification for Gálvez's inspection. Along with the plan, Cruzat sent the British flags and banners he and Chouteau had collected from Indian tribes as tangible evidence of the continuing British interference in Upper Louisiana. No doubt Chouteau also took with him any furs he had acquired in trade, but in view of the past year's developments, it is unlikely that there were many.[72]

Discussions between Chouteau and Gálvez went well, and the governor responded to the urgent appeals for assistance by sending to St. Louis, via Chouteau's boat and a royal barge, eighty additional Spanish soldiers and a supply of much-needed Indian merchandise. Auguste and the others left New Orleans in February 1781, but while en route upriver they took time out to search for suspected British bases being used to plunder Spanish vessels operating on the river. Not surprisingly, the St. Louis trader strongly backed the attempts to halt the British depredations along the Mississippi. In addition to supplying provisions from his own stocks for the undertaking, he also stopped off at the Arkansas Post, where he joined a reconnoitering expedition into British territory on the east bank.[73]

When he finally reached St. Louis in July or August, Auguste was heartened to find morale greatly improved, thanks in part to a successful surprise assault Cruzat had mounted against the British fort at St. Joseph in Michigan. With the fear of attack subsiding, Chouteau prepared to direct more of his attention to the languishing fur trade. Although events of the past two years had forced him to curtail his business operations, the self-assured young merchant had used the hiatus to good advantage. Not only had he gained the confidence of officials in St. Louis, but his missions to New Orleans had solidified his reputation there as well. Auguste Chouteau was already well on his way to becoming Upper Louisiana's best known and most respected subject.

NOTES

1. Spain welcomed the acquisition of Louisiana from France as a means of more effectively safeguarding her valuable possessions in Mexico against foreign encroachment, but financial problems and troop shortages had delayed Spanish occupation of the territory. When the province's first Spanish governor, Don Antonio de Ulloa, finally reached New Orleans in March 1766, he brought fewer than 100 soldiers with him. For the story of the tardy transfer of Louisiana to Spain, see E. Wilson Lyon, *Louisiana in French Diplomacy, 1759–1800* (Norman, Okla., 1934), 39–54.

2. Instructions of Antonio de Ulloa to Francisco Ríu, Jan. 7 and Mar. 14, 1767, in Louis Houck, ed., *The Spanish Regime in Missouri* (Chicago, 1909), I, 1–28.

3. The most comprehensive account of the opposition to the Spanish takeover in New Orleans is John Preston Moore, *Revolt in Louisiana: The Spanish Occupation, 1766–1770* (Baton Rouge, 1976).

4. Billon, *Annals under the French and Spanish,* 42–57; George Morgan to Baynton and Wharton, Dec. 11, 1767, in Clarence W. Alvord and Clarence E. Carter, *Trade and Politics, 1767–1769* (Springfield, Ill., 1921), 135–36; Thomas Gage to General Frederick Haldimand, Apr. 26, 1768, in *ibid.,* 272–73; Ulloa to Marquis de Grimaldi, Aug. 4, 1768, in Houck, ed., *Spanish Regime,* I, 32–34.

5. St. Louis Merchants to Ríu, Jan. 15, 1769, in Houck, ed., *Spanish Regime,* I, 37–38; Moore, *Revolt in Louisiana,* 94–95, 100–101.

6. Ulloa to Marquis de Grimaldi, Aug. 4, 1768, and Report of Don Pedro Piernas, Mar. 10, 1769, in Houck, ed., *Spanish Regime,* I, 33–34, 49–52; Nasatir, *Before Lewis and Clark,* I, 65; John Francis McDermott, "The Myth of the 'Imbecile Governor': Captain Fernando de Leyba and the Defense of St. Louis in 1780," in John Francis McDermott, ed., *The Spanish in the Mississippi Valley, 1762–1804* (Urbana, Ill., 1974), 328.

7. See Moore, *Revolt in Louisiana,* for details of the 1768 rebellion.

8. "Oath of Allegiance to Spain, November 19, 1769," *Louisiana Historical Quarterly* 4 (Apr. 1921), 205–6.

9. Primm, *Lion of the Valley,* 24–27; Louis Houck, *A History of Missouri* (Chicago, 1908), II, 24.

10. Fernando de Leyba to Bernardo de Gálvez, Nov. 16, 1778, in McDermott, "Leyba and the Defense of St. Louis," 333.

11. Even as late as 1847, at the time of a special celebration marking the founding of St. Louis, eighty-eight-year-old Pierre Chouteau could not bring himself to claim Laclède as his true father. For this episode see John F. McDermott's "Pierre Laclède and the Chouteaus," *Missouri Historical Society Bulletin* 21 (July 1965), 279–83.

12. Laclède in favor of the children of Madame Choutaud [*sic*], May 12, 1768, St. Louis Archives, Missouri Historical Society. The Grand Prairie, a set of common fields apportioned in 1765–66, was located approximately two miles west-northwest of the village proper.

13. Billon, *Annals under the French and Spanish,* 150.

14. *Ibid.,* 140–41.

15. Primm, *Lion of the Valley,* 33.

16. Banishment of Amable Litourneau, Aug. 15–24, 1770, and Banishment of Jeanot, Sept. 17, 1770, in Manuscript of Miscellaneous Reports for St. Louis, 1770–1778, St. Louis History Collection, Missouri Historical Society; Billon, *Annals under the French and Spanish,* 124.

17. Abraham P. Nasatir's authoritative studies of Anglo-Spanish relations in Upper Louisiana remain unsurpassed. For a valuable synthesis of his work, see Nasatir, *Borderlands in Retreat* (Albuquerque, 1976). Significantly, Nasatir launched his career with "The Chouteaus and the Indian Trade of the West," M.A. thesis, University of California, Berkeley, 1922.

18. Abraham P. Nasatir, "Ducharme's Invasion of Missouri: An Incident in the Anglo-Spanish Rivalry for the Indian Trade of Upper Louisiana," *Missouri Historical Review* 24 (Oct. 1930), 10–22.

19. *Quebec Gazette,* Aug. 18, 1768, as quoted in Harold A. Innis, *The Fur Trade in Canada,* rev. ed. (New Haven, 1962), 172–73.

20. Thomas Gage to Lord Shelburne, Apr. 24, 1768, in Alvord and Carter, *Trade and Politics,* 267.

21. Captain Pedro Piernas to Governor Alejandro O'Reilly, Oct. 31, 1769, in Houck, ed., *Spanish Regime,* I, 73–74; Inventory of Indian presents, Nov. 27, 1787, in *ibid.,* 268–69; Nasatir, *Borderlands in Retreat,* 33.

22. Ordinance prohibiting sale of spiritous liquor to the Indians, May 8, 1768, in Manuscript of Miscellaneous Reports for St. Louis, 1770–78, St. Louis History Collection.

23. Ordinance against Indian slavery, announced in St. Louis May 1770, in Houck, ed., *Spanish Regime,* I, 249–50.

24. Statement of Dame Choutaud [*sic*], July 3, 1770, in Lawrence Kinnaird, ed., *Spain in the Mississippi Valley, 1765–1794* (Washington, D.C., 1946), I, 173.

25. Leyba to Galvez, Nov. 16, 1778, as quoted in McDermott, "Leyba and the Defense of St. Louis," 353.

26. Maxent to Ulloa, May 8, 1769, and Agreement between Maxent and Laclède to terminate their business partnership, May 8, 1769, both in Nasatir, *Before Lewis and Clark,* I, 66–69. A photostatic copy of the agreement of dissolution is also in the Pierre Laclède Collection, Missouri Historical Society.

27. Laclède to Auguste Chouteau, Dec. 31, 1777, Laclède Collection.

28. *Engagé* contract of Jean Baptiste Vien with Auguste Chouteau, July 4, 1770, Ste. Genevieve Archives, microfilm copy in the State Historical Society of Missouri.

29. John Joseph Mathews, *The Osages: Children of the Middle Waters* (Norman, Okla., 1961), 231–34.

30. Letter from Pierre Chouteau, Sept. 3, 1825, in *North American Review* 22 (1825), n.p.

31. The Osages referred to themselves as the Children of the Middle Waters, or, more informally, as the Little Ones. The term "Osage" was a corruption of the name of one of the subdivisions of the Hunkah element of the tribe, the Wah-Sha-She, which white men had mistaken for the entire nation. Of the Dhegiha Sioux language family, the Osages developed a rich oral tradition to explain the tribe's origins and to account for the twenty-two clans or fireplaces which made up the two grand divisions of the tribe. The Chouteaus were also familiar with the five physical divisions of the tribe. These divisions, often represented by separate villages, cut across the Tzi-Sho and Hunkah tribal divisions and could be traced, according to Osage tradition, to the points of refuge selected by various groups in the tribe at the time of an ancient flood. One such group or physical division was called the Little Osages by the whites, but was known to the tribe as the Down Below People. Although often treated as a separate tribe by whites, the Little Osages were actually part of the larger group, known to whites as the Grand or Big Osages. The Down Below People did, however, tend to follow an existence separate from, although often contiguous to, the other peoples of the Hunkah and Tzi-Sho of the Osage stem. Finally, the Chouteaus knew that the Tzi-Sho provided the peace chief for the nation and the Hunkah the war chief, but that both were guided by a deliberative council known as the Little Old Men. See W. David Baird, *The Osage People* (Phoenix, 1972), 6; Mathews, *The Osages,* 31–52, 103–8, 141–48.

32. Francisco Cruzat's Report on Indian Trade, Nov. 28, 1777, in Houck, ed., *Spanish Regime,* I, 139.

33. Cunningham and Blythe, *Founding Family,* 145, 191. For a more detailed account of the Chouteau genealogy and the family's kinship ties with other illustrious names in the trans-Mississippi annals, see the genealogical appendix. To follow the Chouteau genealogical story through succeeding generations, consult Cunningham and Blythe—a model genealogical work.

34. Pedro Piernas to Luis de Unzaga, Jan. 26, 1775, photostatic copy from Archivo General de Indias, Papeles de Cuba, leg. 81, in John Francis McDermott Mississippi Valley Research Collection; McDermott, "Laclède and the Chouteaus: Fantasies and Facts," 43; *Bernardo Schiloc* vs. *Chouteau (René),* Apr. 20, 1771, in "Index to Spanish Judicial Records of Louisiana," *Louisiana Historical Quarterly* 8 (Apr. 1925), 324–28.

35. Piernas to Unzaga, Jan. 26, 1775, photostatic copy in McDermott Mississippi Valley Research Collection.

36. Francisco Cruzat to Luis de Unzaga, Dec. 10, 1775, photostatic copy from Archivo General de Indias, Papeles de Cuba, leg. 81, in *ibid.*

37. Will of René Chouteau, Apr. 10, 1776, and Inventory of René Chouteau's estate, May 2–6, 1776, photostatic copies in Chouteau Collections; Succession of Raynaldo or Renato Chouteau, in "Index to Spanish Judicial Records of Louisiana," *Louisiana Historical Quarterly* 11 (July 1928), 513–19; power of attorney from Auguste and Pierre Chouteau to Pierre Laclède Liguest, Aug. 4, 1776, power of attorney from Auguste and Pierre Chouteau to Martin Duralde, Sept. 3, 1776, and power of attorney from Madame Chouteau to Martin Duralde, Nov. 23, 1776, St. Louis Archives.

38. Pierre Laclède's note to Louis Marcheteau, Oct. 22, 1776, St. Louis Archives; Billon, *Annals under the French and Spanish,* 145; Pierre Laclède to Auguste Chouteau, Dec. 31, 1777, Laclède Collection; Maxent's account with Auguste Chouteau, Jan. 14, 1779, Chouteau Collections.

39. Pierre Laclède to Auguste Chouteau, Dec. 31, 1777, Laclède Collection.

40. Inventory of Laclède Liguest made at Arkansas Post, May 27, 1778, photostatic copy from Archivo General de Indias, Papeles de Cuba, in Laclède Succession file, McDermott Mississippi Valley Research Collection.

41. Inventory of Laclède's estate, Oct. 12, 1778, photostatic copy in Laclède Collection; Billon, *Annals under the French and Spanish,* 146–47.

42. Account of auction of flour mill to Auguste Chouteau, 1779, Chouteau Collections; Billon, *Annals under the French and Spanish,* 147. An arpent is a French unit of land area equivalent to about .85 acre.

43. Account of auction of Laclède's property to Madame Chouteau, June 20, 1779, Laclède Collection; Billon, *Annals under the French and Spanish,* 147–49.

44. McDermott, *Private Libraries,* 128–66.

45. As executor of Laclède's estate Chouteau paid Louis Marcheteau the 1,200 livres Laclède owed him, Oct. 10, 1778, St. Louis Archives.

46. Billon, *Annals under the French and Spanish,* 148. Believing his brother to have been a wealthy man, Jean de Laclède attempted to claim Pierre's estate since the latter had never legally married. See Nasatir, *Before Lewis and Clark,* I, 63n.

47. Maxent's affidavit, Apr. 20, 1778, Chouteau Collections; Auguste Chouteau's note to Louis Marcheteau, Oct. 11, 1778, and affidavit of payment, Feb. 17, 1779, St. Louis Archives.

48. Maxent's account with Auguste Chouteau, Jan. 14, 1779, Chouteau Collections; affidavit of payment, Auguste Chouteau to Louis Marcheteau, Feb. 17, 1779, St. Louis Archives. In his M.A. thesis, "Auguste and Pierre Chouteau, Fur Trading Magnates," Washington University (St. Louis), 1932, Charles F. Burns cites figures

concerning the Chouteau brothers' business operations between 1778 and 1780 taken from a letterbook in the Missouri Historical Society archives. The book is now missing and archivists there have no record of it. Regrettably because Burns chose to convert all monetary units into American dollars it is impossible to know precisely what the original amounts were. Nonetheless, the figures Burns gives provide an otherwise unavailable glimpse of their transactions during this period. According to Burns, the Chouteaus sold goods valued at $40,965 to Joseph Roy, Rigauche, McCarty, and Cerré in 1778. The next year, he says that the brothers supplied nine different traders, including Joseph Marie Papin, Benito Vasquez, and Gabriel Cerré, with merchandise worth $37,055. The letterbook contained only a partial accounting of the furs they received in exchange. See Burns, "Auguste and Pierre Chouteau," 6–7. Abraham P. Nasatir cites the 161,227-livre figure for 1779 shipments to New Orleans in his "Anglo-Spanish Frontier in the Illinois Country during the American Revolution, 1779–1783," *Journal of the Illinois State Historical Society* 21 (Oct. 1928), 323.

49. Charles Gratiot to John Kay, Apr. 26, 1779, Charles Gratiot Papers, Missouri Historical Society.

50. *Ibid.;* Leyba to Gálvez, July 13, 1779, in McDermott, "Leyba and the Defense of St. Louis," 359.

51. *Ibid.*, 359–60.

52. Jean Baptiste Martigny to Gálvez, Oct. 30, 1779, in Nasatir, *Before Lewis and Clark,* I, 71.

53. Walter B. Douglas, "Jean Gabriel Cerré—a Sketch," in 1903 *Transactions of the Illinois State Historical Society* (Springfield, 1904), 275–88.

54. Nasatir, "The Anglo-Spanish Frontier in the Illinois Country," 291–358.

55. McDermott, "Leyba and the Defense of St. Louis," 356–59.

56. *Ibid.*, 329–31.

57. Chouteau's receipts dated Nov. 19, 1778, Clark Family Papers, Missouri Historical Society.

58. John Montgomery to George Rogers Clark, Feb. 18, 1780, Clark Family Papers.

59. Leyba to Gálvez, Nov. 16, 1778, and Gálvez to Leyba, Jan. 13, 1779, in McDermott, "Leyba and the Defense of St. Louis," 331–33.

60. Leyba to Gálvez, June 8, 1780, in Abraham P. Nasatir, "St. Louis during the British Attack of 1780," in George P. Hammond, ed., *New Spain and the Anglo-American West* (Lancaster, Pa., 1932), I, 243–52.

61. *Ibid.*

62. *Ibid.* According to McDermott a French league was equal to 2.4229 English miles. See John Francis McDermott, *A Glossary of Mississippi Valley French* (St. Louis, 1941), 93.

63. For accounts of the Battle of St. Louis see Nasatir, "St. Louis during the British Attack of 1780," 239–61; McDermott, "Leyba and the Defense of St. Louis," 314–405; Don Rickey, Jr., "The British-Indian Attack on St. Louis, May 26, 1780," *Missouri Historical Review* 55 (Oct. 1960), 35–45; John Francis McDermott, "The Battle of St. Louis, 26 May 1780," *Missouri Historical Society Bulletin* 36 (Apr. 1980), 131–51.

64. Virtutis, Veritatisque Amicus to Governor-General Gálvez, June 19, 23, 1780, and Le Peuple des Illinois to Governor-General Gálvez, 1780, in McDermott, "Leyba and the Defense of St. Louis," 363–72.

65. Inhabitants of St. Louis to Cartabona, July 2, 1780, in Nasatir, "St. Louis during the British Attack of 1780," 254–57.

66. Gálvez to Cartabona and Gálvez to Cruzat, July 25, 1780, in Houck, ed., *Spanish Regime,* I, 171–74.

67. Inhabitants of St. Louis to Cruzat, Sept. 1780, in Nasatir, "St. Louis during the British Attack of 1780," 258–59.

68. Cruzat to Gálvez, Dec. 2, 1780, in Houck, ed., *Spanish Regime,* I, 175.

69. Cruzat's ordinance for St. Louis, Oct. 29, 1780, in *ibid.,* 240–41.

70. Cruzat to Gálvez, Dec. 27, 1780, in *ibid.,* 183.

71. Cruzat to Gálvez, Dec. 18, 1780, in Kinnaird, ed., *Spain in the Mississippi Valley,* I, 408–10.

72. Burns, "Auguste and Pierre Chouteau," 7. Citing figures from the now-missing Chouteau letterbook, Burns stated that it mentioned only two deliveries of pelts in 1780 and 1781.

73. Nasatir, "The Anglo-Spanish Frontier in the Illinois Country," 350–51. The Arkansas Post, established by the French in 1686 and now garrisoned by Spanish troops, was located on the Arkansas River a few miles above the Mississippi. Laclède had died at that trading station in 1778.

Chapter 3

MERCHANT-CAPITALISTS AND AGENTS OF EMPIRE

ALTHOUGH MOMENTARILY the threat of another military invasion had passed, conditions in St. Louis were far from normal when Auguste Chouteau returned there in the summer of 1781. The continuing shortages of merchandise in Spanish Illinois forced merchants and Indians alike to turn more and more to British traders from Canada for scarce supplies. Reluctantly, both Lieutenant Governors Leyba and Cruzat succumbed to local pressures and permitted the illicit trade when goods were not otherwise available.[1]

Items needed for the Indian trade were in short supply in New Orleans, where a partial British blockade of the gulf had disrupted Spanish trade. Even when the scarce goods could be procured, there was no assurance that the shipments would reach St. Louis. Commerce along the lower Mississippi had become extremely hazardous as British fugitives, driven out of Natchez following the Spanish conquest of that post, joined forces with a group of itinerant traders and their Indian allies to pillage boats passing through the area. Chouteau had assisted with efforts to dislodge them, but the elusive bands continued to disrupt river traffic from the relative safety of their wilderness sanctuaries.[2]

In May 1782, near present-day Memphis, a gang of English freebooters seized Lieutenant Governor Cruzat's wife and two sons as they traveled upriver on a boat belonging to the Chouteaus' brother-in-law, Sylvestre Labbadie. After taking both passengers and crew prisoners, the raiders confiscated the ship's cargo and divided the loot, helping themselves to 4,500 pesos in cash intended to pay governmental expenses in Upper Louisiana and a much-needed supply of trade goods destined for St. Louis. As soon as the plunderers released them, Madame Cruzat and Labbadie hurried back to New Orleans to report on their harrowing ordeal.[3] While en route to the capital, they alerted a convoy of three boats on its way to St. Louis to the possible dangers upstream. Since river pirates near Natchez had already attacked one of three vessels—a barge belonging to St. Louis trader Eugene Pourée—he and the other owners decided to return to the Arkansas Post, where they arranged to store their goods until it was safe for them to resume their journey.[4]

Pourée's cargo included a shipment of rum belonging to Auguste Chouteau, and when it finally arrived in St. Louis in November, the boat owner attempted to recoup some of the added expenses he had incurred by billing

Chouteau for extra freight charges. Chouteau denied any responsibility for the additional costs on the grounds that the New Orleans storekeepers from whom he had purchased the rum had paid Pourée to make the delivery. Pourée initiated legal action against Chouteau demanding payment, but the commissioners chosen to decide the case ordered Auguste to pay only a nominal amount to cover storage charges at the Arkansas Post, leaving Pourée to assume all other expenses.[5] Incidents like this one were both aggravating and costly to the parties involved, and it is little wonder that merchants in St. Louis would begin to look elsewhere for their supplies.

The American Revolution had proved disastrous for Spanish trading operations in Upper Louisiana. Backed with superior organization, more capital, fewer governmental restraints, lower taxes, plentiful supplies of merchandise, and better markets for furs, British traders from Canada seized the initiative and overwhelmed their Spanish rivals on both sides of the Mississippi north of St. Louis. At the same time, Spain's weak industrial capability, her overextended lines of supply, and her inability to protect her frontier outposts militarily left her officials in St. Louis and elsewhere powerless to counter the British takeover.[6] These dramatic developments largely redirected the export of furs from the Mississippi valley to London via Montreal and away from the American and French-Spanish markets—a condition that lasted until the Americans finally succeeded in taking charge of much of the North American trade for the United States following the War of 1812.

When the signing of the Treaty of Paris in 1783 formally concluded the American Revolution, the Chouteau brothers found it necessary to readjust to the rapidly changing conditions. With British influence in the Mississippi valley steadily increasing, they turned to the well-stocked Canadian business houses to secure merchandise and to sell their furs. For example, when a Canadian named Marchesseaux opened a store in Cahokia in 1783, Auguste purchased goods from him at an advance of 137 1/2 percent, payable in peltries, even though the northern trader had found it necessary to travel past St. Louis at night to avoid detection by the Spaniards. When Chouteau's furs arrived from the Missouri country the following April, he delivered seventy-four packs to Marchesseaux, who promptly took them to Michilimackinac.[7] Before long Chouteau was dealing directly with merchants in Prairie du Chien, Michilimackinac, Montreal, and London, in an effort to secure articles of trade at still lower prices.[8]

The pricing system for merchandise was very complex. Prices fluctuated from year to year depending upon market conditions, but merchants in St. Louis and Cahokia generally sold their wares at 100 percent or more above the original cost. In contrast, goods could normally be procured at Michilimackinac for an advance in price of between 20 and 75 percent, depending upon the items.[9] Even better prices could be had by purchasing goods from firms in

37

Montreal or London, but shipping delays and related problems also made doing business with the more distant establishments much riskier. Although the Chouteau brothers did from time to time order merchandise directly from trading houses in London and Montreal, they most frequently utilized the services of the suppliers at the Great Lakes posts. Not only was it more convenient, but they also preferred to conduct business in person. In fact, neither Auguste nor Pierre Chouteau ever traveled to Europe or for that matter to Montreal, but they often went to Michilimackinac or one of the other northern trading stations to take a direct hand in supervising their business transactions there.

The Chouteaus were not the only St. Louis merchants to utilize the northern markets. Within a decade following the American Revolution, the new trading patterns had been firmly fixed despite occasional Spanish efforts to redirect the trade to New Orleans. Newcomers from east of the Mississippi such as Charles Gratiot and Gabriel Cerré continued to send their business northward after taking up residence in the Spanish territory. Gratiot, a successful Cahokia trader, had moved to St. Louis in 1781 at the time of his marriage to Auguste and Pierre Chouteau's youngest sister Victoire.[10] Both he and Cerré were known and respected in Canada, and their connections turned out to be especially useful to the Chouteaus.[11]

In addition to providing the St. Louis fur merchants with their best source of Indian merchandise, the British-controlled Great Lakes and Canadian markets also offered other advantages. English dealers generally paid higher prices for fine furs, and the cooler northern climate held out the added promise of reduced losses from spoilage during shipment. In most cases these extra benefits more than offset the higher transportation costs of the longer northern routes.

Although the new commercial patterns deprived Spain of many of Upper Louisiana's best furs, the Chouteau brothers did not entirely abandon their well-established connections in New Orleans. Auguste shipped most of his finer pelts such as beaver and otter to Canada, but he continued to send deer skins and buffalo robes down the Mississippi, where they usually found a ready market. However, as a consequence of his scaled-down trade in the gulf port, Auguste made fewer trips downriver as the years passed. Pierre sometimes went for him, but increasingly both men relied on associates such as John B. and Sylvester Sarpy and later the firm of Cavelier and Petit to handle their transactions in New Orleans.[12]

As the competition for furs intensified, the Chouteaus' diverse operations more than kept them busy. Both as suppliers and traders they sought to garner a major portion of the furs that annually reached the Mississippi River entrepot. Occasionally Indian delegations still brought their furs directly to St. Louis and bartered them for wares, but that became a less common occurrence as a horde of St. Louis traders sought out the Indians in their villages. Foremost among them, the Chouteau brothers and/or their agents regularly spent the winter among the Indian tribes along the lower Missouri and its tributaries swapping trade goods for the valuable pelts. Eager to acquire the merchandise which the traders offered them, the Indians scoured the countryside for animal skins to offer in exchange for the white man's technologically superior goods.

In addition to equipping the men whom they employed in their service, the Chouteaus also supplied many of St. Louis's independent traders and trappers with merchandise and equipment. Each year when the outfits for the Missouri trade were made in late summer, Auguste did a brisk business dispensing everything from muskets to earbobs.[13] The careful attention which he and Pierre gave to the selection of trade goods contributed to their success as suppliers and traders. They knew that the Indians were shrewd and demanding bargainers both in terms of quality and the value of the goods they received. Because they offered the kinds of merchandise the Indians preferred and because they developed a reputation for fair trading, the Chouteau brothers prospered in the highly competitive business.

Very little money ever changed hands at the Chouteau store, where almost all transactions were based on credit. The independent operators simply signed promissory notes due the following spring when they returned with their fur packs. Upon their arrival in St. Louis from their winter quarters, they gathered at the Chouteau trading house to swap stories of life in the wilds and to settle their accounts. In good years, receipts from the sale of their furs more than covered the costs of their outfits, but when yields were poor, the Chouteaus carried the unpaid balances along with necessary advances to purchase goods for the upcoming season.[14]

As the animal skins piled up in the Chouteau warehouse, they had to be sorted, weighed, and repacked in bundles weighing approximately 100 pounds.[15] Once that had been done, they were ready to be sent on the next leg of their journey to the furriers and hatmakers in Bordeaux or London. Without proper care at every step, the precious but perishable commodities could soon rot or be devoured by worms, moths, and rodents. Those that were sent to New Orleans were especially susceptible to such damage because of Louisiana's hot, humid climate.

Though the furs fared better in the cooler northern temperatures, shipping them from St. Louis to Canada was not an easy task. Some shipments from St. Louis went to Michilimackinac by way of the Illinois River, the Chicago portage, and Lake Michigan. From Michilimackinac, which served as a major exchange point, they were usually sent to Montreal via the hazardous Ottawa River.[16] That journey included thirty-six portages, requiring rowers to carry the goods on their backs overland for varying distances.[17] Other shipments were sent up the Mississippi to Prairie du Chien, then on to Michilimackinac via the Fox River and La Baye before continuing on to Montreal. Whatever route they traveled, the long and arduous trip necessitated careful handling of the cargoes to avoid losses during transit.

Those were not the only pitfalls in the fur trade. Fluctuating prices and unpredictable markets constantly tested the business acumen of even skillful traders like the Chouteaus. Erratic shifts in fur prices from one year to the next were common. Likewise the prices charged for merchandise were subject to sudden changes. The perpetual scarcity of liquid capital further complicated frontier business transactions. Just as they extended credit to their customers, the Chouteaus in turn bought their goods from Canadian and European merchants on credit and paid for them with furs and peltries. The vast distances separating Auguste Chouteau from his suppliers made it difficult to settle accounts speedily. During periods of declining fur prices, shipments sent in payment sometimes proved to be insufficient in value to cover the combined costs of merchandise, commissions, and interest charges.

There were numerous other hazards as well. Traders and trappers in the field labored in an often hostile environment where inclement weather, freak accidents, and Indian attacks were commonplace. In the spring of 1780, four hunters employed by Auguste Chouteau and Sylvestre Labbadie returned to St. Louis empty-handed after spending the winter in the vicinity of the Platte River. Blaming the poor showing of their employees on carelessness, Chouteau and Labbadie refused to compensate them for their winter's work. To justify his decision to withhold their pay, Labbadie accused the foursome of disobeying orders and squandering their winter's provisions.[18]

The trappers heatedly denied those allegations and appealed to Jean Baptiste Martigny, a local magistrate, for assistance in collecting their wages. Undoubtedly they expected a sympathetic hearing before Martigny, who the previous fall had denounced Labbadie and Chouteau for bribing officials to secure trading rights. In their defense the petitioners claimed that Indians had twice robbed their camp. When the second raid left them without food, they survived temporarily by cooking and eating beaver skins. They contended that to avoid starvation, they had been forced to abandon their camp and set out in search of game. The fur packets were stolen or destroyed in their absence, but the trappers claimed that they were not at fault.[19] Although the outcome of this suit is unknown, it seems unlikely that the four *hivernants* could have prevailed against their powerful employers.

The close ties which the Chouteaus maintained with the Spanish leaders in New Orleans and St. Louis gave them a decided advantage which they seldom failed to exercise. Both brothers became unusually adept at currying official favor. When Don Manuel Pérez came to Upper Louisiana to succeed Cruzat as lieutenant governor in 1787, he made the trip from New Orleans with Pierre. Pérez, an aging Spanish officer who had participated in numerous North American campaigns following his arrival in New Orleans with General O'Reilly in 1769, was approaching the end of his career in the king's service. No doubt the affable younger Chouteau used the long hours they spent together on the river to cultivate Pérez's friendship and support.[20]

Such efforts did not go unrewarded. When trading licenses were issued for Upper Louisiana, the Chouteau name was always high on the list. In 1786, Cruzat indicated he had awarded them the Kansas trade along with a share of the trading privileges on the Des Moines River. Lieutenant Governor Pérez's order banning all trade with the Osages in 1790 severely curtailed the opportunities for St. Louis traders that year, but in allocating the few available posts, Pérez obligingly selected his friends the Chouteaus to share the Kansas trade with him.[21] Governmental favoritism was not necessarily limited to the issuance of trading licenses. Cruzat once assured Governor-General Esteban Miró that "I shall do my very best to have some of the traders I have named fitted out in the store of Don Augustín [Auguste] Chouteau, for besides your recommendation, he is a boy who is deserving of any favor or help that one can do him. . . ."[22] With such support, it is not surprising that the Chouteaus fared so well.

Business operations commanded most of the Chouteau brothers' attention during the two decades following the American Revolution. Pierre continued his role as the family's agent in the field, while Auguste kept a watchful eye over virtually all facets of their expanding enterprises, which, in addition to the fur trade, included retail sales, real estate, and banking. Operating from quarters on the first floor of his St. Louis mansion, Auguste personally involved himself in the day-to-day tasks of running his business. He hired employees, tended store, supervised the buying, processing, and shipping of furs, corresponded with merchants and suppliers in both North America and Europe, and methodically recorded in his ledgers business transactions ranging from the sale in his store of a spool of thread valued at one piastre to the shipment from his warehouse of a cargo of furs worth more than 40,000 livres. Chouteau recognized that such attention to detail often meant the difference between success and failure in the unpredictable world of mercantile capitalism.

Although the bulk of sales at the Chouteau emporium in St. Louis involved Indian trade goods, local customers could also purchase such diverse items as hardware, chocolate, tea, silk stockings, shoes, all kinds of cloth, stationery, playing cards, and flower and garden seeds. Like most frontier merchants, the Chouteaus accepted a variety of local products including lead, wheat, corn, fruit, and other assorted produce in payment, but furs and peltries remained the stock-in-trade of their business.

In St. Louis's cashless economy, wealth could best be gauged in real and personal property holdings, and Auguste, like so many successful frontier merchant-capitalists, systematically began accumulating real estate.[23] He regularly bought and sold properties in St. Louis and the surrounding area and quickly became the town's largest landowner. Often in attendance when properties were auctioned at the church-house door, Chouteau was a frequent bidder and purchaser.[24] He further augmented his holdings by securing patents to lands from Spanish authorities for various services he rendered and by accepting land titles in lieu of peltries or cash to settle overdue accounts. As St. Louis's leading dealer in property, Auguste frequently assisted both buyers and sellers with their real estate transactions. For example, when village schoolmaster and part-time fur trader Jean Baptiste Truteau and his wife were in the market for a home in St. Louis, they purchased one from Auguste.[25] A short time later, Chouteau paid the departing lieutenant governor, Manuel Pérez, 2,625 pesos in silver for the stone building he and his predecessor, Cruzat, had occupied. Cruzat had bought the structure for use as an official residence when the quarters in Laclède's original trading post deteriorated to the point where they were no longer suitable. The building was a good investment for Chouteau: for years he leased it to the Spaniards and later to the Americans, who used it for their government house.[26] Although Pierre's holdings were never as extensive as his brother's, he also entered the real estate market and through the years acquired substantial properties.[27]

Auguste's growing real estate business helped launch his career in banking. The perpetual scarcity of liquid capital in St. Louis often forced him to carry notes on the property he sold just as he did on the merchandise he sold in his store. As he ventured more and more into the realm of finance, he became, in effect, early St. Louis's unofficial banker.

Both brothers regularly trafficked in slaves. According to the 1791 census, Auguste already owned fifteen slaves and Pierre four.[28] Clearly neither had any qualms about the practice of human bondage. They looked upon their chattels as a necessary but troublesome property and routinely endorsed strong measures for regulating slaves. From every indication, there was little humanity in either of the Chouteaus' attitudes toward blacks. Both regarded them as inferior to whites and Indians, but of the two brothers, Pierre's relationship with his slaves was particularly tempestuous. For the Chouteaus, the buying and selling of slaves was simply another kind of business transaction.

Auguste clearly excelled in business, so it is little wonder that his friends and associates regularly solicited his assistance in handling business and financial matters. Although he lacked formal training in the law, Chouteau often represented his clients in the local courts, where reputation mattered much more than legal expertise. Charles Gratiot granted his new brother-in-law power of attorney in 1782 and sent him to Kaskaskia to collect 11,000 livres from a Monsieur Carbonneaux.[29] When Auguste appeared before the magistrates in Gratiot's behalf, he carried a letter of introduction from Lieutenant Governor Cruzat urging favorable consideration for the claimants.[30] Many others showed similar confidence in Chouteau's abilities, including William Grant, the fur merchant who at this time handled much of the illicit trade between the Chouteaus and others in St. Louis and the Canadian entrepots at Mackinac Island and Montreal. Grant vested Chouteau with his power of attorney in St. Louis and authorized him to oversee large business transactions for his Canadian-based firm.[31] Auguste also frequently served as an executor and administrator in the settlement of estates, and in that capacity he handled some of the largest and most complicated probate cases in early St. Louis.[32]

No strangers to the courtroom, Auguste and the other members of his litigious family never hesitated to press their claims before the bar. Sometimes their celebrated legal battles even pitted one family member against another. For example, after her slave Baptiste was found slain in December 1785, Madame Marie Thérèse Chouteau lost little time in charging her son-in-law Joseph Marie Papin with responsibility for the slave's death and demanding compensation in the amount of $1,000. Baptiste had been accidentally shot as Papin and his brother-in-law Labbadie attempted to apprehend some fugitive Indian slaves who had concealed themselves in Madame Chouteau's barn. The case dragged on for sixteen months before the parties involved agreed to a final settlement requiring the owners of the renegade Indian slaves to contribute the $600 in damages awarded to Madame Chouteau.[33]

Although the Spanish system of justice was simple and direct, the disputes it attempted to resolve often were not. When Daniel McElduff of Ste. Genevieve failed to pay Auguste the 500 piastres he owed him, the St. Louis merchant arranged for McElduff to turn over a slave woman and her two small children as security. Under the plan approved by Lieutenant Governor Pérez, Chouteau was to retain use of the slave until the note had been paid. Claiming prior rights to the slave, McElduff's creditors in Ste. Genevieve protested the agreement and demanded that she be sold immediately to satisfy their demands. The unhappy claimants charged McElduff with working out the deal with Chouteau to circumvent their attempts to force the sale of his slave, but it seems unlikely that their complaints succeeded in altering the governor's decision in the case.[34]

Beyond their operations in St. Louis, the Chouteaus often conducted business in Upper Louisiana's other principal settlement, Ste. Genevieve. Through the years the Chouteaus maintained close ties there with François Vallé and other members of that influential family.[35] The Vallés and their neighbors unexpectedly experienced tragedy in 1785, when the rampaging waters of the Mississippi washed away most of their town and forced its relocation on higher ground farther back from the river. St. Louis's elevated position shielded it from that devastating inundation, which saw the mighty river rise twenty feet above any known previous high-water marks in that locale. Residents on the opposite bank were not so fortunate. When the flood was at its worst in April,

Auguste had to travel by boat through the wooded American bottoms in order to get to Kaskaskia.[36]

St. Louis was spared from flooding in 1785, but the frontier community still had its share of problems. Three years earlier Cruzat had convened an assembly of the village's principal inhabitants to regularize provisions for maintaining streets, bridges, and the fences around the commons. Although a previous citizens' group had initiated some improvements, impassable streets and stray animals roaming through the town remained serious concerns for local residents. Hoping to further remedy those conditions, the 1782 assembly named Auguste Chouteau and six others as syndics empowered to draw up regulations governing the maintenance of streets and the upkeep of village fences. Since they lacked funds to finance the project, the syndics placed the responsibility on local property holders. The new rules required each owner to maintain all streets adjacent to his property in a manner that would make them passable at all times for wagons and carts. Likewise, the syndics assigned individual residents to keep in good repair sections of the palisade around the commons.[37]

Auguste's selection as a syndic provided additional evidence of his growing stature as a community leader. By then both he and the other members of his family enjoyed a special place in their village. As previously noted, his three sisters had married successful, prominent businessmen, and his younger brother's standing was also in the ascendancy in St. Louis. As Auguste's partner, Pierre had become one of the town's rising young traders. His marriage to Pelagie Kiersereau further boosted his personal worth. Pierre was not quite twenty-five when he and the sixteen-year-old Pelagie became husband and wife on July 26, 1783. An only child reared by her grandfather, Joseph Tayon, following the death of her parents, Pelagie Kiersereau was, thanks to her inheritance, a young woman of considerable means. The marriage contract which she and Pierre signed on their wedding day listed the value of his goods and assets at 2,000 silver dollars, while she had possessions worth 1,600 silver dollars plus an undetermined amount still due from her parents' estate.[38] Although Pelagie's untimely death in 1793 cut short the couple's years together, their union produced four children, Auguste Pierre, Pierre Jr., Pelagie, and Paul Liguest.[39]

With four small children to rear, Pierre Sr. did not remain single any longer than custom demanded. On February 17, 1794, he married Brigitte Saucier. Once again Pierre's choice of brides strengthened his connections within the close-knit Mississippi River mercantile community. Two of Brigitte's sisters were married to James and Jesse Morrison, members of the powerful Kaskaskia trading family, while another was wed to the well-known trader and future business associate of Chouteau, Pierre Menard.[40] Pierre Chouteau's new wife, who was only fifteen, had her hands full looking after her husband's family and the five sons she later bore him—François Gesseau, Cyprien, Pharamond, Charles, and Frederick.[41]

Auguste waited until 1786 to marry. Like his brother, he chose his mate carefully. In a community where business was often a family affair, Auguste could scarcely have done better. His bride, Thérèse, was the daughter of prominent merchant Gabriel Cerré. In their nuptial agreement, Auguste listed his net worth as $6,000. Thérèse's parents pledged a dowry of $2,000 in addition to the $3,000 she received from her godfather, Joseph Breaseaux. For his part, Auguste promised his wife $1,000 to use as she saw fit.[42]

Thérèse Cerré, who had been born in Kaskaskia on November 26, 1769, was nearly twenty years Auguste's junior. They repeated their vows in St. Louis on September 21, 1786, with Auguste outfitted in a fashionable embroidered silk vest and pleated frock coat. His bride's elegant matching coral-and-green second-day dress suggests that every effort was made to ensure that it was a celebration befitting a marriage uniting two of the town's leading families.[43] Their marriage, which spanned more than four decades, seems to have been a happy one. The couple had nine children, but the first two, Marie Thérèse and Catherine Emilie, died quite young. The remaining seven, Auguste Aristide, Gabriel Sylvestre or Cerré, Marie Thérèse Eulalie, Marie Louise, Emilie Antoinette, Henry Pierre, and Edward René, were born between 1792 and 1807 and all lived to adulthood.[44]

In addition to their large families in St. Louis, Auguste and Pierre more than likely also had Indian wives and families in the wilderness. As young men they each spent a great deal of time among the Osages, who made them honorary members of influential tribal clans. It certainly would not have been unusual, under the circumstances, if one or both took an Indian wife away from St. Louis.[45] As a case in point, there is every indication that Paul Loise, an Osage half-blood also known as Paul Chouteau, was either Auguste's or Pierre's son.[46]

With growing young families in St. Louis, both the Chouteau brothers had to find suitable places to house them. For a while Auguste and his bride occupied an apartment in his mother's home, but after the birth of their first child in 1788, it quickly became obvious that the relatively small quarters would soon be inadequate. Hoping to remedy that situation, he purchased Laclède's original stone trading headquarters in 1789. He paid Antoine Maxent $3,000 for the structure, the outbuildings, and the square on which they stood.[47]

Through the years the buildings had been poorly maintained. The bill of sale to Chouteau characterized the principal structure as "a stone house sixty by twenty-three feet, falling to ruins, the roof rotten."[48] A stone warehouse also on the lot was in a similarly dilapidated condition with no floors. Chou-

45

teau immediately undertook to convert the decaying headquarters, whose construction he had supervised twenty-five years earlier, into a home for his family and a place for his business. He added a second story and transformed the building into a stately residence befitting St. Louis's most prominent family. Not only did Chouteau give the old trading post a facelift, but he also ordered repairs made on the nearby warehouse, which he used to store his furs. In addition, workmen constructed slave cabins and a stable behind the main house and built a stone wall around the entire square. Many years later, John Darby, an early St. Louis resident, vividly recalled that Chouteau's

> dwelling and houses for his servants occupied the whole square bounded on the north by Market Street, east by Main Street, south by what is known as Walnut Street, and on the west by Second Street. The whole square was enclosed by a solid stone wall two feet thick and ten feet high, with portholes about every ten feet apart, through which to shoot Indians in case of an attack. The walls of Col. Chouteau's mansion were two and a half feet thick, of solid stone-work; two stories high, and surrounded by a large piazza or portico about fourteen feet wide, supported by pillars in front and at the two ends. The house was elegantly furnished, but at that time not one of the rooms was carpeted. In fact, no carpets were then used in St. Louis. The floors of the house were made of black walnut, and were polished so finely that they reflected like a mirror. He had a train of servants, and every morning after breakfast some of these inmates of the household were down on their knees for hours, with brushes and wax, keeping the floor polished.[49]

The refurbished Chouteau mansion, with its glistening floors and its elegant interior furnishings, was much more than a place to live. As in the case of Jefferson's Monticello or many other of the eighteenth-century great houses, it was a center for the entire community. Numerous social events were held there, but it served other purposes too. It was both a place to transact business and an unofficial political headquarters, where local leaders met for strategy and policy-making sessions. Almost without exception, important visitors to the city paid a call there, and the magnificent dwelling and the lavish hospitality which the Chouteaus routinely offered their guests seldom failed to leave a favorable impression.[50]

In 1790 Pierre Chouteau followed Auguste's example and purchased a residence down the street from his brother's new home from Jacques Clamorgan, even then a principal fur-trade figure who would later spearhead a movement among St. Louis traders to enter the upper Missouri country.[51] Although Pierre's house was not as large as Auguste's mansion, it was, nonetheless, an imposing structure equally well appointed. Neither brother, however, found much time to enjoy their new accommodations in St. Louis, since continuing problems with the Osages called them away from home for extended periods of time. Not only had they gained control of much of the Osage trade, but their intimate knowledge of tribal ways and their unparalleled standing within the Osage councils caused government officials repeatedly to seek their services as diplomats and agents to that troublesome tribe.[52]

The Spanish dons in St. Louis and New Orleans considered the Osages the scourge of the prairies. The mere mention of their name aroused anxieties among the inhabitants of Louisiana's isolated and poorly protected settlements. Europeans and Indians alike stood in awe of these numerous and powerful people who roamed the vast territorial expanses south and west of St. Louis. The striking physical appearance of the Osage warriors—tall and muscular, with heads shaved and faces painted—somehow seemed a perfect match for their warlike and aggressive dispositions. It is little wonder that an Osage war party struck fear in the hearts of nearly everyone, or that Spaniards had to devote so much attention to this particular tribe.

Actually, the Osage nation was a people rent by deep divisions near the end of the eighteenth century. Along the banks of the Osage River and its tributaries, the Little Osage and the Marmaton rivers, in present-day Vernon County, Missouri, the Great Osages and the Little Osages or Down Below People maintained separate permanent villages after 1777. Another village developed adjacent to Fort Carondelet after 1795. On extended hunts, however, tribal parties ventured great distances across the prairies of western Missouri, southeastern Kansas, and northeastern Oklahoma. As early as the 1780s, a rebel band, led by a chief whom the French called Le Chenier, or The Oak, broke away from the Osage River towns and settled on a semi-permanent hunting ground in the Three Forks area of northeastern Oklahoma. Finding game plentiful in that region watered by the Arkansas, Neosho, and Verdigris rivers, these Arkansas Osages, or Cheniers as they were often called, defied the authority of the parent tribe and the Spaniards and were, as a result, outlawed by St. Louis officials in 1787.[53] Later, in the 1790s, another dissident chief, Clermont, or Gra Mon, chafing under the Chouteaus' influence on his people, would lead his band to the Verdigris River area and establish a permanent village near the site of the present town of Claremore, Oklahoma. Under changed circumstances, in 1802 a final element of immigrants, numbering perhaps 3,000 in all, nominally directed by Big Track or Cashesegra, joined Clermont's party. As shall be seen later, the Chouteaus helped instigate Big Track's departure from the Missouri towns. From that point on, however, Clermont was the effective leader of all the Arkansas Osages, while White Hair or Paw-Hiu-Skah remained the dominant chief of the Missouri Osages.[54] The Spaniards, like their French predecessors, therefore, encountered considerable difficulty in attempting to control the volatile Osage tribe. Osage chieftains exercised only limited authority in any case, and individual leaders never tired of proclaiming their errant brothers the guilty ones when accused of hostile acts.

Osage depredations were a regular occurrence in Spanish Louisiana. The most frequently heard complaint against them was horse-stealing, but occasionally the charges were more serious, especially when their assaults on rival tribes or isolated white settlements produced human bloodshed. At least some deaths at the hands of the Osages occurred as a result of mourning-war ceremonies organized to secure enemy scalps to hang over the graves of recently deceased tribal members. This practice developed from the belief that the spirit of a dead Osage needed a companion for the journey into the hereafter. Therefore, tribal members who could afford the expense sponsored mourning-war ceremonies to form war parties whenever a family member died. Assisting a departed relative to make the transition into the next world with a scalp brought honor and prestige within the tribe, but in the outside world the tribally sanctioned murders increased hatred for the Osages among both Indians and whites.[55]

In New Orleans and St. Louis Spanish authorities spent much of their time trying to subjugate the nomadic Osages, whose far-ranging assaults occurred from the upper Mississippi to Texas.[56] In 1787 Governor Esteban Miró charged the Osages with perfidy and bad faith and ordered all trade with them halted in an effort to curb their lawlessness. There was little else he could do, since he considered a full-scale military campaign against them both impractical and too costly. Although he sent 200 pounds of gunpowder and 400 pounds of lead shot to St. Louis with Auguste Chouteau for distribution among tribes allied against the Osages, Miró cautioned Lieutenant Governor Francisco Cruzat to avoid making the Osages Spain's permanent adversaries. Treat them, he advised, as errant and disobedient sons rather than as enemies.[57]

After discussing the situation with Miró while he was in New Orleans on business, Auguste returned to St. Louis in 1787 with the governor's instructions for handling the Osages and the supply of gunpowder and lead. Believing that its distribution would have little impact on the Osages and would increase demands for supplies from other tribes, Cruzat decided to hold the ammunition in reserve.[58] He may well have conferred with the Chouteau brothers about the matter before making his decision, since he and his successor Manuel Pérez often looked to them for assistance and counsel in handling Indian affairs.

The seemingly endless Osage hostilities prompted Pérez to encourage the resettlement of Shawnee and Delaware Indians west of the Mississippi as a buffer between white settlements and the marauding Osages shortly after his arrival in late 1787.[59] Yet in spite of the Indian relocations and the prolonged ban on trade with them, the Osages remained defiant. As a practical matter, the Spanish trade sanctions only succeeded in arousing the ire of a growing number of St. Louis traders who resented the loss of the lucrative commerce with the Osages, which accounted for well over half of all Indian sales on the lower Missouri.[60]

48

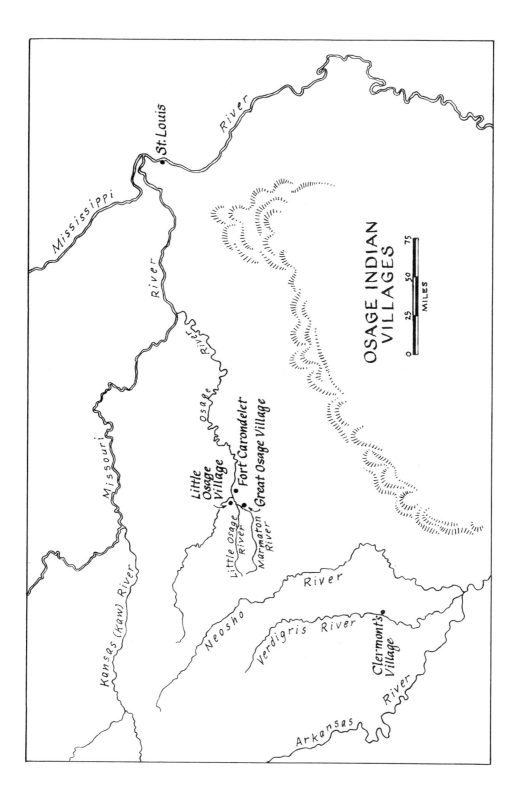

OSAGE INDIAN
VILLAGES

0 25 50 75
MILES

St. Louis

Mississippi River

Missouri River

Osage River

Little Osage Village

Fort Carondelet

Great Osage Village

Little Osage River

Marmaton River

Kansas (Kaw) River

Neosho

River

Verdigris River

Clermont's Village

Arkansas River

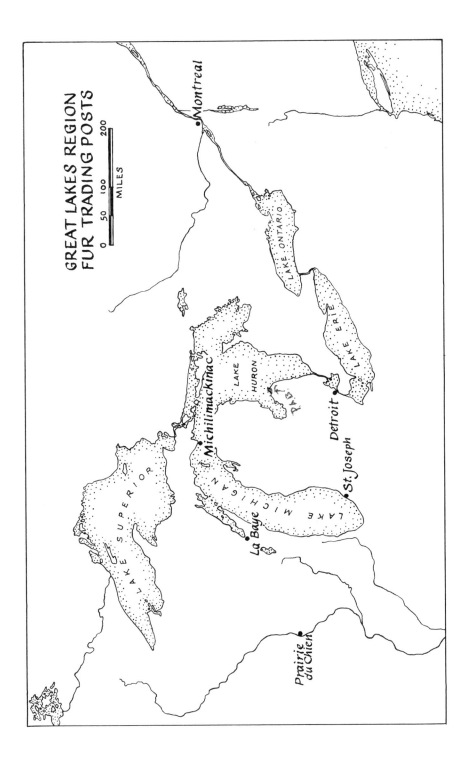

GREAT LAKES REGION
FUR TRADING POSTS

0   50   100   200
MILES

Montreal

LAKE ONTARIO

LAKE ERIE

LAKE SUPERIOR

LAKE HURON

Michilimackinac

La Baye

Detroit

St. Joseph

LAKE MICHIGAN

Prairie
du Chien

Like their counterparts, the Chouteaus experienced a decline in business as a result of the official trade restrictions, but they managed to console themselves with the Kansas trade, which they shared with Lieutenant Governor Pérez.[61] With the Osage villages off limits to traders, Pierre Chouteau passed the winter of 1790–91 at the Kansas village on the Kaw River. All went peacefully enough there until a Sac and Fox trading party sent by British suppliers from east of the Mississippi unexpectedly arrived and began bidding against him for the furs.[62]

To make matters worse, the Sac traders paid a call on the Big Osages and informed them that their friend Cadet Chouteau was wintering with the Kansas. The Osages immediately set out to verify the reports, and on March 1, 1791, more than 100 members of the tribe confronted the younger Chouteau brother at the Kansas village demanding to know why he had not brought them supplies. After listening to their complaints, Chouteau advised them that he had no choice in the matter since the governor had ordered an end to all trade with their tribe as punishment for their recent murders and depredations on the Arkansas River.[63]

The French trader's explanation failed to satisfy some boisterous and unruly younger warriors, and for a moment, things seemed to be on the verge of getting out of hand when they threatened to commandeer his remaining goods. Fortunately cooler heads prevailed, as their chiefs interceded in Chouteau's behalf, but not before all had voiced their dissatisfaction with Spanish policies.[64]

Upon his return to St. Louis, Pierre Chouteau warned Pérez to expect a visit from a large Osage delegation. Pérez, in turn, informed Governor-General Miró that he hoped to placate their anger because "they have the strength to resist if they are received badly."[65] Regrettably, their meeting did little to alleviate tensions. The Osages' refusal to acquiesce to the government's demands prompted Pérez to reject a request from the citizens of Ste. Genevieve to arrange a peace conference between the Osages and rival tribes. Nonetheless, by autumn Pérez had developed second thoughts about Miró's plans for encouraging other Indian tribes to wage war against the Osages. Although he had previously endorsed such a project, concern about the excessive costs for implementing the plan and a growing fear of possible Osage retaliation against outlying settlements caused him to propose as an alternative the construction of a small wooden fort close to the Osage villages to be garrisoned by forty or forty-five men.[66]

Meanwhile, Spanish demands that the Osages send two or three tribal leaders to New Orleans to serve as hostages further widened the rift between the two groups. According to that plan, the chiefs under Spanish custody would have been held responsible for Osage depredations in cases where members of the tribe failed to surrender promptly to the proper authorities the culprits responsible for the misdeeds, but the Indians understandably would have nothing to do with the proposed scheme. When Pérez made compliance with the request a condition for the restoration of trading privileges, an Osage peace delegation angrily departed from St. Louis following a stormy exchange with the lieutenant governor.[67]

Indignant at their treatment, the irate Indians retaliated with attacks on St. Louis traders attempting to reach other nearby tribes. Late in 1791, 200 Osage warriors intercepted a trading party traveling up the Missouri River to the Missouri and Kansas villages and seized their trade goods.[68] Similar incidents followed, and early the next year a determined Pérez ordered an Osage charged with murdering an American near Ste. Genevieve put in chains and brought to St. Louis as an example to other would-be assassins.[69]

Not long afterward, declining health caused Pérez to resign his post in Upper Louisiana, and his successor Zenon Trudeau inherited the unresolved Osage problem. Trudeau, a New Orleans–born professional soldier, quickly earned the admiration and respect of St. Louisans as a popular and efficient administrator. Upon reaching his new post in the summer of 1792, Trudeau immediately conferred with an Osage leader who had been waiting for him in the village for nearly two months. In his conversations with the incoming official, the Big Osage chief adopted a conciliatory posture and apologized for the recent depredations, most of which he blamed on the Little Osages, over whom he had no control. The St. Louis commandant responded, much to the delight of the Chouteau brothers, by agreeing to allow traders to return to the Osage villages, but he warned the tribal leader that if his warriors caused any more damage they could expect a cutoff of all supplies.[70]

In explaining his actions to Louisiana's new governor-general, Francisco Luis Hector, the Baron de Carondelet, Trudeau contended that the attempts to deprive the Osages of all trade goods were not working. When the Spanish traders did not go to their villages, the Osages secured merchandise from traders going to other tribes or from the always-eager British merchants and their Indian confederates.[71] After conferring with Captain Don Joseph Vallier, who for three years had been stationed at the Arkansas Post, Carondelet expressed strong interest in the plan calling for the construction of a small fort in the Osage country previously suggested by Pérez, but the situation deteriorated before any such proposal could be implemented. At the very moment Trudeau was contemplating a relaxation of the sanctions against the Osages in St. Louis, officials in nearby Ste. Genevieve were demanding stronger action to combat recent Osage assaults in their community. These new complaints were too much for Carondelet, whose patience was now exhausted. After deciding to declare war on the Osages, he ordered a continuation of the ban on all trade with the Osages and invited rival tribes to attack them. Trudeau had serious misgivings about the wisdom of Carondelet's latest actions and cautioned the baron not to expect a quick or easy victory over the powerful tribe, which according to his estimate could field 1,250 warriors.[72]

The Chouteaus shared Trudeau's concerns and believed that the governor-general's more aggressive policy would only exacerbate the situation. Throughout the prolonged controversy between the Spaniards and the Osages, Auguste and Pierre Chouteau managed to remain on reasonably good terms with their longtime Indian allies. In March 1792, for example, twelve of the principal Osage chieftains granted Pierre 30,000 arpents of land along the Lamine River in central Missouri. In their florid rhetorical style, the Osage leaders affirmed continuing confidence in their friend the younger Chouteau:

Brother:

As thou hast, since a long time, fed our wives and our children; and that thou has always been good for us, and that thou has always assisted us with thy advice, we have listened with pleasure to thy words; therefore take thou on the river a la Mine, the quantity of land which may suit thee, and anywhere thou pleaseth. This land is ours; we do give it to thee; and no one can take it from thee, neither today nor ever. Thou mayest remain there, and thy bones shall never be troubled. Thou askest a paper from us, and our marks. Here it is. If our children do trouble thine, they have but to show the same paper; and if some nation disturbs thee, we are ready to defend thee.[73]

deed to Pierre Chouteau

Chouteau's arrival at their village with a supply of goods may have inspired their sudden outpouring of gratitude and generosity, for even though the ban on trade remained in effect early in 1792, it would have been unseemly to have greeted them empty-handed. Indeed, in 1793 the Quapaw and Chickasaw Indians complained to Spanish officials that their enemies, the Osages, were decked out in brand-new Limbourg blankets and brandishing shiny new muskets thanks to Pierre Chouteau, who had recently delivered merchandise to their villages in violation of the trade embargo.[74]

Both the Chouteaus and the Osages obviously considered the maintenance of close ties important. The St. Louis traders sought continued access to the Osage fur supply, while the Indians recognized that the two brothers were rich and powerful men whose influence in the white man's world could be very useful to them in their relations with Spanish authorities. Perhaps it was no coincidence that a few weeks after the Osages made their land grant to Pierre, Lieutenant Governor Trudeau temporarily lifted the trade sanctions against them.

The year 1793 was critical in Spanish-Osage relations. Carondelet's attempts to force the tribe into submission not only failed but had the opposite effect, as Osage aggressions increased. In January the Little Osages stole more than twenty horses from settlers in Ste. Genevieve. Tensions were great when fourteen of their leaders came to Chouteau's Town—their name for St. Louis—

feigning sorrow for their inability to prevent the robberies and their failure to secure a return of the horses. News of their presence in the frontier capital brought a party of 200 armed Sac, Fox, Kickapoo, Mascouten, and Winnebago warriors to the scene, and they immediately surrounded and prepared to attack the house where the Osages were staying. Trudeau narrowly averted a bloody battle by luring some of the Mississippi tribesmen outside of town with promises of brandy and by getting the rest of them so drunk that they were unaware when the outnumbered Little Osages quietly departed. Although Carondelet had called for Indian assaults on the Osages, Trudeau felt obligated to protect this Little Osage band, since it had come peacefully under the Spanish banner. More important, he believed that the killing of the visiting chieftains would have invited an attack on St. Louis in retaliation.[75]

Trudeau delayed publication of Carondelet's declaration of war against the Osages until June 23, 1793, to give traders in the field an opportunity to return safely to St. Louis. But in spite of Trudeau's warnings about the possible consequences, the governor-general pressed ahead with plans to destroy the Osages. Whites and Indians alike were asked to join the fight against the recalcitrant tribe.[76] In a further effort to restrict the flow of supplies to the Osages, Carondelet ordered a curtailment of trade with other Missouri River tribes. That announcement was not well received in St. Louis, where Auguste and Pierre Chouteau joined in protesting these latest restrictions. Although they gave tacit approval to the actions against the Osages, the St. Louis merchants admonished the governor-general that unless he reopened the trade with all other tribes, the effects would be disastrous for their frontier community.[77]

Trudeau remained skeptical about the efficacy of Carondelet's plans for waging war against the Osages. Discussions were undertaken with other Indian tribes to launch an expedition against the Osages in the fall of 1793, but when the tribesmen decided to delay the proposed offensive until the following summer, he conjectured that the campaign would never materialize. With conditions in Upper Louisiana steadily worsening, Trudeau advised Carondelet that the Spaniards must either "annihilate the Indians or stop irritating them."[78] Since Trudeau questioned the feasibility of accomplishing the former, he urged the governor-general to reconsider his current course of action.[79]

Trudeau and his friend Auguste Chouteau must have sensed that the time was right to revive the earlier proposal for establishing a fort adjacent to the Osage villages. Trudeau's strong reservations and revolutionary France's declaration of war against Spain in 1793 had given Carondelet second thoughts about his Osage policy. Fearing that if the French invaded Louisiana they might form an alliance with the Osages, Carondelet abandoned his plan to subjugate the powerful tribe militarily.[80] When the Osages volunteered to send a delegation of chieftains to New Orleans to discuss peace proposals, Carondelet accepted their offer. Auguste Chouteau conveniently made himself available to escort the tribal dignitaries to the capital, and Trudeau took advantage of this turn of events to tout the St. Louis trader as the individual best qualified to establish the much-talked-about fort among the Osages.[81]

Chouteau set out for New Orleans in the spring of 1794 confident that the governor was now ready to seriously consider the offer he was prepared to make. Trudeau had already written to endorse the project and to recommend Chouteau as "a rich man, very friendly to the name of Spaniard, and held in the highest esteem by those savages. . . ."[82] Likewise, Chouteau could count upon the full backing of his Osage traveling companions. His plan was simple enough. Chouteau promised to construct, equip, and operate a fort in the heart of the Osage country which was to be manned by twenty militiamen under the command of his brother Pierre. In return, he asked the Spaniards to grant him a monopoly of the Osage trade for a six-year period and to pay him 2,000 pesos a year for maintaining the soldiers stationed at the fort. Chouteau agreed to bear all other expenses.[83]

Auguste's attempt to link his private trading interests with the welfare of the Spanish empire was certainly consistent with a well-established mercantilist tradition stressing the compatibility between imperial needs and those of the merchant-capitalists. By proposing to end wasteful competition and to curb Indian violence through the establishment of a trading monopoly, Chouteau had chosen to follow the familiar pattern of the commercial revolution and national mercantilism.

As anticipated, Carondelet responded favorably. Previous attempts to subdue the Osages had failed, and Chouteau seemed disposed to take all the risks. Once again private entrepreneurs could assist Spain in realizing her imperial objectives at a nominal cost to the royal treasury. During Auguste's audience with the sometimes irascible governor-general, everything went according to plan. The Osage leaders appeared dutifully contrite and gave their consent, the baron placed his stamp of approval on Chouteau's terms, and the remaining details were quickly ironed out.[84]

The final agreement stipulated that Chouteau would construct a two-story fortress, measuring thirty-two feet square and made of brick or stone and wood, to serve as a stronghold and barracks. Other buildings on the site would include a warehouse, a lodging for the commandant, a powder magazine, a bakery, a kitchen, and privies. The entire installation was to be surrounded with a stockade at least twelve feet in height. Finally, Carondelet commissioned Pierre as a lieutenant in the militia and appointed him to assume command of the new fort.[85]

These arrangements seemed to please everyone who participated in the discussions in New Orleans. Carondelet was happy to turn the Osage matter over to the St. Louis merchant. The Osages eagerly looked forward to the establishment of a permanent trading post in their midst, and Auguste Chouteau had successfully cornered for himself a major portion of St. Louis's dwindling fur supply. According to Trudeau's estimate, traders there annually dispatched merchandise valued at 96,000 livres to the Big and Little Osages—well over half of the total Indian trade along the lower Missouri.[86] By securing a six-year monopoly of the valuable Osage traffic at a time when competition for the available posts was forcing profits steadily downward, Chouteau had shrewdly pulled off a major coup that promised to insure his continued domination of the St. Louis–based fur trade.

The ink was scarcely dry on Auguste's contract and Pierre's commission when opposition to the arrangement surfaced in St. Louis. Understandably, the agreement did not sit well with the other traders, who suddenly were denied access to the most important single source of furs in the local market.[87] Likewise, the Indian tribes whom the Spanish had been encouraging to wage war against the Osages resented the establishment of a fortified trading post in the village of their enemy. Upon learning of Chouteau's plan, the Miami chief, Picanne, accused the Spanish of sustaining the Osages in their rogueries. The unhappy chief protested that the Osages "get nothing but caresses and are supplied with everything," in contrast to the harsh reprisals meted out to members of other tribes for their occasional misdeeds.[88]

Other Indians shared Picanne's sentiments, and their anger may have precipitated several incidents early in 1795. A Sac war party attacked and killed ten or twelve Osages somewhere along the Missouri River, while a band of armed Winnebago warriors murdered three settlers on the Meramec River and menaced several travelers, including Auguste Chouteau, in the vicinity of St. Louis.[89]

Meanwhile, the Chouteaus lost no time in opening their new trading establishment. Pierre had gone to the Osage towns in the fall of 1794 to trade and to initiate construction of the fort, which they astutely decided to call Carondelet in honor of the governor. As a site for Fort Carondelet, Cadet Chouteau selected a location on a bluff overlooking the Osage River, and when he returned to St. Louis the following spring, he announced that all of the wood needed for the installation had already been prepared and delivered.[90]

Auguste accompanied his brother to the spot in early June and took personal charge of the ninety laborers at the fort. Construction on the buildings and the palisade had been virtually completed by late August, when the elder brother returned to St. Louis. Only the artillery pieces, sent by Carondelet from New Orleans, remained to be installed. They had arrived too late in the year for transport to the fort on the shallow waters of the Osage River, now diminished by the hot, dry summer.[91]

Significantly, there is no known description of Fort Carondelet, even though at least twenty men were stationed there continuously between 1794 and 1802. Carl Chapman, a recognized authority on the Osages, has speculated that the Chouteaus intentionally kept the precise location and the exact description of

Fort Carondelet a secret because they had failed to follow the specifications which Carondelet had laid down.[92] If that was the case, no one seemed much concerned about it. Trudeau informed Carondelet even before the fort had been completed that "the savages have never been seen as tranquil as they have been this year."[93] Actually, Fort Carondelet had little, if any, strategic or military value. The powerful Osages could have overrun the isolated outpost at any time they wanted. It was, fundamentally, a trading post whose presence near their villages assured the Osages of a constant supply of trade goods and also enhanced their prestige among other tribes who envied their good fortune.[94] As Trudeau noted: "They are proud of having a fort, whites, and domestic animals with them. They regard it all as their own property. Indians have come from very distant nations to compliment them, which has flattered their amour propre [pride] they believing themselves distinguished and with preponderance over the other nations."[95]

Although relations between the Spaniards and the Osages improved markedly following the establishment of Fort Carondelet, occasional reports of Osage misconduct still reached St. Louis. Even with their unparalleled influence, there were times when the Chouteaus simply could not prevail. For example, when the Natchitoches Indians destroyed a Big Osage dwelling and killed Clermont's father-in-law, the St. Louis traders were powerless to dissuade the grieving Osage chief from organizing a war-mourning party for his deceased relative.[96] Pierre moved quickly to chastise Clermont and to undermine his standing among his fellow tribesmen. During the chief's absence, Chouteau lavishly entertained members of the all-important tribal council and provided them with presents and medals. By bestowing medals on rival chiefs of lesser rank, Chouteau increased their power and prestige at Clermont's expense. Undoubtedly the primary beneficiary of his generosity was White Hair, long recognized as a Chouteau protégé. Upon returning and discovering that his authority within the tribe had been eroded, Clermont, as noted previously, moved with his followers to the Verdigris River, where they joined earlier immigrants to establish a village which became the principal town of the Arkansas Osages. This was one of several splits that kept the tribe fragmented and made them even more difficult for the white men to control. For that reason, Pierre Chouteau took great pains in later years to persuade Clermont and his people to rejoin White Hair and the other Big Osages at their former villages in the upper Osage valley.[97]

Despite Clermont's departure for the Arkansas basin, conditions remained generally peaceful in 1795. Auguste assuredly claimed credit for the diminution in Osage hostilities when he paid a visit to Carondelet in New Orleans the following spring. He also used the occasion to prevail upon the governor-general to reject trader Andrew Todd's bid to open trade with the Sac and Fox nations west of the Mississippi, but that proved a small setback to the Canadian, who subsequently managed to pull off a far more grandiose scheme under which the Spaniards granted him full control of the upper Missouri fur trade.[98]

Auguste Chouteau was as adept in dealing with Spanish officials as he was in working with tribal leaders. When Carondelet's expected promotion to a post in Havana failed to materialize, Chouteau massaged the temperamental governor's ego with assurances that the advancement undoubtedly would be forthcoming in another year. In the same breath, Chouteau stressed his personal satisfaction at having an opportunity to continue to work with Carondelet, and as a token of his esteem he sent the baron some apples from his orchards with an apology that a small crop had prevented him from sending more.[99]

Not everything went so smoothly, however. When an Osage party went on the rampage in 1797, Chouteau's rivals lost little time in attempting to place the blame for the incident on him. Chouteau reacted by urging Carondelet to ignore their allegations, saying that he found it difficult to imagine that he would be held accountable for the behavior of a few bad persons. Kings, he immodestly noted, were not responsible for the misdeeds of their subjects. Since even the most polished societies were bothered with troublesome persons, how could he be expected to restrain completely "a numerous people who deem these murders an honor and who are like children of nature"?[100] All he could do under the circumstances was to keep the bulk of the nation in check. He considered it unreasonable for his opponents to suggest that he should control those "insubordinate individuals who break loose from the general mass to abandon themselves to the excesses of their barbarism."[101]

Like most traders, the Chouteaus considered the Indians to be childlike savages. As Auguste later advised Carondelet's successor, Manuel Gayoso de Lemos, "This is a tribe that will give trouble for a long time because it is so brutal, and too far away from civilization to become a good people or for one to hope for a change in them except in the course of time."[102] Chouteau's comments were directed toward his superiors in New Orleans at a time when he was under fire for failing to subdue the Osages. Clearly he hoped to impress upon them the difficulty of his task.

Actually, while the Chouteau brothers did not blindly admire the Indians, neither did they consider them to be murderous vermin whose destruction was essential for the advancement of civilization. Repeatedly, both men sought leniency for wayward Indians charged with violating the white man's laws. Their view was paternalistic. Like stern fathers, they regarded justice and discipline as essential for maintaining peace, order, and material well-being. As Auguste told Gayoso, "Present circumstances demand they should be treated firmly."[103] The Chouteaus' respect for Indian culture was conditional. Their approval and support depended upon the tribe's continued loyalty and obedience to them and their enterprises.

At the same time, however, the Chouteaus made what they believed was an honest effort to consider Indian needs and demands. Because they realized that callousness and dishonesty would destroy their credibility and usefulness as traders and government agents, they insisted on fairness in all transactions with the Indians. They also labored to provide adequately for the material wants of their Indian friends, and their close association at Fort Carondelet further strengthened ties between the Chouteau brothers and their redskinned companions. In 1798 Lieutenant Governor Trudeau referred to the Chouteaus' "accredited ascendancy," which suggested that the Osages had awarded the brothers honorary membership in one of the twenty-two hereditary tribal clans.[104] Thus, despite the willingness of both sides to attempt to manipulate one another for reasons of self-interest, it seems obvious that a genuine sense of affection and goodwill existed between them. Certainly without it the Chouteaus could not have commanded Osage respect and allegiance for so many years.

Auguste responded to the criticism of his handling of the Indian problems by carefully outlining the steps he and his brother had taken to counteract the Osage misbehavior. In 1797 he reported that Pierre had left his sickbed, at a possible risk to his health, to demand the surrender of the culprits responsible for some murders committed on the Arkansas River. According to Auguste, Pierre's firmness and bearing persuaded tribal leaders to surrender the guilty parties even though they were related to important chiefs. Consequently, Pierre had the murderers in tow even before Carondelet's call for action.[105]

The senior Chouteau seized upon his brother's successful handling of this incident to argue vigorously against a proposal to open trade with the Osages along the Arkansas River to other persons. Insisting that it would be unfair to hold him accountable for future depredations if his authority to control the trade was eroded, Chouteau cleverly threatened to toss the Osage problem back to the governor by suggesting that he would defer to his judgment in the matter if Carondelet was willing to "shield him from blame" whenever something went awry.[106] The ploy worked, and the governor-general quietly scrapped any plans for amending the contract.

Increasingly, the Chouteaus' strategy for dealing with the Osages seems to have been to direct their depredations away from settled areas in the vicinity of St. Louis and the Mississippi River and toward the sparsely populated interior regions. Despite the strong stand they had taken against the Osages charged with the Arkansas River murders, the Chouteaus subsequently pressed for their release after they had been kept in chains in St. Louis for several weeks. This gesture, they insisted, would have a positive effect on future Indian-white relations.[107] In supporting the Chouteaus' position in the matter, Trudeau cryptically observed, "It seems to be that a handful of hunters on the Arkansas River might be better forgotten for an instant in order to let prosper a country which is going to become, perhaps the most consequential in the province."[108] Apparently concurring with the politics of expediency, Spanish officials freed the two accused warriors. They may have been swayed by Chouteau's offer to provide a force of 500 Osages under Pierre's command for the defense of Upper Louisiana should the province come under attack.[109]

In his 1798 report to Gayoso, Trudeau continued to give the Chouteaus high marks for their handling of the Osages, because, in his words, "Don Auguste Chouteau found the means of diverting and dissuading them by good counsels and by means of the accredited ascendancy which he has among both tribes [Big and Little Osages]."[110] Gayoso undoubtedly concurred with Trudeau's favorable assessment of their conduct, but in a move to economize he suggested that the Chouteaus rely on their hunters to guard Fort Carondelet. This would have made it possible for the Spanish government to eliminate the 2,000-peso-a-year subsidy it paid the fort's proprietors for maintaining twenty militiamen there.[111] Since the fort had long since been completed, Gayoso assumed that it was not unreasonable for the Chouteaus to bear this added expense in return for their continued rights to exclusive trading privileges with the Osages.

Auguste Chouteau strenuously protested the governor's proposal to alter the terms of his contract. Claiming that the agreement was not making him rich, he recounted the sacrifices he and his brother had been forced to make to maintain their post among "the intractable savages." Surely, he concluded, neither the king nor the governor intended for Chouteau to ruin himself because of his devoted service, and that, he insisted, would be the result of transferring the entire cost for defending the fort to him.[112] Auguste's pleadings persuaded the governor to continue the payments.

Although Chouteau grossly understated the benefits he derived from the Osage trade, fluctuating prices in the erratic fur market had left him temporarily in arrears to some of his Canadian and British suppliers. His financial situation failed to improve when several Mississippi River tribes invaded the Osage hunting grounds and substantially curtailed that tribe's hunting activities in 1799. The resulting shortage of animal skins that year prompted Chouteau to ask Gayoso for 3,000 pounds of gunpowder to help offset his losses. Gayoso's response to Auguste's request is unknown, so it remains unclear whether the St. Louis merchant's gift to Madame de Gayoso of the furs of six martens and a black fox influenced the governor-general's decision.[113]

After their poor showing in 1799, the Chouteaus eagerly looked for the return of traders and trappers to St. Louis with their fur packs in the spring of 1800. Not only were they anticipating an upswing in the fur harvest, but the spring thaws also promised to signal an end to the worst winter that anyone in the Mississippi valley could remember. During that memorable season in 1799–1800, the temperature in St. Louis had dipped as low as 32° below zero, according to Auguste's recollection.[114] While he and his brother had shivered in the unseasonably cold temperatures, however, they had undoubtedly had more on their minds than the weather. Their contract with the Spanish gov-

ernment to operate Fort Carondelet was about to expire, and they did not want
to take any chances on losing it. Fortunately, they soon won over Upper Louisiana's new lieutenant governor, Don Carlos Dehault Delassus, a French-speaking
officer in the Spanish army whose father had fled his native Flanders and come
to Louisiana following the outbreak of the French Revolution. Delassus urged
his superiors in New Orleans to continue the agreement with the Chouteaus
for another six years. As had his predecessors on so many occasions, he praised
the Chouteau brothers' loyalty to the Spanish government and their influence
among the Osages.[115] Delassus's commendation came after he had observed
their conduct during a council with 200 Osages in the late summer of 1800.
The Indians had come to St. Louis to deliver the leader of a band charged with
committing two recent murders on the Meramec River.[116]

As soon as the Osages arrived, the Chouteau brothers took charge of the
proceedings, sparing no effort to impress all in attendance with their diplomatic skills. On August 29 nearly 100 of the Indian delegates crowded into
the government chamber to observe the ritualized exchanges between their
chiefs and the newly arrived Spanish leader. They heard Lieutenant Governor
Delassus urge the Arkansas chieftain Le Chenier and his followers to rejoin
White Hair, the Big Osage leader on the Osage River. Since the Arkansas band
had been responsible for most of the recent depredations, the Chouteaus believed that they could more easily control the group's comings and goings once
they returned to their former villages. Following Delassus's remarks, Le Chenier rose to say that he favored the move, but his young warriors would not
listen to him. After reminding the lieutenant governor that he had delivered
the Osage commander responsible for the Meramec raid, he asked the Spanish
leader to take pity upon the accused warrior. One by one the other chiefs
addressed Delassus in a similar fashion. At that point, Pierre ceremoniously
presented the Osage prisoner, who stoically proclaimed, "I am a man and I do
not fear death. Do with me what thou wilt."[117]

After briefly lecturing the assembled Osages about the evils of this man's
actions, Delassus ordered him put in chains and taken to the fort. He also
asked the Indians to return at the same time the following day for further
discussions. That night the Spanish leader invited White Hair, Le Chenier,
and two other head men to join him in his quarters for dinner, along with
members of his officer corps and Auguste and Pierre Chouteau. When the
evening's festivities concluded, Delassus observed that the chiefs had been well
satisfied.[118]

Upon returning to the government house the next day, members of the
delegation found the room filled with presents which Delassus had purchased
for them from Auguste. During the speeches, the Indians nodded in approval
as their chiefs assured Delassus that their friends the Chouteaus should in no
way be held responsible for the misdeeds of a few of their incorrigible mem-

bers. Delassus reiterated his comments from the previous day and invited his guests to divide among themselves the muskets, clothing, blankets, vermilion, tobacco, tools, implements, and other assorted merchandise he had selected for them.[119] After loading themselves down with presents the Indians left, praising their new Spanish leader's generosity and thanking Auguste and Pierre, whom they credited with making it all possible.

The Chouteau brothers certainly had not neglected the visiting Osages. They feasted and entertained them repeatedly throughout their week-long stay in St. Louis, seeing to it that they were amply supplied with food and merchandise. The two traders also added presents of their own to the gifts which Delassus had provided.[120] Prior to their departure the Osage leaders conferred briefly with representatives of several neighboring tribes, and on their final night in St. Louis they reached an accord pledging to end hostilities and to live together in peace. In celebration, the Osages joined the others in tribal dancing and thus provided a fitting climax to the week's events.[121]

All of this impressed Delassus, who wrote to Gayoso's replacement in New Orleans, the Marquis de Casa Calvo, "I must not forget to tell Your Lordship that I have been greatly surprised at seeing the confidence which this tribe places in the Messrs. Chouteau, and the manner in which they get along with them."[122] Just before the end of the year, Casa Calvo informed the lieutenant governor in St. Louis that he had "conceded the Osage trade for four years to Auguste Chouteau, because he is really worthy of it."[123] Although it was not the six-year extension he had sought, the elder Chouteau must have been pleased with the news.

Along with the monopoly of the Osage trade, Auguste also held a contract for supplying provisions to the government posts at New Madrid and St. Louis.[124] As in the past, merchants and traders who failed to share in the governmental largess complained about the preferential treatment afforded to the Chouteaus and the other members of the privileged St. Louis establishment, but until the brash young Spanish trader, Manuel Lisa, arrived on the scene in the late 1790s, officials successfully managed to ignore the grumblings. The ambitious Lisa could not be so easily put off, however, and he joined forces with St. Louis traders Joseph Robidoux, François Marie Benoit, Charles Sanguinet, and Jacques Chauvin in calling for the abolition of the monopolistic grants and the establishment of free trade. The assault on the closed trading system rankled the Chouteaus and their allies, most notably Lieutenant Governor Delassus and the Spanish storekeeper, Manuel Gonzalez Moro. Delassus considered their criticism unjustified and so informed his superiors in New Orleans.[125]

When Lisa failed to make headway in St. Louis, he traveled down the Mississippi in October 1801 with a petition bearing the signatures of more than thirty persons supporting his campaign for free trade. But after receiving Delassus's warning to be wary of Lisa and his schemes, officials in the provincial

60

capital summarily dismissed the Spanish trader's request to overturn the monopoly system and reprimanded him for criticizing the government's policy.[126] Although they rejected Lisa's plan for altering the trading system, the economy-minded Spaniards did not close the door on his separate offer to supply Upper Louisiana's military outposts at lower prices than those the Chouteaus currently were charging the government. Juan Ventura Morales, the Spanish intendant, declined to transfer the supply contract to Lisa immediately, but he forwarded a copy of Lisa's proposals to Delassus with instructions for him to accept the offer unless he could secure better terms locally.[127]

After Lisa arrived back in St. Louis in January 1802 boasting that free trade would soon be instituted and that he had been awarded the contract for provisioning the local garrisons, Delassus labeled his conduct as "impudent and seditious."[128] Taking no chances, the lieutenant governor hastily conferred with Chouteau and awarded him a new three-year contract for supplying merchandise for the government, but Morales subsequently insisted on modifications in the agreement when he discovered that Chouteau's St. Louis prices were still well above those in New Orleans.[129]

Lisa's machinations had succeeded in complicating matters for the Chouteaus, but that was to be only the beginning. Once he realized that the Spaniards intended to continue the trading monopolies in force, Lisa changed his strategy and set his sights on capturing the biggest prize of all—the coveted Osage monopoly. In partnership with Sanguinet, Benoit, and Gregory Sarpy, he made a bid to wrest control of that lucrative trade from the Chouteaus. Lisa and the others knew that since Auguste Chouteau had agreed to construct Fort Carondelet in 1794, he had not provided the Spanish government with any additional compensation for the trading privileges he enjoyed. On the contrary, the wealthy St. Louis merchant had on occasion solicited supplemental assistance for maintaining the installation. Sensing that Chouteau's growing tendency to take his favored status for granted could be the key to his undoing, Lisa and his partners boldly seized the initiative and drafted a plan offering the government more tangible remuneration for the Osage trading rights than it was receiving from the Chouteaus.[130]

Lisa returned with Sanguinet to New Orleans, where on June 4, 1802, they presented the governor-general with their proposal, along with a petition criticizing Chouteau's handling of the Osage trade. Casting themselves as public servants eager to serve their king and to improve their community, they promised in exchange for the Osage monopoly to build a water mill in St. Louis capable of making flour as fine as that of the Anglo-Americans and to waive the 2,000-peso annuity currently paid to the Chouteaus from the royal treasury.[131] The offer was too attractive for Louisiana's new governor-general, Manuel de Salcedo, to resist. Another mill promised to lessen Upper Louisiana's growing dependence upon American suppliers for flour, and the proposed reduction in governmental expenses was equally welcome. On June 12 Salcedo announced his decision to transfer Osage trading rights from the Chouteaus to Lisa and his partners. In canceling the contract with the Chouteaus two and a half years before its expiration date, the governor sought to justify his actions with the observation that it was just that all honorable and powerful residents have an opportunity to profit from the Indian trade.[132]

The triumphant Lisa arrived in St. Louis in early August, flaunting Salcedo's orders conceding the Osage trade to him for five years. Delassus clearly disapproved of the decision to oust his friend Chouteau, but there was little he could do about it. He summoned Lisa and Benoit for a meeting with Chouteau in his office to discuss the terms of the new agreement giving the Lisa group exclusive trading rights with the Osages of the Missouri.[133]

The stunned Chouteau acceded to the governor's order, but as Delassus made clear to Salcedo, the St. Louis merchant believed he had been badly treated. The loss of the Osage trade was a powerful blow to Auguste, who acted to protect his other interests as best he could under the circumstances. After determining that his contract to supply all governmental installations including Fort Carondelet remained in effect, he and Pierre carefully pondered their next moves.[134] Though stricken, the Chouteaus were not ready to be counted out.

When Delassus had reviewed the provisions of Lisa's contract with him, Auguste detected an important distinction between that agreement and his earlier concession for the Osage trade. Since Lisa's grant applied only to the Osages on the Missouri, it did not affect Chouteau trading rights with members of that tribe residing on the Arkansas River. Therefore, despite their recent entreaties to the Arkansas Osages to return to their former villages, the Chouteaus abruptly reversed themselves and encouraged the Missouri Osages to make the Arkansas basin their permanent home. Intent upon looking after their business interests, the Chouteaus made it clear by their actions that they considered their obligation to assist the Spaniards with Indian problems ended with the cancellation of their contract.

Despite Pierre's importuning, their old friend White Hair decided to remain at the Osage River Village, perhaps fearing that the move might prompt his rival on the Verdigris, Clermont II, to challenge openly his authority within the tribe. Nonetheless, nearly half of the Missouri Osages did follow the lesser chief Big Track to the Three Forks area in 1802. The impressive migration, which numbered as many as 3,000, clearly demonstrated the Chouteau brothers' continuing influence with the tribe, but they unknowingly may have benefited more from Clermont's presence in the Arkansas valley than from any assistance they received from their new ally Big Track.[135]

The departure of the sizable Osage band for the Arkansas was not the only mischief Lisa and his partners encountered at the hands of the Chouteaus.

When José Ortíz attempted to slip up the Missouri to engage in illicit trade with the Osages, Lisa suspected, probably with justification, that Auguste Chouteau was the venture's real sponsor.[136] Chouteau's ally, Delassus, ignored Lisa's strong protests, and the Spanish trader unleashed a stinging denunciation of the lieutenant governor which so angered that official that he ordered Lisa imprisoned. Lisa's subsequent apology to Delassus, along with his assurances that he would conduct himself properly in the future, led to his release, but his troubles were not over yet.[137]

His nemesis, Auguste Chouteau, had still another surprise for him. Lisa and his partners had borrowed money to help launch their new enterprise. Chouteau promptly acquired a 1,500-dollar note they had signed, and when it came due on April 30, 1803, he demanded immediate payment.[138] By this time Sanguinet and Sarpy had virtually withdrawn from the venture, and they, along with Benoit, agreed to give Chouteau the $375 that each owed as their share of the obligation.[139] In contrast, Lisa, who was short of cash because of the company's poor initial returns, caused in part by Big Track's move to the Arkansas River, refused to pay. Chouteau's legal action to collect the debt prompted Delassus to order the payments made. Lisa again declined, saying he would await the New Orleans superior court's decision in the case, but when the lieutenant governor ordered Lisa's partners to assume responsibility for his share, he relented and paid his debt along with the court costs.[140]

It was perhaps small consolation for the losses he had sustained at Lisa's hands, but Auguste undoubtedly savored the momentary embarrassment he had caused his ambitious rival. Moreover, since he had learned late the previous year that Spain had retroceded Louisiana to France, Chouteau sensed that the final chapter in the episode was yet to be written.[141] What he could not have suspected was that on the day he filed suit against Lisa in St. Louis, France had agreed to sell the vast territory to the United States.

Whatever changes came, the Chouteaus could be counted upon to do everything possible to capitalize upon them. So too, of course, could Lisa, who continued to feud with Auguste and Pierre over the Osage trade even after the American takeover. Marie Philippe Le Duc, Lieutenant Governor Delassus's former private secretary, who had remained in St. Louis and had married Auguste and Pierre's niece Marguerite Papin, reported in January 1805 that Pierre Chouteau and Lisa "were in open warfare."[142] Lisa's attempts to circulate disparaging reports concerning Pierre's conduct of the Osage trade, at the time that the younger Chouteau brother was seeking to persuade the incoming U.S. officials to place all Indian trade in Upper Louisiana under his control, further strained their already troubled relationship.[143]

Once it became apparent, however, that the Americans had no intention of granting exclusive trading rights to anyone, Lisa moved to patch up his differences with the powerful merchant family. Although their reconciliation remained tentative, Lisa was on good enough terms with the Chouteaus in February 1805 for Pierre to invite him to join a whist game at his residence.[144] The Chouteau-Lisa feud, and particularly its tranquil termination, suggests that on the Upper Louisiana trading frontier, commercial alliances and rivalries were conditional and influenced by the shifting tides of market forces. Similarly, while business competition could lead to personal animosity, such as that between Lisa and the Chouteaus, the circumscribed nature of the St. Louis mercantile world required a certain level of civility and restraint. Today's competitor might be tomorrow's partner, and in any event, the Spanish and French entrepreneurs represented the values of civilization in a deep wilderness. The Chouteaus were businessmen, but they were also self-consciously gentlemen. As gentlemen, and as men who kept an eye on tomorrow, the Chouteaus simultaneously moved to extend their hospitality to the unpredictable Lisa and to the even more unpredictable Americans.

NOTES

1. McDermott, "Leyba and the Defense of St. Louis," 360; Nasatir, *Borderlands in Retreat,* 34.

2. James B. Musick, *St. Louis as a Fortified Town* (St. Louis, 1941), 64–66; Nasatir, "The Anglo-Spanish Frontier in the Illinois Country," 350–51.

3. Esteban Miró to Bernardo de Gálvez, June 5, 1782, and Testimony of Madame Cruzat, May 30, 1782, in Houck, ed., *Spanish Regime,* I, 211–34.

4. *Ibid.; Pourée* vs. *Auguste Chouteau,* 1782, Chouteau Collections, Missouri Historical Society.

5. *Pourée* vs. *Chouteau,* 1782, Chouteau Collections.

6. Abraham P. Nasatir, "The Anglo-Spanish Frontier on the Upper Mississippi, 1786–1796," *Iowa Journal of History and Politics* 29 (Apr. 1931), 161; Nasatir, *Borderlands in Retreat,* 33–35.

7. John Sharpless Fox, ed., "Narrative of . . . Jean Baptiste Perrault," *Historical Collections and Researches Made by the Michigan Pioneer and Historical Society* 37 (1910), 515–18.

8. Among the earliest documents directly linking Chouteau with traders in Canada are A. Tabeau's secret contract with Joseph Marie Papin, Sept. 3, 1789, and William A. Todd to Auguste Chouteau, May 5, 1791, both in Chouteau Collections.

9. For example, Frederick Groeter of Cahokia, Mons. Gagnon of St. Louis, and Isidore LaCroix and Company of Cahokia all charged Auguste Chouteau a 100 percent benefice for goods they sold him in the 1790s. There were, of course, variations depending upon the items and their scarcity. In 1797 Clamorgan, Loisel and Company charged Pierre Chouteau 120 percent above original cost for some miscellaneous merchandise he bought from them in St. Louis, but in the same year Pascal Detchemendy charged Auguste only a 50 percent markup on a lot of hats that he sold him in St. Louis.

In contrast with St. Louis prices, the markup for similar goods purchased in the

Great Lakes posts tended to be considerably less. For example, a 1795 invoice for goods Andrew Todd supplied from Michilimackinac included only a 33⅓ percent benefice for certain items of clothing, while iron pails, chocolate, padlocks, saltpeter, and priming wires were advanced only 20 percent. The same invoice, however, included a 75 percent additional charge for rifles, gunpowder, sails, canoes, and sugar. All records and invoices cited are in the Chouteau Collections.

10. Warren Lynn Barnhart, "The Letterbooks of Charles Gratiot, Fur Trader: The Nomadic Years, 1769–1797" (Ph.D. diss., St. Louis University, 1971), 81.

11. *Ibid.;* Douglas, "Jean Gabriel Cerré," 279–80, 283.

12. For example, see Sarpy to Auguste Chouteau, May 10, 1790, and Feb. 10, 1791, in Chouteau Collections.

13. Edward F. Rowse, "Auguste and Pierre Chouteau" (Ph.D. diss., Washington University, St. Louis, 1936), 73–74. See also Pierre Lavigeure's note, Aug. 30, 1782, Jean Casanave's note, Sept. 16, 1782, Jean Baptiste Dufrene's note, Aug. 11, 1790, Pierre Bernier's note and account, Sept. 20, 1790–Apr. 18, 1791, Louis Amelin's account, Sept. 25, 1790, and promissory note of Joseph Peres and Charles Dutor, Oct. 19, 1790, all in Chouteau Collections.

14. *Ibid.*

15. Petition for a change in the custom of weighing packs of peltries, Mar. 4, 1776, in "Manuscript of Miscellaneous Reports for St. Louis, 1770–78," St. Louis History Collection, Missouri Historical Society.

16. Arthur St. Clair to President George Washington, Mar. 5–June 11, 1790, in William H. Smith, ed., *The St. Clair Papers: Life and Public Services of Arthur St. Clair* (Cincinnati, 1882), II, 174–75; Wayne E. Stevens, *The Northwest Fur Trade, 1763–1800* (Urbana, Ill., 1928), 150–56.

17. Zenon Trudeau's Report on English Commerce with Indians, May 18, 1793, in Nasatir, *Before Lewis and Clark,* I, 175–79.

18. Petition of Solomon Petit, Frederic, Vaseur, and Brion to Jean Baptiste Martigny, June 28, 1780, Chouteau Collections.

19. *Ibid.*

20. Abraham P. Nasatir, "Indian Trade and Diplomacy in the Spanish Illinois, 1763–1792" (Ph.D. diss., University of California, Berkeley, 1926), 283.

21. De Volsay to Francisco Cruzat, July 18, 1786, cited in Nasatir, *Before Lewis and Clark,* I, 72; Manuel Pérez to Esteban Miró, Aug. 23, 1790, in *ibid.,* I, 134–35.

22. Cruzat to Miró, [1786], cited in Nasatir, "Indian Trade and Diplomacy," 216.

23. John Jacob Astor, the founder of the American Fur Company, invested heavily in real estate and became the richest man in America. On other American frontiers the merchant-capitalist often followed a similar pattern. For example, Lewis Atherton demonstrates that on the cattleman's frontier, the successful cattle barons became heavily involved in real estate and banking. See Atherton, *The Cattle Kings* (Bloomington, Ind., 1961). In a similar vein, Jerome O. Steffen has noted that merchant-capitalists sought to control their economic fortunes through diversification of function and efficient administration. See Steffen, *Comparative Frontiers: A Proposal for Studying the American West* (Norman, Okla., 1980), 37.

24. Account of auction of estate of Jacques Noise, Apr. 15–29, 1792, Chouteau Collections.

25. The St. Louis Archives, Missouri Historical Society, contain numerous land and property transactions involving Auguste Chouteau. For examples see Account of auc-

tion of house and land of Louis Motar to Auguste Chouteau, Mar. 1, 1782, Auguste Chouteau to Louis Bourris, Aug. 28, 1784, Augustín La Comba to Auguste Chouteau, Oct. 10, 1789, Auguste Chouteau to Joseph Lemoin Burgeon, June 22, 1790, Auguste Chouteau to Jean Baptiste Truteau and wife, July 5, 1792, and many others.

26. Manuel Pérez to Auguste Chouteau, July 23, 1792, St. Louis Archives; *Hunt's Minutes,* I, 121–22; Billon, *Annals under the French and Spanish,* 245.

27. See the St. Louis Archives for examples of Pierre Chouteau's land transactions.

28. Both the Chouteau Collections and the St. Louis Archives contain records of numerous slave transactions involving Auguste and Pierre Chouteau; 1791 Census, typescript in Census Papers, Missouri Historical Society.

29. Francisco Cruzat to Magistrates at Kaskaskia, Aug. 24, 1782, in Clarence W. Alvord, ed., *Kaskaskia Records, 1778–1790,* (Springfield, Ill., 1909), 298–99.

30. Cruzat to Magistrates, Sept. 1, 1782, in *ibid.,* 300.

31. William Grant's power of attorney to Auguste Chouteau, Apr. 29, 1797, St. Louis Archives.

32. Aside from Laclède's, one of the earliest estates that Chouteau handled was that of Louis Robert in 1788. Some of the largest estates he helped administer included those of Sylvestre Labbadie, Joseph Robidoux, and Julien Dubuque. Both the Chouteau Collections and the St. Louis Archives contain many documents related to Auguste's role as an administrator.

33. See documents pertaining to the killing of Baptiste, 1785–87, in Billon, *Annals under the French and Spanish,* 233–43.

34. Agreement of Daniel McElduff and Auguste Chouteau, Oct. 31 and Nov. 12, 1789, Helen Blouin to Don Henry Peyroux de la Coudrenière, civil and military commandant of Ste. Genevieve, Nov. 11, 1789, and McElduff to Peyroux, Nov. 16, 1789, all in Ste. Genevieve Archives, microfilm copy in the State Historical Society of Missouri.

35. See Chouteau Collections and Vallé Papers, Missouri Historical Society.

36. *Hunt's Minutes,* I, 126.

37. Accounts of the Sept. 22 proceeding can be found in the Delassus Papers, Sept. 29, 1782, Missouri Historical Society, and Billon, *Annals under the French and Spanish,* 216–20. There is also a copy of the Regulations for the maintenance of St. Louis streets in the Ste. Genevieve Archives.

38. Marriage contract for Jean Pierre Chouteau and Pelagie Kiersereau, July 26, 1783, Chouteau Collections; Cunningham and Blythe, *Founding Family,* 59.

39. Cunningham and Blythe, *Founding Family,* 60.

40. Houck, *History of Missouri,* II, 89n20. The other Morrison brothers were William, Robert, Samuel, and Guy. William, who had come to Kaskaskia in 1790, formed with his uncle, Guy Bryan of Philadelphia, a trading partnership known as Bryan and Morrison. That powerful mercantile firm operated from Canada to the Gulf of Mexico and from Pittsburgh to the Rockies. The Chouteaus often conducted business with William Morrison and his brothers. In 1809 William Morrison and his fellow Kaskaskia trader Pierre Menard joined Manuel Lisa, Pierre Chouteau, Chouteau's son Auguste Pierre, and several other well-known merchants to form the St. Louis Missouri Fur Company. For the story of Morrison's trading operations consult John L. Tevebaugh, "Merchant on the Western Frontier: William Morrison of Kaskaskia, 1790–1837" (Ph.D. diss., University of Illinois, 1962).

41. Cunningham and Blythe, *Founding Family,* 59–60.

42. Marriage contract of Auguste Chouteau and Marie Thérèse Cerré, Sept. 21, 1786, Chouteau Collections.

43. Those fashionable wedding garments are now in the Missouri Historical Society's costume collection.

44. Cunningham and Blythe, *Founding Family,* 6.

45. Relying on the tribe's oral traditions, John J. Mathews says that both men married Osage women. See Mathews, *The Osages,* 285. The practice of keeping an Indian wife for the wilderness and a white one for the city (St. Louis) was manifested in its most tragic and dramatic form in Manuel Lisa's wilderness marriage to Mitain of the Omahas, the prototype of Clay Basket in James A. Michener's *Centennial.*

46. See Donald Jackson, ed., *Letters of the Lewis and Clark Expedition with Related Documents, 1783–1854* (Urbana, Ill., 1962), 305n.

47. Billon, *Annals under the French and Spanish,* 148–50.

48. *Ibid.,* 149.

49. John Darby, *Personal Recollections* (St. Louis, 1880), as cited in John Francis McDermott, "Auguste Chouteau: First Citizen of Upper Louisiana," in McDermott, ed., *Frenchmen and French Ways in the Mississippi Valley* (Urbana, Ill., 1969), 9. McDermott notes that Darby was incorrect on one minor point: according to the inventory of Auguste Chouteau's estate they had at least one carpet.

50. McDermott, "Auguste Chouteau," 8–13.

51. *Hunt's Minutes,* II, 3.

52. Carl Chapman's account of the Osages in Spanish Illinois provides useful insights concerning the relationship between that tribe and the Chouteau brothers. See Chapman, "The Indomitable Osages in Spanish Illinois (Upper Louisiana) 1763–1804," in McDermott, ed., *The Spanish in the Mississippi Valley, 287–313.*

53. See Grant Foreman, *Indians and Pioneers: The Story of the American Southwest before 1830,* rev. ed. (Norman, Okla., 1936), 16–18. According to Mathews neither tribal nor gentile memory recalls the identity of the chief whom the French called Le Chenier. Mathews, *The Osages,* 300.

54. Considerable confusion surrounds both the date and the circumstances under which Clermont or Gra Mon or Arrow-Going-Home (as he was variously called) left his village on the Osage River and took up permanent residence in the vicinity of the Verdigris River. In 1777 Francisco Cruzat identified "Cleromon" as the chief of the Great Osage village on the banks of the Osage River. See Cruzat's report, Nov. 15, 1777, in Houck, ed., *Spanish Regime,* I, 144. In late 1806, James B. Wilkinson reported that Clermont's son, Clermont II or Builder of Towns, was the greatest warrior and most influential man among the Arkansas Osages. According to Wilkinson, White Hair or Paw-Hiu-Skah had usurped Clermont II's authority when the latter was still a child. See James B. Wilkinson's report, Apr. 6, 1807, in Donald Jackson, ed., *The Journals of Zebulon Montgomery Pike with Letters and Related Documents* (Norman, Okla., 1966), 16–17, and Savoie Lottinville, ed., *Thomas Nuttall's A Journal of Travels into the Arkansas Territory during the Year 1819* (Norman, Okla., 1980), 194. Carl Chapman has speculated that the problem originated in the 1790s, when the Chouteaus used medals and gifts to elevate the standing of their ally White Hair at Clermont's expense after the latter assembled a war-mourning party over their protests. According to his account, Clermont I and some of his followers may at that point have moved permanently to the Verdigris. See Chapman, "The Indomitable Osages," 290, 299–300. If that was the case, it seems probable that Clermont's son Clermont II (who died in

67

1828) accompanied his father to the Verdigris in the 1790s and thus was already in the region when Big Track arrived there in 1802. Although it seems highly unlikely that Clermont II, who had no particular fondness for the Chouteaus, would have lent his support to the 1802 migration which Pierre Chouteau organized, his presence in the region might in reality have helped persuade many of the Missouri Osages to make the move. In fact, following Big Track's arrival, Clermont II took steps to assert his claims to tribal leadership over the newcomer from the Osage towns, who like White Hair was considered to be one of Chouteau's chiefs. As Terry P. Wilson demonstrates (despite his failure to distinguish between Clermont I and Clermont II), Clermont II became the recognized leader of the Arkansas Osages after the 1802 migration. See Terry P. Wilson, "Claremore, the Osage, and the Intrusion of Other Indians, 1800–1824," in H. Glenn Jordan and Thomas M. Holm, eds., *Indian Leaders: Oklahoma's First Statesmen* (Oklahoma City, 1979), 141–57.

Although the Chouteaus traded with the Arkansas Osages or Cheniers from the earliest period, the claims that Pierre Chouteau founded a trading post at the Three Forks region near present-day Salina, Okla., in 1795–96 are without foundation. For a summary of the evidence on this controversy see "Minutes of the Meeting of the Board of Directors of the Oklahoma Historical Society," Oct. 23, 1944, *Chronicles of Oklahoma* 22 (Winter 1944–45), 475–80, and "Founding of the First Chouteau Trading Post in Oklahoma at Salina, Mayes County," *ibid.* 24 (Winter 1946–47), 483–91. In fact, the Chouteaus established their first trading post in the area sometime after Big Track and his followers moved into the region in 1802. In subsequent years, Pierre's son Auguste Pierre developed a thriving trading house near Salina. For details concerning his operations and those of other traders in the vicinity see two articles by Wayne Morris, "Auguste Pierre Chouteau, Merchant Prince at the Three Forks of the Arkansas," *Chronicles of Oklahoma* 48 (Summer 1970), 155–63, and "Traders and Factories on the Arkansas Frontier, 1805–1822," *Arkansas Historical Quarterly* 28 (Spring 1969), 28–48.

55. Chapman, "The Indomitable Osages," 294–95.

56. Nasatir has thoroughly investigated the Spanish efforts to control the Osages. In addition to his numerous published accounts, his "Indian Trade and Diplomacy" remains a valuable source of information, and his forthcoming book with Gilbert Din, *The Imperial Osage,* will no doubt stand as the definitive work on this important topic.

57. Esteban Miró to Francisco Cruzat, May 15, 1787, in Kinnaird, ed., *Spain in the Mississippi Valley,* II, 201–3.

58. Nasatir, "Indian Trade and Diplomacy," 280.

59. Nasatir, *Borderlands in Retreat,* 42.

60. Manuel Pérez to Esteban Miró, Aug. 23, 1790, in Nasatir, *Before Lewis and Clark,* I, 134–35.

61. *Ibid.*

62. Manuel Pérez to Esteban Miró, Apr. 5, 1791, in *ibid.,* I, 143–44. In an effort to avoid detection, the British traders sometimes used Indian intermediaries to conduct trade for them along the lower Missouri.

63. Manuel Pérez to Esteban Miró, Apr. 5, 1791, in Nasatir, *Before Lewis and Clark,* I, 143–44.

64. *Ibid.*

65. *Ibid.*

66. Manuel Pérez to Residents of Ste. Genevieve, Apr. 26, 1791, Vallé Papers;

Pérez to Miró, Oct. 5, 1791, in Kinnaird, ed., *Spain in the Mississippi Valley*, II, 414–17, additional copy in Osage Indian file, John Francis McDermott Mississippi Valley Research Collection, Lovejoy Library, Southern Illinois University at Edwardsville.

67. Pérez to Miró, Nov. 8, 1791, in Nasatir, *Before Lewis and Clark*, I, 149–50.

68. *Ibid.*

69. Pérez to François Vallé, Mar. 20, 1792, Vallé Papers; Pérez to Louis Lorimier, May 4, 1792, in Houck, ed., *The Spanish Regime*, II, 44.

70. Zenon Trudeau to the Baron de Carondelet, July 25, 1792, in Nasatir, *Before Lewis and Clark*, I, 156–57.

71. *Ibid.*

72. Joseph Vallier to Carondelet, Feb. 14, 1792, and Carondelet to Don Luis de las Casas, Feb. 26, 1792, in Osage Indian file, McDermott Mississippi Valley Research Collection; Trudeau to Carondelet, Oct. 21, 1792, Carondelet to Trudeau, Dec. 22, 1792, and Trudeau to Carondelet, Apr. 10, 1793, in Kinnaird, ed., *Spain in the Mississippi Valley*, III, 94, 107, 148; Trudeau to Manuel Gayoso de Lemos, Dec. 20, 1797, in Nasatir, *Before Lewis and Clark*, II, 526.

73. Concession to Pierre Chouteau, Mar. 17, 1792, in *American State Papers, Public Lands*, VI, 839.

74. Diary of Captain Don Pedro Rousseau, Feb. 9, 1793, in Abraham P. Nasatir, *Spanish War Vessels on the Mississippi, 1792–1796* (New Haven, Conn., 1968), 167–70.

75. Trudeau to Carondelet, Mar. 2, 1793, in Nasatir, *Before Lewis and Clark*, I, 167–69.

76. Proclamation of Zenon Trudeau, June 23, 1793, typescript copy in Ste. Genevieve Papers, Missouri Historical Society.

77. Merchants of St. Louis to Carondelet, June 22, 1793, in Nasatir, *Before Lewis and Clark*, I, 181–84.

78. Trudeau to Carondelet, Sept. 28, 1793, in *ibid.*, I, 197–201.

79. *Ibid.*

80. Carondelet to Don Luis de las Casas, Dec. 2, 1795, in Houck, ed., *Spanish Regime*, II, 100–101. Another copy is in the Osage Indian file, McDermott Mississippi Valley Research Collection.

81. *Ibid.*

82. *Ibid.*

83. Contract between Auguste Chouteau and the Baron de Carondelet, May 18, 1794, in Houck, ed., *Spanish Regime*, II, 106–10.

84. Carondelet to the Duke of Alcudia, May 31, 1794, in *ibid.*, 103–6.

85. Contract between Chouteau and Carondelet, May 18, 1794, in *ibid.*, 106–10; Pierre Chouteau's commission, May 21, 1794, Delassus Papers, Missouri Historical Society.

86. Trudeau's Report on Trade in St. Louis, May 1–3, 1794, in Nasatir, *Before Lewis and Clark*, I, 209–11.

87. Trudeau to Gayoso, Dec. 20, 1797, in *ibid.*, II, 526.

88. Picanne's speech in Louis Lorimier's Journal, Aug. 22, 1794, in Houck, ed., *Spanish Regime*, II, 95–96.

89. Trudeau to Carondelet, Mar. 12, 1795, in Nasatir, *Before Lewis and Clark*, I, 318–19; Trudeau to François Vallé, Mar. 24, 1795, Vallé Papers.

90. Trudeau to Carondelet, Apr. 18, 1795, in Nasatir, *Before Lewis and Clark*, I,

320. Carl Chapman has conducted extensive archaeological investigations which tend to confirm Halley's Bluff in Vernon County, Mo., as the site for Fort Carondelet. See Chapman, "The Indomitable Osages," 303–7.

91. Trudeau to Carondelet, May 27, July 20, and Aug. 30, 1795, in Nasatir, *Before Lewis and Clark,* I, 214–15, 343–44, 345–46.

92. Chapman, "The Indomitable Osages," 303.

93. Trudeau to Carondelet, Apr. 18, 1795, in Nasatir, *Before Lewis and Clark,* I, 320–21.

94. Chapman, "The Indomitable Osages," 300–301.

95. Trudeau to Carondelet, Apr. 18, 1795, in Nasatir, *Before Lewis and Clark,* I, 320–21.

96. Trudeau to Carondelet, Aug. 30, 1795, in *ibid.,* 345–46.

97. For a discussion of the importance of Indian medals and diplomacy see John Ewers, "Symbols of Chiefly Authority in Spanish Louisiana," in McDermott, ed., *The Spanish in the Mississippi Valley,* 272–84; Chapman, "The Indomitable Osages," 299; Trudeau to Carondelet, May 30, 1795, in Nasatir, *Before Lewis and Clark,* I, 325–27; Perry Wallis to Frederick Bates, Dec. 18, 1808, Bates Papers, Missouri Historical Society. According to Wallis, Clermont II declared in 1808 "White Hare and Shoto are his mortal enemies, the one because his father was the only great chief of the Osages and that dignity belonged to him (Claremont) and the other because he wished him to leave his village on the Arkansas River and move over to Missouri which he never would. . . ."

98. The Baron de Carondelet to Jacques Clamorgan, May 11, 1796, Clamorgan Papers, Missouri Historical Society. Todd's activities are discussed in Chap. 4 below.

99. Auguste Chouteau to Carondelet, Dec. 8, 1796, Chouteau Collections.

100. Auguste Chouteau to Carondelet, Apr. 18, 1797, Chouteau Collections.

101. *Ibid.*

102. Auguste Chouteau to Manuel Gayoso de Lemos, June 24, 1797, Chouteau Collections.

103. *Ibid.*

104. Chapman, "The Indomitable Osages," 300.

105. Auguste Chouteau to Carondelet, Apr. 18, 1797, Chouteau Collections.

106. *Ibid.*

107. Auguste Chouteau to Gayoso de Lemos, July 29, 1797, Vasquez Papers, Missouri Historical Society.

108. Trudeau to Carondelet, May 26, 1797, in Nasatir, *Before Lewis and Clark,* II, 521.

109. Auguste Chouteau to Gayoso de Lemos, June 24, 1797, Chouteau Collections; Chouteau to Gayoso de Lemos, July 29, 1797, Vasquez Papers.

110. Trudeau to Gayoso de Lemos, Jan. 15, 1798, in Nasatir, *Before Lewis and Clark,* II, 538.

111. Auguste Chouteau to Gayoso de Lemos, July 22, 1798, Chouteau Collections.

112. *Ibid.*

113. Auguste Chouteau to Gayoso de Lemos, Apr. 14, 1799, Chouteau Collections.

114. *Hunt's Minutes,* I, 126.

115. Carlos Dehault Delassus to the Marquis de Casa Calvo, Nov. 29, 1800, in Nasatir, *Before Lewis and Clark,* II, 623–24.

116. Delassus to Casa Calvo, Sept. 25, 1800, in Houck, ed., *Spanish Regime,* II, 301–7.

117. *Ibid.*

118. *Ibid.*

119. Presents to Osage Indians, Sept. 6, 1800, in *ibid.,* 310–11.

120. Delassus to Casa Calvo, Sept. 25, 1800, in *ibid.,* 306–7.

121. *Ibid.*

122. *Ibid.*

123. Casa Calvo to Delassus, Dec. 30, 1800, in Nasatir, *Before Lewis and Clark,* II, 628.

124. Juan Ventura Morales to Delassus, Jan. 26, 1802, Chouteau Collections.

125. The story of Lisa and his activities can be found in Richard E. Oglesby, *Manuel Lisa and the Opening of the Missouri Fur Trade* (Norman, Okla., 1963). For this episode see pp. 18–22, but that account should be supplemented with Walter B. Douglas, *Manuel Lisa,* ed. Abraham P. Nasatir (New York, 1964), 17–19.

126. *Ibid.*

127. Douglas-Nasatir, *Manuel Lisa,* 25–26, 40–41.

128. *Ibid.,* 19.

129. *Ibid.,* 26.

130. *Ibid.,* 20–21; Manuel Lisa, Charles Sanguinet, François Marie Benoit, and Gregory Sarpy to Manuel de Salcedo, June 4, 1802, in Nasatir, *Before Lewis and Clark,* II, 677–80.

131. *Ibid.*

132. Salcedo to Lisa and partners, June 12, 1802, in *ibid.,* 687–89.

133. Delassus to Salcedo, Aug. 28, 1802, in *ibid.,* 705; Douglas-Nasatir, *Manuel Lisa,* 21.

134. Morales to Delassus, June 18, 1802, Chouteau Collections; Douglas-Nasatir, *Manuel Lisa,* 21.

135. Lottinville, ed., *Nuttall's Journal,* 105n10; Wilson, "Claremore, the Osage, and the Intrusion of Other Indians, 1800–1824," 142–46.

136. Lisa to Delassus, Mar. 14, 1803, in Nasatir, *Before Lewis and Clark,* II, 716–18; Douglas-Nasatir, *Manuel Lisa,* 22; Oglesby, *Manuel Lisa,* 25.

137. Oglesby, *Manuel Lisa,* 25–26; Douglas-Nasatir, *Manuel Lisa,* 27–28.

138. Oglesby, *Manuel Lisa,* 26–27; Douglas-Nasatir, *Manuel Lisa,* 22–23; *Chouteau vs. Lisa,* 1803, in Billon, *Annals under the French and Spanish,* 334–38.

139. Douglas-Nasatir, *Manuel Lisa,* 23, 39.

140. *Ibid.*

141. Cavelier and Son to Auguste Chouteau, Oct. 28, 1802, Chouteau Collections.

142. Marie Philippe Le Duc to Delassus, quoted in Douglas-Nasatir, *Manuel Lisa,* 31–32.

143. *Ibid.*

144. *Ibid.,* 32–33.

FURS AND FOREIGN WARS

THE 1790S were an uncertain decade for the Chouteaus and for their community. Since its founding in 1764, St. Louis had grown and developed steadily, but midway in its third decade that changed. The city's population was no longer increasing, and its economy was on the verge of stagnating.[1] Not only did Upper Louisiana's agricultural output continue to lag, but the fur trade, long the economic mainstay, was also on the wane. Increasingly continental preoccupations had forced the great European powers to rely more heavily upon their traders to sustain their claims to North American territorial possessions. Unfortunately, Spain's inability to supply its French-speaking adventurers in the wilderness with the trade goods and imperial largess necessary for holding the Indians to the Spanish flag placed its emissaries at a decided disadvantage.

The better-equipped British traders gradually captured control of the Indian trade on both sides of the Mississippi north of St. Louis. Neither the efforts of Lieutenant Governors Francisco Cruzat, Manuel Pérez, and Zenon Trudeau nor the activities of traders such as Jacques Clamorgan and Louis Tesson Honoré proved sufficient to check the British intrusions into the northern country.[2] With a reported 150 traders operating out of Michilimackinac as early as 1792, St. Louisans found themselves relegated to an ever-shrinking trading zone. As competition for the dwindling fur supply intensified, profits tumbled sharply. Whereas a few years earlier St. Louis traders sometimes reaped returns of between 300 and 400 percent, they now had to be satisfied with 25 percent.[3]

As Upper Louisiana's principal merchants, the Chouteaus fared better in the highly volatile fur market than many of their rivals, but they too experienced numerous problems. Because the traffic in furs was international in scope, conflicts among nations often disrupted the trade and compounded the risks. At no time was that more evident than during the war-wracked 1790s, when the repercussions of the French Revolution, then convulsing Europe, spilled over onto the North American continent. Even after the Spaniards awarded him a monopoly of important Osage trade in 1794, Auguste Chouteau had to struggle to remain solvent amidst the uncertainties of an international market buffeted by distant events completely beyond his control. If that were not bad enough, Auguste and his brother sometimes found themselves forced to choose between conflicting national loyalties. They were, after all, at one and the same time Frenchmen by birth, language, and culture, Spanish subjects and imperial agents, and businessmen closely linked to British suppliers and fur dealers in Canada and England.

The multinational character of the Chouteaus' business activities made it imperative for them to stay abreast of the latest developments abroad. When the revolutionary French National Assembly's declaration of war on Austria in 1792 triggered a full-scale European conflict, the experienced St. Louis merchants sensed that the expanding struggle posed a serious threat to the North American fur trade and, more to the point, to their own trading ventures. Nonetheless, Auguste and Pierre attempted to carry on business as usual in 1793. Although illness prevented Pierre from undertaking his annual trip to Michilimackinac that spring, the two brothers dispatched fifty-six packs of assorted skins to the Great Lakes post, including one large shipment which Auguste described as "fine quality peltries from the upper Missouri traders."[4] The elder Chouteau asked Charles Gratiot to act as their agent at Michilimackinac in Pierre's absence. He empowered his brother-in-law to do whatever was necessary to get a fair price for the peltries, but he suggested that Gratiot give preference to Etienne Campion of Grant, Campion and Company. That firm had handled the Chouteau account in previous years, and Auguste had already drawn a bill of credit on them for current expenses. Experience had taught him it was wise to work with the Michilimackinac agents whenever possible.[5]

Since the Chouteaus were sending most of their furs northward by this time, the Canadian connection had become a vital part of their operations. Fortunately, Lieutenant Governor Trudeau, like his predecessors, continued to look the other way as St. Louis merchants dealt with Canadian and American suppliers.[6] The Chouteaus and other community leaders applauded the popular official's willingness to consider local needs and urged the king to retain him in his post indefinitely.[7]

While the Chouteaus waited for word from Gratiot concerning the arrangements he had made for their furs in Michilimackinac, reports reached their town in 1793 that Great Britain had joined the war against France. The news prompted Auguste and Pierre to dispatch a letter to their brother-in-law advising him that they still wanted the goods they had ordered from London.[8] England's status was crucial, and the Chouteaus knew it. Not only did British manufacturers provide virtually all of the Indian trade goods, but England was also the hub of the European fur market. Most American furs first went to London, where brokers resold a substantial portion to buyers from the Continent. Any disruption of the continental markets drastically reduced the demand for furs in England.

It did not take long for the effects of the Anglo-French conflict to be felt in St. Louis. Gratiot reported from Michilimackinac in mid-summer that depressed fur prices there had made it impossible for him to reach a satisfactory agreement with Grant, Campion and Company. After much haggling, Campion had proposed to buy Chouteau's furs at 25 percent below the previous year's prices, but Gratiot held out for only a 15 percent reduction. When Campion rejected that offer, Gratiot declined to sell to him and opted to send the furs to Montreal, where he hoped to secure a better return. If prices were equally low there, then Gratiot intended to ship them directly to John Henry Schneider, a London fur merchant in whom he had great confidence.[9]

Word of declining fur prices was not the only bad news Gratiot had to relay from the Great Lakes outpost. He predicted that the war-related interruption of commerce between England and Canada would boost the cost of English trade goods in North America for the coming year by as much as 25 to 30 percent.[10] Equally unsettling were Gratiot's reports concerning Campion's reaction to his decision to send Chouteau's furs directly to Montreal. The loss of that substantial account so angered the Canadian trader and his partner, William Grant, that in an effort to "revenge themselves" they attempted to hire away all the *engagés* Chouteau had previously retained in his service at Michilimackinac.[11]

Gratiot, who had already warned Chouteau to expect "trade-spoilers," now predicted that the Michilimackinac traders would compete actively with him for the Missouri trade. Fearing that the Chouteau brothers might be overstocked with trade goods, he suggested that Auguste undercut Grant and Campion in outfitting the Missouri trade, presumably even if this meant selling at a loss. This would, he concluded, soon "weary them and disgust them with their undertaking."[12] It seems unlikely that the conservative Chouteau thought much of his brother-in-law's idea. Such a scheme could unleash a ruinous trade war in the already volatile fur market. Besides, if his plans for the Osage trade materialized, as he assumed they would, he would have a place for all of his merchandise and more.

The matter with Grant, Campion and Company was still not settled by autumn, when Gratiot, then on his way to Europe, arrived in Montreal. Gratiot had sent the Chouteau furs to the Canadian firm's offices there, but company representatives refused to release them until Auguste's accounts with them had been paid in full. Since his clients could not possibly settle their accounts until they sold their furs, Gratiot went to court seeking to recover possession of the disputed pelts.[13] The legal proceedings meant additional costs, for as Gratiot advised two of his other St. Louis clients also involved in the action, "It is impossible to obtain justice without money and . . . lawyers don't feed themselves on prayers."[14]

Even after the Canadian firm agreed to open the fur packs, rebale them, and ship them to London to be sold for the accounts of Chouteau and his creditors, Gratiot insisted that he intended to sue the company for damages and costs resulting from their illegal seizure of the furs.[15] Gratiot departed for Europe at the end of October, and the Chouteau brothers apparently declined to press the issue further, leaving their account with Grant, Campion and Company unsettled until Auguste met with William Grant in Cahokia more than three years later and agreed to renew their business relationship, after amicably resolving their long-standing differences.[16]

Initially, however, the dispute with Grant had not helped Chouteau's reputation or that of the other Illinois traders among the more influential Montreal firms. In mid-1794 a representative of the powerful Todd, McGill and Company advised Isaac Todd's nephew Andrew Todd, who was then in St. Louis, against involving himself in the trade there: "As you seem to have a view of fixing some plan of Trade with Messrs. Chouteau & of buying Furs with Mr. Bleakley, we request you to recall to your memory the idea of your uncle of the Illinois Furs: He says that He would not send a light canoe for a load of them to that Country and we perfectly coincide with him in opinion; besides Monsr. Chouteau must now be largely in debt and it is next to impossible that He can get out of it until a great change in Furs takes place a thing that no one can foresee the time when it shall happen. . . ."[17] The conventional wisdom at the time was that immensely rich though they were, the southern fur lands—Missouri, Arkansas, present Oklahoma, and Louisiana—could not match the northern, cold-country pelts of Michigan, Iowa, Wisconsin, and the upper Missouri. Young Todd, who replaced Campion as the Chouteau's principal agent at Michilimackinac, obviously assessed the situation differently as he began receiving the first returns from Chouteau's new Osage monopoly.

Meanwhile, Charles Gratiot had arrived in London in December 1793, and the following spring he confirmed what the Chouteaus already knew—the war had been especially hard on the fur business. He admonished his North American kinsmen to send only the finest skins and furs to London because those of lesser quality would not return a profit.[18] Gratiot also encountered problems in securing the merchandise the Chouteaus had asked him to send from London. British wartime regulations prohibited the export of guns and powder, so using the line of credit extended to Chouteau by Schneider and Company, he arranged for Todd, McGill and Company in Montreal to furnish those items from their stock.[19]

Gratiot was able to buy from various London dealers most of the non-contraband items his brothers-in-law had ordered, including such diverse commodities as iron pails, cutlery, tools, pewter utensils, blankets, shoes, leather canes, cloth of all kinds and colors, ladies' silk stockings, garden seeds, tea, and assorted medicines. The shipment also included an elegant silver-studded saddle and bridle engraved with Pierre Chouteau's initials, made especially for him by Samuel Beazley and Company.[20] Not only did such custom-made finery suit the Chouteau brothers' patrician tastes, but it also accented their aristo-

cratic bearing and made it abundantly clear that any egalitarian impulses born
of the frontier experience had not received their countenance.

When the supplies Gratiot had purchased in England were ready for shipment, he had difficulty finding a boat to carry them across the Atlantic because
of the war. He finally arranged to dispatch them on a vessel sailing under the
protection of convoy, thereby saving the Chouteaus a substantial sum thanks
to reduced insurance costs.[21]

As these events unfolded, Lieutenant Governor Trudeau, in concert with the
Baron de Carondelet, launched yet another campaign to revitalize the languishing fur trade in St. Louis and to counter British incursions into Spanish
territory. Carondelet's new program, first unveiled in 1792, proposed to end
the monopolistic system by allowing any resident of Illinois who purchased a
license from the government to engage in the fur trade.[22] In October 1793,
Trudeau summoned all of Upper Louisiana's traders to a meeting in St. Louis
to review a detailed set of proposed regulations which Carondelet hoped would
eliminate the inequities of the previous system and improve the overall effi-
ciency of Spanish trading operations.[23] The Chouteaus obviously favored reten-
tion of the closed system, but in view of Auguste's plans to seek control of the
Osage trade in return for the construction of a fort, they said little in public
on the subject, choosing instead to air their disagreements privately with the
proper officials in St. Louis and New Orleans.

In their meeting the St. Louis traders recommended that Carondelet's proposed rules be modified to allow local merchants to secure additional goods
from British and American sources when they were not otherwise available.
Almost certainly the Chouteau brothers backed that resolution, but they showed
considerably less enthusiasm for a proposal calling for the organization of a
company with the exclusive right to control trade along the upper Missouri—
a region heretofore largely untapped by the Spanish. Yet, in spite of Auguste
and Pierre's coolness to the suggested new company, a majority of the assembled traders endorsed the idea and so informed Carondelet. The governor-
general reviewed the St. Louis group's suggestions and incorporated most of
them in the final directives he issued shortly thereafter.[24]

When Upper Louisiana's traders reconvened in the government assembly
hall in St. Louis on May 3, 1794, to reassign trading rights in accordance with
Carondelet's newly revised policies, the Chouteau brothers found themselves
in the unusual situation of being on the defensive. The decision to distribute
the Missouri trade equally among all the region's licensed traders would force
them to curtail their trading operations substantially, but for the moment
there was little they could do about it. Both Auguste and Pierre attended the
meeting, presided over by trade syndic Jacques Clamorgan. The traders set the
value of the Missouri trade at 175,000 livres annually. According to their

estimates, the Big and Little Osage trade accounted for 96,000 livres, with the remaining amount divided variously among the Kansas, Republicans, Otos, Pawnees, Loups, and Omahas.[25]

In conformity with Carondelet's directives, the group decided to divide the trade into twenty-nine equal shares, each worth approximately 6,000 livres. That amounted to one share for each of the twenty-five St. Louis and three Ste. Genevieve licensed merchants who were present for the meeting and, according to custom, one share for Lieutenant Governor Trudeau. In the drawings that were held, Pierre was one of twelve traders authorized to trade with the Big Osages, and Auguste was awarded trading rights with the Republican nation.[26]

Two days later the Chouteaus were back at the government house for a meeting convened by Clamorgan to consider plans for an organization to initiate trade along the upper Missouri. The glib and aggressive Clamorgan dazzled Spanish officials and members of the St. Louis merchant community with a grandiose scheme for driving the British from the upper Missouri and reestablishing the hegemony of Spanish traders in the region, but the always-cautious Chouteaus were not so impressed. After listening to Clamorgan's proposal, they declined to participate in the venture because they considered it too risky.[27]

In any event, Auguste Chouteau had other things in mind. Almost immediately after Clamorgan's meeting, the elder Chouteau left for New Orleans, where, as previously mentioned, he won Carondelet's approval for his plan to establish a fort among the Osages. That agreement, in effect, overturned the recently approved trade assignments and gave Chouteau exclusive control over sixteen of the twenty-nine shares of trade allocated to the Missouri traders.[28]

While the Chouteaus concentrated their energies on exploiting the familiar Osage trade, they nervously eyed Clamorgan's attempts to enter the upper Missouri under the auspices of the newly formed Company of Explorers of the Upper Missouri. Despite the Chouteaus' decision not to participate, eight other merchants had joined Clamorgan in this venture, which promptly won Carondelet's unqualified endorsement.[29] Even Lieutenant Governor Trudeau borrowed 2,000 piastres from Auguste to invest in the enterprise, dismissing Chouteau's skepticism about the new company's chances for success.[30]

In 1794 and 1795 the Missouri Company sent out three expeditions, but each encountered stiff resistance from Indian tribes in the region which caused them all to fail. The company's poor initial showing dashed hopes in St. Louis for a speedy Spanish takeover of the northern Indian trade. Many investors blamed Clamorgan for their losses, but he successfully fended off his critics and through skillful maneuvering secured complete control of the faltering Missouri Company. With the backing of the powerful British merchant Andrew Todd, Clamorgan won Carondelet's approval for extending the firm's monopoly to include Indian trade on the upper Mississippi as well as the upper Missouri despite the growing opposition in St. Louis to his continued leadership.[31]

Todd, who handled the Chouteau shipments in Michilimackinac after 1794, had switched his allegiance to Spain when Great Britain acquiesced to American demands and withdrew her remaining troops from the U.S. Northwest Territory. The Britisher moved his headquarters from Michilimackinac to New Orleans in return for numerous concessions from Carondelet, who now looked to him for assistance in reestablishing Spanish control along the upper Mississippi and Missouri. By joining forces with Todd, Clamorgan hoped to revitalize his languishing northern enterprises. With his friend Regis Loisel, a onetime clerk of the Chouteaus at Michilimackinac, Clamorgan formed Clamorgan, Loisel and Company as a successor to the nearly defunct Missouri Company. The new firm agreed to make Todd its sole supplier. In return, Todd promised to supply only Clamorgan, Loisel and Company and the Chouteau brothers in St. Louis.[32] Understandably, Todd had insisted on the right to continue doing business with the Chouteau brothers, who made purchases from him totaling more than 75,000 livres between July 1794 and November 1795.[33]

Todd's unexpected death in New Orleans from yellow fever in November 1796 shocked and saddened his associates and brought Clamorgan, who had borrowed heavily from him, to the verge of bankruptcy. Because Chouteau was actively involved in settling Todd's affairs in St. Louis, Clamorgan found it necessary to look to him for assistance. Realizing that Clamorgan's financial demise would unleash a chain reaction and ruin many others in his town, Chouteau came to Clamorgan's rescue in 1799 in spite of their previous differences.[34]

While Clamorgan struggled unsuccessfully to extend trading operations in St. Louis to the headwaters of the Missouri, military and diplomatic developments in Europe brought the conflict abroad ever closer to the wilderness capital on the Mississippi. Spain's declaration of war against France in 1793 raised the specter of a French campaign to regain control of Louisiana. With its sparse population and its limited resources, the North American province seemed particularly vulnerable. That such fears might be justified became evident when the representative of the French revolutionary government in the United States, Citizen Edmond Genêt, granted military commissions to George Rogers Clark and other lesser-known American adventurers in an effort to mount expeditions against Louisiana and Florida.[35] Although the proposed invasions never materialized, the rumors of French attempts to liberate Louisiana in the name of revolutionary principles understandably alarmed Spanish authorities in the predominantly French-speaking province.

In addition to the possible French threat, Spanish officials in Louisiana also had to concern themselves with the continuing dangers posed by the British on the north and the rapidly expanding American republic to the east. As governor, Carondelet devoted much of his attention to planning for the region's defense. Among other things, he authorized the formation of a Spanish fleet to patrol the Mississippi River in an effort to thwart possible assaults against Spanish territory.[36] He also directed Lieutenant Governor Trudeau to strengthen the military fortifications in St. Louis, which by 1792 had fallen into disrepair and ruin once again. Trudeau opted to build a wooden fort surrounding Fort San Carlos, the old stone tower originally constructed in the Mississippi River settlement just prior to the British invasion of 1780.[37] Likewise, concerns about a possible attack prompted Carondelet to attempt to defuse the volatile Osage situation by contracting with Chouteau to build a fortification in the heart of the Osage country as a step toward restoring peace with that powerful Indian nation.

In 1795 Carondelet dispatched Manuel Gayoso de Lemos, the governor of Natchez, on an inspection tour of Upper Louisiana. By sending Gayoso and the naval squadron to Spanish Illinois, Carondelet hoped to secure a firsthand report on conditions in that district and at the same time to impress Indians and local inhabitants with Spanish power, lest some of them be tempted to cast their lot with Spain's enemies. Although Jacobinism was never a serious problem in St. Louis, the Spaniards worried a great deal about the loyalty of their subjects in the remote province, and directed Gayoso to keep a careful lookout for any signs of revolutionary activity.[38]

A salute fired from the guns atop Fort San Carlos announced Gayoso's arrival in St. Louis on October 30. Many of the village's inhabitants, led by Lieutenant Governor Trudeau and Auguste Chouteau, turned out to welcome their distinguished visitor.[39] As one of Gayoso's principal hosts during his sojourn in Upper Louisiana, the eldest Chouteau brother was an almost constant companion of the mild-mannered and polished governor of Natchez. He accompanied Gayoso on horseback from St. Louis to St. Charles, where they celebrated the king's birthday with a special mass and other appropriate ceremonies before inspecting the countryside around the small Missouri River settlement. Since Auguste was as familiar with the Illinois country as any single individual, he was a logical choice to guide the Spanish official during his reconnaissance mission. After completing their inspection in the vicinity of the strategic Missouri junction, Gayoso and his party boarded the Spanish vessel *La Vigilante*, which had been sent to St. Charles to pick them up; and when they reached the Mississippi, they ascended it as far north as the Illinois River before returning to St. Louis. Aside from Fort Carondelet, which he could not reach because of low water, Gayoso visited all military installations in Upper Louisiana during his travels.[40]

Chouteau and the others spared no effort to impress the visiting Spanish dignitary and to convince him of their loyalty to Spain. As always, the famed

Chouteau hospitality and charm worked its magic and the two men became fast friends. When Auguste hosted what Gayoso described as "a magnificent assembly" at his refurbished mansion, the Spaniard carefully scrutinized the guests but could find no signs of revolutionary ardor. There were no tricolored ribbons or similar adornments except for the dress of three colors worn by Madame Robidoux, wife of Joseph Sr., a well-known trader, but Gayoso brushed that aside as merely a result of the lady's "bad taste," since he judged her garment to be older than the French Revolution.[41]

The only person who might possibly have been tainted with Jacobin sentiments was Chouteau's brother-in-law Joseph Marie Papin, but according to Gayoso there was no reason to fear him because his "relatives and friends keep him under control."[42] Gayoso left St. Louis reassured by all that he had heard and seen and impressed most of all by Auguste Chouteau, about whom he wrote, "Likewise I find it impossible to forget the well-known enthusiasm of Mr. Chouteau as well as his enterprising and ready character regarding whatever interests the royal service."[43] In the future the Chouteaus would not hesitate to call upon Gayoso for assistance, especially after he succeeded Carondelet as the provincial governor-general in 1797.[44]

Although Gayoso's reports helped allay fears of a possible revolt against Spanish authority in St. Louis, the overall situation was by no means tranquil. Clamorgan's failure to open trade along the upper Missouri rekindled Spanish anxiety over the continuing British domination of trading activities throughout the upper Mississippi valley, and events in Europe did not alleviate that concern. In 1795, following two years of unsuccessful fighting, Spain decided to come to terms with France. The Treaty of Basel, which officially ended hostilities between those two nations, prepared the way for Spain to go to war with Great Britain a year later. This shift in alignments forced the Spaniards once again to consider the possibility of a British attack from Canada against Louisiana.

Moreover, the visit of the French general Victor Collot to St. Louis in 1796 aroused old fears about French intentions in the region. Reports that Collot, who was engaged in military surveillance for his government, had received a warm welcome from St. Louisans convinced Carondelet that he needed to take decisive steps to counter both British and French threats to Spanish territory.[45] Consequently, he ordered a force of more than 100 Spanish regulars to accompany Lieutenant Colonel Don Carlos Howard to St. Louis. Carondelet had selected Howard to assume personal control of all military operations in Upper Louisiana. The colonel's instructions called for the deportation to New Orleans of any suspected French agitators, the destruction of any British establishments along the Missouri or Mississippi rivers, the organization of militia companies in Upper Louisiana, and the strengthening of fortifications at St. Louis. Before Howard headed up the Mississippi, Carondelet made it a point to recommend the two Chouteau brothers as persons deserving of his confidence and capable of providing assistance.[46]

Auguste welcomed Howard to St. Louis in 1797. The Spaniard's conversations with the St. Louis merchant and others quickly convinced him that the rumors of local insurrection had been greatly exaggerated. In his estimation, the greatest danger to the Mississippi River settlement continued to come from the British in Canada. An offer from the Chouteaus to raise a force of 500 Osages to assist in defending Upper Louisiana in case of an enemy attack impressed Howard even more than their elegant reception and gracious hospitality.[47]

To further augment the St. Louis defenses, Howard supervised the construction of four stone towers and also launched an unsuccessful military raid against the British post at Prairie du Chien. Despite the mission's failure, fears of a British invasion in St. Louis gradually subsided. Nonetheless, when the king of Spain issued a plea to Louisiana's citizens in 1799 for donations to the royal treasury to assist with the province's defenses, Auguste saw to it that his hundred-peso contribution was twice that of any of the other local townspeople. In addition, Pierre pledged another fifty pesos. Although neither man was known for being free with his money, they were in the process of requesting an extension of their Osage monopoly and could not afford to appear unduly penurious in their support of His Majesty's government.[48]

Neither the unsettled conditions in Louisiana nor the difficulties of transacting business during wartime deterred the Chouteaus from actively participating in the fur trade. According to one estimate, the average value of furs annually brought to St. Louis during the 1790s exceeded $200,000.[49] As the city's leading merchants, Auguste and Pierre handled many of those furs. No other traders in St. Louis could match their reputation among the numerous Canadian and English firms that frequently solicited their business. In 1798, Schneider and Company officials assured Auguste that they were not apprehensive about his unpaid accounts, "first because you are a man of great fortune, and second, and more important, your honor is of the first rank."[50] Even James and Andrew McGill overcame their earlier doubts about Chouteau's standing. In 1801 those prominent Montreal merchants informed him: "Your observations on the causes which have rendered commerce with your territory less desirable than with other parties are correct, and it is possible that the good merchants there have been confounded with the bad. Candor sometimes requires that we declare that you, at least, have not been in that number. So we are well persuaded that you fulfill your engagements with all the exactitude of a merchant instructed by the greatest honesty."[51]

Although it is impossible to gauge the exact amount of the Chouteau brothers' fur sales during those years, the total would be substantial. Enough of their business records are extant to indicate that they routinely shipped large quantities of furs and peltries to Canada and New Orleans. For example, their records in 1796 show that Andrew Todd and Company credited their account with 37,950 livres for the sale of an assortment of skins and furs that included deer, beaver, otter, bear, fox, and lynx.[52] In the same year, Cavelier and Petit, a New Orleans firm, sold a collection of furs and peltries for the Chouteaus worth 21,160 livres.[53] The next year, Grant, Campion and Company reported the sale of furs for the Chouteaus valued at 33,888 livres.[54] From year to year the amounts fluctuated considerably, but even in the worst years their sales probably outdistanced those of their major competitors in St. Louis by a sizable amount.

Despite such a volume of business, declining fur prices and shipping delays resulting from the Anglo-French war, along with deductions for commissions, interest charges, and packing and transportation costs, often left the Chouteaus with large deficits in their fur-trade accounts. Those deficits, however, do not tell the entire story. Because the Chouteau brothers sometimes accepted items other than furs in payment for their goods and services, their net worth continued to increase. Auguste Chouteau's role as the community's unofficial banker provided yet another source of income. He remained the largest landowner in Upper Louisiana, and his brother Pierre was not far behind in the amount of property he owned.

Auguste also dabbled in other ventures as well. In 1795 Gayoso reported that despite frequent breakdowns, Chouteau's St. Louis mill ground all of the flour in St. Louis and St. Charles along with a substantial amount from nearby Ste. Genevieve.[55] Then, in 1800, the elder Chouteau brother began operating St. Louis's first distillery. The St. Louis merchant's difficulties in securing alcoholic spirits from his New Orleans suppliers may have prompted his decision to build his own still.[56] Work on the distillery got under way in 1799, and early the next year Lieutenant Governor Delassus gave the new venture his official blessing. Declaring it to be an establishment of public utility and benefit, he granted Chouteau 1,281 arpents of land to provide a source of fuel.[57] Its usefulness to the community might be debatable, but the Chouteaus must have found a ready market for the whiskey, brandy, grain alcohol, applejack, and other assorted liquors they were able to run off in their new still.

In the same year that Auguste Chouteau opened his distillery, Pierre secured confirmation from Delassus for a grant of twenty arpents of land above St. Charles, where he established another gristmill. Even though the undertaking folded the following spring after a flood washed away the dam at the mill site, he retained his claim to the land.[58] In fact, in an economy where specie and currency were virtually nonexistent, the Chouteau brothers' expanding real and personal property holdings provide the best indicators of their general prosperity even in hard times.

Still, with so much of their capital tied up in non-liquid assets, unpaid accounts occasionally posed problems for the Chouteaus. When the balance of Auguste Chouteau's account with Schneider and Company had remained unpaid for several years, the English firms turned it over to American fur merchant John Jacob Astor for collection.[59] Astor had already taken advantage of the unsettled European situation to enter the Canadian market. After purchasing some of Chouteau's pelts in Montreal, he invited the St. Louis merchant to ship furs directly to him in New York.[60] Fearful of the possible consequences of the powerful American's entry into the St. Louis market, or perhaps worried that Astor might use these transactions to collect the unpaid accounts with Schneider and Company, Chouteau declined Astor's offer, stating that he preferred to continue selling his furs in Canada. Despite Auguste's disinclination to allow Astor into the St. Louis market, Charles Gratiot remained eager to do business with the wealthy American merchant, but following his rebuff at the hands of the Chouteaus and their allies Astor abandoned his efforts to establish direct ties with the western fur-trading center for nearly a decade.[61]

All the while the Chouteaus continued to do a brisk business. Even the loss of Osage trading rights to Manuel Lisa and his associates in 1802 proved to be only a temporary setback for them. Not only did they trade with the Arkansas Osages, whose numbers had been augmented by the arrival of Big Track and his followers, but they sought out new fur sources. In 1801 Auguste joined Jacques Clamorgan in outfitting and equipping Regis Loisel and Hugh Heney for an expedition up the Missouri. With backing from Chouteau and Clamorgan, Loisel and trader Pierre Antoine Tabeau built Post aux Cedres at the mouth of the Bad River on the upper Missouri in 1802.[62]

The temporary cessation of hostilities in Europe following the collapse of the Second Coalition and the signing of the Peace of Amiens was particularly beneficial for fur traders. In contrast with the disappointing returns of previous years, furs sent to England in 1802 brought premium prices.[63] McGill and Company optimistically predicted that the restoration of peace would at long last bring stability to commercial affairs, but other observers, conditioned by long years of uncertainty, sounded a more cautious note.[64] While reporting on the exceptionally good prices paid in 1802, Auguste's brother-in-law Pierre Louis Panet warned of a possible renewal of hostilities between Great Britain and France. He concluded his letter with the guarded observation, "but who can foresee what will happen after all the strange events we have seen occur in the last few years."[65] In a similar vein, Canadian trader George Gillespie cautioned that the previous year's high profits might well produce unwarranted speculation which could result in substantial losses, especially if the unpredictable European situation changed again.[66]

Gillespie's reservations proved to be well founded. The resumption of fighting between Great Britain and France in 1803 deflated hopes for continued prosperity in the fur trade. Napoleon's decision to resume the conflict with

Great Britain that year came as no surprise, but his sudden agreement to sell the Louisiana Territory, over which he had only recently regained control, caught nearly everyone unaware, including the Chouteaus. When the transfer became inevitable, however, the resourceful brothers lost no time in taking steps to court the favor of the unpredictable Americans who would soon take charge.

NOTES

1. Holt, "The Shaping of St. Louis," 491, 495, 497–98.

2. Honoré, who went to the Iowa country in the 1790s, did wonders when neither medals nor money were available, but neither he nor the other Spanish traders could fully block the growing British influence. Honoré's activities are briefly mentioned in Nasatir, *Borderlands in Retreat*, 61–62.

3. Zenon Trudeau to the Baron de Carondelet, Nov. 12, 1792, and May 31, 1794, in Nasatir, *Before Lewis and Clark*, I, 162, 230.

4. Auguste Chouteau to Charles Gratiot, May 27, June 4, June 7, and June 12, 1793, and Auguste and Pierre Chouteau to Gratiot, June 20, 1793, in Barnhart, "The Letterbooks of Charles Gratiot," 402–7.

5. Auguste Chouteau to Gratiot, May 27, 1793, in *ibid.*, 402–3.

6. Nasatir, "The Anglo-Spanish Frontier on the Upper Mississippi," 192, 195, 196n.

7. Inhabitants of Spanish Illinois to the King, July 7, 1793, in Kinnaird, ed., *Spain in the Mississippi Valley*, III, 181–90.

8. Auguste and Pierre Chouteau to Charles Gratiot, June 20, 1793, in Barnhart, "The Letterbooks of Charles Gratiot," 406.

9. Charles Gratiot to Auguste Chouteau, July 12, July 18, and July 19, 1793, in *ibid.*, 407–16. Barnhart's historical introduction to the letterbooks provides a valuable summary of Gratiot's activities during this period.

10. Gratiot to Auguste Chouteau, July 12, 1793, in *ibid.*, 409.

11. Gratiot to Auguste Chouteau, July 18, 1793, in *ibid.*, 412–15.

12. Gratiot to Auguste Chouteau, July 12 and Sept. 15, 1793, in ibid., 409, 427–29.

13. Gratiot to Auguste Chouteau, Aug. 27, 1793, in *ibid.*, 418–21.

14. Charles Gratiot to Benito and Roy, Sept. 8, 1793, in *ibid.*, 435.

15. Gratiot to Auguste Chouteau, Sept. 8, 1793, in *ibid.*, 421–27.

16. Account of Auguste Chouteau with Grant, Campion, and Company, May 17, 1793–Dec. 10, 1796, Chouteau Collections, Missouri Historical Society.

17. Todd McGill and Company to Andrew Todd, Aug. 26, 1794, Fur Trade Papers, Missouri Historical Society.

18. Charles Gratiot to Auguste and Pierre Chouteau, Mar. 5, 1794, in Barnhart, "The Letterbooks of Charles Gratiot," 438–41.

19. Gratiot to Auguste and Pierre Chouteau, Mar. 30, 1794, in *ibid.*, 442–56.

20. Invoice for "diverse merchandise purchased by order of Charles Gratiot and charged to the account and risk of Messrs. Auguste and Pierre Chouteaux of St. Louis in Illinois . . . ," Mar. 27, 1794, Chouteau Collections.

21. Gratiot to Auguste and Pierre Chouteau, Mar. 30, 1794, in Barnhart, "The Letterbooks of Charles Gratiot," 442–56.

22. Carondelet's instructions to Trudeau, Mar. 28, 1792, and Proclamation of Zenon Trudeau, July 25, 1792, in Nasatir, *Before Lewis and Clark*, I, 151–52, 155–56.

23. Regulations for the Illinois Trade, Oct. 15, 1793, in *ibid.*, I, 186–94.

24. Abraham P. Nasatir, "The Formation of the Missouri Company," *Missouri Historical Review* 25 (Oct. 1930), 10–22.

25. Distribution of Missouri Trading Posts, May 1–3, 1794, in Nasatir, *Before Lewis and Clark*, I, 209–11.

26. *Ibid.* The Republicans were a major division of the Pawnee tribe known as the Kitkehahki or Republican Pawnee. See Jackson, ed., *Journals of Pike*, I, 325–27n86.

27. Articles of Incorporation of the Missouri Company, May 5, 1794, in *ibid.*, 218–25. For a summary of Clamorgan's efforts see Abraham P. Nasatir, "Jacques Clamorgan, Colonial Promoter of the Northern Border of New Spain," *New Mexico Historical Review* 17 (Apr. 1942), 101–12.

28. Zenon Trudeau to Carondelet, Apr. 18, 1795, in Nasatir, *Before Lewis and Clark*, I, 321.

29. For the full story of this venture see Nasatir, "Formation of the Missouri Company," 10–22.

30. Trudeau to Carondelet, June 4, 1795, in Nasatir, *Before Lewis and Clark*, I, 328.

31. Trudeau to Manuel Gayoso de Lemos, Dec. 20, 1797, in *ibid.*, II, 527–28; Nasatir, "Jacques Clamorgan," 107–8.

32. Minutes of Council of State, May 27, 1796, and Agreement between Andrew Todd and Clamorgan, Loisel and Company, Oct. 26, 1796, in Nasatir, *Before Lewis and Clark*, II, 435–36, 464.

33. Account of Auguste and Pierre Chouteau with Andrew Todd, July 30, 1794–Nov. 14, 1795, Chouteau Collections.

34. See Nasatir, "Jacques Clamorgan," 111; Account of Daniel Clark, Jr., with Auguste Chouteau relative to affairs of Clamorgan, Loisel and Company, July 27, 1798–Dec. 1, 1800, Chouteau Collections.

35. F. R. Hall, "Genêt's Western Intrigue, 1793–1794," *Journal of the Illinois State Historical Society* 21 (1928), 359–81.

36. For a discussion of Carondelet's defensive measures see Nasatir, *Spanish War Vessels.*

37. *Ibid.*, 306–7n40.

38. *Ibid.*, 291n9; Ernest R. Liljegren, "Jacobinism in Spanish Louisiana, 1792–1797," *Louisiana Historical Quarterly* 22 (1939), 83–97.

39. Diary of Manuel Gayoso de Lemos, Oct. 30–Nov. 10, 1795, in Nasatir, *Spanish War Vessels*, 304–9.

40. *Ibid.;* Report of Gayoso de Lemos, Nov. 24, 1795, in *ibid.*, 331–41.

41. Report of Gayoso de Lemos, Nov. 24, 1795, in *ibid.*, 333–34.

42. *Ibid.*, 334.

43. *Ibid.*

44. Auguste Chouteau to Gayoso de Lemos, June 24, 1797, and July 22, 1798, Chouteau Collections.

45. Nasatir, *Borderlands in Retreat*, 61–62.

46. The Baron de Carondelet to Don Carlos Howard, Nov. 26, 1795 [1796], in Houck, ed., *Spanish Regime*, II, 123–32.

47. Auguste Chouteau to Manuel Gayoso de Lemos, June 24, 1797, Chouteau Collections; Auguste Chouteau to Gayoso, July 29, 1797, Vasquez Papers, and ———— to Don Carlos Howard, Apr. 15, 1797, Delassus Papers, Missouri Historical Society.

48. Juan Ventura Morales to Zenon Trudeau, Mar. 1, 1799, Chouteau Collections; Subscription to Patriotic Defensive Fund, Oct. 6, 1799, in Houck, ed., *Spanish Regime,* II, 299–300.

49. Amos Stoddard, *Sketches, Historical and Descriptive of Louisiana* (Philadelphia, 1812), 297–98. Stoddard's estimate was likely based on information supplied him by the Chouteaus.

50. Schneider and Company to Auguste Chouteau, Apr. 9, 1798, Chouteau Collections.

51. James and Andrew McGill to Auguste Chouteau, Feb. 12, 1801, Chouteau Collections.

52. Account of sale of peltries by Andrew Todd for Auguste Chouteau, 1796, Chouteau Collections.

53. Account of Auguste Chouteau with Cavelier and Petit, May 13, 1796, Chouteau Collections.

54. Account of sale of goods of Chouteau sold at auction by Grant, Campion and Company, Sept. 1, 1797, Chouteau Collections.

55. Report of Gayoso de Lemos, Nov. 24, 1795, in Nasatir, *Spanish War Vessels,* 340.

56. Cavelier and Petit to Auguste Chouteau, July 26, 1798, Chouteau Collections.

57. Account of Joseph Labbadie with Auguste Chouteau, Oct. 1, 1799, Chouteau Collections; *American State Papers, Public Lands,* II, 443.

58. *American State Papers, Public Lands,* II, 455.

59. Schneider and Company to Auguste Chouteau, Apr. 11, 1799, Chouteau Collections.

60. John Jacob Astor to Auguste Chouteau, Jan. 28, 1800, Chouteau Collections.

61. Charles Gratiot to John Jacob Astor, Apr. 1, 1800, Gratiot Letterbook, Missouri Historical Society; Kenneth Wiggins Porter, *John Jacob Astor: Business Man* (New York, 1966), I, 60–62.

62. Articles of Agreement between Regis Loisel and Hugh Heney, July 6, 1801, and Account of Jacques Clamorgan relative to equipment furnished Loisel and Heney, June 20, 1805, Chouteau Collections. See also Annie Heloise Abel, *Tabeau's Narrative of Loisel's Expedition to the Upper Missouri* (Norman, Okla., 1939), 24–27.

63. Pierre Louis Panet to Auguste Chouteau, May 9, 1803, and George Gillespie to Auguste Chouteau, July 16, 1803, Chouteau Collections.

64. James and Andrew McGill and Company to Auguste Chouteau, Oct. 8, 1802, Chouteau Collections.

65. Pierre Louis Panet to Auguste Chouteau, May 9, 1803, Chouteau Collections.

66. George Gillespie to Auguste Chouteau, July 16, 1803, Chouteau Collections.

Auguste Chouteau (1749–1829).

Missouri Historical Society

Pierre Chouteau, Sr. (1758–1849).

Madame Marie Thérèse Bourgeois Chouteau (1733–1814).

Missouri Historical Society

Pierre de Laclède Liguest (1729–78).

Auguste Chouteau Mansion.

Missouri Historical Society

Thérèse Cerré Chouteau (1769–1842).

Missouri Historical Society

Laclède's original St. Louis trading headquarters, later used by the Spaniards
as the government house. Auguste Chouteau purchased the building in 1789,
added a second story, and transformed it into the city's most fashionable residence.

Missouri Historical Society

Partial View of S.t Louis

St. Louis in 1814, from the present Walnut to Pine streets.

Courtesy of Historical Pictures Service, Inc.

St. Louis in 1770 as seen from the Illinois side.

Francisco Luis Hector, the Baron de Carondelet.

Missouri Historical Society

Carlos Dehault Delassus,
Upper Louisiana's last Spanish lieutenant governor.

Missouri Historical Society

Charles Gratiot, Sr. (1752–1817).

Missouri Historical Society

Manuel Lisa.

Missouri Historical Society

Meriwether Lewis.
Pastel by Charles B. J. F. de St. Mémin.

Missouri Historical Society

William Clark. Painting by Chester Harding.

Missouri Historical Society

Chief White Hair (Paw-Hiu-Skah) of the Osages.
Portrait by Charles B. J. F. de St. Mémin.

Courtesy of the New-York Historical Society, New York City.

Chief Big Track (Cashesegra) of the Osages.
Portrait by Charles B. J. F. de St. Mémin.

Courtesy of the New-York Historical Society, New York City.

WELCOMING THE AMERICANS

T HE HISTORIC TRANSFER of the Louisiana Territory from Spain to France, and then from France to the United States, confronted Auguste and Pierre Chouteau with new and unexpected challenges more difficult, in many ways, than any they had encountered in developing the Indian trade or in serving the Spanish colonial government. Although St. Louis was remote from the councils where the decision to sell Louisiana was made, the new arrangements affected the Chouteaus and their neighbors more directly than anyone in Paris, Madrid, or Washington. The French-speaking inhabitants of the vast territory could not escape the potentially tragic consequences of the unfolding drama, which threatened to undermine their entire way of life.

The problem was particularly compelling for the Chouteaus. As the foremost traders and merchants in St. Louis, they naturally desired to retain their preeminent positions and well-established influence on the trans-Mississippi frontier, but for Frenchmen who long ago had become accustomed to the authoritarian Spanish regime, citizenship in the American republic necessitated dramatic alterations in their life-styles. To their credit, the Chouteaus again exhibited remarkable adaptability as they adjusted to the requirements of an alien culture, government, and language. Such flexibility made it possible for them to live long and productive lives under the new order which they now eagerly sought to serve. Thus, when representatives of the various governments involved in the Louisiana Purchase called upon them for assistance in the delicate operations of dismantling Spanish authority and affirming the control of the United States, the two brothers responded willingly.

At the behest of Napoleon Bonaparte, who momentarily dreamed of reviving France's colonial empire in the western hemisphere, Spain retroceded Louisiana in the Treaty of San Ildefonso on October 1, 1800. Although the terms of the agreement were kept secret, unconfirmed rumors of the transaction were abroad in America by 1801. In Upper Louisiana, the news was unsettling to the great landowners, traders, and colonial officials who for almost forty years had been constructing, often at great cost, a society in the wilderness. Despite their French heritage, the St. Louis magnates undoubtedly pondered what their fate might be under the authority of a military dictator in a nation committed to revolutionary action. Would France's First Consul upset the balance of forces and the distribution of power and wealth in their community? Auguste and Pierre certainly turned such thoughts over in their minds at the dawn of the new century.

Confirmation of Louisiana's reversion to France reached St. Louis late in 1802, and early the next year Pierre Clément Laussat, the French prefect, came to New Orleans to supervise the transfer for his government. Not long after his arrival, the colonial official sought information about conditions in Upper Louisiana from Pierre Chouteau, who was then in the capital city on business. Laussat gave the St. Louis trader a lengthy questionnaire which formed the basis for later discussions between the two men. Their talks went so well that Pierre returned home in mid-1803 with the prefect's assurances that the Chouteaus had nothing to fear and much to gain from the forthcoming French takeover.[1]

But those expectations were never to be realized, because before Spain officially surrendered control of Louisiana to France, Napoleon abandoned his designs on North America and sold the immense territory to the United States. The reasons for his unexpected decision were complex, but the French ruler's zeal for reforming France, his growing preoccupation with the perfidious British and their European allies, and his need for money to finance his continental campaigns had diverted his attention from the New World. In any case, Napoleonic dreams of an American empire already had been dashed on the hard rock of Santo Domingo. Added to these considerations were the pressures from the government of the rapidly expanding United States to ensure that its citizens would have continued access to the Mississippi River and the port of New Orleans, and Bonaparte's desire to forestall any possibility of an Anglo-American rapprochement.

Since Spanish resistance to American demands to navigate the river and to deposit goods at New Orleans had been a source of friction for years, the sudden prospect of the more aggressive French assuming control of the neighboring colony understandably had alarmed President Thomas Jefferson. When the American president quietly launched a diplomatic offensive in Paris designed to persuade Louisiana's new French rulers of the expediency of recognizing U.S. rights on the vital waterway, he even hinted that a British alliance might be America's only alternative if the French proved recalcitrant. Nevertheless, neither Jefferson nor his advisers had been prepared for the shocking news in October 1802 that the Spaniards, who had not yet turned New Orleans back to the French, had closed the port to all foreign nations.

The sudden Spanish initiative demanded an American response. In an effort to settle the issue once and for all, Jefferson dispatched James Monroe as an *envoi extraordinaire* to France to join resident minister Robert Livingston, who was already conferring on the matter. On the day before Monroe arrived in Paris, the French foreign minister Talleyrand stunned Livingston with his inquiry as to whether the United States would be interested in purchasing the entire Louisiana Territory. Although Napoleon had not authorized Talleyrand to make such an offer, he had, in fact, decided to sell Louisiana and had so informed his minister of finances, François de Barbe-Marbois, whom he designated to handle the arrangements.

The American commissioners had not been empowered to negotiate such a sweeping transaction, but they did not hesitate to accept the French offer. Further discussions were necessary, however, before the two sides agreed upon a final sale price of fifteen million dollars. On May 2, 1803, representatives of the two nations confirmed the terms of sale and signed the Treaty of Cession stipulating that the Louisiana Territory would be made a part of the United States and that its inhabitants would enjoy full rights and privileges as American citizens.[2]

In St. Louis the Chouteaus learned of the American acquisition in August of 1803, when William Henry Harrison, governor of the Indiana Territory, notified Upper Louisiana's Lieutenant Governor Don Carlos Dehault Delassus of the transaction.[3] The astonishing announcement took St. Louisans by surprise, and a mood of uncertainty quickly gripped the city. Previous concerns about the consequences of a change from Spanish to French control suddenly paled to insignificance as the city's leaders faced the prospect of adjusting their lives to accommodate the incoming Americans. Typically, however, Auguste and Pierre prepared to meet the challenge with vigor, if not enthusiasm.

As Upper Louisiana's new governors, the Americans needed to know a great deal about the region, its inhabitants, its trade arrangements, its flora and fauna, and its general character. With that in mind President Jefferson pressed ahead with the plans he previously had made to dispatch the Lewis and Clark expedition to explore the trans-Mississippi West. Since St. Louis was the obvious starting point for that mission, the American explorers turned to citizens in that town for advice and assistance. As experienced traders familiar with western Indian tribes, St. Louis's French merchants offered a ready source of information concerning the conditions the Americans might encounter during their trek to the Pacific. Beyond that, the loyalty and support of the city's leading traders could be a crucial factor in persuading Louisiana's French and Indian populace to accept American control. Under these circumstances, the Chouteau brothers stood ready to demonstrate their usefulness to the region's new rulers. Few, if any, individuals had more experience in trade and Indian relations, and certainly no one commanded more respect or honor in Upper Louisiana.

After receiving his instructions from the president, Captain Meriwether Lewis arrived in St. Louis in December 1803 to arrange for his forthcoming mission. Since the Americans lacked Spanish passports, and the formal ceremonies of transfer had not yet taken place in Upper Louisiana, Lieutenant Governor Delassus declined to grant Lewis and his fellow commander William Clark permission to set off on their westward journey. From their camp at Wood River, Illinois, opposite the mouth of the Missouri, Lewis and Clark continued with preparations for their expedition while they awaited the demise of Spanish and French authority across the Mississippi. During their stay at Camp Wood River, which lasted from December to May, both men often traveled to St. Louis, where they passed many pleasant hours in the comfortable homes of Auguste and Pierre Chouteau. In fact, Pierre's residence served the American explorers as an unofficial domicile in the city.[4] From the beginning, the association between the leaders of the exploring party and the members of St. Louis's first family was cordial and mutually beneficial.

The Chouteau gentility and gracious hospitality favorably impressed the American officers. Besides providing a welcome diversion from camp life, their visits with the Chouteaus also gave them an opportunity to expand their knowledge about the immense trans-Mississippi territory. Accordingly, Lewis wrote to Auguste on January 4, 1804, requesting answers to a series of questions about the region and its people.[5] Of course the Americans solicited similar information from other knowledgeable traders including Manuel Lisa, Joseph Robidoux, Regis Loisel, and Louis Tesson Honoré, but the Chouteaus made the most of their frequent contacts to acquaint Lewis and Clark with their personal views on matters ranging from appropriate forms of government— they preferred a military one—to Indian policy. The Chouteaus also took advantage of their new friendships to strike bargains for the sale of merchandise to outfit the upcoming expedition.

Clark may have had reservations about the degree of enthusiasm for the cession among some St. Louis merchants who he believed feared losing control of the Indian trade, but he had no qualms about the character or loyalty of the Chouteau brothers.[6] Of Pierre he wrote: "He is a gentleman deservedly esteemed among the most respectable and influential citizens of Upper Louisiana. M. Choteau's zeal to promote the public welfare . . . promptitude and fidelity . . . intitle him to an emanant degree to the particular attention and best services, not only of yourself but of his fellow citizens generally. . . ."[7] Lewis also regarded the younger Chouteau highly. He readily accepted Pierre's offer to travel to the Osage villages to acquaint members of that tribe with Louisiana's imminent transfer to the United States, and in accordance with President Jefferson's direction, he invited him to escort a delegation of the powerful chieftains to visit government leaders in Washington D.C.[8] Well aware of Pierre's long experience with the Osages and his influence in their councils, Captain Lewis understood that no other white man could serve so well in convincing their leaders to visit the capital or to observe American authority.

The Chouteaus assisted in other ways as well. In response to a request from

Pierre Clément Laussat, Pierre Chouteau arranged for an inventory of Spain's governmental properties in Upper Louisiana. Pierre appointed a militia officer, Don Francisco Riche Dupin, to supervise the necessary appraisals for him in New Madrid, but in St. Louis he needed no assistance, since the Spanish government owned no public structures of significant value there. The headquarters building belonged to his brother Auguste, who leased it to the government, and the old Spanish fort on the outskirts of the city was in ruins. Although Pierre had conducted the survey for French officials, he also communicated his findings directly to Captain Amos Stoddard, the U.S. army officer named to oversee the transfer of control in St. Louis for his government.[9]

Pierre Chouteau's part in the inventory of Spanish property and his cooperation with the new American commandant provided further evidence of his desire to get off to a good start with the Americans. At the same time, both he and his brother began to sever their ties with the territory's former rulers. For example, when the Spanish royal storekeeper, Manuel Gonzalez Moro, attempted to lease one of Pierre's large barges to transport the departing troops and their artillery to New Orleans, the younger Chouteau brother declined, on the grounds that his vessel would have to return to St. Louis empty. Chouteau did offer to sell the barge to Spanish officials for $1,200, but he insisted on cash terms inasmuch as the royal treasury already owed him money.[10] The Spaniards rejected his offer, and the issue was not finally resolved until October 1804, when Auguste consented to oversee construction of the necessary boats for them. The elder Chouteau also took charge of supervising the removal of whatever Spanish property remained at Fort Carondelet after Manuel Lisa refused to cooperate in the evacuation of that installation. Although Auguste contracted to assist the Spaniards, he, like his brother, refused to accept Spanish certificates in payment for his services.[11] Perhaps the Spaniards noticed the irony of the situation when the departing Lieutenant Governor Delassus, on his way to New Orleans late in 1804, encountered Pierre Chouteau heading up the Mississippi in the company of William Henry Harrison, Upper Louisiana's new territorial governor.[12]

The Chouteaus' behavior in 1804 did not, however, signify ill will against Spanish authority. Though their confidence in the outgoing regime may have been shaken by their earlier loss of the Osage monopoly, they sincerely regretted the departure of their friend Delassus and the retreat of Spain's power. Nonetheless, since the Americans were now to be the source of authority in Louisiana, the new realities had to be faced and handled in a way that would preserve the St. Louis trading class's vital interests. As always, the Chouteaus had chosen the most practical course for furthering their larger interests. Thus, even before the Americans assumed control in St. Louis, the Chouteaus had already established themselves as the friends and servants of the United States.

The long-awaited transfer of authority in that city did not take place until

March 9 and 10, 1804. Captain Stoddard reached St. Louis on February 24, but the illness of Lieutenant Governor Delassus and the tardiness in the arrival of Stoddard's men caused by ice on the river had forced a postponement of the formal ceremonies of transfer. On March 9 the members of the Spanish garrison stood at attention before the government house in full dress uniforms as the royal Spanish standard was lowered for the last time to the accompaniment of drum rolls and cannon fire. Stoddard, acting as a stand-in for French officials, signed the necessary documents before addressing the crowd that had gathered to observe the solemn proceedings.[13]

Within twenty-four hours, Captain Stoddard marched his company of soldiers through the town and formally took charge of the territory for the United States. The American flag was raised and a salute was fired. Stoddard reported that there were tears in the eyes of the assembled natives but denied that they were tears of regret—a conclusion that was probably more patriotic than accurate.[14] Even so, a new era had begun for the people of Louisiana. For the Chouteaus, however, it was already well under way. That evening the Chouteaus and their fellow St. Louisans feted the new American commandant with a public dinner and ball to mark the occasion. Feeling obliged to repay their generous hospitality, Stoddard reciprocated by hosting a gala affair for community leaders at his residence. Sparing no expense to insure a successful evening, the commandant had to borrow money from Pierre Chouteau to pay for the festivities, which cost him over $600.[15]

The dramatic events of March were followed closely by the equally notable departure of the Lewis and Clark expedition. In the rush of last-minute preparations, the Chouteaus continued to assist the American explorers. Shortly before they were ready to depart, Lewis informed Clark that Mr. Chouteau had procured seven *engagés* to accompany them as far as the Mandan villages on the upper Missouri.[16] On May 14 Clark headed up the wide Missouri, while Lewis remained temporarily in St. Louis to finalize arrangements for the Osage delegation's departure for Washington under Pierre's command. Once that group was safely on its way to the capital, Lewis was ready to embark upon his journey to the Pacific. On May 20 he bade farewell to his hostess of the past several months, "that excellent woman, the spouse of Mr. Peter Chouteau," and then in the company of Captain Stoddard, two of his officers, Auguste Chouteau, Charles Gratiot, Sylvestre Labbadie, Jr., and several other "respectable inhabitants" of the city, he set out to join his companion Clark, who was waiting for him at St. Charles, where they rendezvoused late that afternoon in a driving rain.[17] The following day the two explorers and their party began the historic trek to the cheers of the crowd of well-wishers who had gathered to see them off.[18] As Chouteau, Gratiot, and their associates mingled freely with Captain Stoddard, Lieutenant Milford, Lieutenant Worrall, and the other Americans on the Missouri riverbank, Lewis and Clark's departure symbolized the true beginning of a long and successful partnership uniting the old French inhabitants and the American newcomers in a common effort to develop the trans-Mississippi frontier.

Already the region around St. Louis was experiencing the tonic effects of the American presence. In 1804 Stoddard estimated that Upper Louisiana contained some 12,000 white residents and two-thirds of them were Americans.[19] The once-small village of St. Louis peopled by a few merchants and *engagés* was on its way to becoming a great metropolis. It boasted over 200 houses, including many well-constructed stone dwellings of ample proportions. By the American commandant's reckoning the land was rich, and the natives were intelligent, generous, charming, and sociable.[20] Given sound policies and co-operation between the old and new orders, there was every reason for St. Louis and Upper Louisiana to prosper.

Actually, for all their sentimental attachments to the old order, powerful trading families like the Chouteaus stood to gain much from the influx of American immigrants. Not only were prospects good for selling merchandise to the newly arriving settlers, but lucrative government-supply contracts seemed to promise tidy profits, as did the provisioning of the expanding American trade with the Indians. Also not to be overlooked were the opportunities for handsome returns to large landowners, whose properties seemed likely to appreciate in value. Because Auguste and Pierre recognized those opportunities and took advantage of them, they continued to prosper under the new regime.

For example, the assistance which the Chouteau brothers provided in outfitting and financing the Lewis and Clark expedition is a prime instance of their aplomb in turning the American arrival to their profit. The financial records of the mission exhibit the extent of their assistance in furnishing local support. Lewis purchased gunpowder, blankets, bullets, knives, paint, clothing, vermilion, hair pipes, and other goods from them. Equally important, the brothers extended credit to the Americans for paying wages to workmen and soldiers and for outfitting the Osage delegation for its journey to Washington.[21] While most of Lewis's drafts on the treasury in favor of the Chouteaus were for Pierre's expenses in preparing for the Osage enterprise, it is significant that those funds were paid to the Chouteaus rather than to the proprietors of other trading houses.

Undertakings such as the Lewis and Clark trip and the Indian visit to Washington were understandably expensive, and the Chouteaus were sufficiently clever to garner for themselves a handsome share of the lucrative governmental expenditures for outfitting these ventures. Although the Chouteaus' haste to capitalize on these opportunities provoked jealousy among rivals and later raised suspicions of impropriety, especially when Pierre was appointed Indian agent, their important financial assistance also contributed undeniably to the success of the new government's initial activities in Louisiana. That the brothers turned the business to their economic advantage was hardly a surprise. It was neither the first nor the last time they would combine official activity with private gain. If this eventually seemed reprehensible to some Americans, it simply indicated the gulf of misunderstanding that initially separated the two white cultures in Louisiana.

During the months that Lewis and Clark were making their way to the Pacific, the Chouteaus continued to build a good relationship with the American authorities. Pierre successfully completed his journey to Washington, and despite the misgivings of some high-ranking federal officials, he returned as Louisiana's first American Indian agent. He and Auguste also directed the warm welcome the citizens of St. Louis prepared for the new civilian governor, William Henry Harrison, when he arrived on October 12. Auguste's St. Louis mansion was the setting for a lavish reception honoring Harrison and his entourage, and, like Lewis, Clark, and Stoddard before him, Harrison found the patriarch to be an estimable gentleman whom he commended to the president as "the first citizen of Upper Louisiana."[22] Harrison obviously had not regretted the decision he had made before leaving Vincennes designating the elder Chouteau as a justice of the peace and a judge of the court of quarter sessions for the St. Louis district.[23]

Likewise, Harrison seconded Captain Lewis's suggestion that Auguste send Jefferson an account describing commercial operations and Indian customs in Upper Louisiana. Chouteau, however, planned to travel to the capital to confer with the American president personally, not only on these matters but also to air local grievances created by the change in governments, especially concerning the growing opposition to the confirmation of Spanish land titles.[24] Armed with a glowing letter of introduction from Harrison, the senior Chouteau left for Washington in November 1804, but an attack of gout forced him to abandon the undertaking before he reached Vincennes.[25] Clearly, however, the relationship between the Chouteaus and the Americans was developing so well that both brothers felt at ease in corresponding directly with the president.

In Washington, President Jefferson was naturally hungry for any news on the progress of the American mission up the Missouri. The Chouteaus did their best to keep him informed of the whereabouts of the explorers and served as a conduit for the specimens of animal and plant life they sent to Jefferson. Even before the expedition left St. Louis, Lewis obtained a variety of items from the Chouteau brothers for the president, including samples of silver, lead, rock crystal, and salt.[26] Those mineral specimens only whetted Jefferson's well-known scientific curiosity, and he was grateful to the Frenchmen for forwarding, by way of New Orleans, the magpies, sharp-tailed grouse, and prairie dog Lewis dispatched from the upper Missouri.[27] No doubt the president also appreciated the horn spoon and buffalo robes Pierre later sent him.[28]

Actually, the Chouteaus displayed a keen interest of their own in the advancement of knowledge. Auguste's library, the finest in Upper Louisiana, would certainly have won Jefferson's approbation, as would Pierre's efforts to collect mastodon and mammoth bones.[29] An entry in Auguste's 1797 account with Father Pierre Joseph Didier of St. Louis recording Pierre's purchase of an otherwise unidentified "electric machine and a magic lantern lamp" provides yet another intriguing glimpse of their far-ranging scientific interests.[30] Similarly, in 1804 Auguste experimented with raising silkworms for cloth production, while for his part Pierre cultivated a garden in which he raised wild plum and Osage orange or bois d'arc trees supplied by his friends the Osages. Lewis found those plants so extraordinary that he sent Jefferson cuttings for his garden.[31]

Fascinated as he was by the flow of new forms of minerals and life from the prairies, Jefferson was no doubt more immediately concerned with the disposition of the Lewis and Clark column. Here again the Chouteaus proved to be his best source of information. Acquainted with Missouri River traders and Indians arriving in St. Louis at various intervals, the Chouteaus were in a unique position to send news of the explorers' progress. How delighted the president must have been to learn from Auguste in November 1804 that Lewis and Clark had arrived "without accident" at the Mandan villages some 850 miles above the mouth of the Missouri, where they were wintering safely, and that the Indian nations along the way had received them warmly.[32] And after several more months of waiting, the president was relieved to be informed by the elder Chouteau in March 1805 that the American force was still safe and at least fifty miles north of the Mandan towns. In late 1805 Pierre communicated to Jefferson that Indian reports placed Captain Lewis near the "Southern Sea."[33]

Since the bearers of good news are always welcome, it is safe to assume that the Chouteaus' assistance in providing reports of the project that Jefferson so earnestly wished to succeed only enhanced his regard for them. It was only fitting that when Lewis and Clark finally returned to St. Louis in late September 1806, the Chouteau brothers once again hosted their stay. On their first full day in the city, Clark commented that they had dined with "Mr. Chotaux," and the next day he reported that all of their skins had been sunned and stored away in Pierre's storeroom. That night the Chouteau brothers joined in honoring the explorers with a gala dinner and ball.[34] The mission had been a resounding triumph for the United States, but it also constituted an important achievement for the St. Louis Chouteaus.

It was fortunate that the Chouteaus were building up a reservoir of credit in Washington, because in the important matter of territorial administration, their predilections placed them in opposition to both Jefferson's plans for the area and the general mood of the Congress. The question of Louisiana's form of government and its relationship to the Union vexed all parties from the beginning. The Chouteaus and other St. Louis magnates had esteemed the Spanish regime for its clear and direct lines of authority and its avoidance of taxes. The new government was unlikely to be as aloof or as generous. Therefore, even as they endeavored to court American authorities, the Chouteaus hoped to hold the administration to Article III of the Treaty of Cession, guaranteeing Louisianans the rights and privileges of American citizenship while securing a territorial system that would confirm existing property claims and minimize popular government.

The architect of the Louisiana Purchase entertained a broader vision. Imbued with the Enlightenment's ideals and a passion for system, Jefferson saw Louisiana as a laboratory for republican institutions and a place where some of the nation's most perplexing problems might be resolved successfully. In particular, the president believed the vast lands of Louisiana would provide a perfect refuge for the depleted and endangered Indian tribes of the eastern United States. But Jefferson was no European monarch; he had to counter the arguments of those who doubted the constitutionality of his actions and to secure congressional approval for the purchase.

To deal with these problems, the president drafted a proposed constitutional amendment authorizing Louisiana's incorporation into the United States and protecting the region's Indian tribes. The amendment called for a division of the territory along the thirty-first parallel, north latitude. Jefferson proposed to create a separate territory for the more populous regions south of that line, whose inhabitants would have a territorial government as determined by Congress and would enjoy the same rights as American citizens. Upper Louisiana, on the other hand, was to be closed to white settlement, in order to permit a relocation of eastern tribes there. White settlers in the area were to be offered tracts of land east of the Mississippi comparable to their existing holdings.[35] In this fashion the eastern part of the country would be completely settled, and the northern portion of Louisiana would be held in reserve for a later and well-planned, orderly settlement. In the meantime, the Indians would enjoy the protection of the United States and be gradually prepared for incorporation into the mainstream of American life.

The amendment won only limited support within the president's own cabinet, and Upper Louisianans regarded it with horror. But the Congress and especially the members of the opposing Federalist party posed the most immediate obstacle to the Louisiana Purchase. They argued that both the president and the Congress lacked constitutional authority to incorporate the residents of Louisiana into the Union. Moreover, they feared that American settlement of the northern territory could not realistically be prevented. Once that vast region from the Gulf of Mexico to the Canadian border was populated, they warned, its size, diversity, and remoteness from the remainder of the nation would lead to secession and a disruption of the Union. In reply, the Republicans could only reaffirm their view that the actual settlement of Louisiana would take a very long time. In the meantime, they argued, the removal of the Indians to the West would foster tranquility in the existing states.[36]

The debate over the legal status of Louisiana notwithstanding, Congress authorized the president to take possession of the territory and to establish a temporary government for its citizens. While William C. C. Claiborne was named governor of all Louisiana, Captain Amos Stoddard was made Upper Louisiana's acting commandant. In effect, Upper Louisiana was to have a military government for the time being. Stoddard was to be directly subordinate to Claiborne and to General James A. Wilkinson, the ranking officer in the U.S. Army. Still, Stoddard had room to maneuver in his administrative decisions, and his administration proved to be quite popular in Upper Louisiana, even though it lasted but a short time.[37]

Stoddard's standing with the ruling families of his territory was very high from the beginning. Pleased by the graciousness of the Chouteaus and their associates, he reassured them that Article III of the Treaty of Cession would be honored, that the United States would deal fairly with them, and, most important to the French leaders, that the United States would honor Spanish land titles.[38] Stoddard could have promised nothing that would have endeared him more to the St. Louis commercial interests. Unhappily, his promises that all land claims would be confirmed could not be fulfilled immediately, and the resulting land disputes placed the old French elite and the American government at odds over this issue for years to come.

Captain Stoddard exercised both civil and military authority in Upper Louisiana until he relinquished military command to Major James Bruff, who arrived in St. Louis in the summer of 1804. In civil affairs, Stoddard, with Claiborne's approval, elected to retain in office most of the district commandants who had held office under the Spanish regime. In practice, however, Stoddard found it necessary to make most important governmental decisions. He did so with admirable skill, particularly in view of the serious problems confronting him. The complicated issue of determining the validity of Spanish land grants, especially those conferred after the Treaty of San Ildefonso, demanded his immediate attention. So did the many Indian delegations who descended on St. Louis expecting to receive gifts from the new government as they had from the previous one.[39] In addition, a possibly dangerous confrontation between the Osages and their arch rivals the Sacs and Foxes threatened to trigger a violent outburst at any moment. Spurred on by British traders, the Sacs and Foxes accused the Americans of favoring the powerful Osages at their expense. So serious was the problem that many white inhabitants feared a general war was imminent.[40]

On the whole, Stoddard dealt ably with these issues during his abbreviated command. Although none of the critical problems had been eliminated when Upper Louisiana's new government took effect in October, a creditable beginning had been made toward their resolution. Among other things, he had initiated an investigation of the land claims issue and had impounded many of the pertinent records. Most significantly, Stoddard had secured the loyalty of a majority of the territory's white citizenry, who now regretted his departure.[41] Without question, the Chouteaus and their fellow French landowners and merchants would have preferred to retain his military regime. However, as 1804 wore on, Congress moved in the direction of establishing a more republican framework for Upper Louisiana's government.

In Washington, concerns over maintaining the nation's commitment to self-government caused most national leaders to ignore the views of French Louisiana's inhabitants as they attempted to formulate a new government for the region. Jefferson, it is true, favored the continuation of a military government on the grounds that it would facilitate the resettlement of eastern Indian tribes in the region while preventing any further influx of white settlers. He therefore persuaded Senator John Breckinridge of Kentucky to introduce a measure in Congress that essentially would have perpetuated Upper Louisiana's temporary government.[42] The bill touched off a long and lively debate over the merits of self-government, which ended only when it was agreed to divide Louisiana into two territories, the Territory of Orleans and the District of Louisiana. The measure stipulated that the District of Louisiana, formerly Upper Louisiana, would be governed by officials of the Indiana Territory. In addition, the new law authorized the president to appoint commandants to administer each of the district's political subdivisions. All existing laws of the district were to remain in force unless repealed or changed by the governor and judges of the Indiana Territory, but a particularly controversial proviso declared all land grants made in Louisiana after October 1, 1800, to be null and void. Finally, the law authorized the president to begin negotiations which would implement a policy of removing eastern tribes to new tracts of land west of the Mississippi River.[43]

As the debate in the capital progressed, reports that the government was considering basic alterations in the administration of Upper Louisiana dismayed St. Louis's French residents. When word reached the city that the territory was likely to pass under the authority of Indiana's officials, that settlement was to be restricted, that eastern Indian nations were to be relocated in Louisiana, and, most ominously, that Spanish land grants issued after 1800 were to be annulled, resistance to the proposed bill began to mount within the French community. The Chouteaus and their friends had been content to wait upon American justice until now. They had listened with equanimity to Stoddard's reassurances and had endeavored to demonstrate their acceptance of the new government, but the news from Washington concerning the Louisiana bill stirred them to action.

Before dispatches announcing the bill's final passage on March 26, 1804, reached St. Louis, an inner circle of the city's leading citizens gathered on April 2 at the home of David Delaunay to formulate a plan for informing the American government of the intense local opposition to the Louisiana bill. After deciding that the measure's provisions would be injurious to the interests of the district's inhabitants, the group appointed Auguste Chouteau, Charles Gratiot, Peter Provenchere, Louis Labeaume, and Bernard Pratte as a committee to convene a general meeting to apprise the citizens of St. Louis of the situation and to secure their endorsement for registering the community's distaste for the proposed new law. Those at the April 2 meeting also agreed to publish an account of their deliberations in English and French and to inform Captain Stoddard of their actions and intentions.[44]

Auguste Chouteau took the lead in organizing the proceedings. Not only did he preside at the April 2 gathering, but the follow-up meeting, to which all interested citizens had been invited, was held in his home on April 15. Pierre's name was missing from the list of participants only because at the time he was in the East with the Osage delegation. After selecting Auguste Chouteau to preside, those who attended the general meeting of the 15th endorsed the position taken at the earlier session and added the names of Charles Sanguinet and James Rankin to the original five-member committee as they prepared to enter the lists against the bill.[45]

Unfortunately for the Chouteau committee, the Louisiana bill had become law even before they met, and when that news became known their campaign against its provisions stalled momentarily. But a report that Governor Harrison of the Indiana Territory planned to visit the district in October to officially launch the new government inspired the Chouteau committee to draft a circular calling for the election of a convention composed of representatives from all parts of the District of Louisiana to confer with the incoming governor upon his arrival and to express their dissatisfaction with the recent legislation. Although the Chouteau committee sought to enlist support from throughout the district, its scheme for allocating representation ensured that the St. Louis delegation would be able to control the convention.[46]

As the St. Louisans pondered the implications of the new legislation, rumors began to circulate that the institution of slavery might be in jeopardy in the territory. The Chouteaus, like others in their class, were longtime slaveowners whose commitment to the peculiar institution was firmly fixed. A realization that Congress had specifically sanctioned slavery in the Territory of Orleans but had omitted any mention of it in regard to Upper Louisiana prompted the creation of yet another committee headed by the elder Chouteau. That group petitioned Stoddard to declare the black code from the previous regime in force.[47] Although Stoddard complied with their request, the demon issue that was to plague the nation for half of its history was already lurking in the shadows of the trans-Mississippi frontier.[48]

Meanwhile, the call for delegates to meet with Governor Harrison displayed a widening division between the older French and newer American settlers. In Ste. Genevieve, an American-dominated assembly rejected the St. Louis circular after charging that the proposed scheme was an unpatriotic attempt by a small clique to maintain the favored position it had held under Spanish auspices.[49] In spite of the controversy, the convention assembled in St. Louis on September 14, though only twelve of the proposed seventeen delegates attended. Following Charles Gratiot's selection to preside, the assembly members attempted to allay all suspicions of disloyalty by persuading Captain Stoddard to administer to them an oath of allegiance to the United States, its laws, and its Constitution.[50]

The deepening gulf separating them from both the American settlers in Louisiana and the national government in Washington worried the more responsible members of the French camp. Gratiot urged all citizens to respect the law and to obey those in authority. Asserting that Congress was unfamiliar with the actual conditions in the district, Chouteau's brother-in-law affirmed his conviction that if moderation prevailed, all disputes could be amicably settled. In a similar manner, Auguste cautioned against an ill-advised scheme to request France or Spain to intervene to force American compliance with the Treaty of Cession. He also insisted that Stoddard help edit the petition which the convention had drafted to forward to Washington.[51] Once the harsh language of the original version had been toned down, Chouteau joined in supporting the final document, which sought a congressional repeal of the act of March 26 on the grounds that it denied the citizens of Upper Louisiana the right to self-government and the rights of free men. Among other provisions, the petition specifically asked for the protection of slavery in the district, the confirmation of all Spanish land titles, and the permanent division of Upper Louisiana from all other territories, granting it its own officials and delegate to Congress.[52] In light of his critical role in the proceedings, it was appropriate that the delegates selected Auguste Chouteau, along with Eligius Fromentin, a French emigré who had recently come to Louisiana in search of new opportunities, to take the resolution to Washington and speak on its behalf. As noted earlier, however, illness interrupted his journey and saddled Fromentin with full responsibility for completing the important mission.[53]

Meanwhile, the governance of Upper Louisiana proceeded under the terms of the law of March 26, 1804. Auguste's cordial reception welcoming Governor Harrison to St. Louis in October convinced the American officer that Chouteau was a man to be trusted. Moved by the spirit of cooperation that he encountered following his arrival, Harrison lent his support to their petition to Congress and so advised Jefferson in a letter stating that "nine-tenths of the people of this Country are warmly attached to the Government of the United States."[54] Others remained suspicious, however, including Rufus Easton, a newly appointed territorial judge, who cautioned the president that the French clique was not to be trusted, that they wanted military government and the protection of "fraudulent antedated grants" of land.[55]

When Fromentin submitted the protest of his countrymen to the national legislature in January 1805, the citizens of Upper Louisiana received a lesson in the operations of a democratic government. Although the atmosphere in Washington regarding the petition encouraged both Fromentin and Harrison, the reports of sedition emanating from the district still threatened to cause the government to reject all suggestions for altering the Louisiana act. The president's support along with Governor Harrison's probably turned the issue in favor of the petitioners. Congress decided in March 1805 to grant the District of Louisiana, which it renamed the Territory of Louisiana, its own government modeled after the first stage of government outlined in the Northwest Ordinance of 1787.[56] The citizens of St. Louis and the old district did not obtain all they might have wished, however, because Congress also enacted a separate bill providing stringent procedures and regulations for ascertaining the validity of Spanish land titles.[57]

Even so, the national government had demonstrated its good faith and its determination to redress the grievances of its new citizens. For the Chouteau family, and for other old French settlers, the events of March 1805 constituted a qualified success. The land claims issue was hardly settled, and there was to be no military government for Louisiana, but neither was the door closed to them. They would have every opportunity to secure their vital interests if they could learn to work within the American system and turn it to their further advantage.

NOTES

1. Pierre Clément Laussat to Pierre Chouteau, Apr. 30 and Aug. 24, 1803, Delassus Collection, Missouri Historical Society. In addition, Pierre Louis Panet's letter to Auguste Chouteau suggested that the Chouteaus had expected to benefit greatly from the restoration of French control. Panet to Auguste Chouteau, May 18, 1804, Chouteau Collections, Missouri Historical Society.

2. Accounts of the negotiations with France and the Louisiana Purchase can be found in Harry Ammon, *James Monroe: The Quest for National Identity* (New York, 1971), 203–24, and Dumas Malone, *Jefferson the President: First Term 1801–1805* (*Jefferson and His Time,* vol. V, Boston, 1970), 239–363.

3. William Henry Harrison to Don Carlos Dehault Delassus, Aug. 2, 1803, Delassus Collection. There is also a copy in the Chouteau Collections. Auguste Chouteau

confirmed this date in his testimony before Theodore Hunt in 1825. *Hunt's Minutes,* I, 126.

4. Don Carlos Dehault Delassus to Manuel de Salcedo and the Marquis de Casa Calvo, Dec. 9, 1803, in Nasatir, *Before Lewis and Clark,* II, 719–20; John L. Loos, "William Clark's Part in the Lewis and Clark Expedition," *Missouri Historical Society Bulletin* 10 (July 1954), 490–511; William Clark to William Croghan, May 2, 1804, Clark Family Papers, Missouri Historical Society.

5. Meriwether Lewis to Auguste Chouteau, Jan. 4, 1804, in Jackson, ed., *Letters of Lewis and Clark,* 161–63. Although no copy of Chouteau's response has been found, in view of his close association with Lewis it seems highly likely that he replied in some form to the inquiry.

6. William Clark to William Croghan, Jan. 15, 1804, Clark Family Papers.

7. William Clark to William Croghan, May 2, 1804, Clark Family Papers.

8. Meriwether Lewis to William Clark, Feb. 18, 1804, Clark Family Papers. See Chap. 7 below regarding Jefferson's instructions to Lewis and Clark for the sending of Indian delegations to the capital and for Pierre Chouteau's part in the expedition.

9. Pierre Clément Laussat to Pierre Chouteau, Jan. 12, 1804, Delassus Collection; Report of valuation of royal buildings in New Madrid, Campo de la Esperanza, and Arkansas etc., Feb. 25, 1805, and related documents in Houck, ed., *Spanish Regime,* II, 336–43.

10. Manuel Gonzalez Moro to Carlos Dehault Delassus, July 13, 1804, and Certificate of Royal Treasury, Apr. 28, 1803, Chouteau Collections.

11. Houck, *History of Missouri,* II, 364–65; Douglas-Nasatir, *Manuel Lisa,* 30.

12. Diary of Don Carlos Dehault Delassus on the evacuation of Upper Louisiana, entry dated Nov. 17, 1804, Delassus Collection.

13. Order to Troops of St. Louis, Mar. 8, 1804, Delassus Collection.

14. Amos Stoddard to William C. C. Claiborne and General James A. Wilkinson, Mar. 26, 1804, Amos Stoddard Papers, Missouri Historical Society.

15. Amos Stoddard to Phoebe Reade Benham, June 16, 1804, Stoddard Papers.

16. Meriwether Lewis to William Clark, May 2, 1804, in Jackson, ed., *Letters of Lewis and Clark,* 177–78.

17. Rueben Gold Thwaites, ed., *Original Journals of the Lewis and Clark Expedition, 1804–1806* (New York, 1904–5), I, 22–23.

18. *Ibid.,* 25.

19. Amos Stoddard to Phoebe Reade Benham, June 16, 1804, Stoddard Papers.

20. *Ibid.*

21. Financial Records of the Lewis and Clark Expedition, Aug. 5, 1807, in Jackson, ed., *Letters of Lewis and Clark,* 419–31.

22. William Henry Harrison to Thomas Jefferson, Nov. 6, 1804, Thomas Jefferson Papers, Library of Congress. Unless otherwise noted all subsequent citations of the Jefferson Papers refer to the L.C. holdings.

23. Houck, *History of Missouri,* II, 383.

24. Auguste Chouteau to Thomas Jefferson, Nov. 20, 1804, Jefferson Papers. For a full discussion of the grievances regarding territorial status and land claims and the role of the Chouteaus in the affair see pp. 98–101 below.

25. Auguste Chouteau to Thomas Jefferson, Nov. 20, 1804, and William H. Harrison to Thomas Jefferson, Nov. 6, 1804, Jefferson Papers.

26. Meriwether Lewis to Thomas Jefferson, May 18, 1804, in Jackson, ed., *Letters of Lewis and Clark,* 192–94.

27. Pierre Chouteau to Thomas Jefferson, June 12, 1805, and Pierre Chouteau to William Clayborn [Claiborne], June 15, 1805, Pierre Chouteau Letterbook, Missouri Historical Society.

28. William Simmons to Thomas Jefferson, Mar. 30, 1808, Thomas Jefferson Papers, Missouri Historical Society. For a comprehensive discussion of Jefferson's interest in the American West see Donald Jackson, *Thomas Jefferson and the Stony Mountains: Exploring the West from Monticello* (Urbana, Ill., 1981).

29. Thwaites, ed., *Journals of Lewis and Clark,* VI, 32.

30. Account of Auguste Chouteau with Didier, Sept. 18, 1797, Chouteau Collections.

31. Edward Coles to Richard Rush, Nov. 15, 1826, in Everts B. Greene and Clarence W. Alvord, eds., *The Governors' Letterbooks, 1818–1834* (Springfield, Ill., 1909), IV, 113–14; Meriwether Lewis to Thomas Jefferson, Mar. 26, 1804, in Jackson, ed., *Letters of Lewis and Clark,* 170–72. Specimens of the Osage orange (*Maclura pomifera*) still thrive in the vicinity of Monticello. See Jackson, *Jefferson and the Stony Mountains,* 161n52.

32. Auguste Chouteau to Thomas Jefferson, Nov. 20, 1804, Jefferson Papers.

33. Auguste Chouteau to Thomas Jefferson, Mar. 2, 1805, in Jackson, ed., *Letters of Lewis and Clark,* 219–20n.

34. Thwaites, ed., *Journals of Lewis and Clark,* Sept. 24–25, 1806, V, 394–95; Pierre Chouteau to Thomas Jefferson, Dec. 1, 1805, Pierre Chouteau Letterbook.

35. Amendment to the Constitution, 1803, Jefferson Papers.

36. For a fuller discussion of the debate over Louisiana see William E. Foley, "Territorial Politics in Frontier Missouri, 1804–1820" (Ph.D. diss., University of Missouri, 1967), 11–18; William E. Foley, *A History of Missouri, 1673–1820* (Columbia, Mo., 1971), 66–70.

37. Foley, "Territorial Politics in Frontier Missouri," 24–30.

38. Amos Stoddard to Louisianans, Mar. 10, 1804, Stoddard Papers.

39. Amos Stoddard to William C. C. Claiborne, Mar. 26, 1804, Stoddard Papers.

40. Amos Stoddard to Henry Dearborn, June 3, 1804, Stoddard Papers.

41. Convention of Deputies of Louisiana to Amos Stoddard, Sept. 30, 1804, Stoddard Papers.

42. Thomas Jefferson to John Breckinridge, Nov. 24, 1803, Jefferson Papers; *Annals of Congress,* 8 Cong., 1 Sess., 245 (Feb. 2, 1804).

43. See Foley, "Territorial Politics in Frontier Missouri," 33–39.

44. Proceedings of a meeting of the inhabitants of St. Louis, Apr. 2, 1804, in Clarence E. Carter, ed., *Territorial Papers of the United States,* vol. XIII, *Louisiana-Missouri, 1803–1806* (Washington, D.C., 1948), 35–37.

45. Proceedings of a meeting of the inhabitants of St. Louis, Apr. 15, 1804, in *ibid.,* 37.

46. Committee of Inhabitants of St. Louis to the Citizens of Upper Louisiana, July 28, 1804, in *ibid.,* 33–35.

47. J. Rankin, tr., to Amos Stoddard, Translation of petition of St. Louis Committee, Aug. 4, 1804, Stoddard Papers.

48. Amos Stoddard to Auguste Chouteau, president of St. Louis Committee, Aug. 6, 1804, Stoddard Papers.

49. Resolutions of a Committee of Ste. Genevieve and New Bourbon, Sept. 2, 1804, in Carter, ed., *Territorial Papers,* XIII, 41–43.

50. Minutes of a meeting at St. Louis, Sept. 14, 1804, in *ibid.,* 43–46.

51. Michael Amoureux to Albert Gallatin, Nov. 2, 1804, and anonymous paper concerning the attitude of French inhabitants of Louisiana, Nov. 4, 1804, in *ibid.*, 65, 68–71.

52. *Representation and Petition of the Representatives Elected by the Freemen of the Territory of Louisiana* (Washington, D.C., 1805).

53. *American State Papers, Miscellaneous,* I, 404–5; Auguste Chouteau to Thomas Jefferson, Nov. 20, 1804, Jefferson Papers. Fromentin, a former Catholic priest, had fled France during the Reign of Terror. After coming to the United States he left the priesthood to study law. He settled permanently in New Orleans, where he embarked upon a successful political career that included election to the U.S. Senate from Louisiana in 1813. For a number of years he and Chouteau argued over who should bear the costs for the 1804 trip to Washington. See Eligius Fromentin to Auguste Chouteau, July 25, 1807, Chouteau Collections.

54. William Henry Harrison to Thomas Jefferson, Nov. 6, 1804, Jefferson Papers.

55. Rufus Easton to Thomas Jefferson, Jan. 17, 1805, Jefferson Papers.

56. Eligius Fromentin to Auguste Chouteau, Jan. 12 and Feb. 14, 1805, Chouteau Collections; William Henry Harrison to Auguste Chouteau, Dec. 21, 1804, in Logan Esarey, ed., *Governors' Messages and Letters: Messages and Letters of William Henry Harrison* (Indianapolis, 1922), 113–14. Also see Foley, *History of Missouri,* 93–95.

57. Foley, *History of Missouri,* 95–96.

Chapter 6

A FRENCH ENTREPRENEUR AS
AN AMERICAN INDIAN AGENT

OF THE MANY thorny problems attendant upon the Louisiana Purchase, none proved more perplexing to U.S. officials than establishing American control over the trans-Mississippi Indian tribes. Numerous, combative, and independent nations such as the Osages, the Pawnees, the Sioux, the Arikaras, the Mandans, and a host of others constituted a formidable presence west of the Mississippi and a substantial barrier to the Americanization of Upper Louisiana. Spanish and British officials and traders had gained their allegiance by combining trade with a generous policy of distributing gifts and honors, but at no time had they managed to subdue the plains Indians. Collectively, those tribes could match any force that the United States could afford to muster against them in 1804. The situation demanded caution and diplomacy, and the Jefferson administration wisely shunned the use of raw power as much as possible. Accordingly, the president and his advisers sought assistance from the established trading houses of St. Louis, whose long-standing dealings with the Missouri tribes gave them ready access to the Indian's world.[1]

Because the Americans knew so little about western tribal customs and the complex relationships existing among the diverse trans-Mississippi nations, they astutely chose to employ the willing services of Pierre Chouteau. Chouteau's status in tribal councils made him an obvious choice to represent the United States in its initial negotiations with the western Indians. When the French trader visited Washington with the first delegation of Osage chieftains in the summer of 1804, Secretary of War Henry Dearborn commissioned him as U.S. Indian agent for Upper Louisiana's tribes.[2]

Chouteau's appointment to the Indian agency represented a personal triumph for the St. Louis merchant and his family. Hopeful that his new position would enable him to retain his influence with the tribesmen and that this in turn would make it easier for the family to sustain its lucrative fur-trading operations, Pierre Chouteau welcomed Dearborn's decision. Moreover, because Chouteau's selection signaled an American willingness to trust a key member of Louisiana's ruling French elite, leading members of the St. Louis community greeted the news with similar enthusiasm.

Pierre Chouteau's 1804 trip to the national capital was not simply a matter of chance. Even before the Louisiana Purchase, President Jefferson had suggested that Meriwether Lewis invite selected western Indian chieftains to travel to Washington for conferences with American officials in the hope that the journeys would induce the tribesmen to respect the strength and authority of the United States. After the territory passed into American hands, the proposed Indian visits seemed even more necessary, especially after reports reached the capital city of British and Spanish operatives openly defying the official agreements recently concluded with the European powers.[3]

The 1804 Osage delegation was the first of three trans-Mississippi Indian groups to visit Washington during the Jefferson administration. In October 1805 Captain Amos Stoddard conducted a second and larger collection of chiefs representing twelve separate tribes to the East in a visit long remembered in the nation's capital for the colorful chieftains' boisterous arrival. The final deputation, consisting of the Mandan chief, Shahaka, and another group of Osages, set out for the federal city in the fall of 1806. For the last mission, which coincided with Lewis and Clark's return from the Pacific, the Americans once again called upon Pierre Chouteau to accompany the Osage leaders in the party.[4] Because of his unparalleled standing among the Osages, Pierre made two journeys which presented him with unique opportunities to confer directly with the president and other high-ranking officials.

If Chouteau regarded the trips as occasions to plead his causes in Washington, Jefferson's immediate objective in bringing western tribesmen to the national capital was to impress them with the size, power, and wealth of the nation whose lands they now inhabited. This, the president trusted, would make them more amenable to American control.[5] His plan also called for the Indians to behold the wonders of such prosperous eastern cities as Baltimore, Philadelphia, New York, and Boston. Hoping to overawe them with the nation's might, the organizers always saw to it that the Indians' itinerary included carefully staged demonstrations of American military prowess.[6] In reality, however, the decision to invite the Indians to the East was taken, at least in part, because American authorities did not possess the military strength to coerce recalcitrant tribes. Jeffersonian officials believed a massive deployment of armed force west of the Mississippi would be both too costly and contrary to republican principles. By combining the visits to Washington with the distribution of gifts and the benevolent activities of government traders and agents assigned to assist the tribesmen in making a gradual transition to the white man's ways, they expected the western Indian nations to accept American authority peacefully.[7]

In seeking to reconcile national interests with national ideals, the country's leaders struggled to achieve American aggrandizement without destroying the

Indians. Never doubting that native ways would give way to civilization, J̣
ferson concluded that the Indian's survival depended upon his gradual assim
lation into the expanding American society. By persuading tribesmen to abandon
their traditional ways in favor of agriculture, limited ownership of land, and
peaceful coexistence, he hoped to transform them from nomadic hunters and
gatherers into independent farmers. Although the experiences of the dwindling eastern tribes, forced off their lands, did not offer much reason for optimism, the acquisition of the Louisiana Territory revived expectations among
the philanthropic Jeffersonians that within its vast open spaces the Indians
could be saved through the slow process of acculturation.[8] From that perspective, the trips to the capital presented the added attraction of introducing the
technologically backward western Indians to the wonders of the white man's
world which one day they would be expected to join.

The Jeffersonian vision of the peaceful establishment of republican civilization in the Louisiana Territory contained many contradictions.[9] Not only did
ordinary frontiersmen, with their eyes fixed upon Indian lands, not share Jefferson's benevolent attitudes, but most tribesmen displayed little interest in
surrendering their traditional cultures. In addition, the frontier administrators
assigned to oversee the conduct of Indian-white relations in Upper Louisiana
openly questioned the efficacy of the civilizing mission.[10]

Auguste and Pierre Chouteau certainly doubted that the president's goals
could be achieved. Content to trade with the Indians, they entertained no
thoughts that the tribesmen could transcend the savage state. Decades of experience had impressed upon them a vision of the natives as childlike in rela-
tion to white men and condemned by their own codes to a life of conflict.
Auguste Chouteau dismissed any notion that Indians might dwell in harmony
with themselves or with white society, holding that it was their nature to be
violent to "barbarous excess."[11] Nor did his younger brother consider the Indians likely candidates for conversion to the refinements of the Enlightenment
world. Although Pierre welcomed American assistance and protection for the
tribes—especially the Osages—he calculated that the primary consequences of
that aid would be the orderly continuation of the St. Louis–based fur trade.

Pierre Chouteau and the first Osage delegation, headed by the Chouteau
protégé White Hair, crossed the Mississippi on their way to consult with the
president a short time before Lewis and Clark embarked upon their westward
trek. This chief was the original White Hair who died in 1809. He received
his name from a gray wig which he had seized from the pate of an unfortunate
American during the 1791 battle in the Northwest Territory in which Little
Turtle and the Miami Indians defeated General Arthur St. Clair. According to
a contemporary: "He [White Hair] had grasped at the wig's tail in the melee
of the battle, supposing it the man's hair, and that he should have him by that

hold. It instantly became in his hand a charmed thing, a grand medicine. Supposing that in a like case it would always effect a like deliverance, he afterwards wore it, as a charmed thing, rudely fastened to his own scalp."[12]

Captain Lewis had attempted to smooth the way for Chouteau and his companions with letters of introduction to American officials along their route.[13] But overland travel in the early nineteenth century was a tedious and sometimes dangerous business. Traveling by barge and on horseback, Chouteau's party did not reach Frederickstown, Maryland, until July 9, and an impatient Henry Dearborn sent word that the delegation should make haste to arrive in the capital before the president left the muggy city for a vacation in Virginia.[14] Within three days Jefferson welcomed the visitors from Missouri in the federal city and exchanged greetings with them.[15] His formal address to the Osages, delivered on July 16, followed a pattern which became standard for subsequent occasions of this kind. He promised the dignitaries American protection and assistance in return for friendship and trade. Reminding his guests that the power of France and Spain had been removed from Louisiana forever, the president stressed that as nations inhabiting the same continent, the Americans and the Osages shared a common destiny. Seeking to allay any fears of his intentions, he said: "On your return tell your people that I take them all by the hand, that I become their father hereafter, that they shall know our nation only as friends and benefactors. That we have no views upon them but to carry on commerce useful to them and us; to keep them in peace with their neighbors, that their children may multiply, may grow up and live to good old age, and their women no longer fear the tomahawk of any enemy."[16]

Prompted no doubt by Chouteau's counsel, White Hair responded warmly to his new "Father's" sentiments, affirming that his people took pride in their attachment to the United States and expressing gratitude that they were no longer to be given "bad counsel" by the Europeans.[17] In truth, a French colonial steeped in European traditions, who only recently had become a U.S. citizen himself, was about to become their principal adviser, but this new American was a longtime friend whose nomination obviously pleased them. Secretary Dearborn made it official the next day when he formally designated Chouteau as Indian agent for Upper Louisiana.[18]

Chouteau's commission granted him broad powers and responsibilities in conducting Indian affairs and assigned him to represent the United States in all matters pertaining to the tribes located north of the Arkansas River. Dearborn charged him with maintaining peace among the various tribes and between Indians and whites, encouraging the tribes to take up agricultural pursuits, providing the tribes with tools and other gifts, and, more immediately, procuring the blacksmith Jefferson had promised to send the Osages. Beyond that, the secretary of war advised Chouteau to attempt to heal the breach between the main body of the Osage nation and the disaffected bands that had settled in the Arkansas drainage area.[19]

It was ironic that Pierre Chouteau was given the task of reconciling these groups, since he had played a role in the departure of the two principal Arkansas River bands. However, because these tribal divisions now threatened to complicate his tasks of maintaining the peace and securing Osage compliance with American policy, the newly installed Indian agent pressed for the tribe's reunification under White Hair's leadership. Although he succumbed to the temptation of seeking to impose the white man's sense of order in the red man's world, Pierre Chouteau knew better than anyone how difficult the task would be. Within the tribe the Osage chief had only limited powers, thus making it virtually impossible for any individual leader to exercise authority singlehandedly over his fellow tribesmen.[20] Nonetheless, he pushed ahead with plans to reunite the tribe.

Perhaps Pierre's eagerness to end the split stemmed from the administration's obvious concern about the schism. Plans were already in place for an American expedition to explore the Arkansas River, and Jefferson feared that Big Track and his 400 warriors would oppose the American party's passage. For that reason the president urged Chouteau to utilize his influence and skill to forestall hostilities with the breakaway Osages.[21]

A final section of Pierre's commission cautioned him to keep regular accounts, to be economical in expenditures, and to correspond with Governor Harrison on all subjects relating to Indian affairs. Dearborn made it clear that, without exception, the administration expected Chouteau to follow Harrison's instructions.[22] These last instructions indicated that American authorities were undecided about their new agent's trustworthiness. After all, at the very moment Pierre was in Washington conferring with them, his brother and other members of Upper Louisiana's mercantile elite were launching a protest against the administration's recently approved arrangement for governing their territory in an effort, many believed, to preserve the special privileges they had long enjoyed under the previous regime. Moreover, rumors from the West suggested that Pierre Chouteau's closest associates were attempting to defraud the United States of large tracts of public land granted under questionable circumstances after the transfer of the territory from Spain. An interview between Chouteau and Secretary of the Treasury Albert Gallatin in which Chouteau suggested that Upper Louisiana should be subjected to a military government did little to lay those suspicions to rest. Gallatin reported his misgivings to the president:

> At the request of Gen. Dearborn, I had two conversations with Chotteau. He seems well disposed, but what he wants is power and money. He proposed that

he should have a negative on all the Indian trading licenses and the direction and all the profits of the trade carried on by Government with all the Indians of Louisiana replacing only the capital. I told him this was inadmissable, but his last demand was the exclusive trade with the Osages, to be effected by granting licenses only to his agents, but that he should not be concerned in the trade with any other nation. . . . As he may be either useful or dangerous I gave him no flat denial to his last request, but told him to modify it in the least objectionable shape and to write to Gen. Dearborn from St. Louis which he said he would do.[23]

Clearly Chouteau had not made a favorable impression on Gallatin, and under normal circumstances it is unlikely that Jefferson would have consented to his appointment as Indian agent. Given the exigencies pressing on the government, however, the president decided to employ the Frenchman. As Pierre left the city to conduct the Osages on to Baltimore, Philadelphia, and New York, it was evident that federal officials had every intention of scrutinizing carefully the new Indian agent's conduct.

In line with the president's desire, the eastern journey made a great impression on both the visiting Indians and their French escort. After the simplicity of life in St. Louis, Pierre Chouteau could not have failed to notice the energy and potential of the young nation whose cities he beheld in the early autumn of 1804. But if the strange sights of the East stirred the visitors from the West to wonder, the appearance of the "savages" from the plains also excited their American hosts. Enthusiastic citizens welcomed White Hair and his fellow chiefs in all of the cities on their itinerary; wherever they went their encounters with both civil and military officials were uniformly friendly. Yet much of the praise and admiration heaped upon the Indians by their curious white hosts was tempered with a sense of caution or even perhaps dread. Although an air of goodwill and comradery masked the cultural shock of both visitors and hosts, these initial encounters suggested that Jefferson's vision of a peaceful merging of the two peoples appeared a distant prospect indeed. Thus the Osage delegation of 1804 established a pattern which was repeated in the subsequent expeditions of 1805 and 1806. Prompted by both practical and idealistic considerations, the visits simply underscored the absence of any common ground between the two peoples now in fateful confrontation.

During their 1804 visit, the Osages conferred with members of Congress, witnessed naval and military displays, performed their traditional war dances before enthralled white audiences, and partook of the fancy cuisine and wines laid out for them at numerous receptions and parties.[24] In every way official Washington endeavored to persuade the chiefs of the American government's good intentions and its high regard for their people. At every stop their hosts lavished them with gifts, including medals, uniforms, proclamations, merchandise, and Bibles, but the Indians could not have failed to notice that a major part of their entertainment consisted of military exhibitions. Even so, Chouteau's mission appears to have been completed without a hitch. Jefferson was informed in August that the delegation had been as far north as New York and had left Philadelphia en route to St. Louis. All the chiefs were healthy, and "nothing happened to frustrate the object contemplated by the government."[25] By October, Pierre Chouteau and the Osage leaders were safely back in St. Louis. In Chouteau's opinion, at least, the trip had been a success. To the president he reported that the Osages were well, favorably disposed toward the United States, and convinced that many benefits would come from the experience.[26]

Pierre Chouteau seemed equally well disposed toward the United States. If he had detected any coolness among his American colleagues, he chose not to mention it publicly. Rather, he dutifully saw to it that the Osages were sent on their way from St. Louis to their villages. According to plan, he hired a blacksmith for the Indians and equipped him with a forge and other essential items. A short time later, Chouteau reminded the president of his promise also to provide the Osages with a mill for their village. Unfortunately, like other commitments made to Indian leaders in Washington, its delivery was long delayed despite repeated inquiries from the Osages.[27] Perhaps the lassitude with which the government acted to uphold its pledges to the Indians was a result of its usual reluctance to spend public funds, but more likely, once the delegations had left the federal city, officials simply lost interest. In any case, the tribesmen did not forget broken promises, and that made the work of officials like Chouteau all the more difficult.[28]

While federal authorities procrastinated, Chouteau turned his attention to other matters. On his return to Louisiana he heard the discouraging news that several traders had been active among the Arkansas Osages. If unchecked, this development threatened to frustrate his design to coerce the dissidents to return to their former villages along the Osage River by depriving them of merchandise.[29] Moreover, the arrival in St. Louis of the new territorial governor, William Henry Harrison, coincided with a renewal of violence between the Osages and the envious Sac and Fox tribes. Under the circumstances, Pierre decided not to accompany White Hair and his chiefs from St. Louis to their village.[30] As Indian agent, it was his responsibility to try to suppress the hostilities between the feuding tribes. At the same time, the Chouteaus recognized the importance of convincing Governor Harrison of their regard and their readiness to serve. Predictably, therefore, they welcomed the new governor to St. Louis with profuse statements of esteem and entertained him in a manner which their family alone could provide. From Pierre's point of view, it was no time to be away in an Indian village.

Although Harrison wisely refused their offer of a business partnership,[31] he did not hesitate to use the Chouteau brothers' talents to end the dangerous warfare initiated by the Sacs and Foxes. The fighting had begun early in 1804, when a dispute over hunting grounds precipitated an attack that left several Osage braves dead and others in captivity. Captain Amos Stoddard's investigation of the incident disclosed that the Sacs and Foxes deeply resented what they considered to be the American government's preferential treatment of the Osages. Demanding the construction of a U.S. government factory in their territory, the belligerent Indians hinted that they were in touch with British officials in Canada, a point not lost on apprehensive American leaders. Relations did not improve, however, and the pressure mounted when an assault on a white settlement north of St. Louis led to the death of three Americans. In Captain Stoddard's words, the Sacs were assuming a "pretty elevated tone."[32] Some settlers demanded retaliatory strikes, but Major James Bruff, the region's ranking military officer, opted instead for a more cautious policy. Rather than sending a punitive expedition, Bruff ordered the Sacs to surrender the warriors responsible for the murders. Although the tribal leaders admitted the involvement of four of their braves in the incident, they refused to turn them over for trial. Apparently, the hostile Indians believed that the Osages had gained American favor by virtue of the threat they represented to nearby settlements. If the Osages were securing favor in proportion to the fear they inspired in the whites, the Sacs and Foxes had no intention of allowing themselves to be taken for granted.[33]

Harrison naturally wanted peace in the new jurisdiction under his authority, but he also had instructions from Secretary Dearborn to conclude a treaty with the Sacs and Foxes which would bring large tracts of their land directly into American hands. With Pierre Chouteau installed as Indian agent, Harrison hoped that the warring tribes would listen to their old friend and be persuaded to negotiate an end to the crisis. In response to Pierre Chouteau's summons, a wary party of Sac chiefs appeared in St. Louis, but they were prepared to surrender no more than one of the guilty braves to the Indian agent. Harrison imprisoned the Sac warrior, but to appease the tribe he pardoned the remaining three murderers. Seeking to calm the Indians' remaining doubts, he promised to petition the president for a pardon for the brave in custody. The pardon was eventually obtained, but it came too late to save the Sac prisoner, who was killed during an escape attempt in May 1805.[34]

In the meantime, Harrison and Chouteau took advantage of the cordial atmosphere created by the initial pardons to present a treaty to the chiefs for their approval. After the Chouteau brothers distributed over $2,000 worth of gifts among the tribal leaders and gave assurances that they would be protected from the Osages, the Sacs and Foxes consented to surrender all of their lands east of the Mississippi River along with a considerable expanse west of the stream. The agreement further stipulated that the two tribes would receive a 1,000-dollar annuity and could continue to live and hunt on the ceded ground.

For their part the Sacs and Foxes also promised to terminate all fighting with the Osages. Finally, at the specific request of the Chouteaus, the treaty included a proviso stipulating that the cession would in no way invalidate Spanish land grants in the ceded territory.[35]

The Sac and Fox treaty was a triumph for Harrison, but it indebted him to the Chouteaus, whose assistance had greatly facilitated the negotiations. For the Chouteaus, the conclusion of the treaty greatly improved their position with the Americans in general and with Harrison in particular. Unfortunately, as was so often the case, the formal treaty did not forestall future difficulties among the signatories. Early in 1805, Pierre received word that a large and warlike assembly of northern tribes, including the Sacs, the Foxes, and the Iowas, was about to gather on the Des Moines River.[36] Fearing that white traders were seeking commercial advantage by stirring up the old ghost of preferential treatment for the Osages, Chouteau decided to proceed to the meeting and "to bring them back to a peaceful frame of mind."[37] In outlining his plans to the president and the secretary of war, Chouteau argued that the root of the troubles lay in the policy of permitting traders to move among the Indians in an uncontrolled manner. The Frenchman's solution was the same one he had suggested to Gallatin in Washington. As Indian agent, he should be granted strict control over the issuance of all trading licenses.[38] Had government leaders accepted his suggestion, Pierre Chouteau would have gained a decided advantage over Upper Louisiana's other Indian traders.

No more receptive to Chouteau's recommendation than they had been before, however, American officials in Washington considered another remedy for easing frontier tensions. Since the Osage visit of the previous year seemed to have been an effective diplomatic move, they contemplated bringing a second Indian delegation to the federal city in an attempt to prevail upon the various tribes to sign a series of treaties which would end hostilities in Upper Louisiana while securing large blocs of land for the long-term policy of resettling eastern tribes west of the Mississippi.

The idea for the second Indian delegation to visit the capital, however, did not originate solely from the angry actions of the Sac and Fox tribes. Plans had long before been made for Lewis and Clark to invite key tribal leaders they encountered on their journey to proceed to St. Louis and thence to Washington. Now, in 1805, American authorities concluded that if the Sac and Fox chiefs could be persuaded to join the others on the trip to the East, they also might decide that American strength was too great to resist.

Chouteau reported to the president as early as November 1804 that dignitaries from the Iowa nation were in St. Louis, and that Lewis had told them and Sioux leaders that Chouteau would conduct them to Washington.[39] Since the Sacs desired to make the trip as well, Chouteau volunteered to lead the Indians to the seat of government if the president wished. In the meantime, he distributed gifts to the visiting Indians and told them he would consult with the administration to learn its intentions. For his part, the Indian agent encouraged the government to authorize the expedition on the grounds that it would have the same beneficial effect on these Indian travelers as the first visit had had on the Osages.[40] Since he had returned from the capital only one month previously, Chouteau appeared unusually eager to return to Washington. He was restless and ill at ease, almost certainly believing that the Americans could bear more persuasion of the correctness of his views regarding alterations in Upper Louisiana's government and its economy.

In anticipation of the arrival of various chiefs in St. Louis, Dearborn instructed Chouteau to have a house constructed to accommodate the visitors, but the secretary admonished him to keep down expenses.[41] It was not the only time that federal officials ordered the Frenchman, whom they considered something of a spendthrift when it came to public funds, to economize. In February 1805, Dearborn instructed Chouteau to consult with Governor Harrison, who was also superintendent for Indian affairs, on all questions involving the disbursement of funds.[42] But, asserting that it would afford him better control of the Indians while they tarried in St. Louis, Chouteau proceeded to have the house built on his own property and at his own expense. Having obtained Harrison's approval in the matter, Chouteau did not hesitate subsequently to charge the secretary of war rent for housing the Indians.[43]

As the number of Indians arriving in St. Louis increased almost daily in the late winter of 1805, Pierre suffered a great personal tragedy. On the night of February 15, a terrible fire left his house, along with all of his personal property and papers, in ashes. He wrote to the president that the "flames destroyed the fruits of twenty-five years of work."[44] A disgruntled female slave apparently set the blaze deliberately. Insisting that he had not mistreated her, Chouteau turned the slave woman over to the St. Louis general court while he tried to pick up the pieces.[45] After requesting Dearborn to send him a new supply of medals, flags, and patents, along with a new commission, Pierre set about the difficult business of rebuilding his home and accommodating the chiefs sent down the river by Lewis and Clark.[46] Fortunately the dwelling that he had built to house the visiting Indians had escaped the conflagration.

Although Pierre coveted a second journey to Washington, he concluded that the various Indian leaders congregating in St. Louis would fare poorly on such a difficult trip during the hot and humid summer months. Therefore, in March he advised Dearborn that it would be best to delay the visit until autumn in order to reduce the risks of fatalities which might be expected from the rigors of an overland march in the midyear heat.[47] He also suggested that a mixed delegation of chiefs from several nations be received instead of a series of separate delegations, in order to preclude unnecessary tribal jealousies. While he awaited final instructions from his superiors regarding the Indian travelers, other pressing matters demanded his attention.

His primary concern remained the Osages. Although the main body of the tribe seemed generally satisfied with the results of White Hair's visit with the president, scattered Osage attacks on whites continued, as did their skirmishes with the Kansas tribe. Moreover, the Arkansas Osage factions remained defiantly detached. Pierre determined to go to their villages and effect a general peace settlement that would end the divisions, but when the Sacs and Foxes appeared in force in St. Louis in April demanding to see their imprisoned warrior, who remained in federal custody, Chouteau temporarily canceled his trip. A running dispute with Major James Bruff over the jurisdiction of the military forces and the Indian agency exacerbated the already tense situation. The two men had never been very compatible, and Bruff's refusal to supply twenty soldiers to assist Chouteau during his discussions with the Indians so angered the agent that he turned to the local militia for assistance. Bruff, in Chouteau's opinion, did not understand the necessity of displaying a firm resolve to the Indians. Moreover, the Indian agent had to intervene personally before Bruff allowed the visiting tribesmen to see their kinsman. Chouteau also castigated the military commander for failing to notify him when the Sac prisoner escaped two days later. Chouteau argued that had Bruff informed him of the breakout immediately, the escapee could in all likelihood have been recaptured. Such unnecessary calamaties did nothing to promote good relations, Chouteau affirmed, and were the result of a situation in which "the different heads to whom authority is confided are not always disposed to aid each other."[48] The full dimensions of the debacle became clear when Chouteau belatedly discovered that the Sac warrior had been shot while fleeing, "the victim of an unjust and barbarous vengeance."[49]

Once again Pierre Chouteau prepared to embark upon his trip to the Osage villages, but before he could get under way, a delegation of forty-five Indians dispatched downriver by Captain Lewis arrived in St. Louis with instructions that they be escorted to the federal capital. For the next few weeks the Indian agent had to devote his time to making arrangements to accommodate the latest visiting dignitaries. With a wave of smallpox sweeping the eastern states that spring and with some of the chiefs in St. Louis already suffering from colds and dysentery, Chouteau again recommended that their departure be delayed until fall. His superiors wisely acquiesced in his appraisal and postponed the trip. Having received suitable gifts from Chouteau, many of the Indians left St. Louis promising to return in the autumn. Others, however, including several Otos, Sioux, and Missouris, chose to remain in the city, requiring the harried Indian agent to attempt to amuse them, which he did by outfitting a wagon to convey them on periodic hunting trips in the vicinity.[50]

In the midst of all this uncertainty Pierre Chouteau learned that in accordance with the provisions for the new territorial government recently approved by Congress, the Territory of Louisiana, formerly known as Upper Louisiana, was about to have a new governor. The president had named the controversial General James Wilkinson to assume that post. Since Wilkinson would be Pierre Chouteau's immediate superior, the Frenchman and his family took steps to ensure that their relationship began on a positive note.[51]

Shortly before Wilkinson's arrival, a Sac and Fox party 160 strong came to the territorial capital to confer with the new governor about the fate of their recently murdered warrior and to receive gifts. Apparently too impatient to wait for Wilkinson to reach St. Louis, Chouteau took three of the Sac chieftains with him down the Mississippi and intercepted the governor's party near Kaskaskia.[52] After briefing Wilkinson on the situation, the Indian agent explained that because of the expense and inconvenience of entertaining such a large delegation in St. Louis, he had decided to come downriver for a meeting in order to expedite the return of the Sacs to their villages.[53] It was a plausible story, but the fact remains that the ploy allowed Chouteau to obtain a private audience with the new governor before he had an opportunity to make contacts with Major Bruff or any of Chouteau's other critics in St. Louis.

When Wilkinson entered St. Louis in early July to take up his new duties, the Chouteaus and their associates showered him with a gala round of receptions in the same generous style they earlier had accorded Governor Harrison. The new governor's obliging acceptance of their hospitality annoyed Americans like Major Bruff, who suspected the loyalty of the older element in St. Louis. Even so, Pierre found Wilkinson less accommodating than Harrison.[54] Wilkinson was certainly a forceful personality, and he rapidly detected Chouteau's jealous resentment of competition where Indian matters were concerned. Moreover, Chouteau was, in Wilkinson's judgment, "ambitious in the extreme" and "by no means regardless of his private interests."[55] But despite those qualities—ones with which Wilkinson could easily identify—the new territorial executive was prepared to place his trust in Chouteau, whose zeal and loyalty to the United States he commended.[56] If the expenditures of the Indian agency sometimes seemed excessive, Wilkinson explained, it was because Chouteau was steeped in "Spanish habits" and was inexperienced in American ways.[57] All things taken into account, the new governor pronounced Chouteau's "principles rather more chaste than those of three-fourths of his Country men."[58] Once again Chouteau charm and ability had prevailed, and the brothers could expect an air of cordiality to surround their relations with Governor Wilkinson. Unfortunately, Wilkinson himself was shortly to become a storm center on the frontier, and the Chouteaus could not escape the gales which would rush around him.[59]

A more immediate effect of Wilkinson's residence in St. Louis, however, was

Chouteau's long-delayed mission to confer with the Arkansas Osages. Wilkinson discussed the matter with Pierre in July and instructed him to seek permission from the Osages to erect military posts on their lands. He also directed Chouteau to explore the country as well, investigating the waterways, soil, timber, and other resources.[60] At about the same time, Louisiana's new governor sent Lieutenant Zebulon Pike on a parallel mission to explore the far reaches of the Mississippi River. Chouteau's expedition, however, was to be a brief one, for Wilkinson ordered him to be back in St. Louis by October, in order to assist in negotiations for a general treaty to end all Indian hostilities and to accompany the second deputation of tribal dignitaries scheduled to depart then for Washington.[61] In fact, the governor intended the Chouteau visit to the Osages to be a goodwill mission and a prelude for the government's designs for obtaining direct American control over the Osage territories. Wilkinson's instructions that Pierre discover the routes and distances from the Osage villages to the Spanish settlements in New Mexico presaged Lieutenant Pike's forthcoming expedition to the Southwest.[62]

In early August the often-postponed Osage mission finally got under way. A confident Pierre Chouteau departed from St. Louis believing that the following autumn would find him en route to Washington for a second time. Chouteau made his way up the Missouri and down the Osage along the natural highway to the Osage villages accompanied by a small party of troops under the command of George Peter, an officer at Cantonment Belle Fontaine.[63] Following an uneventful trip, Chouteau met in council on September 3 with over 1,000 Osages, apparently comprising braves from the major tribal factions.[64] Chouteau entreated the Arkansas bands to abandon their separate villages and return to White Hair's authority. Surprisingly, perhaps, Big Track's forces consented to do so the following spring. But Chouteau's success was limited to securing this single verbal promise, and Big Track's assembly rejected Chouteau's suggestion that a delegation from their numbers accompany him to visit the president.[65] Chouteau intended to follow the Arkansas warriors to their village to press his case, but the sudden arrival of 100 Pawnees and Omahas seeking traders for their nations necessitated a change in plans. Instead of chasing after the recalcitrant Big Track, the Frenchman characteristically and decisively chose the more positive alternative of prevailing upon his unexpected visitors to provide a corps of chiefs to descend to St. Louis with him for the autumn peace conference.[66] On September 22, he was back in St. Louis with seven Pawnees and twenty Osages, including White Hair, all of whom were prepared to participate in the conference and perhaps go to the federal city as well.[67]

Although Chouteau had secured a promise from the Arkansas Osages to return to their parent village the following spring, they had no intention of keeping their bargain. When spring came they reneged and remained at the

Arkansas site. Pierre had no way of knowing that at the time, but their refusal to grant permission for the construction of a fort in their territory did suggest that serious problems remained to be resolved.[68] But a much greater disappointment awaited Chouteau on his return to St. Louis. On August 5, the secretary of war had informed Wilkinson that the administration did not want Pierre to escort the new Indian delegation to the capital.[69] The War Department explained that Pierre's services in the territory were too important to spare for the long trek to the East. In fact, there seems little doubt that suspicions of Chouteau's propriety and perhaps his loyalty lay at the root of the rebuff. Wilkinson reported that the Indian agent was "much disappointed," but had accepted the decision "with good grace."[70]

The import of the government leaders' resolution to keep him in St. Louis, however, was not lost upon Pierre Chouteau. But it is likely that the distant officials failed to realize the loss of face their policy implied for their subaltern. Pierre Chouteau had personally invited a number of Indian leaders to go to the president in his company. His chagrin at being publicly embarrassed by the denial of his planned visit must have been severe indeed, but he managed it as he managed other setbacks. His annoyance surfaced only in his criticism of the government for sending inferior merchandise for the Sacs and Foxes and in his impatience with Dearborn's inability to comprehend the genuine costs of supplying the Indians with sufficient provisions and presents.[71] Yet whatever his private feelings, Chouteau understood that the greater interests of his family lay in accommodating the Americans. Thus, he once again pledged his best efforts for the administration, claiming that "whatever be the destinations of the duty my superiors give me, I shall always be satisfied. . . ."[72] He would continue to serve and by his services make himself indispensable to the Americans.

NOTES

1. According to Howard R. Lamar, the trader's world served as the focal point of Indian-white relations in North America between 1600 and 1850. For a discussion of the trader's crucial role see Lamar, *The Trader on the American Frontier: Myth's Victim* (College Station, Tex., 1977).

2. Henry Dearborn to Pierre Chouteau, July 17, 1804, and Commission of Pierre Chouteau as Indian agent, July 17, 1804, in Carter, ed., *Territorial Papers*, XIII, 31–33.

3. Thomas Jefferson to Meriwether Lewis, June 20, 1803, and James Wilkinson to Henry Dearborn, Oct. 27, 1805, in Jackson, ed., *Letters of Lewis and Clark*, 64, 265–66.

4. For a complete account of the Indian visits to the capital in this period see William E. Foley and Charles David Rice, "Visiting the President: An Exercise in Jeffersonian Indian Diplomacy," *American West* 16 (Nov./Dec. 1979), 4–16, 56.

5. Thomas Jefferson to Robert Smith, July 13, 1804, Jefferson Papers.

6. Foley and Rice, "Visiting the President," 10.

7. Thomas Jefferson to William Eustis, June 25, 1805, in Jackson, ed., *Letters of Lewis and Clark,* 249.

8. Bernard W. Sheehan, *Seeds of Extinction: Jeffersonian Philanthropy and the American Indian* (Chapel Hill, N.C., 1973), 245–46. Sheehan's work provides the most extensive account of Jeffersonian Indian policy, but for a different perspective one should also consult Robert F. Berkhofer, Jr., *The White Man's Indian: Images of the American Indian from Columbus to the Present* (New York, 1978), 134–53, and Reginald W. Horsman, *Expansion and American Indian Policy, 1783–1812* (East Lansing, Mich., 1967), 104–14.

9. For examples of some of the difficulties in what the author refers to as "Expansion with Honor" see Berkhofer, *White Man's Indian,* 134–53.

10. Meriwether Lewis was among those who questioned federal policy. See Meriwether Lewis to Henry Dearborn, July 1 and Aug. 20, 1808, in Carter, ed., *Territorial Papers,* XIV, *Louisiana-Missouri, 1806–1814* (Washington, D.C., 1949), 200, 214.

11. Auguste Chouteau to the Baron de Carondelet, quoted in Lewis O. Saum, *The Fur Trader and the Indian* (Seattle, Wash., 1965), 93.

12. Timothy Flint, *Recollections of the Last Ten Years . . . in the Valley of the Mississippi,* 155, quoted in Foreman, *Indians and Pioneers,* 20n.

13. Meriwether Lewis to Major William Preston, May 3, 1804, in Jackson, ed., *Letters of Lewis and Clark,* 179.

14. Henry Dearborn to Thomas Cushing, July 9, 1804, in *ibid.,* 198.

15. Jefferson's Greeting to White Hair and the Chiefs and Warriors of the Osage Nation, July 12, 1804, Jefferson Papers.

16. Jefferson's Address to White Hair and the Chiefs and Warriors of the Osage Nation, July 16, 1804, Jefferson Papers.

17. White Hair's Reply to Jefferson's Address, July 16, 1804, Jefferson Papers.

18. Henry Dearborn to Pierre Chouteau, July 17, 1804, in Carter, *Territorial Papers,* XIII, 31–33.

19. *Ibid.*

20. Chapman, "The Indomitable Osages," 293–94.

21. Jefferson's Address to White Hair and the Chiefs and Warriors of the Osage Nation, July 16, 1804, Jefferson Papers; Henry Dearborn to Pierre Chouteau, July 12, 1804, cited in Jackson, ed., *Letters of Lewis and Clark,* 203n.

22. Henry Dearborn to Pierre Chouteau, July 17, 1804, in Carter, ed., *Territorial Papers,* XIII, 31–33.

23. Albert Gallatin to Thomas Jefferson, Aug. 20, 1804, Jefferson Papers.

24. See Foley and Rice, "Visiting the President," 10–11.

25. Hezekiah Rogers to Thomas Jefferson, Aug. 21, 1804, in Jackson, ed., *Letters of Lewis and Clark,* 208–9.

26. Pierre Chouteau to Thomas Jefferson, Oct. 12, 1804, Jefferson Papers.

27. Pierre Chouteau to Thomas Jefferson, Nov. 7, 1804, and Pierre Chouteau to Henry Dearborn, Nov. 7, 1804, both in Pierre Chouteau Letterbook, Missouri Historical Society; Pierre Chouteau to Thomas Jefferson, Nov. 19, 1804, Jefferson Papers. Unlike most other members of the Siouan linguistic group, the Osages, through their women, were large producers of corn. For that reason the breach of promise vis-à-vis the mill was a serious matter for the Osages. For references to the importance of corn culture within the tribe see Pierre Chouteau's observations as reported in M. P. Le Duc

to Frederick Bates, Dec. 30, 1815, in Carter, ed., *Territorial Papers, XV, Louisiana-Missouri, 1815–1821* (Washington, D.C., 1954), 98–99; Zebulon Pike's observations in Donald Jackson, ed., *Journals of Pike,* II, 34; Francis LaFlesche, *Rite of the Chiefs* (Washington, D.C., 1921), 134–37.

28. For a fuller account of the administration's neglect of its engagements with tribal delegations see Foley and Rice, "Visiting the President," 14, 56.

29. Pierre Chouteau to Thomas Jefferson, Nov. 7, 1804, Pierre Chouteau Letterbook.

30. *Ibid.*

31. Freeman Cleaves, *Old Tippecanoe* (New York, 1939), 43.

32. Amos Stoddard to Henry Dearborn, June 3, 1804, Stoddard Papers, Missouri Historical Society; Foley, *History of Missouri,* 76–77.

33. Like the Osages, the Sacs and Foxes historically were a scourge to whites. A complete account of the Sac and Fox negotiations in St. Louis can be found in Jackson, *Jefferson and the Stony Mountains,* 203–17.

34. *Ibid.;* Pierre Chouteau to the Chiefs of the Sac and Fox Nations, Oct. 18, 1804, and Pierre Chouteau to Henry Dearborn, Nov. 7, 1804, and May 11, 1805, Pierre Chouteau Letterbook.

35. *American State Papers, Indian Affairs,* I, 693–94; William H. Harrison to Auguste Chouteau, Jan. 4, 1806, Lucas Collection, Missouri Historical Society; William T. Hagan, "The Sauk and Fox Treaty of 1804," *Missouri Historical Review* 51 (Oct. 1956), 1–7; Jackson, *Jefferson and the Stony Mountains,* 208–17.

36. Pierre Chouteau to Thomas Jefferson, Jan. 31, 1805, Pierre Chouteau Letterbook. At the time Pierre thought the hostility of the tribes stemmed from the policy of removing eastern tribes for resettlement west of the Mississippi River.

37. Pierre Chouteau to William H. Harrison, Mar. 9, 1805, and Pierre Chouteau to Henry Dearborn, Mar. 11, 1805, Pierre Chouteau Letterbook.

38. Pierre Chouteau to Henry Dearborn, Mar. 11, 1805, Pierre Chouteau Letterbook. A copy was sent to Jefferson.

39. Pierre Chouteau to Thomas Jefferson, Nov. 4, 1804, Pierre Chouteau Letterbook.

40. *Ibid.*

41. Henry Dearborn to Pierre Chouteau, July 18, 1804, Records of the Office of the Secretary of War, Letters Sent, Record Group 75, Microfilm 15, Indian Affairs, Vol. B, National Archives, Washington, D.C.

42. Henry Dearborn to Pierre Chouteau, Feb. 10, 1805, in Carter, ed., *Territorial Papers,* XIII, 443.

43. Pierre Chouteau to Henry Dearborn, Feb. 16, 1805, Pierre Chouteau Letterbook.

44. Pierre Chouteau to Thomas Jefferson, Mar. 11, 1805, Pierre Chouteau Letterbook.

45. Pierre Chouteau to Henry Dearborn, Mar. 11, 1805, Pierre Chouteau Letterbook.

46. Pierre Chouteau to Henry Dearborn, Mar. 2, 1805, Pierre Chouteau Letterbook.

47. *Ibid.*

48. Pierre Chouteau to Henry Dearborn, May 5, 1805, Pierre Chouteau Letterbook.

49. Pierre Chouteau to William H. Harrison, May 31, 1805, Pierre Chouteau Letterbook.

50. Pierre Chouteau to Henry Dearborn, May 22, 1805, and to William H. Harrison, May 31 and June 12, 1805, Pierre Chouteau Letterbook; William H. Harrison to Henry Dearborn, May 27, 1805, and to Pierre Chouteau, May 27, 1805, in Esarey, ed., *Messages and Letters of William Henry Harrison,* 132–34, 135–36.

51. Henry Dearborn to Pierre Chouteau, May 29, 1805, in Carter, ed., *Territorial Papers,* XIII, 134.

52. James Wilkinson to Henry Dearborn, June 27, 1805, in *ibid.,* 144–45.

53. Pierre Chouteau to Henry Dearborn, July 27, 1805, Pierre Chouteau Letterbook.

54. Rowse, "Auguste and Pierre Chouteau," 193–94.

55. James Wilkinson to Henry Dearborn, Nov. 26, 1805, in Jackson, ed., *Journals of Pike,* I, 251.

56. James Wilkinson to Henry Dearborn, July 27, 1805, in Carter, ed., *Territorial Papers,* XIII, 168–69.

57. *Ibid.*

58. James Wilkinson to Henry Dearborn, Nov. 26, 1805, in Jackson, ed., *Journals of Pike,* I, 251.

59. For a discussion of Wilkinson's tumultuous gubernatorial career see William E. Foley, "James A. Wilkinson: Territorial Governor," *Missouri Historical Society Bulletin* 25 (Oct. 1968), 3–17.

60. James Wilkinson to Henry Dearborn, July 27, 1805, in Carter, ed., *Territorial Papers,* XIII, 170–71.

61. James Wilkinson to Henry Dearborn, Aug. 10, 1805, in *ibid.,* 182.

62. Instructions of Governor Wilkinson to Pierre Chouteau, July 30, 1805, in *ibid.,* 184.

63. James Wilkinson to George Peter, Aug. 6, 1805, Folder 7605, University of Virginia Archives.

64. George Peter to James Wilkinson, Sept. 8, 1805, in Carter, ed., *Territorial Papers,* XIII, 231–32.

65. *Ibid.*

66. *Ibid.*

67. James Wilkinson to Henry Dearborn, Sept. 22, 1805, Letters Received by the Secretary of War, Record Group 107, Microfilm 221, Main Series 1800–1870, National Archives.

68. *Ibid.*

69. Henry Dearborn to James Wilkinson, Aug. 5, 1805, in Carter, ed., *Territorial Papers,* XIII, 179.

70. James Wilkinson to Henry Dearborn, Oct. 8, 1805, in *ibid.*

71. Pierre Chouteau to William H. Harrison, Oct. 8, 1805, to James Wilkinson, Oct. 8, 1805, and to Henry Dearborn, Oct. 1, 1805, Pierre Chouteau Letterbook.

72. Pierre Chouteau to Henry Dearborn, Oct. 1, 1805, Pierre Chouteau Letterbook.

DIFFERENT NOTIONS OF JUSTICE

I N THE COURSE of his continuing efforts to maintain peaceful relations with the Indians, Pierre Chouteau asked Governor James Wilkinson in June 1806 to defer the scheduled execution of two condemned Kickapoo braves. Although Chouteau did not think their sentence unjust, he reminded Wilkinson that "the Indian nations have such different notions of justice from ours. . . ."[1] This succinct observation epitomized Chouteau's constant dilemma as Indian agent. Charged with the task of smoothing relations between the tribesmen and the growing number of white settlers in the region, the American agent frequently found himself attempting to strike an uncertain balance between two incompatible worlds. All along the extended frontier where the contrasting cultures uneasily meshed, any misstep could mean disaster. To further complicate matters, Chouteau was a product of a cultural milieu markedly different from that of his employers. Accustomed to the relaxed Spanish style of business and government, he was unprepared for the Americans' notions of virtue and their republican expectations. Moreover, though Chouteau appreciated and understood the cultural and tribal divisions that separated the Indians under his jurisdiction, few Americans were as perceptive as Captain Amos Stoddard, who noted that the Sacs and Osages were as different from one another as either was from "a Esquimaux."[2] On the contrary, most ordinary white settlers regarded all Indians at best as nuisances or at worst as deadly savages.

Thomas Jefferson might well see the Native American as a sturdy son of a superior American habitat and blame disruptions of the peace on unscrupulous white traders, but the president was far away.[3] Pierre Chouteau had to deal with Indians who stole horses, robbed traders, made war on one another, and occasionally killed whites. He also had to contend with the realities of white prejudice, the ambitions of politicians and soldiers, the enterprise of traders and trappers, and, of course, the demands of his own financial and political interests. That Chouteau managed to continue his duties for many years and that he was often successful in them is a tribute to his skill and his perseverance.

Not all of the Indian agent's time was filled with such dramatic activities as maintaining the peace, negotiating treaties, and escorting Indian delegations to Washington. Much of the work was time-consuming and routine. The agent employed and supervised sub-agents and interpreters in his region.[4] When in the spring of 1805 the administration dispatched William Ewing as a special agricultural agent charged with instructing the Sacs in the arts of cultivation, Chouteau had to outfit him with farming equipment and supplies and hire an interpreter to accompany him.[5] Chouteau also licensed all traders doing business with the Indians under his jurisdiction, even though, as previously noted, he would have preferred to have retained all trading rights for himself.[6] On occasion, the Frenchman had to invoke his agency's authority to settle individual grievances, especially in cases where Indians had victimized whites. Local authorities often called upon him to assist in recovering stolen property or to bring Indians accused of crimes to St. Louis for trial.[7] At the same time, the Indians, mindful of American promises of protection, sometimes appealed to Chouteau for letters of safe conduct, relief from enemy tribes, or security from renegade whites.[8]

Pierre spent much of his time supplying the tribes under his jurisdiction with the merchandise, gifts, and other symbols of favor which the American government had promised them in an attempt to retain their goodwill. The task was frequently difficult. An agent's failure to exercise good judgment in distributing those objects could create serious problems. For instance, the agent had to decide which chiefs should be awarded Indian medals for their merit and loyalty while at the same time taking care not to offend any of the powerful tribal dignitaries by a profligate distribution of the prized symbols.

The American agent also had to counter English and Spanish influence in the villages by persuading the Indians to accept U.S. medals and flags in exchange for any European symbols in their possession. When chieftains demanded replacements, as some Sioux leaders did in 1805, Chouteau had to secure them in order to avoid risking their displeasure.[9] Claiming that he needed a hundred or more American flags in 1806, Chouteau kept the seamstresses of St. Louis busy with his orders.[10] Even so, as late as 1811, eight years after the Louisiana Purchase, American factor George Sibley found Spanish papers, medals, and flags from Santa Fe on display in a Pawnee village.[11] Such matters could not be taken lightly, since Indian acceptance of these symbols indicated at least tacit acquiescence to the donor's authority.

Less symbolic, but equally important, were the provisions of food and manufactured goods which the American government had pledged to make available to the Indians in various treaties and understandings. After the Americans first took possession of Louisiana, Indian provisions were delivered directly on the national government's orders, as in 1804 when Daniel Vertner supplied Amos Stoddard with 10,000 pounds of tobacco and 620 gallons of whiskey from Kentucky.[12] But after Pierre rejected a shipment of goods which federal authorities sent for the Sacs and Foxes because the items contained in it were inferior in quality, he increasingly insisted on purchasing all Indian supplies locally in order to forestall discontent among the discriminating tribesmen.[13] Because the agent's favor with the natives often rested upon their trust in his word, Chouteau had no intention of allowing shoddy merchandise to undermine his standing with them. The practice of buying from local dealers also had a tonic effect on the region's economy. The records indicate that Chouteau patronized a number of firms in ordering wares for the tribes under his administration. Although he apparently made an effort to spread the government's business around, he seems to have favored kinsmen and longtime associates including Auguste, Charles Gratiot, Bernard Pratte, Sylvestre Labbadie, Jr., Joseph Robidoux, John Mullanphy, Jacques Clamorgan, and William Morrison.[14] Morrison, one of Pierre's partners in the Missouri Fur Company, did a brisk business with the Indian agent for well over a decade. Between 1811 and 1813, for example, Chouteau arranged for Morrison to provide the Osages with 10,000 pounds of flour, 18,000 pounds of pork, 260 gallons of whiskey, and similar quantities of beef and salt.[15]

Chouteau had significantly less control over supplies that could not be procured locally. He particularly experienced difficulty in obtaining heavy equipment such as blacksmith's tools, forges, and horse mills, which the administration had promised to provide for the tribes. In 1809 Chouteau finally received some blacksmith's implements for the Osages, but as late as 1811 a long-promised mill had not yet been erected at their village.[16]

Funneling large amounts of treaty goods to the Indians entailed a considerable cost, particularly for a republican administration philosophically committed to frugality in its expenditures. Federal officials repeatedly pressed their Indian agent in Upper Louisiana concerning the extravagant costs of his agency. At least some of the criticism of Pierre Chouteau's alleged prodigality perhaps stemmed from a frustration born of the difficulties in fulfilling the substantial treaty and other obligations to which the American government had committed itself. In reality, Indian diplomacy had always been a costly business. Chouteau estimated that the Spanish annually had disbursed about $15,000 in provisions and presents among a lesser number of tribes than the United States now wished to influence.[17] He advised Governor Wilkinson in 1806 that the American government would need to spend a minimum of $8,000 a year for that purpose in addition to its normal outlays for the salaries and wages of employees, ordinary supplies for the tribes, and incidental costs. Altogether, Chouteau concluded that the expenses of the Indian agency could amount to as much as $30,000 per year.[18]

Despite Pierre's objections that his superiors did not appreciate the magnitude of expenditures necessary to pursue government policies among the trans-Mississippi tribes,[19] Secretary of War Dearborn frequently admonished him to spend less and to obtain the approval of his supervisors in all transactions.[20] On August 5, 1805, the secretary informed Governor Wilkinson that he and

Chouteau would be limited to a budget of $2,000 for Indian matters until Congress approved a new appropriation.[21] Under the circumstances, Chouteau unsuccessfully tried to shift the burden for handling the agency's accounts to Wilkinson, observing that only the governor could authorize the use of funds anyway.[22] Chouteau's trepidations were understandable, inasmuch as the bill he submitted to Dearborn in November covering the period since his appointment as agent amounted to $2,645.[23]

In fact, Chouteau was not responsible for the high costs of Indian policy in Upper Louisiana. In 1808, for example, after Chouteau's role in Indian matters had been reduced considerably, the total expenses for affairs in the territory exceeded $20,000, an amount far above what the War Department deemed necessary.[24] The following year federal officials turned down William Clark's request to add several new positions in the Indian agency with the pointed admonition that the expenses for Indian relations in Louisiana already amounted to four times those of the territory's civil government.[25] Evidently, federal employees were as prone to cost overruns in the nineteenth century as they are today.

If Pierre Chouteau did not merit censure for the expensive federal Indian policy, he was more vulnerable to criticism for his tendency to blend private trade with official duties. In the Spanish era colonial administrative officials customarily involved themselves in commercial operations. Indeed, it was a valuable perquisite of office. Officials in Washington, by contrast, questioned the propriety of public servants exerting their power and influence for personal profit. To some American observers, at least, Chouteau appeared to be more zealous in fostering his trade with the Indians than in administering federal policies among them. By the spring of 1806, rumors reached the federal city that the Indian agent had been making payments for services performed in the Indian department in goods rather than in cash and at prices calculated to make a profit for himself. If the charges were true, Chouteau had clearly violated the instructions he received at the time of his appointment.

Dearborn considered the allegations sufficiently serious to fire off a stinging letter to Chouteau threatening to remove him from office if such conduct did not come to a halt.[26] Pierre answered that the entire affair was based on the false report of an interpreter named Dorion, who had claimed that Chouteau never paid him or the other employees in money.[27] At Chouteau's behest Dorion appeared before Governor Wilkinson and denied having made the statements attributed to him. To further bolster his position, the Indian agent also collected written declarations from his other employees and forwarded them to Dearborn in such profusion that the secretary finally replied that no more justifications were necessary. All that was required, Dearborn wrote, was for Chouteau to declare that he was not procuring a personal profit by supplying goods to his own agency.[28]

Although on the surface Dearborn's communication seemed to imply continued confidence in Chouteau's capacity and integrity, the letter's formal and aloof tone hinted that the administration might, nonetheless, be entertaining second thoughts about the wisdom of his appointment. Whether or not those in power believed Chouteau's explanations and protestations of innocence regarding his alleged private trading operations, criticism of the agent continued to surface. Even though Wilkinson's own standing in Washington was by then in doubt, the general's testimony the previous year that Chouteau resented any rivals in Indian affairs remained a matter of record.[29] More severe criticism came from American army officers, who frequently took issue with the Indian agent's conduct in office. Major James Bruff repeatedly clashed with Pierre over jurisdictional disputes, and it was a Lieutenant Hughes who allegedly had passed on to his superiors word of Chouteau's rumored private dealings in his Indian agency.[30]

More serious were the charges leveled by Lieutenant Zebulon Pike, the famous military explorer whom Wilkinson had sent on expeditions to the upper Mississippi in 1805 and to the Arkansas and Red rivers in 1806. No friend of the Chouteaus, Pike resented their influence among the Osages and believed them to be masquerading as friends of the United States. He blamed Pierre Chouteau for creating the divisions among the Osages,[31] and concluded that the French trader had no intention of reuniting them. As proof, he cited Chouteau's failure to end the tribal divisions during his 1806 visit to their villages. Believing Chouteau to be an intriguer, Pike also criticized Pierre's nominees for appointments in the Indian service. For example, he refused to employ Noel Mongrain, an Indian half-blood, claiming that Mongrain was a "perfect creature" of Chouteau. Likewise, Pike branded White Hair as a Chouteau lackey, more loyal to Pierre than to the government he served.[32]

In time, the growing disenchantment with the Chouteaus became commingled with the suspicions surrounding their ally, Governor Wilkinson. Wilkinson attributed Major Bruff's disaffection to a belief that the governor had slighted him in favor of the Chouteaus.[33] But one of Zebulon Pike's biographers asserts that there was more to it than that. John Upton Terrell claims Wilkinson promoted the Chouteaus' commercial interests and was their "confederate behind the lines," using his authority, especially his power to grant licenses for the fur trade, to the Chouteaus' benefit.[34]

There is reason to believe that Wilkinson and the Chouteaus had arrived at some understanding, but the exact nature of their association is unknown.[35] What is clear is that Wilkinson favored the Old French elements in the factional politics of the territory and thereby earned the suspicion and resentment of those opposing the commercial and political power of families like the Chouteaus.[36] Federal officials became concerned about the growing discord and about Wilkinson's running dispute with territorial judges Rufus Easton and

John B. C. Lucas. After carefully scrutinizing the conduct of all parties involved in the disagreement, Jefferson declined to reappoint Easton as a judge. But since Wilkinson momentarily seemed to be possessed of too much political influence, the administration decided not to move against him openly.[37] In these struggles, Governor Wilkinson enjoyed the vocal support of the Chouteaus and other members of the French community, who bombarded Wilkinson's superiors in Washington with letters and petitions in his behalf. Significantly, Auguste also served on the St. Louis grand jury that precipitated Easton's dismissal from the territorial court by indicting him on a land-fraud charge.[38] Wilkinson went on to win Senate confirmation as governor in March 1806, but his position was actually deteriorating by then. Not only was the government displeased with Wilkinson's meddling in the land-claims controversy and his feuding with other officials, but the governor's failure to quell the continuing Indian conflict in the territory added to the administration's discontent. Most ominous, however, was the suspicion that the governor was involved in a conspiracy with Aaron Burr to create an independent western state.

Burr and Wilkinson had talked in St. Louis in September 1805, and though no direct evidence exists to prove that a plot was formed, the president had become convinced that the controversial general had to go. In a move to minimize Wilkinson's authority, Secretary Dearborn ordered him in May to assume command of military forces in the Orleans Territory. When Wilkinson finally left St. Louis in August, his tenure as governor of Louisiana was in effect ended.

Wilkinson's removal constituted a serious political defeat for the Chouteaus. They had clashed with the rising new men in the territory, most of whom were Americans, in a contest to save their benefactor and to uphold their political and business interests. In the process, the Chouteaus and their allies incurred the enmity of powerful newcomers like Lucas, who openly criticized them in letters to Washington.[39] Zebulon Pike had even reported that Pierre had counseled the Indians not to cooperate with the Americans because he expected that the territory would soon be returned to Spain.[40]

More outrageous, if less damaging, were the charges leveled by the deposed and discredited Wilkinson, who, besides turning on Burr, now joined the chorus against the Chouteaus as well. He repeated, for instance, Pike's allegations that the Chouteaus were unreconciled to the American possession of Louisiana. More specifically, the former governor claimed that Pierre had made Big Track chief of the dissident Osages in order to obtain another invitation to Washington, where he hoped to gain approval for an "illicit trade with Santa Fe."[41] In fact, Wilkinson went on, Clermont was the genuine chief of the Arkansas Osages, but he had refused to visit the president in the autumn of 1805 in defiance of Chouteau's pleas.[42] Wilkinson later expanded on this theme, alleging that although Clermont was a friend of the Americans, Chouteau's appointee, White Hair, had usurped his legitimate power as chief of the Big Osages.[43] Thus, the governor blamed Chouteau for the ongoing divisions in the tribe and for the unrestrained violence of the younger braves. Nor did Wilkinson consider the Frenchman innocent regarding the Little Osage tribe. His report specified that Chief Tuttasuggy, also known as The Wind, had testified that Pierre treated him contemptuously during an 1806 visit to his village because of his loyalty to the Americans. This insult was capped, Tuttasuggy was quoted as saying, when Chouteau took the chief's younger brother Nezuma to Washington and attempted to place him in control of the tribe.[44]

The flurry of damaging charges against the Chouteaus, and especially against Pierre's actions as Indian agent, came at a time when the government feared treason on the frontier. Consequently, well before the accusations peaked in 1807, the administration decided to discipline its Indian agent in St. Louis. In May 1806, as previously noted, Dearborn reprimanded Chouteau for his alleged private exchanges within the Indian agency. Then, in August the War Department rejected many of the agent's expense reports, charging that his accounting methods were unacceptable.[45] The most telling blow, however, fell on March 7 of the following year, when the administration informed Chouteau that henceforth his duties would be confined to serving as agent for only the Big and Little Osage tribes.[46] Jefferson selected William Clark to replace Chouteau as agent for all of the remaining tribes in the territory. The reduction of his duties also carried with it a cut in salary from \$1,500 to \$1,200 per year. Chouteau could not have missed the point. He had been demoted, and his ambitions had been severely checked. On the other hand, Dearborn had stopped short of dismissing him altogether, and as agent for one of the most powerful tribes in the region Chouteau continued to occupy a strategic position. His influence among the Osages and his general knowledge of Indian affairs was simply too valuable for the Jefferson administration to dispense with even if it doubted his propriety. In fact, during the subsequent absences of Governor Meriwether Lewis, who replaced Wilkinson, and Lewis's successor, Benjamin Howard, frontier necessities compelled acting Governor Frederick Bates to return virtually all responsibility for Indian affairs to Pierre Chouteau.[47]

In the wake of the Burr-Wilkinson affair, the Chouteau brothers surmounted much of the opposition against them by publicly rejecting all schemes to separate the territory from American political control. Pike and Wilkinson's charges against Pierre notwithstanding, Auguste Chouteau had refused to deal with Burr's agent, Colonel Julien de Pestre, when he visited St. Louis in October 1806. Upon being offered a commission by the Frenchman de Pestre, Chouteau had attempted to throw it into a fire. Moreover, although they briefly supported territorial secretary Joseph Browne, Burr's brother-in-law, as a candidate to replace Wilkinson, the Chouteaus joined others in the community in demanding official action to forestall the threatened conspiracy.[48] Indeed, no direct evidence exists linking the Chouteaus with the Burrite plot, and Wilkinson's bitter denunciations of Pierre's activities in his 1807 report may well have reflected the general's own frustrated aspirations.

In the midst of these momentous events, Louisiana's ongoing Indian problems had continued to demand Pierre Chouteau's attention. Upon Chouteau's return from the Osage villages in the fall of 1805, American authorities attempted to effect a general pacification by convening a conference in St. Louis attended by chiefs from the Delaware, Miami, Potawatomi, Kickapoo, Kaskaskia, Sioux of the Des Moines River, Iowa, Sac, Fox, Pawnee, Oto, Arikara, and Osage tribes. Although the Indian leaders agreed under great pressure to a pact pledging a cessation of intertribal hostilities, they had scarcely departed when the fighting between the Sacs and the Osages resumed.[49]

Even before the abortive St. Louis conclave, federal officials had authorized the construction of a fort and government trading factory on the Missouri River about four miles above its junction with the Mississippi. They assumed that by supplying goods to the Indians at reasonable rates, the new government factory could help offset the nefarious operations of the private traders, whom Jefferson believed to be a principal cause of Indian unrest.[50] In addition to Cantonment Belle Fontaine, as the new military and trading installation was first called, Governor Wilkinson urged the construction of additional forts in the interior as a means of establishing American authority. Cost-conscious leaders in the administration temporarily vetoed all such proposals, but in time they relented and established additional fortified government trading posts at Arkansas Post, located in the present state of that name on the Arkansas River a short distance above its confluence with the Mississippi River, Fort Madison, located on the Mississippi River at the site of the present city of Fort Madison, Iowa, and Fort Osage, situated on a high bluff overlooking the Missouri River near the present town of Sibley, Missouri.

Actually, the Indian hostilities along the trans-Mississippi frontier emanated from a more complex set of factors than Jefferson supposed. In the first place, intertribal jealousies had deep historical roots. Moreover, the American designs on the Indian lands and the plans calling for the resettlement of various eastern tribes on the western side of the Mississippi understandably generated resentment and ill will, which British and Spanish operatives in the territory seized upon to advance their interests. With his usual vigor, Wilkinson had tried to control the movements of outsiders among the tribes through a policy of issuing trading licenses only to American citizens. Unfortunately, the program proved ineffective in checking British commercial operations in Louisiana. Wilkinson also had to back down from his attempt to ban the use of firearms in the Indian trade. The St. Louis fur traders, led by the Chouteaus, Manuel

Lisa, and Bernard Pratte, convinced the governor that a prohibition of firearms from the fur trade would cause the entire business to collapse and that unfriendly tribes would obtain the weapons anyway.[51]

Having failed to halt the flow of weapons to the tribes, the American government persisted in its attempts to thwart the law of supply and demand by trying to prevent the sale of liquor to the Indians. This effort was perhaps more quixotic than the embargo on arms, for as can be seen in the accounts of the British North West Company, the Indians were avid consumers of strong spirits. In 1803 that firm supplied eager tribal customers with 16,299 gallons of liquor, and its agents estimated that between 1806 and 1810 the yearly Indian consumption averaged 9,700 gallons.[52] Naturally, the St. Louis merchants had no intention of forfeiting their business by ignoring their customers' demands for alcohol. The traders developed various subterfuges to circumvent the regulation, and in 1811 William Clark admitted that he could not enforce the American government's ban on liquor in the Indian trade. According to him, nine out of ten traders had no respect for the prohibition law.[53]

If frontier conditions thwarted American authorities in their efforts to calm the Indians and stabilize the political situation in Louisiana, they continued, nonetheless, the policy of summoning Indian leaders to confer with them in Washington. In the waning months of 1805, Captain Amos Stoddard set out for the federal city with the expedition of tribal dignitaries which Pierre Chouteau had originally expected to escort. A much more varied company than Chouteau's Osage delegation of the previous year, the assembly contained representatives from at least eleven Indian nations. Some of them were delegates originally sent down the Missouri by Lewis and Clark and now returned to St. Louis, as promised, with the passing of summer. Others had accompanied Chouteau to the city following his journey to the Osage towns in August and September. Wilkinson forwarded a number of British and Spanish trade articles with the deputation as evidence of the need to conciliate the tribes and to shore up American authority in the area.[54] The governor regretted that the Oto and Arikara chiefs would not be with Stoddard, but, mistakenly as it turned out, he thought there would be no untoward results of their decision to forgo the trip.[55] The Indian envoys created a great stir among the curious Americans who turned out to greet them, but otherwise their visit with the president and their tour of eastern cities were carried off without incident.[56]

For a government beset with many problems, not the least of which was maintaining the security of the vast Louisiana Territory in a time when Europe was once again convulsed in war between Napoleon I and the British-inspired Third Coalition, the policy of consulting with Indian chieftains seemed the preferable alternative. Thus, the euphoria created by the impending return of the highly successful Lewis and Clark expedition, along with the apparent

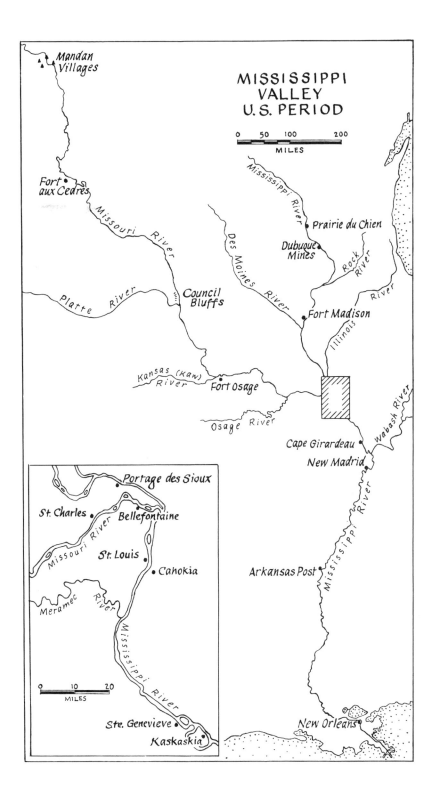

MISSISSIPPI
VALLEY
U.S. PERIOD

0   50   100   200
MILES

Mandan
Villages

Fort
aux Cedres

Missouri River

Platte River

Council
Bluffs

Kansas (Kaw) River

Fort Osage

Osage River

Des Moines River

Mississippi River

Prairie du Chien

Dubuque
Mines

Rock River

Fort Madison

Illinois River

Wabash River

Cape Girardeau

New Madrid

Mississippi River

Arkansas Post

New Orleans

Portage des Sioux

St. Charles

Bellefontaine

Missouri River

St. Louis

Cahokia

Meramec River

Mississippi River

Ste. Genevieve

Kaskaskia

0   10   20
MILES

achievements of the previous Indian visits to the capital, moved the administration to invite a third delegation to Washington. In St. Louis, Paul Loise,
the mixed-blood interpreter who had gone to the capital with Stoddard, informed Pierre Chouteau that the president would welcome a conference with
leaders of the Arkansas River Osages.[57]

As previously noted, Chouteau's standing in Washington had begun to
plummet by 1806, so he warmly endorsed the proposal and volunteered to
escort Big Track and, if the administration wished, leaders of the unfriendly
Sacs, Foxes, and Kickapoos as well. He believed he could better inform his
supervisors of the Indian situation in person, and, in any event, he wished to
have precise instructions regarding the limits of his duties.[58] The Frenchman
had no way of knowing when the administration endorsed his second visit to
the capital that the result would be his demotion and Clark's appointment as
agent for all tribes except the Osages.

The exciting events in St. Louis during the summer of 1806 left Chouteau
with little time to brood about his future. With Wilkinson removed from
authority, the Burr conspiracy unraveling, Indian fighting raging, Lewis and
Clark expected in St. Louis, and Pierre called to Washington for a second time,
there was plenty to keep him occupied. After hastily preparing for a trip to
the Osage villages to persuade the Arkansas leaders to accompany him on the
upcoming trip to Washington, Pierre set out from St. Louis in late August.[59]
When he arrived at White Hair's village on the Marmaton River (or south fork
of the Osage) a few days later, his son Pierre Jr. was already on his way to the
Osage village on the Verdigris River to arrange for a meeting with Big Track.[60]
Pierre Sr. prevailed upon White Hair to go with him to the Arkansas Osage
camp to assist with the negotiations, but once they got there the results of
their discussions were not altogether satisfying.[61] Claiming that he was seriously ill, Big Track declined to make the journey to Washington, but he did
agree to send his son and five other tribal leaders in his place.[62] However,
despite their earlier promise, the Arkansas Osages gave no indication that they
intended to rejoin White Hair at their former village on the banks of the
Marmaton.

A month later Pierre and the Osage delegates who had agreed to accompany
him were back in St. Louis preparing to join the recently arrived Lewis and
Clark for a triumphant march to the national capital.[63] Much had changed
since Auguste Chouteau had cheered the famous explorers as they departed
from St. Charles nearly two and a half years before, but upon their return to
St. Louis in September 1806 they found the Chouteau hospitality as inviting
as ever. They dined at the home of one of the brothers on their first night in
St. Louis, and on the following evening the pathfinders attended a ball given
by the Chouteaus and other prominent St. Louisans in their honor.[64] During

the festivities, their genial hosts listened intently to the reports of what they had seen. For Pierre, the preparations for his return to Washington made the occasion doubly enjoyable.

Another celebrant eagerly awaiting the trip east was the talkative, light-skinned Mandan chief, Shahaka. This animated Indian had joined the American explorers on their homeward trek and planned to go on with them to the capital. As the leader of a tribe whose support the U.S. government considered vital, Shahaka was a welcome guest. The chieftain had displayed a benevolent interest in the Americans when Lewis and Clark wintered near the Mandan village on their outward journey, and now he, his wife and son, and Canadian interpreter René Jusseaume and his family had acceded to Clark's requests that they accompany the party to Washington.[65]

By October 21, Chouteau and the Osage chiefs, Lewis and Clark, and Shahaka and his party had taken leave of St. Louis and headed eastward to the warm greetings of well-wishers, who turned out to salute the returning explorers. Jefferson, obviously delighted with his countrymen's achievements, sent word ahead that he anxiously awaited his friends and the Mandan chief, whom he invited to pay a visit to Monticello while en route to the federal city.[66]

The two main elements of the party separated at Frankfort, Kentucky. Chouteau and the Osages took the more direct route through Lexington to Washington, while Captain Lewis and the others traveled by way of Charlottesville, Richmond, Fredericksburg, and Alexandria, taking time out to visit friends and relatives. Consequently, Chouteau and the Osage delegation had already reached the capital when Lewis's seasoned wayfarers arrived there on December 28.

The ringing celebrations which greeted the travelers from the Missouri added to the normally festive holiday season in Washington. Jefferson formally welcomed Shahaka on the 30th, and on New Year's Eve he treated Chouteau's Osages to his standard address to Indian delegations. Amid the White House receptions, Washington dinner parties, and theater performances, Chouteau attempted to repair his strained relations with the administration. On January 14 he attended the jubilant banquet honoring Lewis, where he joined with some of the most powerful men in America in their many toasts, including one to "The Red People of America—under an enlightened policy, gaining by steady steps the comforts of the civilized, without losing the virtues of the savage state."[67]

Agreeable as the New Year festivities were, the year 1807 did not prove to be particularly fortunate for either Chouteau or the United States. Not long after returning to St. Louis, Chouteau received word that his duties would henceforth be confined to acting for the Osages alone. Having failed in his attempts to shore up his position while in Washington, he found himself increasingly isolated and even ignored. He later recollected that he had been reduced to being "a mere nominal agent, without Powers to exercise or duties to perform."[68] Pierre Chouteau may be excused if he exaggerated the impact of his demotion. Actually, even in his reduced capacity he remained active in Indian affairs, as demonstrated by his important role in securing final approval for the Osage treaty the following year.

For the U.S. government, the New Year marked the beginning of a long and frustrating period in Indian relations in the Louisiana Territory. From 1807 until the outbreak of the War of 1812, the trans-Mississippi frontier presented a montage of escalating violence among various tribes and between Indians and whites. Although the machinations of Spanish and British agents were partly to blame for the unsettled conditions, the relentless pressures of an expanding white population which threatened the land, the resources, and even the existence of the Indians lay at the heart of the problem. The Jeffersonian calculation that the trans-Mississippi West would not be heavily populated with whites for generations to come proved to be hopelessly inaccurate—tragically so for the Indian nations, who in desperation turned for assistance in resisting the American assault to Great Britain, the United States' most formidable rival in North America. A common desire to check American expansion helped forge an uneasy alliance between the red men and the Red Coats. Fighting for her survival in Europe following Napoleon's smashing victories at Jena in October 1806 and at Friedland in June 1807, Britain desperately needed to maintain her commercial and strategic position in North America. Fighting to preserve their way of life, the Indians increasingly preferred the distant menace of British power to the ominously present danger from the United States.

As America's standing with the tribes deteriorated, Pierre Chouteau spent much of his time countering British and Spanish efforts to woo the Osages from their American allies.[69] The continued intrusions on their lands by white settlers and rival tribes alike enraged the younger Osage braves, who angrily challenged White Hair's leadership. As the dissident warriors killed cattle, burned houses, stole horses, and attacked whites in remote settlements, the bitter tribal divisions intensified.[70] It was in an effort to stabilize the political situation in Louisiana and to reverse the drift toward general war that President Jefferson selected Meriwether Lewis to succeed Wilkinson as territorial governor. And it was upon Lewis's suggestion that his famous colleague, William Clark, replaced Chouteau as Indian agent for all tribes except the Osages, and also assumed command of the territorial militia. Clearly the chief executive hoped that the celebrated explorers could end the feuding within Louisiana and restore some of the diminished luster to the territory. The skills required to explore Louisiana, however, were quite different from those required to govern it. And, as Chouteau reported to the War Department in the autumn of 1807, the level of Indian unrest was intensifying.[71]

Lewis did not arrive in St. Louis to take up his new duties until 1808, and in the meantime a series of shocks rolled across the frontier. In May 1807 a band of Osages descended on St. Louis announcing that Spanish emissaries had been in their villages seeking their support and that neighboring tribal leaders were urging them to take up arms.[72] Chouteau warned them to remember their proper allegiance, but he could only apologize because a promised mill had not arrived.[73] That summer officials in St. Louis ordered all white men to arm themselves,[74] and in August Pierre learned of attempts to form a general coalition of the Mississippi tribes against the United States.[75] September saw the mobilization of part of the territorial militia,[76] while Chouteau decided to attend a forthcoming council of potentially hostile tribes at the Des Moines River in an effort to discourage further disorders.[77] First, however, the Osage agent planned to visit members of that tribe to pay them for horses requisitioned earlier for Lieutenant Pike and to dissuade them from enlisting in any anti-American coalition.[78] During his stay at the principal village on the forks of the Osage River, a party of Sacs and Potawatomis launched a murderous assault against the town which left three Osages dead in a lodge next to Chouteau's own quarters. Enraged by this treachery, the Osages turned their wrath on the American agent, charging that the United States talked of peace but allowed enemy tribes to kidnap and kill their people. It was a fearful moment, and Chouteau's safety appeared in great jeopardy. But disregarding the dangers to his own life, Chouteau displayed his rare diplomatic gifts and overcame the Osage hostility. He persuaded them to reject the invitation to attend the council at the Des Moines River and to undertake a tribal hunt instead. It was a master stroke of diplomacy which probably prevented the formation of a more ominous anti-American alliance.[79]

Impressive as Chouteau's performance at the Osage towns was, neither he nor his friend White Hair could prevent dissident braves from making further raids. Ignoring Pierre's renewed entreaties to rejoin their northern brethren, the Arkansas Osages remained obstinately rebellious. Therefore, when Governor Lewis, never one to suffer Indian recalcitrance patiently, finally assumed his duties in St. Louis, he declared the Osage nations outside of American protection, cut off all trade with them, and invited rival tribes to make war on them.[80] Since the president was uneasy with this punitive policy, Lewis tempered his stringency by promising the Osages a government trading factory in return for their submission and loyalty.

Lewis selected Clark to supervise the construction of the fortified trading post, which they called Fort Osage.[81] The new governor consulted with Pierre Chouteau about its location, but otherwise he had bypassed the Osage agent's services in the matter.[82] Perhaps Lewis simply had more confidence in his old associate, but Chouteau may be excused if he regarded the move as another sign of his waning esteem in administration circles. Meanwhile, as the Osages experienced the effects of Lewis's sanctions against them, they seemed anxious to placate the Americans in order to reopen the trade and secure the promised new factory. Clark capitalized upon this favorable turn of events to conclude a treaty with the Big and Little Osages on Fire Prairie on September 13, 1808, which fulfilled the American government's desire to extract territorial concessions from the Osages. In the agreement, Clark persuaded them to relinquish to the United States an immense tract of land between the Missouri and Arkansas rivers in the Louisiana Territory.[83]

Not long after Clark's apparent success, Lewis learned from Pierre that many Osages objected to the treaty. Misunderstandings concerning the provisions of the agreement and dissatisfaction occasioned by the failure of White Hair and the other chiefs to obtain the tribal council's consent before accepting Clark's terms generated mounting opposition to the treaty within the tribe. Governor Lewis was dubious of the Osage objections, but he consented to new negotiations to deter further hostilities.[84]

This time Lewis took the precaution of consulting with Chouteau before drafting a new treaty, but he denied the Frenchman's appeal that the revised document include a provision confirming his Spanish title to 30,000 arpents of land in the ceded area. Once the treaty had been revised, Lewis dispatched Chouteau to obtain the Osages' agreement. Employing his superior knowledge of the tribe's customs, the Osage agent secured the consent of the chiefs to Lewis's terms on November 10, 1808.[85] The revised treaty reaffirmed the Osage land cession, and in return the United States agreed to establish a permanent trading factory for supplying the tribe with merchandise, to erect a blacksmith shop and mill for Indian use, to grant an annual 1,500-dollar stipend to the tribe, and to restore them to the protection of the United States.

By any measure, the Osage treaty of 1808 was a triumph for Pierre Chouteau and for the American government. Nevertheless, as was so often the case, Chouteau's role in the negotiations proved to be quite controversial. For one thing, the insistence of the Osage chiefs that the treaty include a provision validating Pierre's title to land in the area caused William Clark to conclude that Chouteau had persuaded them to reject the first treaty.[86] Lewis could uncover no conclusive evidence that Chouteau had prejudiced the Osages against Clark's accord, but he reported that the affair had produced "a want of cordiality and confidence" between Chouteau and Clark.[87] There were other critics too. George Sibley, the government factor at Fort Osage, disapproved of Chouteau's methods in securing Osage assent to the second treaty. Asserting that Chouteau lacked Clark's patience and understanding, he accused the Frenchman of forcing the negotiations and employing threats to make the Indians sign the document. In fact, Sibley's resentment toward Chouteau emanated more from his belief that Chouteau had attempted to use the treaty for personal gain than from objections to the agent's negotiating tactics.[88]

Pierre Chouteau almost certainly encouraged the Osages to demand inclusion of the article concerning his land grant, but the efforts to blame him for the misunderstandings and disagreements surrounding the proceedings seem misplaced. The agreement did, after all, compel the Osages to surrender sizable parts of their traditional tribal lands, and Pierre, above all others, must have appreciated the sacrifices his old friends were being asked to make.[89] Once the tribesmen understood the magnitude of those concessions, it is little wonder that they registered their objections to the original treaty. At their insistence, the provision for the 1,500-dollar annuity was inserted in the revised document along with additional articles concerning hunting grounds, the surrender and punishment of Indian and white criminals, and the recovery of stolen property. Even with those changes, it is doubtful that final acceptance could have been won without Chouteau's diligent efforts. Sibley's charges that Chouteau had coerced the chiefs to ratify the pact suggests that widespread opposition to it persisted. Moreover, in criticizing Pierre's handling of the negotiations, the new factor at Fort Osage failed to mention that the Osage agent had followed Governor Lewis's instructions to the letter. And if the Osages disliked Chouteau's high-pressure tactics, they also knew that bad as it might be, the final treaty was decidedly more favorable to them than the one General Clark had pressed upon them.

The pacification of the Osages was a timely success for the United States in 1808. It was, moreover, almost a unique achievement, because elsewhere American interests were undergoing severe strain. For half a decade the young republic had been given the time to develop a satisfactory policy toward the trans-Mississippi Indian nations and to reconcile their "different notions of justice" with those of the white man's world. Faraway events and great challenges now moved rapidly to end that respite. Rumors of war raced across the land like a summer prairie fire, and no American could confidently predict the allegiance of the tribal nations should that test come. Thanks to the efforts of Pierre Chouteau, however, the chances were better than even that the Osage nation would stand by the United States.

NOTES

1. Pierre Chouteau to James Wilkinson, June 7, 1806, Pierre Chouteau Letterbook, Missouri Historical Society.

2. Stoddard, *Sketches,* 429. The Sacs are Algonquians, the Osages Siouan.

3. Thomas Jefferson to Henry Dearborn, Aug. 30, 1802, in Carter, ed., *Territorial Papers,* VII, *Indiana, 1800–1810* (Washington, D.C., 1939), 72.

4. For example, see Pierre Chouteau's appointment of Reuben Lewis as sub-agent, Oct. 12, 1809, Meriwether Lewis Papers, Missouri Historical Society. The appointment of Meriwether's only brother was certainly not an impolitic move at the time.

Although Meriwether had died the day before the appointment was made, Chouteau had no way of knowing that.

5. Pierre Chouteau to William H. Harrison, May 14, 1805, Pierre Chouteau Letterbook; Zebulon Pike to James A. Wilkinson, Aug. 20, 1805, in Jackson, ed., *Journals of Pike,* I, 230–32.

6. Jefferson desired to establish government trading factories among the tribes to undersell private traders because he thought they swindled the Indians and sowed discord among them. See Jefferson's Message to Congress, Jan. 18, 1803, in Jackson, ed., *Letters of Lewis and Clark,* 11. The licensing process, however, could reduce the number of private dealers and, as in May 1805, when Pierre Chouteau refused to issue a permit to British merchant Allan Wilmot, help prevent foreign influence among the tribes. See Jackson, ed., *Journals of Pike,* 125n.

7. For example, in May 1805 some Sioux chiefs brought in one of their members charged with murdering two French Canadians on the St. Pierre River. See Pierre Chouteau to William H. Harrison, May 11, 1805, Pierre Chouteau Letterbook. Many other cases involved the Sacs, Foxes, and Osages. See, for example, Henry Dearborn to Pierre Chouteau, Mar. 23, 1805, concerning the robbery of one Pierre Jarda by the Osages, in Records of the Office of the Secretary of War, Letters Sent, Record Group 75, Microfilm 15, Indian Affairs, Vol. B, National Archives; and Jackson, ed., *Journals of Pike,* II, 164n, concerning an Osage theft of horses and goods belonging to William T. Lamme. In 1805, for instance, Chouteau furnished a safe-conduct letter to a Sioux chief named Wabasha and his companions, who were traveling to Prairie du Chien. See Jackson, ed., *Journals of Pike,* I, 26–27n.

8. In 1810 the Osages sent a chief to St. Louis to complain that more and more Americans were daily settling on their lands. Pierre Chouteau to William Eustis, Apr. 26, 1810, Pierre Chouteau Letterbook.

9. In this case Chouteau was fortunate to have the necessary medals, since most of his supply had been destroyed when his residence burned. Luckily, however, he had seven medals at the goldsmith's at the time of the fire. Pierre Chouteau to Henry Dearborn, May 11, 1805, Pierre Chouteau Letterbook.

10. James Wilkinson to Henry Dearborn, May 27, 1806, in Jackson, ed., *Journals of Pike,* 278, 279n.

11. Thomas D. Isern, ed., "Exploration and Diplomacy: George Champlin Sibley's Report to William Clark, 1811," *Missouri Historical Review* 73 (Oct. 1978), 93.

12. Henry Dearborn to Amos Stoddard, May 8, 1804, Stoddard Papers, Missouri Historical Society.

13. Pierre Chouteau to Henry Dearborn, Oct. 1, 1805, and to William Henry Harrison, Oct. 8, 1805, Pierre Chouteau Letterbook.

14. For examples of Chouteau's disbursements for the Indian agency see Pierre Chouteau to Henry Dearborn, May 23, July 27, and Aug. 5, 1805, and Jan. 6 and Apr. 12, 1806, Pierre Chouteau Letterbook.

15. Tevebaugh, "Merchant on the Western Frontier," 179. Also see Pierre Chouteau's account with Morrison, Sept. 30, 1808, Chouteau Collections, Missouri Historical Society.

16. Henry Dearborn to Tench Coxe, Aug. 10, 1809, Clark Family Papers, Missouri Historical Society; Pierre Chouteau to William Eustis, Jan. 17, 1811, Pierre Chouteau Letterbook.

17. Pierre Chouteau to Henry Dearborn, Nov. 12, 1805, Pierre Chouteau Letterbook.

18. Pierre Chouteau to James Wilkinson, Apr. 12, 1806, Pierre Chouteau Letterbook.

19. Pierre Chouteau to Henry Dearborn, Oct. 1, 1805, Pierre Chouteau Letterbook.

20. Henry Dearborn to Pierre Chouteau, Feb. 10 and Dec. 20, 1805, in Carter, ed., *Territorial Papers,* XIII, 443, 316.

21. Henry Dearborn to James Wilkinson, Aug. 5, 1805, in *ibid.,* 179.

22. Pierre Chouteau to Henry Dearborn, Nov. 12, 1805, Pierre Chouteau Letterbook.

23. *Ibid.*

24. Foley, *History of Missouri,* 135.

25. William Eustis to William Clark, Aug. 7, 1809, in Carter, ed., *Territorial Papers,* XIV, 289–90.

26. Henry Dearborn to Pierre Chouteau, May 12, 1806, in Carter, ed., *Territorial Papers,* XIII, 510.

27. Pierre Chouteau to Henry Dearborn, July 1806, Pierre Chouteau Letterbook. Dorion was almost certainly the mixed-blood Pierre Dorion who often acted as an interpreter.

28. Henry Dearborn to Pierre Chouteau, Aug. 17, 1806, Records of the Office of the Secretary of War, Letters Sent, Record Group 75, Microfilm 15, Indian Affairs, Vol. B, National Archives.

29. James Wilkinson to Henry Dearborn, Nov. 26, 1805, in Jackson, ed., *Journals of Pike,* I, 251.

30. Pierre Chouteau to Henry Dearborn, July 1806, Pierre Chouteau Letterbook.

31. Pike's Dissertation on Louisiana, in Jackson, ed., *Journals of Pike,* II, 32–33.

32. Zebulon Pike to James Wilkinson, Sept. 23, 1805, and Aug. 28, 1806, in *ibid.,* I, 239, and II, 143.

33. James Wilkinson to Henry Dearborn, Dec. 31, 1805, in Carter, ed., *Territorial Papers,* XIII, 370.

34. John Upton Terrell, *Zebulon Pike: The Life and Times of an Adventurer* (New York, 1968), 43.

35. For an account of Wilkinson's role in private trade see Alvin M. Josephy, Jr., *The Nez Perce Indians and the Opening of the Northwest* (New Haven, 1965), 657–60.

36. Foley, "James A. Wilkinson," 3–17.

37. Foley, *History of Missouri,* 107.

38. Presentment of the Grand Jury of the Territory of Louisiana, Oct. term, 1805, Petition on behalf of Governor Wilkinson, Dec. 27, 1805, Minutes of a meeting of inhabitants at St. Louis, Jan. 4, 1806, and Auguste Chouteau and others to the President, Jan. 6, 1806, all in Carter, ed., *Territorial Papers,* XIII, 248–51, 333–34, 338, 385–86.

39. John B. C. Lucas to Albert Gallatin, Feb. 13, 1806, in *ibid.,* 444.

40. Weston Arthur Goodspeed, *The Province and the States* (Madison, Wis., 1904), I, 340.

41. James Wilkinson to Henry Dearborn, Oct. 17, 1806, in Jackson, ed., *Journals of Pike,* II, 154.

42. *Ibid.*

43. James Wilkinson's report, Apr. 6, 1807, in *ibid.,* II, 16–17.

44. *Ibid.,* II, 12.

45. Pierre Chouteau to W. Simmons, Aug. 18, 1806, Pierre Chouteau Letterbook.

46. Henry Dearborn to Pierre Chouteau, Mar. 7, 1807, in Carter, ed., *Territorial Papers*, XIV, 107–8.

47. William Clark to William Eustis, July 20, 1810, Clark Family Papers.

48. Clarence E. Carter, "The Burr-Wilkinson Intrigue in St. Louis," *Missouri Historical Society Bulletin* 10 (July 1954), 447–64; Auguste Chouteau to the President, July 15 and Aug. 24, 1806, in Carter, ed., *Territorial Papers*, XIII, 550–51.

49. Foley, *History of Missouri*, 115.

50. See Jefferson's confidential message to Congress, Jan. 18, 1803, in Jackson, ed., *Letters of Lewis and Clark*, 11.

51. Merchants of St. Louis to Governor Wilkinson, Aug. 24, 1805, in Carter, ed., *Territorial Papers*, XIII, 202–3.

52. G. C. Davidson, *The Northwest Company* (Berkeley, 1918), 91.

53. Francis Paul Prucha, *American Indian Policy in the Formative Years: The Indian Trade and Intercourse Acts, 1790–1834* (Cambridge, Mass., 1962), 108.

54. James Wilkinson to Henry Dearborn, Oct. 8, 1805, Letters Received by the Secretary of War, Record Group 107, Microfilm 221, Main Series 1800–1870, National Archives.

55. James Wilkinson to Henry Dearborn, Oct. 27, 1805, Record Group 107, W 515, Microfilm M221, Roll 2, National Archives. An Arikara chief named Ankedoucharo did make the trip but died suddenly in the East. No Arikaran appears in the list of delegates prepared by Wilkinson nor in the account in the *National Intelligencer*, Dec. 18, 1805, but Dearborn's letter to Wilkinson of Mar. 14, 1806, Records of the Office of the Secretary of War, Letters Sent, Military Affairs, MC, Roll 2, National Archives, said an Arikara chief was in Philadelphia.

56. For a full account of Stoddard's expedition see John C. Ewers, "'Chiefs from the Missouri and Mississippi' and Peale's Silhouettes of 1806," *Smithsonian Journal of History* 1 (1966); and Foley and Rice, "Visiting the President," 4–14, 56.

57. Pierre Chouteau to Henry Dearborn, June 17, 1806, and to Thomas Jefferson, June 17, 1806, Pierre Chouteau Letterbook.

58. *Ibid.*

59. Pierre Chouteau to Henry Dearborn, Aug. 18, 1806, and to William H. Harrison, Aug. 19, 1806, Pierre Chouteau Letterbook.

60. Pike's Journal of the Western Expedition, entry for Sept. 21, 1806, in Jackson, ed., *Journals of Pike*, I, 312–13.

61. *Ibid.* Jackson notes that White Hair later wrote to the president saying that he had arrived home "with my brother Chouteau" from the Arkansas.

62. Pierre Chouteau to Henry Dearborn, Oct. 14, 1806, Pierre Chouteau Letterbook.

63. *Ibid.*

64. Clark's Journal, Sept. 24, 1806, in Thwaites, ed., *Journals of Lewis and Clark*, V, 394–95.

65. For a full account of the events surrounding Shahaka's journey to Washington and his belated return to his village see William E. Foley and Charles David Rice, "The Return of the Mandan Chief," *Montana, the Magazine of Western History* 29 (July 1979), 2–15. Jusseaume had served as an interpreter for the Lewis and Clark expedition along with Toussaint Charbonneau, Sacagawea's husband.

66. Thomas Jefferson to Meriwether Lewis, Oct. 26, 1806, in Jackson, ed., *Letters of Lewis and Clark*, 350–51.

67. *National Intelligencer and Washington Advertiser,* Jan. 16, 1807. Clark, who had not yet arrived from his stopover in Virginia, missed the banquet.

68. Pierre Chouteau to William Eustis, Dec. 14, 1809, Pierre Chouteau Letterbook.

69. William Clark to Henry Dearborn, May 18, 1807, in Carter, ed., *Territorial Papers,* XIV, 122.

70. Meriwether Lewis to Henry Dearborn, July 1, 1808, in *ibid.,* 196–97.

71. Pierre Chouteau to Henry Dearborn, Aug. 4, 18, and Sept. 24, 1807, Pierre Chouteau Letterbook.

72. Frederick Bates to Henry Dearborn, May 15, 1807, in Thomas M. Marshall, ed., *The Life and Papers of Frederick Bates* (St. Louis, 1926), I, 119–23.

73. William Clark to Henry Dearborn, May 18, 1807, in Carter, ed., *Territorial Papers,* XIV, 122.

74. Frederick Bates to William Clark, July 25, 1807, in Marshall, ed., *Bates Papers,* I, 168.

75. Pierre Chouteau to Henry Dearborn, Aug. 4, 1807, Pierre Chouteau Letterbook.

76. Frederick Bates to William H. Harrison, Sept. 16, 1807, in Marshall, ed., *Bates Papers,* I, 190–91.

77. Pierre Chouteau to Henry Dearborn, Sept. 24, 1807, Pierre Chouteau Letterbook.

78. *Ibid.*

79. Pierre Chouteau to Frederick Bates, Oct. 6, 1807, Pierre Chouteau Letterbook.

80. Meriwether Lewis to Henry Dearborn, July 1, 1808, in Carter, ed., *Territorial Papers,* XIV, 196–202.

81. For the story of Fort Osage see Kate L. Gregg, "The History of Fort Osage," *Missouri Historical Review* 34 (July 1940), 439–88.

82. Charles T. Jones, Jr., *George Champlin Sibley: The Prairie Puritan, 1782–1863* (Independence, Mo., 1970), 42–43.

83. According to the treaty, the western boundary of the cession was a north and south line beginning at Fort Osage and running south to the Arkansas River. The Indians ceded to the United States all land between this line and the Mississippi, east and west, between the south banks of the Arkansas and Missouri River, north and south.

84. *American State Papers, Indian Affairs,* II, 763–67.

85. Perhaps Chouteau was not invited to take part in the original negotiations because of his well-known objections to the government-supported factory system. As private traders, the Chouteaus did not appreciate the competition of government trading posts.

86. Meriwether Lewis to Thomas Jefferson, Dec. 15, 1808, in *American State Papers, Indian Affairs,* II, 766–67.

87. *Ibid.*

88. Jones, *George Sibley,* 52–54.

89. The Osage agreement to relinquish their lands in present Arkansas and Missouri set the stage for the American government's attempts a decade later to relocate the Choctaws and the Cherokees in the region. See Lottinville, *Nuttall's Journal,* 105n.

Thomas Jefferson. Portrait by George Caleb Bingham.
State Historical Society of Missouri

Henry Dearborn. Painting by Charles Willson Peale.

Courtesy Independence National Historical Park

General James A. Wilkinson. Painting by Charles Willson Peale.

Courtesy Independence National Historical Park

Jean (John) B. C. Lucas.

Missouri Historical Society

Jean Gabriel Cerré.

Missouri Historical Society

Wedding garments worn by Auguste and Thérèse Cerré Chouteau,
September 21, 1786.

Auguste Chouteau's European-style buckskin coat
with quillwork decoration in Indian design.

Missouri Historical Society

Pierre Chouteau's commission
as lieutenant and commandant of the militia
at Fort Carondelet, May 21, 1794.

Missouri Historical Society

Note issued by the Bank of Missouri and signed by
Auguste Chouteau.

Missouri Historical Society

Satin banner prepared for the celebration of the anniversary of
the founding of St. Louis, February 15, 1847.

Missouri Historical Society

Fort San Carlos, constructed on the outskirts of St. Louis in 1780.

Missouri Historical Society

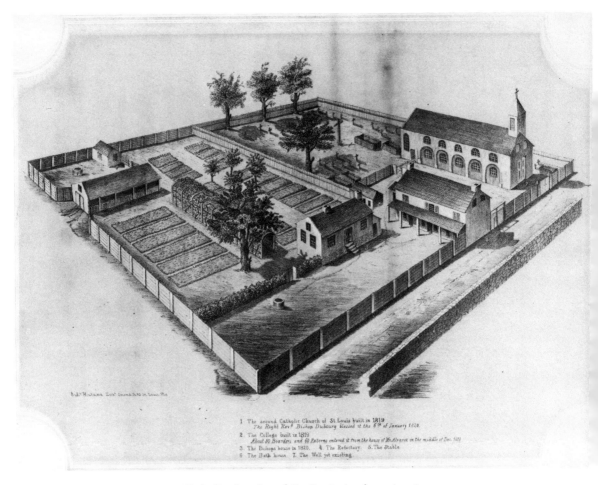

1 The second Catholic Church of St. Louis built in 1819
  The Right Rev.d Bishop Dubourg blessed it the 6th of January 1820.
2 The College built in 1819
  About 50 Boarders and 60 Externs entered it from the house of Mr. Alvarez in the middle of Dec. 1819
3 The Bishops house in 1820.   4 The Refectory.   5 The Stable
6 The Bath house   7 The Well yet existing.

Catholic church and St. Louis Academy in 1820.
Lithograph by Jules Hutana.

1840 view of St. Louis. Drawing by J. C. Wild.

Missouri Historical Society

Mackinaw or cordelle boat.

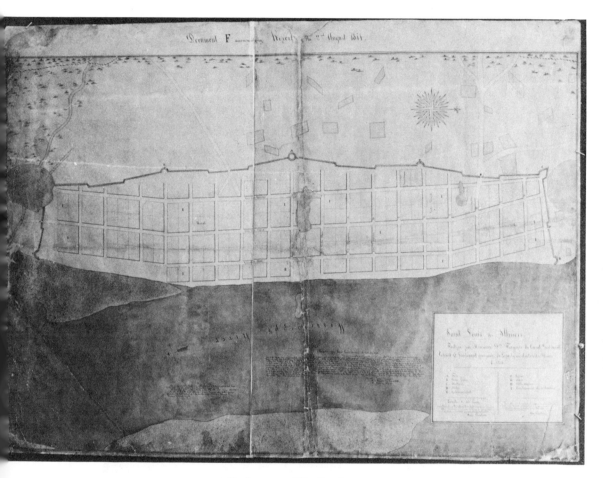

Early map of St. Louis,
drawn from an original sketch by Auguste Chouteau.

Missouri Historical Society

Chief Shahaka of the Mandans.
Portrait by Charles B. J. F. de St. Mémin.

American Philosophical Society.

Chapter 8

SOLDIERS AND PEACEMAKERS FOR
THE AMERICAN REPUBLIC

FROM THE MOMENT when the stars and stripes replaced the French colors over the parade ground at St. Louis in 1804, U.S. officials wrestled with the knotty problems of defending the Louisiana Territory and safeguarding American interests in the region. Hostile Indian tribes sought to impede the white man's penetration of their lands, while Spanish and British agents continued to challenge U.S. authority west of the Mississippi. The situation steadily worsened as the European disorders unleashed by Napoleon Bonaparte's imperial ambitions further muddied western America's already troubled waters.

As the westward stream of white settlers swelled far beyond expectations, the need for a credible military force in the Louisiana Territory became painfully evident. Because it was equally clear that any such force would be expensive to establish and maintain, American authorities, reflecting the Jefferson administration's philosophical aversion to large public expenditures, shied away from costly military programs and opted instead for a policy utilizing diplomacy and trade as alternatives to armed conflict. Though praiseworthy in some respects, the decision to deploy only a minimal fighting force in the sprawling territory placed a great burden upon local officials charged with maintaining peace along the troubled frontier. Under the circumstances, they found themselves compelled to rely heavily on persuasion, personal diplomacy, and trade sanctions for resolving disputes and curbing violence.

In cases such as the Osage agreement of 1808, the policy seemed to work, but ultimately the time came when the U.S. government found it necessary to pay a price in blood to hold its trans-Mississippi possessions. As always, Auguste and Pierre Chouteau stood ready to defend their new nation. In the face of danger, they willingly offered their services as soldiers and as diplomats, and when at the conclusion of the War of 1812 the great heartland of the continent was irreversibly in American hands, the citizens of the expanding republic owed them a measure of gratitude for their assistance.

Although many of Louisiana's inhabitants lived under an intermittent dread of violence and death between 1804 and 1815, federal officials only grudgingly allocated resources for their protection. Shortly after the Americans had taken charge of the territory, Secretary of War Henry Dearborn directed Captain Amos Stoddard to construct in St. Louis a temporary barracks for his men until the War Department could decide where to build a permanent fort and government trading post.[1] It was not until the following summer that the newly appointed territorial governor, General James Wilkinson, selected a site on the Missouri River four miles above the Mississippi junction and launched construction of the post which was known as Cantonment Belle Fontaine.[2] Meanwhile, Major James Bruff's small command in St. Louis suffered from shortages of stores, medicine, and clothing.[3]

As a military officer, Wilkinson expressed concern for the territory's safety and called for the establishment of additional military outposts at the mouth of the Wisconsin River and at the Mandan villages high on the Missouri.[4] But despite the governor's repeated pleas, federal authorities contented themselves with the completion of Cantonment/Fort Belle Fontaine until 1808.[5] Before he was forced to surrender his governorship, Wilkinson dispatched Lieutenant Zebulon Pike on separate reconnaissance expeditions up the Mississippi and into the Southwest, but the effectiveness of those isolated displays of force as a deterrent to either Indian or European challenges remains in doubt. Still, Wilkinson exhibited more zeal for establishing U.S. military power in the West than any of his predecessors, even to the point of reducing his small St. Louis garrison when necessary. In 1805 he sent thirty-two troopers stationed there to the Oto villages on the Platte River to insure the safe return of several chiefs who had called upon him in the territorial capital. His goal, he wrote, was to "increase our friends and extend our influence."[6]

By the time William Clark arrived in the territory in May 1807 to take charge of the militia and to assume his duties as Indian agent, America's western defenses appeared more precarious than ever. After only a cursory examination, Brigadier General Clark discovered that the local militia was sadly deficient as a fighting force. He proposed immediate changes in the militia law designed to improve its state of readiness.[7] By September he reported that a complete reorganization had been effected, but even after the implementation of those changes Clark continued to worry, estimating that half of the territory's 2,433 militiamen were still unarmed and widely scattered. Should an Indian war erupt, he confided to Jefferson, "they would be in a very defenceless State."[8]

As leaders in Louisiana's French community, the Chouteaus responded to the American call for help in organizing the territory's defenses. Drawing upon their experiences from the American Revolution, Auguste and Pierre lent their considerable talents and influence to the campaign to shore up the territorial militia. In 1806 Governor Wilkinson appointed Auguste, who had commanded a militia company during the Spanish regime, as a lieutenant colonel in the American militia, and in July of the following year acting Governor

Frederick Bates issued a commission affirming Auguste's appointment and placing him in command of the first militia regiment of the Louisiana Territory.[9] Pierre was named a captain in the militia cavalry in 1806 and was elevated to the rank of major at the outbreak of the War of 1812.[10] In addition, Auguste's sons, Auguste Aristide and Gabriel Sylvestre, and Pierre's sons, Auguste Pierre, Pierre Jr., and Paul Liguest, saw service in various capacities in the territorial forces.[11]

Despite the experience and the enthusiasm which the Chouteaus brought to their military assignments, at least some Americans doubted that they could be counted upon to do much actual fighting if war came. Frederick Bates politely approved Colonel Chouteau's request to parade the St. Louis volunteers in 1807, but he confided to Secretary of War Dearborn that only the Americans possessed sufficient martial spirit to defend the territory.[12] According to Bates, the French "knew nothing of the duties of a soldier and could never be dragged into action either with the Spaniards or the Indians."[13] Bates's cultural bias led him to underestimate the fighting qualities of a people whose European brothers were at that moment the masters of a vast military empire.

During the summer of 1807, relations between the United States and Great Britain steadily worsened. In St. Louis news of an unprovoked attack upon the *U.S.S. Chesapeake* lent credibility to rumors that the Shawnee leaders Tecumseh and his brother Tenskwatawa, the Prophet, were, with British encouragement, urging Indians in the Old Northwest to unite for a war against the United States. Under the circumstances, the private thoughts of American officials about their French-speaking constituents could not be allowed to stand in the way of cooperation between the two groups. Should war come, St. Louis would be an almost certain target for the British and Indian forces from the north, and in that event the services of every ablebodied person would be needed.

Although Meriwether Lewis's arrival in early 1808 to assume his duties as governor and Pierre Chouteau's subsequent treaty with the Osages relieved some of the insecurity in St. Louis, throughout the year Lewis still felt compelled to call for frequent musters of the territorial militia. The governor ordered the Chouteau brothers and the other militia officers to assemble their commands in St. Louis and St. Charles in April, August, October, and again in early 1809.[14] Reacting to a war scare in April, when stories of an impending Winnebago assault on Fort Belle Fontaine reached St. Louis, Lewis moved to expand the militia by directing Colonel Chouteau and Colonel Timothy Kibby to enroll two new companies of riflemen.[15]

When the young men of the territory displayed no enthusiasm to rally to the colors, Colonel Chouteau convened a court-martial in June and issued fines to several citizens who had failed to respond to the governor's summons.[16] All things considered, the limited forces at Lewis's disposal could hardly guarantee

Upper Louisiana's safety, and it is understandable that the worried governor implored Dearborn "not to lose sight of the safety of our defenceless and extended frontier."[17]

If that were not enough, Governor Lewis had yet another problem to deal with when he came to St. Louis in 1808. Hostile Indians had forcibly prevented the Mandan Chief Shahaka from rejoining his people along the upper Missouri. Subsequently, the chief and his family were lodged at Fort Belle Fontaine awaiting new arrangements to see them home safely. Difficulties had begun following a successful visit to Washington in 1806–7, when Shahaka and his party had returned to St. Louis with Ensign Nathaniel Pryor, a veteran of the Lewis and Clark expedition. After designating Pryor to head a small military contingent assigned to escort the chief, Secretary Dearborn instructed William Clark to complete preparations for the trip. In an effort to minimize federal expenditures without unduly endangering Shahaka, Dearborn suggested that Clark encourage private traders to accompany the Pryor expedition upriver. For assisting with the mission, the secretary promised the traders exclusive trading rights with the Mandans.

Pierre Chouteau's eldest son, Auguste Pierre, had accepted Dearborn's offer and organized a trading party to travel with the Pryor expedition to the Mandan villages. Lewis and Clark's estimates of the potential for the fur business in that country had intrigued the Chouteaus, who were determined not to forfeit the trade there to their rival, Manuel Lisa, who recently had headed up the Missouri with a trading party. Unfortunately, Auguste Pierre's maiden venture in the far north had to be abruptly terminated when misfortune struck his expedition at the Arikara villages. On September 9, 1807, a large band of angry Arikaras and Sioux assaulted the Pryor-Chouteau party, sending it reeling downstream in retreat with three dead and several wounded.[18]

Convinced that the Pryor debacle had sullied American honor, both President Jefferson and Governor Lewis considered it imperative to deliver the Mandan chief safely to his people and to punish and bring to submission the errant Arikara and Sioux warriors. Actually, anger over the recent death of the Arikara chief, Ankedoucharo, during his visit to the U.S. capital and lingering Arikara animosities against their traditional enemies, the Mandans, had provoked them to attack the Pryor-Chouteau party. Nonetheless, American authority and prestige had to be upheld, and the United States remained determined not to abandon the upper Missouri to the British, who had long been active in the region.[19]

Manuel Lisa's expedition had proven more fruitful than the ill-fated Chouteau venture. When the Spaniard returned to St. Louis in 1808, his impressive cargo of pelts convinced even the cautious Chouteaus that it was time to organize a commercial operation to tap the rich new source of furs in the Rocky Mountains. After careful negotiations, Pierre Chouteau and his son Auguste Pierre agreed to join forces with Lisa and his partners, William Morrison and

Pierre Menard, along with William Clark, Reuben Lewis, the governor's brother, Benjamin Wilkinson, the former governor's brother, Sylvestre Labbadie, and Andrew Henry to form the St. Louis Missouri Fur Company.[20] At the time, apparently neither Pierre nor Clark had any misgivings about undertaking a private commercial venture while serving in an official capacity for the U.S. government. Likewise, Governor Lewis, under pressure to return Shahaka to his people, did not hesitate to employ the company's services in accomplishing the project, even though it is likely that he was also a secret partner in the firm. From their perspective, there was nothing wrong with enlisting private enterprise to assist in achieving national goals—a view not shared by their superiors in Washington.

The contract, worked out with Governor Lewis, called for the Missouri Fur Company to organize and outfit 125 militiamen, including forty expert American riflemen, under Pierre Chouteau's command, to escort the Mandan chief and his family home. The St. Louis firm also promised to transport upriver an unspecified quantity of merchandise for distribution among the Indians. In return, the federal government agreed to pay the company $7,000, and, as a further incentive, Lewis stipulated that he would not issue licenses for trade above the mouth of the Platte River to other merchants until after the Missouri Fur Company party's scheduled departure.[21]

Chouteau, Shahaka, and their militia column left St. Louis on May 17, 1809, after many delays. Pierre's orders instructed him to overawe the Arikaras, to arrest those responsible for the deaths of Pryor's men, and to escort his Indian charges safely to their Mandan village.[22] Lewis, sharing the commonly held opinion of frontier society that Indian attacks on whites required a decisive response, was determined to redeem the honor of the United States.

Eventually Chouteau fulfilled his mission, but only after overcoming many unexpected obstacles. On the outward leg of the journey, he encountered sullen members of the Pawnee, Oto, and Kansas tribes, who complained of a scarcity of traders. More menacing were the 350 Sioux who threatened to seize Chouteau's merchandise in lieu of promised but as yet undelivered trade goods. Only the timely intervention of a friendly band of Prairie Sioux, who remembered Pierre's hospitality when they had visited St. Louis, prevented bloodshed.[23]

Dissension between the French and American boatmen accompanying the expedition further complicated matters. The Americans particularly disliked Manuel Lisa, who was in charge of the commercial unit. Rumors that Lisa's unfriendly actions among the Indians had contributed to Pryor's misfortune combined with resentment against his stern discipline to foster an ugly mood among the Americans. Unwilling to tolerate such insubordination, Chouteau confronted the most vocal of the dissidents, James Cheek. After an unpleasant scene, Chouteau ordered Cheek to quit the expedition at a point 1,200 miles up the Missouri. The order shocked Cheek's fellow Americans, who then took up their weapons in defense of their countryman.[24] Fortunately, Chouteau chose not to press the matter. But animosities continued to fester beneath the surface. When Cheek later assaulted a supply keeper at a Gros Ventre village, the volatile Chouteau exploded in rage. Having sufficient difficulties to deal with already, he could suffer Cheek's insubordination no longer. He probably would have shot the American had his French comrades not physically restrained him. Cheek responded with threats to kill both Chouteau and Lisa.[25] Though the tensions gradually subsided and Cheek later lost his life in a clash with Blackfoot warriors, the confrontation between the French and American members of the Mandan expedition provided yet another indication of the deep antagonisms remaining between Louisiana's two principal white cultures.

Subsequent events on the mission proved to be anticlimactic. The Arikaras offered no resistance to Chouteau's well-armed force, and Shahaka ended his three-year absence with a joyful reunion at his village on September 24, 1809. Undoubtedly Chouteau's generosity in distributing gifts of powder, ammunition, vermilion, and tobacco enlivened the celebrations at the Mandan town.[26] Having fulfilled its contractual obligations, the Missouri Fur Company was then free to direct its undivided attention to the commercial side of its mission and to begin trading for furs. But in far-off Washington, federal officials did not consider the case closed.

Returning to St. Louis, Pierre Chouteau expected to receive plaudits from the government for a job well done. Instead, he found letters from the new secretary of war, William Eustis, charging him and his partners with improprieties in the financial arrangements for the expedition.[27] More stunning was the news that his associate, Meriwether Lewis, was dead, probably by his own hand.[28] Although Pierre knew of the American government's strictures against combining public and private business and had already had brushes with officials on the subject, he justifiably did not think himself culpable in the Mandan matter. After all, Lewis and Clark had encouraged the operation, and the earlier Pryor expedition offered a precedent of sorts.

Eustis did not see it that way. While Chouteau was heading up the Missouri, the secretary refused to honor a number of bills which Lewis had submitted to cover the costs of the expedition. Later, Eustis dispatched a letter to Lewis suggesting in a rather insulting tone that the governor had knowingly sent an armed force into either British or Spanish territory for the purpose of promoting a private trading company.[29] The letter left Lewis shaken. Believing that President James Madison's new administration had questioned his honor and integrity, Lewis, in the return post, tried to explain that there had been no violations of foreign territory for the benefit of the Missouri Fur Company or for any other purpose. He also rejected Eustis's allegation that a bill for $500, payable to Chouteau for Indian merchandise, was out of order. The goods had been purchased, Lewis wrote, to employ Indian auxiliaries if they were needed to counter hostile Cheyennes known to be friendly to the Arikaras.[30] But fearful that his explanations might not suffice, a distraught Lewis still thought it necessary to depart for Washington and to defend himself in person before the new government. Tragically, his journey ended with his untimely death at Grinder's Tavern on the Natchez Trace.

The Eustis allegations touched off a shock wave of anxiety in St. Louis even before Lewis's death and Chouteau's return from the Mandan town. Reflecting that mood, Pierre Chouteau, Jr., wrote Eustis a long excusatory letter attempting to justify his father's actions. The young man reminded the secretary that his father's superior, William Clark, was also a member of the Missouri Fur Company. Moreover, displaying his irritation with the manner in which the War Department had treated the elder Chouteau, Pierre Jr. accused the government of ignoring the Osage agent for over a year, even to the point of making appointments in the agency without first conferring with him.[31]

Upon his return to St. Louis in late November, Pierre Chouteau moved to vindicate himself. In a barrage of letters to officials in Washington, he provided detailed reports describing the successful conclusion of his mission, explaining his conduct, and seeking permission to come to the capital city to answer any charges against him.[32] Repeating Lewis's account of the reasons for the purchase of the extra merchandise, he pointed out that since only a small portion of the supplies had been needed for distribution among the Indians, he had sold the remaining goods to the Missouri Fur Company for $745.50. This, he argued, saved the government the expense of transporting the surplus items back to St. Louis.[33] Although Chouteau's explanation for selling the merchandise seemed plausible, he neglected to mention that the availability of additional trade goods deep in Indian country had undoubtedly been a windfall for the company in which he held a partnership.

Eustis initially remained unimpressed with Chouteau's justifications of the Mandan enterprise and the shuffling of government money and supplies it had occasioned. To Chouteau's dismay, the secretary ordered him to reimburse the firms from which the goods had been purchased with his personal funds. But Pierre continued to proclaim his innocence and to protest the injustice of the War Department's verdict in the matter.[34] At last a weary Eustis relented, and on June 10, 1810, he informed Chouteau that his bills would be honored. Eustis also apologized for any inconvenience arising from Lewis's protested drafts. The secretary now seemed willing to allow the deceased Lewis to take the blame.[35]

The passing of the Mandan incident meant that once again Pierre Chouteau had weathered a grave crisis in his relationship with the U.S. government. Initially, however, it did not seem so. Toward the end of 1809, Chouteau had indicated that the War Department had dismissed him as Osage agent and expressed regret over the government's loss of confidence in him, but the secretary unexpectedly relented. Eustis retained Chouteau in office, but only after Clark personally interceded in his behalf.[36]

In fact, Chouteau's influence among the Indians was too important to overlook at the beginning of 1810, and Clark had managed to convince the Madison administration that such was the case. War seemed likely to break out at any time, and the United States needed all of the Indian support it could muster. A growing restlessness among the Missouri tribes seemed ominously disturbing. Not even the Osages could be counted on to uphold their agreements with the American government in the event of a war with the British. Although some Americans still harbored suspicions that Pierre was maneuvering to monopolize trade with that tribe,[37] federal officials also recognized that without him, the United States might forfeit all claims on the Osages' goodwill.

Actually, at the moment the Osages appeared anything but cordial. In July, for example, they robbed employees of Auguste Chouteau and his nephew Sylvestre Labbadie of $735 in goods.[38] Hoping to deal with this and other problems, including a threatened war between the Osages and the Shawnees, Pierre traveled to their respective villages. Again the Chouteau charm worked, and by October he had managed to convince both sides to accept a settlement.[39] Nonetheless, all was not well with the Osages. Congress's failure to ratify promptly the Osage treaty of 1808 and the consequent nonpayment of the promised annuity caused some of the tribesmen to conclude that the treaty was null and void.[40] The Arkansas Osages still had not returned to the upper Osage valley, and armed clashes between the Osages and various Mississippi River tribes occurred with regularity.[41] The spring of 1811 found the Osage nation tense and uneasy. Complaining that Pierre had neglected them, some of the Osages participated in scattered outbreaks of violence, including the burning of Pierre's own barn in St. Louis.[42]

In July, Congress finally ratified the Osage treaty of 1808, but Chouteau worried that the tribe had by then turned its back on the agreement.[43] George Sibley told Clark that the Big Osages had rejected the treaty because they mistakenly believed that they were to receive no annuity. Sibley seemed inclined to suggest that Chouteau had misled the tribe in order to spoil the treaty.[44] Pierre countered that the Osages believed they had been ignored and were confused regarding some of the treaty provisions.[45] Finally, in August came the long-delayed federal order to distribute the Osage annuities. In short succession the United States also shipped a corn mill and a forge for delivery to the tribe. Secretary Eustis seized upon that occasion to admonish Pierre in a stern manner to forward all accounts and bills to Clark for his approval.[46] Thus, despite his apparent willingness to exonerate Chouteau in the Mandan affair, the secretary of war had no intention of granting the Osage agent a free hand in financial matters.

As the American authorities made progress with the Osages, other Indian nations drifted toward war with the United States. In June 1811 a Potawatomi attack left two whites dead near St. Louis, and a month later a band of Ottawas threatened Pierre himself.[47] A pitched battle at Tippecanoe in Indiana Territory followed in November, and though the engagement which later helped make the Chouteaus' friend William Henry Harrison a celebrity was a nominal American success, it did not remove the threat of a broader conflict involving Great Britain. In St. Louis, acting Governor Bates ordered Colonel Auguste Chouteau to place the First Regiment in a state of readiness for war.[48]

President Madison had appointed Benjamin Howard as Lewis's successor in 1810, but the new governor was frequently absent from the territory. The looming menace of war, however, compelled him to return to St. Louis to take charge of the area's defenses. In early 1812 Howard ordered the construction of blockhouses at strategic frontier locations, the formation of additional militia units, and the commissioning of a special company of rangers.[49] The U.S. Congress declared war on Great Britain in June, and a short time later word reached St. Louis that during an Indian council held at the Rock River Sac villages, the Winnebago, Kickapoo, Potawatomi, Shawnee, and Miami nations agreed to wage war against the United States.

Following the outbreak of war, the United States suffered military reverses in a number of engagements, including the loss of the strategic post at Michilimackinac. In the Missouri Territory residents worried that a major British or Indian attack could come at any time. Characteristically, the Chouteaus were among those taking the initiative to prepare for the worst. In July Governor Howard sent Pierre to Prairie du Chien to assess the level of British activity there and to gauge the mood of the Indians.[50] The news he brought back was not reassuring. He predicted that the British in Canada soon might launch a general offensive against the United States.[51]

With this danger in mind, Pierre again journeyed to the main Osage village to supervise the installation of the recently delivered mill and forge and to discuss with the tribe the possibility of constructing a blockhouse to defend their town.[52] Fearing further assaults from the Mississippi tribes, the Osages fully agreed that Chouteau should seek permission from Washington to build the fortification. After passing much of the autumn with the tribe and trying to secure their continued loyalty, Pierre returned to St. Louis as winter began. He honored his promise to ask the War Department for the blockhouse for the Osages, and he also took the opportunity to request that his eldest son, Auguste Pierre, be named as the resident sub-agent at the Arkansas Osage village. This arrangement, Chouteau explained, would eliminate the frequent and tiresome trips he was forced to make from his headquarters in St. Louis to the Osage town.[53] But as conditions in the territory worsened, Pierre decided to return to the Osages before the end of February.

While Pierre anxiously labored to hold that tribe's loyalty, Auguste helped alert the citizens of St. Louis to the dangers threatening their city. Rumors that the British planned to attack with artillery sometime the following spring led to the convening of a town meeting to examine the state of the city's defenses.[54] The assembled citizens chose a seven-person Committee of Safety to supervise the construction of fortifications, to organize the town's defensive preparations, and to see to the fair distribution of work and costs. In selecting Auguste Chouteau to chair the committee, they added weighty burdens to the responsibilities he already bore as commander of the militia.[55] He accepted nonetheless, possibly remembering that similar preparations had saved the city in 1780. Auguste's committee took steps to repair the dilapidated Spanish blockhouses along the city's outskirts and to mount the few available cannons, but when the conditions improved slightly they abandoned their costly plan to surround the village with a stockade of pickets.

Although St. Louis did not come under attack during the War of 1812, other frontier settlements were not so lucky. In July 1814 the American post at Prairie du Chien fell to a combined Anglo-Indian force. But since hard-pressed American officials had been unable to station any substantial federal force in the territory, local authorities had to continue to rely on the militia. Unfortunately, the U.S. government's failure to pay rangers and militiamen for their services at the frequent musters made it almost impossible to raise a credible body of troops during the last year of the war.[56] As a result, for the duration of the conflict, settlers beyond St. Louis remained especially vulnerable to Indian attack, and uneasy territorial residents continued to press for assistance in shoring up the region's limited defenses.

Meanwhile, Pierre had his hands full with the Osages. Dispatched by acting Governor Bates to recruit an Osage force to oppose tribes hostile to the United States, Auguste's younger brother once more proved his worth to the American government.[57] After sending his son Auguste Pierre to solicit cooperation from the Arkansas Osages, Pierre persuaded the Missouri Osages to furnish 260 well-armed braves to help defend the northern frontier.[58] After these faithful warriors completed a 360-mile march to the mouth of the Osage River, Governor Howard preemptively overruled Bates and directed that the force be dismissed.[59] Apparently Howard considered the presence of a large armed Indian force in the vicinity of St. Louis too great a risk to take for the help they might render. The governor's decision to disband the Osage party embarrassed Chouteau, and Howard's orders to close Fort Osage compounded the problem.

Since the outbreak of the war, federal officials had favored closing that installation because its remoteness made it so difficult to defend.[60] Although the

Osages also found the place inconvenient and would have preferred a trading factory at their old town, they were not in a positive mood. They resented the repeated delays in the payment of their annuities and continued to demand the construction of blockhouses for their defense.[61] By promising the chiefs that they would have their annuities and blockhouses, and by further stipulating that another government factory would be established, but not on Osage lands, Chouteau managed to obtain their agreement to the terms outlined by Governor Howard. During his negotiations, Chouteau cautioned the Osages against attending a Choctaw council to discuss the common interests of red men.[62] The following year, William Clark underscored the importance of Chouteau's understanding with the Osages when he informed Secretary of War James Monroe that "should only the half of their force [Osages] be turned against these Territories, the scattered population within it will not be adequate to their defence against such a herd of Savages."[63] Even after the war had ended, Clark continued to praise Pierre for his work with the Osages.[64]

Regardless of his crucial role in maintaining the Osage alliance during the war, Pierre remained suspect in some camps. In 1813 George Sibley implied that Chouteau wanted to close the trading factory at Fort Osage because it successfully competed with his own mercantile activities.[65] And William L. Lovely, the U.S. agent among the Cherokees, later wrote to Clark that Clermont, the Arkansas Osage chief, had told him that troubles between his band and the Cherokees could be traced to Chouteau, White Hair, and their "unfriendly disposition" toward the United States.[66] As Governor Clark noted at the time, however, the Arkansas Osages had recently murdered a number of white men and had refused to turn the murderers over to Chouteau after repeated demands.[67] It was not surprising that Clermont, a chief never friendly to the Chouteaus and their ally White Hair, sought to undercut the agent's standing in Washington.

Chouteau eventually forced Clermont to surrender the braves charged with the murders.[68] In fact, while Pierre was at the Osage villages, a Sac delegation arrived at one of them displaying a British flag. Major Chouteau ordered the Osages to eject the Sac party immediately, adding that if the British flag were raised there, "he would go himself immediately to the village, tear the flag to pieces, and throw it into the fire."[69] The Osages obeyed without hesitation.

This incident indicates that Chouteau had no intention of turning the Osages against the United States. Indeed, throughout the war both his activities and those of his elder brother demonstrated that they were reconciled to American control of the Missouri Territory. Still, their staunch support of the United States did not prevent them from trying to advance their commercial interests, as in the case of Pierre's transparent request in 1813 that the U.S. government refrain from placing a factory on Osage lands.[70] Although he claimed that the presence of a factory on their lands would lead other tribes to trespass on Osage territory, he had a much more obvious reason for opposing its establishment. Without a government factory at the Osage villages, his family could expect to monopolize the lion's share of their trade.

The war with Great Britain formally ended in December 1814 when the two sides agreed to terms at Ghent, but the fighting in North America could not be concluded so easily. Andrew Jackson's famous victory at New Orleans was yet to come, and it required months to restore peace along the Missouri Territory's exposed frontier. Still, the news from the Belgian city gave reason for optimism. The American republic could begin to regard its lands across the Mississippi with less alarm. If nothing else, the war had guaranteed that the vast prairies and plains of the mid-continent would remain American territory.

As the people of St. Louis looked forward to the future with renewed hope in 1815, Auguste and Pierre could also look back with pride and claim credit for their part in upholding U.S. authority in the trans-Mississippi West. Although it was a natural time for them to pause and reflect upon their lengthening careers, the cessation of hostilities by no means signaled an end to their active involvement in the region's affairs as public servants and as entrepreneurs. On the contrary, both men continued to display a lively interest in the world around them. By most measures of the time they were approaching old age, but the Chouteau vitality that had propelled their family to the forefront of St. Louis society showed no signs of diminution. In the councils of white men and red men alike the Chouteau name still commanded respect, even as a new generation stood ready to inherit and maintain the luster of that name.

As if to underscore the point, shortly before his sixty-fifth birthday, Auguste embarked upon a belated but highly successful career as diplomat and peacemaker for the United States when President James Madison tapped him to serve as one of three commissioners assigned to conclude treaties with various western Indian nations. Although Pierre's position as Osage agent and his notable contributions to the war effort made him seem a more likely candidate for the post, federal officials bypassed him in favor of his elder brother. Pierre's relations with the War Department had always been stormy, and the lingering suspicions concerning his conduct during the 1808 Osage negotiations and the 1809 Mandan expedition, while not justified, weighed heavily nonetheless against his appointment. Perhaps it was inevitable that as the frontier became more tranquil, the American government would gradually decrease its reliance on the services of the more volatile Chouteau brother.

In contrast, U.S. officials considered Auguste less likely to embarrass the administration. Highly esteemed in St. Louis and Washington, Auguste remained the principal representative and spokesman for the Missouri Territory's still-important French community. Beyond that, he also had proved himself a loyal defender of the American cause during the war. Thus, Madison viewed Auguste as the more acceptable candidate as peacemaker in 1815.

Much remained to be done to bring tranquility to America's western frontier. Britain's Indian allies had to be informed of the agreement at Ghent, and satisfactory accords had to be reached with all of the Missouri and Mississippi River tribes. Beyond that the Americans already had plans for acquiring title to additional tracts of Indian lands. Madison had instructed Secretary of War James Monroe to choose three commissioners to direct those efforts. Governor William Clark of the Missouri Territory and Governor Ninian Edwards of the Illinois Territory had been obvious choices for the assignment, but Monroe experienced more difficulty in selecting the third commissioner. Acting upon Colonel Alexander McNair's advice, Monroe chose Auguste Chouteau. In fact, McNair, a highly respected soldier and future governor of Missouri, had been Monroe's first choice for the position, but he had declined to serve and suggested that Chouteau be appointed instead.[71] McNair's marriage into a French mercantile family, the Reilhes, and his association with St. Louis's old trading elite had given him a high regard for the St. Louis merchant, and although he later broke with the St. Louis establishment, McNair's influence paved the way for Auguste's appointment in 1815.[72]

McNair personally informed the three commissioners of their nominations and gave them each a copy of the Treaty of Ghent. He also passed along Monroe's instructions directing them to inform the Indians that the United States planned to construct forts and trading houses on the upper Mississippi and on Lake Michigan, a clear indication that the secretary intended for the commissioners to put the Indians on notice that the United States meant to occupy and hold its legitimate territory.[73]

After receiving his official appointment from Monroe on May 26, Chouteau drafted a letter of acceptance within twenty-four hours.[74] The immediacy of his reply, however, did not represent a hasty reaction on his part, for he and the other commissioners were already well along with preparations for convening peace talks with the various western tribes. Shortly after receiving word of their nomination from McNair, Chouteau, Clark, and Edwards had met in St. Louis on May 11 to plan a course of action.[75] Even though some of the tribes were still on the warpath, the commissioners dispatched thirty-seven messages to various Indian nations, summoning them to meet at Portage des Sioux, near the junction of the Missouri and Mississippi rivers, for a general council to terminate all hostilities.[76] Auguste could not have foreseen it at the time, but the initial meeting of the peace commissioners in St. Louis was only the opening scene in a sequence of diplomatic maneuvers to settle Indian affairs that would occupy much of his attention for the next six years.

The peacemaking process encountered difficulties from the outset. The unrelenting enmity of the Rock River Sac and Fox posed the most serious challenge for the American commissioners. When members of those tribes murdered several white settlers in St. Charles County, Chouteau and his colleagues called upon federal authorities to use force to subdue them and to end their atrocities.[77] Dissident Indians also attacked and robbed officers sent to deliver the invitations for the Portage des Sioux conference. The commissioners attributed their daring to the intrigues of British agents, who had persuaded the tribes that His Majesty's government intended to resume the war in the near future.[78] Unquestionably, such actions helped keep the hostile tribes in a state of agitation, but a fundamental distrust of the Americans and their officials fueled the Indian animosity. Never at ease with the provisions of their 1804 treaty, the Rock River tribes believed they had been cheated out of their best lands. Driven by their hatred, they rejected all peace proposals as long as any hopes for effective resistance lingered.

Despite these setbacks, the three commissioners arrived at Portage des Sioux in early July, after news reached St. Louis that between 2,000 and 3,000 Indians had already assembled there. The colorful spectacle of the Sioux, Omaha, Iowa, Shawnee, Delaware, and various other delegations encamped at the site, attired in their diverse costumes and inhabiting the temporary lodges they had erected, greeted the American commissioners upon their arrival. Missing, however, were delegations to speak for the Winnebagos, the Menominees, and the Chippewas.[79] Reports that the Rock River Sac and Fox nations remained arrogantly defiant and rumors that the Kickapoos might prove equally recalcitrant made it clear that the task confronting American authorities would not be an easy one. Be that as it may, Chouteau, Clark, and Edwards prepared to begin the lengthy business of negotiating with the tribes on hand.

If the commissioners worried about the dangers posed by the absent tribes, a reassuring message from the War Department, indicating that if the belligerent Indians refused to come to terms General Jackson would be ordered to undertake military operations against them, improved their position and buoyed their hopes.[80] More to the point, the commissioners had arranged to station two fully manned gunboats and a force of 275 regulars under the command of Colonel John Miller at Portage des Sioux as a precaution against possible trouble. In addition, the War Department had authorized them to call upon the mounted militia at nearby Fort Belle Fontaine if the situation demanded it.[81]

Even though the war was officially over, most Americans continued to believe that major military operations would be required to break Indian resistance to American authority, and the Rock River tribes' open contempt for the Americans did nothing to modify that view. Such defiance provoked men like Colonel Daniel Bissell to call openly for an armed showdown with the red men.[82] Clearly, the shift in the military balance of power in the Missouri Territory since 1812 left the dominant Americans more disposed toward a military solution for resolving Indian problems than they had been before the war.

Fortunately, at Portage des Sioux no force of arms was needed to bring about peace between the United States and most of the tribes in attendance. In conformity with their instructions, Chouteau and his fellow commissioners initially confined themselves to restoring peace, even though they believed a more wide-ranging and lasting settlement was possible. Clark opened the conference on July 6 with a forceful address in which he left no doubt that the United States was now the unquestioned master of the Mississippi basin. Edwards and Chouteau reinforced this fundamental point, with Chouteau emphasizing that since the British had deserted the Indians, they could only find peace and wellbeing under U.S. protection.[83] Resplendent in his scarlet officer's coat with gold braid and brass buttons, Chouteau spoke to the assembled nations in an idiom shaped by decades of commerce and deliberations with them. For the ranks of Indian dignitaries, the scene must have seemed familiar in many ways. Facing them were old adversaries and old friends: William Clark, Auguste Chouteau, Ninian Edwards, and Manuel Lisa, who had brought in the eastern Sioux delegates—all figures from a shared past. At the same time, the more perceptive among them sensed that a turning point in time was at hand. The faces were familiar, and the bundles of government gifts were there as always, but this time things were not the same.[84] The Sacs and Foxes might continue to fight, and the Winnebagos, Iowas, and Kickapoos remain sullenly aloof, but most somehow knew that effective resistance was impossible. Great Britain's failure to defeat the Americans left the trans-Mississippi tribes naked to the irresistible onrush of white settlement. Whether the participants perceived it or not, that was the meaning of the peace discussions at Portage des Sioux.

On July 22 the commissioners informed federal officials in Washington that settlements had been made with the Potawatomis, Sioux of the Lakes, Piankashaws, Yankton and Teton Sioux, Omahas, Ottawas, Shawnees, Wyandottes, Miamis, Delawares, and Senecas. The terms included an end to all hostilities, mutual forgiveness, perpetual peace and friendship, the return of prisoners, the reaffirmation of earlier treaties, and U.S. protection for Indians accepting the terms.[85] In September Pierre Chouteau arrived at Portage des Sioux with delegations from the Osages and Missouri Sacs and Foxes.[86] Guided by the ever-persuasive younger Chouteau, they were predisposed to give their consent to an agreement even before the formal discussions got under way. In short order they accepted the same commitments already approved by the other tribes, and the hesitant Kansas, Kickapoos, and Iowas soon followed their example and came to terms.[87] Although the Rock River Sacs, encouraged by the arrival of British traders and merchandise, breathed fiery defiance on into the autumn, the commissioners had information that even that tribe was divided on the desirability of making peace.[88]

In October the peace commissioners returned to St. Louis, where they prepared a report outlining their work for the War Department. Full peace had not yet been achieved, but much had been accomplished toward that goal. Many tribes had been restored to submission, and much had been learned about their grievances and their disposition to part with title to their lands.[89] With the military situation improving, Auguste resigned his command in the territorial militia in early 1816. He also took advantage of his brief respite in St. Louis during that winter to compile a set of notes for the War Department describing the approximate territorial boundaries of the various western tribes. That remarkable document provided yet another example of the elder Chouteau's vast fund of knowledge regarding Indian matters and explains why he was frequently called upon to assist with tribal negotiations.[90]

Meanwhile, as pressure built on the hold-out tribes to settle with the Americans, Auguste took the opportunity to express his concern about the expanded program for establishing government factories in Indian territory. In a lengthy report to Secretary of War William H. Crawford in November, Chouteau denounced the policy. According to his report, the factories had produced a decline in trade, led the Indians to favor British traders over Americans, dried up necessary sources of credit for the tribes, and denied the Indians easy access to goods. The correct policy, according to Chouteau, would be to establish a central store in St. Louis to outfit at moderate prices twenty-five to thirty traders working the Mississippi and Missouri river areas. Those selected should be men who understood "perfectly well the Indian trade, and who should also know exactly what suits every nation in particular."[91] While Chouteau was undoubtedly sincere in his apprehensions, it did not require a great deal of insight to grasp that he and his St. Louis associates would be the most likely beneficiaries of his proposed scheme. In any case, after cautioning federal officials that private traders imposed excessively high prices on the Indians and discouraged their industry in the fur trade, Cherokee Indian agent Return J. Meigs, whose son and namesake briefly served as a territorial official in St. Louis, counseled them against the kind of trading policy Chouteau championed.[92] Actually, neither plan succeeded in preventing British traders from continuing to cash in on the Indian trade. Frustrated officials first tried to impose heavy fines or prison sentences on the interlopers, but after 1816 they accepted the law of supply and demand and agreed to license them as interpreters and boatmen.[93]

With the return of good weather, the last serious obstacle to peace dissipated as the Rock River tribes at last reconciled themselves to coming to terms with the Americans. The discussions with the tribal leaders threatened to break down at several points, but the patient work of the Sac agent, Nicholas Boilvin, combined with the construction of a fort near the mouth of the Rock River by a St. Louis infantry force, sufficed to bring about a settlement. On May 13 the Sacs signed a treaty requiring them to implore mercy, confirm the treaty of 1804, and deliver up all property taken from American citizens on pain of losing all annuities due them from the federal government forever.[94] By summer's end, Chouteau, Clark, and Edwards had effected similar accords with eight bands of Sioux, Winnebagos, Ottawas, Chippewas, and Potawa-tomis. In addition to the standard terms, the last three tribes agreed to cede all lands south of a line due west from the southern end of Lake Michigan to the Mississippi River and other lands in the vicinity of the Fox and Kankakee rivers and Chicago Creek.[95] Thus, by 1816, Chouteau and his colleagues had broadened their negotiations from dealing with simple peace terms to includ-ing land cessions as well. For Auguste and the other commissioners, and for the United States, the year's negotiations had been fruitful. But Chouteau's work as a treaty-maker had just begun.

The commissioners scarcely had time to initial the Sac agreement before they faced a host of new challenges involving disputes of Quapaw land claims, dis-agreements between the Osages and the Cherokees, and administration de-mands to obtain more land cessions from various tribes.[96] Still more pressing was the need to have lines run and surveyed delineating the area ceded to the United States by the Osages in 1808. Tribal leaders had requested that the line be mapped on several occasions, apparently because they believed that the cession included less territory than it did.[97] As it happened, the tribes had ceded a vast portion of their lands, including much of the present states of Missouri and Arkansas.

Both Auguste and Pierre Chouteau took part in this project. As one of the peace commissioners, Auguste helped supervise the overall plan, while as Osage agent, Pierre managed the actual survey. As was often the case in matters involving the Osages, the project was not easily accomplished. When it dawned upon the Indians that the survey line did not meet their expectations, Pierre had to draw upon his reserve of influence in a conference at Fire Prairie to prevent them from forcibly halting the survey.[98]

The completion of the Osage survey brought a temporary respite to Au-guste's work for the War Department, but Pierre found that the affairs of the great tribe filled his agenda as much as ever. The most worrisome Osage issue in those years was the arrival of the eastern Cherokees on the hunting grounds of the Arkansas. As this advanced tribe, gradually being removed from its southeastern homelands, pushed its way onto Osage territory beginning in 1810, violent incidents erupted between the two nations and between both bands and the Quapaws, a small people caught in the middle. By 1816 the confrontation had precipitated a crisis which threatened to disrupt the fragile peace on the Missouri frontier. Stung by Cherokee complaints about the im-potence of the United States in halting attacks by Clermont's warriors, the Cherokee agent, Major William Lovely, engaged in a spirited correspondence with Pierre Chouteau. As the situation steadily worsened, Pierre promised to attend a conference at Clermont's village with Lovely, the Cherokees, and the Osages in an attempt to work out an agreement.[99] Unfortunately, the episode occurred while Pierre was recuperating from "a violent cold and a Sciatick,"[100] and also at a time when he was engaged in a dispute with the War Department over its decision to require its agents to reside in the villages of the tribes they represented.[101] As a consequence, Chouteau failed to keep the rendezvous, but Lovely nevertheless negotiated a treaty by which the Arkansas Osages ceded a portion of their territory to the United States for use by the Cherokees. This cession of land, known as Lovely's Purchase, did not prevent the recurrence of hostilities, however, and in the autumn of 1817 the Cherokees, led by a white member of the tribe, John D. Chisholm, fell upon Clermont's village while the chiefs and warriors were absent on a hunt. The resulting slaughter of unarmed women, children, and elderly Osages guaranteed a bitter war would ensue.[102]

Although a misunderstanding concerning Auguste's compensation for his work as a peace commissioner in 1815–16 had created ruffled feelings in Washington, and public criticism of the government's expenditures on the Indians and the "Indian-treaty men" had surfaced in St. Louis, the resumption of Indian fighting and rumors of British intrigue prompted Secretary of War John C. Calhoun to recommission Auguste Chouteau and Ninian Edwards to settle renewed conflicts among tribes in the Illinois region.[103] Ironically, Chouteau was again the War Department's second choice for the post, since Governor Clark had previously declined to serve.[104] It was just as well, however, for Clark was shortly given a joint appointment with Auguste to settle the Quapaw problem by negotiating a land cession from that tribe.[105] As the governor well understood, a Quapaw settlement hinged upon the outcome of efforts to conclude the new war raging between the Osages and the Cherokees.

But as Clark and the elder Chouteau took up their new tasks, orders from Washington relieving Pierre of his duties as Osage agent undoubtedly took them by surprise.[106] Secretary Calhoun's terse dismissal letter, directing Pierre to surrender all papers and monies relating to the agency, offered no explanation for the action. In retrospect, it seems that Pierre's refusal to abide by the policy which required agents to reside in the tribal towns, along with his failure to take action to prevent the Osage-Cherokee bloodshed, prompted federal authorities to remove him. Long a source of controversy, and known for neither his furtiveness nor his docility, the Frenchman appeared more expendable than he had in the precarious pre-war era. The absence of any record of complaint on his part suggests that Pierre received his dismissal with the same capacity for adaptation and adjustment that characterized his entire life.

Even as he wrapped up his affairs as Osage agent, however, Pierre lent his support to his brother and to Clark in winning a peace settlement in the Osage-Cherokee-Quapaw dispute. In August, Clark and Auguste persuaded the Quapaws to submit to American authority and to part with a great tract of land along the Arkansas and Mississippi rivers.[107] In the following weeks agreements with the Peoria, Kaskaskia, Michigamea, Cahokia, and Tamaroa tribes followed—all negotiated by Auguste and his fellow commissioner, Ninian Edwards.[108] On September 25, Pierre was in attendance as Clark won the Osages' acceptance for a treaty ceding a sixty-mile-wide strip of land north of the Arkansas River which would eventually be used by the Cherokees.[109] The following week, Pierre attended the formal ceremonies ending the Osage-Cherokee war.

Flushed with success, and no doubt appreciative of the years of service his old friend had given to the United States, Clark informed Calhoun that at long last the Osages had determined to reunite in one village, and he urged him to reappoint Pierre as their agent.[110] As far as can be determined, Calhoun simply ignored the recommendation.

Despite his removal from the War Department's official lists of Indian agents, Pierre continued to affect tribal affairs indirectly as an adviser to Auguste in his work as peace commissioner and by his influence over his son Paul Liguest, who subsequently served as sub-agent and agent to the Osages.[111] Pierre also continued to correspond with federal officials on matters concerning the Osage nation, and it is evident that Calhoun, the official who had terminated his services, continued to rely upon the former agent for advice in handling the Osages.[112] Chouteau's willingness to offer his knowledge and influence to assist the government that had rejected him for further official employment was a mark of his generous nature.

Complicated men like the Chouteau brothers can of course never be explained in simple terms. By the end of the War of 1812, they were reconciled to the permanence of the Americans in the Missouri hinterland. It was also evident to them that they had to accept some American ideas about government, trade, and Indian affairs with which they fundamentally disagreed. Be that as it may, peace between Indians and whites was as much in their interest as it was in the interest of the United States. The fur trade, the growth of St. Louis, and the prosperity of the mercantile families depended upon safe access to the resources in Indian territory. So the Chouteaus worked to pacify the tribes and to make their post-war resettlement on new lands as tranquil as possible. This coincidence in interests helps to account for Pierre's cooperation with federal officials, and it also helps explain Auguste's diligence in the laborious effort to reach agreement with tribes reluctant to see their way of life disrupted forever.

Therefore, between 1818 and 1820 the elder brother negotiated with the Pawnees, Poncas, and Kickapoos.[113] The Kickapoos, antagonistic toward Americans for years, proved a particularly serious test for the diplomatic skills of Chouteau and his fellow commissioner, Benjamin Stephenson. Opposed to an American proposal calling for them to take up residence on the western side of the Mississippi, and fearful of a Potawatomi attack if they crossed the river, the Kickapoos finally relented, but only after obtaining better terms from the

United States than those accorded to most other tribes at the time.[114] Yet the completion of negotiations, which involved much traveling between St. Louis and Edwardsville, did not end the matter for the aging commissioner, who found it necessary to conduct a further round of consultations after the U.S. Senate objected to parts of the initial agreement. In fact, the entire tedious episode dragged on until 1821.[115]

To his weariness, however, Chouteau had to add the extra burden of disappointment. Undoubtedly expecting some reward for his lengthy and effective service, in early 1820 he applied for the position of superintendent of Indian affairs for Missouri which his friend Clark, as an announced candidate for governor, might soon have to give up. Unfortunately, Calhoun informed him that Missouri's forthcoming entry into the federal Union would, in accordance with the federal statutes, eliminate the position. Chouteau probably took little consolation from Calhoun's assurances that he believed him to be well qualified for the soon-to-be-discontinued post.[116]

To the casual observer, the many years of service which Auguste and Pierre Chouteau donated to the United States in conducting Indian affairs may seem to have gone unrewarded. Except for their official salaries, neither man received any special compensation or commendation. There were no appointments to higher office, no medals, no gifts of land, and no pensions. Indeed, as in the case of the Osage treaty of 1808, the government had specifically disallowed some special claims on land grants. On the other hand, it should be recalled that when the United States took possession of Louisiana in 1804, the Chouteaus were not only outsiders, they were well-known agents of a foreign power and scions of a retreating regime. The opportunities the American republic afforded them to serve in handling Indian affairs were not extended out of sheer generosity, of course. The United States eagerly exploited their wealth of experience and influence. Even so, the Chouteaus profited from the readiness of the United States to accept the French element in St. Louis into the relatively open American system. Like the Spanish before them, the Americans wisely chose not to exclude the leadership elements of a previous government from the counsels of political decision. The Chouteaus assumed important responsibilities commensurate with their talents and experience. Had the Americans denied them their confidence, the brothers might have sustained their commercial activities, but it seems unlikely that they could have maintained their unique position among the Indians or in St. Louis society. If their world had changed, the Chouteaus had changed too.

Unlike that other relic of old Louisiana, the Indian hunter and trapper, St. Louis's first family had accustomed itself to the passing of one world and the advent of another. As Missouri prepared to take its place as an equal state in the American Union, the Chouteau legacy was being passed gradually to a vigorous line of heirs. Auguste and Pierre Chouteau were full of years, but they were filled with life as well. Like the city they had done so much to build, they were moving on. But after the state's entry into the Union, life would move at a pace unprecedented in the experience of the Chouteaus or of St. Louis.

Rising as always to the challenge, the brothers faced the coming deluge of post-war American settlers and the submerging of their old Creole culture with the Gallic logic and high spirits that had braced them through a lifetime on the edge of the wilderness. And, equally characteristically, they tried to turn the new tides to their political advantage and to their personal profit.

NOTES

1. Henry Dearborn to Amos Stoddard, May 4, 1804, Stoddard Papers, Missouri Historical Society.
2. Kate L. Gregg, "Building of the First American Fort West of the Mississippi," *Missouri Historical Review* 30(July 1936), 347, 353.
3. Report of James Wilkinson to Henry Dearborn, Dec. 13, 1804, in Carter, ed., *Territorial Papers*, XIII, 80.
4. Francis Paul Prucha, *The Sword of the Republic: The United States Army on the Frontier, 1783–1846* (New York, 1969), 75.
5. *Ibid.*, 76.
6. James Wilkinson to Henry Dearborn, Oct. 8, 1805, in Carter, ed., *Territorial Papers*, XIII, 236–37.
7. William Clark to Henry Dearborn, May 18, 1807, in *ibid.*, XIV, 122–25.
8. William Clark to Thomas Jefferson, Sept. 20, 1807, Jefferson Papers.
9. Commission of Auguste Chouteau as lieutenant colonel of militia, Jan. 1, 1806, Wilkinson Papers, Missouri Historical Society; Appointment of Auguste Chouteau as lieutenant colonel in command of the First Regiment of militia of Louisiana Territory, July 8, 1807, Chouteau Collections, Missouri Historical Society.
10. Joseph Browne to Thomas Jefferson, July 14, 1806, in Carter, ed., *Territorial Papers*, XIII, 548; *Missouri Gazette*, Dec. 5, 1812.
11. Index to Military Service, War of 1812, M602, No. 39, National Archives; *Missouri Gazette*, June 12, 1813.
12. Frederick Bates to Auguste Chouteau, May 27, 1807, copy in Billon Collection, Missouri Historical Society; Frederick Bates to Henry Dearborn, May 30, 1807, in Marshall, ed., *Bates Papers*, I, 132–34.
13. Frederick Bates to Henry Dearborn, May 30, 1807, in Marshall, ed., *Bates Papers*, I, 132–34.
14. Militia orders, Apr. 3, Aug. 18, and Nov. 28, 1808, and Apr. 21, 1809, in Carter, ed., *Territorial Papers*, XIV, 258–59, 211, 237–38, 263; *Missouri Gazette*, Aug. 24, 1808; Houck, *History of Missouri*, II, 410.
15. *Missouri Gazette*, Apr. 5, 1809.
16. *Ibid.*, Apr. 12 and Oct. 19, 1809.
17. Meriwether Lewis to Henry Dearborn, July 1, 1808, in Carter, ed., *Territorial Papers*, XIV, 196–203.
18. For a complete account of the Mandan affair see Foley and Rice, "The Return of the Mandan Chief," 2–14.

19. William Clark to Henry Dearborn, May 18, 1807, in Jackson, ed., *Letters of Lewis and Clark*, 412–13.

20. For a full discussion of the organization of the Missouri Fur Company, see Oglesby, *Manuel Lisa*, 65–73.

21. Missouri Fur Company Articles of Agreement, Feb. 24, 1809, Chouteau Collections.

22. Meriwether Lewis to Pierre Chouteau, June 8, 1809, in Jackson, ed., *Letters of Lewis and Clark*, 451–56.

23. Pierre Chouteau to William Eustis, Dec. 14, 1809, Pierre Chouteau Letterbook, Missouri Historical Society.

24. Thomas James, *Three Years among the Indians and Mexicans* (Waterloo, Ill., 1846); reprint: Milo M. Quaife, ed. (New York, 1966), 21–22.

25. *Ibid.*, 32–33, 43–44.

26. Pierre Chouteau to William Eustis, Dec. 14, 1809, Pierre Chouteau Letterbook.

27. William Eustis to Meriwether Lewis, July 15, 1809, in Jackson, ed., *Letters of Lewis and Clark*, 456–57.

28. Although Lewis's biographer, Richard Dillon, disputes the suicide claim, there is much evidence to the contrary. See Richard Dillon, *Meriwether Lewis: A Biography* (New York, 1965). For the other viewpoint see Jackson, ed., *Letters of Lewis and Clark*, 574–75n; and Dawson A. Phelps, "The Tragic Death of Meriwether Lewis," *William and Mary Quarterly*, 3rd ser. 13 (July 1956), 305–18.

29. William Eustis to Meriwether Lewis, July 15, 1809, in Jackson, ed., *Letters of Lewis and Clark*, 456–57.

30. Meriwether Lewis to William Eustis, Aug. 18, 1809, in *ibid.*, 459–61.

31. Pierre Chouteau, Jr., to William Eustis, Sept. 2, 1809, Pierre Chouteau Letterbook.

32. Pierre Chouteau to William Eustis, Nov. 22 and Dec. 14, 1809, and Jan. 10 and Apr. 12, 1810, and Pierre Chouteau to William Simmons, Nov. 23, 1809, Pierre Chouteau Letterbook.

33. Pierre Chouteau to William Eustis, Jan. 10, 1810, Pierre Chouteau Letterbook.

34. Pierre Chouteau to William Eustis, Apr. 12, 1810, Pierre Chouteau Letterbook.

35. William Eustis to Pierre Chouteau, June 16, 1810, Records of the Office of the Secretary of War, Letters Sent, Record Group 75, Microfilm 15, Indian Affairs, Vol. C, National Archives.

36. William Clark to Pierre Chouteau, Feb. 20, 1810, Chouteau Collections.

37. James McFarlane to William Clark, Feb. 20, 1809, in Carter, ed., *Territorial Papers*, XIV, 268–69.

38. Record of Claims, 1807–30, Records of the Office of the Secretary of War, Indian Affairs, Vol. 11, National Archives.

39. Pierre Chouteau to William Eustis, July 19 and Oct. 13, 1810, Pierre Chouteau Letterbook; William Clark to William Eustis, Sept. 12, 1810, in Carter, ed., *Territorial Papers*, XIV, 412–13.

40. Pierre Chouteau to Benjamin Howard, Oct. 14, 1810, Pierre Chouteau Letterbook.

41. White Hair's son to Pierre Chouteau, Mar. 4, 1811, in Carter, ed., *Territorial Papers*, XIV, 467–68.

42. *Ibid.; Missouri Gazette,* May 30, 1811.

43. Pierre Chouteau to William Eustis, July 2, 1811, Pierre Chouteau Letterbook.

44. George Sibley to William Clark, July 22, 1811, Sibley Papers, Missouri Historical Society.

45. Pierre Chouteau to William Eustis, Aug. 7, 1811, in Carter, ed., *Territorial Papers,* XIV, 465–66.

46. William Eustis to William Clark, Aug. 28, 1811, in Records of the Office of the Secretary of War, Letters Sent, Record Group 75, Microfilm 15, Indian Affairs, Vol. C, National Archives.

47. Daniel Bissell to William Eustis, June 28, 1811, Bissell Papers, Missouri Historical Society; Ninian Edwards to Pierre Chouteau, July 14, 1811, Chouteau Collections.

48. Auguste Chouteau to acting Governor Frederick Bates, Nov. 27, 1811, in Carter, ed., *Territorial Papers,* XIV, 494.

49. Benjamin Howard to William Eustis, Mar. 19, 1812, in *ibid.,* 531–34.

50. Pierre Chouteau to William Eustis, July 26, 1812, Pierre Chouteau Letterbook. The most comprehensive treatment of the War of 1812 in Missouri is Kate L. Gregg, "The War of 1812 on the Missouri Frontier," *Missouri Historical Review* 33 (Oct. 1938, Jan. and Apr. 1939), 3–22, 184–202, 326–48.

51. *Missouri Gazette,* Aug. 29, 1812.

52. Pierre Chouteau to William Eustis, Nov. 18, 1812, Pierre Chouteau Letterbook.

53. Pierre Chouteau to William Eustis, Jan. 27, 1813, Pierre Chouteau Letterbook.

54. Christian Wilt to Joseph Herzog, Feb. 20, 1813, Christian Wilt Letterbook, Missouri Historical Society.

55. *Missouri Gazette,* Feb. 20, 1813.

56. Foley, *History of Missouri,* 160.

57. Frederick Bates to Benjamin Howard, Feb. 27, 1813, and Pierre Chouteau to John Armstrong, Mar. 5, 1813, in Carter, ed., *Territorial Papers,* XIV, 633, 639–40.

58. Pierre Chouteau to John Armstrong, May 20, 1813, in *ibid.,* 671–73.

59. *Ibid.*

60. Fort Osage Officers to William Eustis, July 16, 1812, in *ibid.,* 587–88.

61. Pierre Chouteau to Benjamin Howard, May 11, 1813, Pierre Chouteau Letterbook.

62. Pierre Chouteau to John Armstrong, May 20, 1813, in Carter, ed., *Territorial Papers,* XIII, 671–73.

63. William Clark to James Monroe, Nov. 1814, James Monroe Papers, Library of Congress.

64. William Clark to William H. Crawford, Dec. 11, 1815, in Carter, ed., *Territorial Papers,* XV, *Louisiana-Missouri, 1815–1821* (Washington, D.C., 1954), 95–96.

65. George Sibley to William Clark, Nov. 30, 1813, in Carter, ed., *Territorial Papers,* XIV, 712–14.

66. William L. Lovely to William H. Crawford, May 27, 1815, in Carter, ed., *Territorial Papers,* XV, 52–53; William L. Lovely to William Clark, May 29, 1815, and to Return J. Meigs, May 29, 1815, Clark Papers, Missouri Historical Society.

67. William Clark to William L. Lovely, June 15, 1814, in Carter, ed., *Territorial Papers,* XV, 52–53.

68. *Missouri Gazette,* May 28, 1814.

69. *Ibid.*, June 25, 1814.

70. Pierre Chouteau to John Armstrong, May 20, 1813, in Carter, ed., *Territorial Papers*, XIV, 671–73.

71. James Monroe to William Clark, Mar. 11, 1815, Clark Family Papers.

72. "Alexander McNair," in Dumas Malone, ed., *Dictionary of American Biography* (New York, 1933), XII, 147.

73. James Monroe to Indian Commissioners, Mar. 11, 1815, in Carter, ed., *Territorial Papers*, XV, 14–15; James Monroe to William Clark, Mar. 11, 1815, Clark Papers.

74. Auguste Chouteau to James Monroe, May 27, 1815, in *American State Papers, Indian Affairs*, II, 7.

75. *Ibid.* A complete account of these negotiations can also be found in Robert L. Fisher, "The Treaties of Portage des Sioux," *Mississippi Valley Historical Review* 19 (Mar. 1933), 495–508.

76. Report on Activities as Peace Commissioners to Mississippi Indians, Oct. 18, 1815, in *American State Papers, Indian Affairs*, II, 9–11.

77. Commissioners Clark, Edwards, and Chouteau to James Monroe, May 22, 1815, in *ibid.*, 7.

78. Report on Activities as Peace Commissioners, Oct. 18, 1815, in *ibid.*, 9–11.

79. *Ibid.*; *Missouri Gazette*, July 8, 1815.

80. A. F. Dallas to Clark, Edwards, and Chouteau, June 11, 1815, Records of the Office of the Secretary of War, Letters Sent, Record Group 75, Microfilm 15, Indian Affairs, Vol. C, National Archives.

81. Fisher, "Treaties of Portage des Sioux," 499–501.

82. Daniel Bissell to Major General Andrew Jackson, July 2, 1815, Bissell Papers.

83. Fisher, "Treaties of Portage des Sioux," 499–503.

84. The U.S. government allocated $20,000 in presents for negotiations at Portage des Sioux. See Foley, *History of Missouri*, 161.

85. *American State Papers, Indian Affairs*, II, 1–5, 9.

86. *Missouri Gazette*, Sept. 9, 1815.

87. Commissioners Clark, Edwards, and Chouteau to William H. Crawford, Sept. 18, 1815, in *American State Papers, Indian Affairs*, II, 9; *Missouri Gazette*, Sept. 9, 1815.

88. Commissioners Clark, Edwards, and Chouteau to William H. Crawford, Sept. 18, 1815, in *American State Papers, Indian Affairs*, II, 9.

89. *Ibid.*, 9–11.

90. William Clark to Auguste Chouteau, Feb. 27, 1816, Chouteau Collection, Mercantile Library, St. Louis, Mo., photostatic copy in John Francis McDermott Mississippi Valley Research Collection, Lovejoy Library, Southern Illinois University at Edwardsville; Grant Foreman, ed., "Notes of Auguste Chouteau on Boundaries of Various Indian Nations," in Missouri Historical Society's *Glimpses of the Past* 7 (Oct.– Dec. 1940), 119–40.

91. A Report on Conducting the Indian Trade by Auguste Chouteau, and Ninian Edwards to William H. Crawford, Nov. 1815, in *American State Papers, Indian Affairs*, II, 66–67.

92. Return J. Meigs to William H. Crawford, Feb. 17, 1816, in Carter, ed., *Territorial Papers*, XV, 121–23.

93. Cardinal Goodwin, "A Larger View of the Yellowstone Expedition, 1819–1820," *Mississippi Valley Historical Review* 4 (Dec. 1917), 300–301.

94. William T. Hagan, *The Sac and Fox Indians* (Norman, Okla., 1958), 81–82; Treaty with Sacs of Rock River, May 13, 1816, in *American State Papers, Indian Affairs,* II, 94–96.

95. Treaty with Sioux, June 1, 1816, and Treaty with Ottawas, Chippewas and Potawatomi, Aug. 24, 1816, in *ibid.,* 94–96.

96. William H. Crawford to Indian Commissioners, May 27, 1816, in Carter, ed., *Territorial Papers,* XV, 136–37.

97. William Clark, Ninian Edwards, and Auguste Chouteau to William H. Crawford, Dec. 7, 1816, Clark Papers.

98. *Ibid.;* Indian Commissioners to William H. Crawford, Nov. 4, 1816, in Carter, ed., *Territorial Papers,* XV, 201–2.

99. William Lovely to William Clark, Jan. 20, 1816, Clark Papers; Pierre Chouteau to Major William Lovely, May 2, 1816, and William Lovely to William Clark, Sept. 22, 1816, Chouteau Collections.

100. Marie Philippe Le Duc to Frederick Bates, Dec. 30, 1815, in Carter, ed., *Territorial Papers,* XV, 98–99.

101. *Ibid.;* Pierre Chouteau to William Clark, Dec. 8, 1816, photocopy in Indian Papers, Missouri Historical Society.

102. Lottinville, *Nuttall's Journal,* 150n.

103. George Graham to Auguste Chouteau, Feb. 14, 1817, Records of the Office of the Secretary of War, Letters Sent, Indian Affairs, Vol. D, National Archives; *Missouri Gazette,* Apr. 12 and Oct. 4, 1817; Department of War to Auguste Chouteau, Mar. 7, 1818, Chouteau Collections.

104. John C. Calhoun to Ninian Edwards, Mar. 7, 1818, Records of the Office of the Secretary of War, Letters Sent, Indian Affairs, Vol. D, National Archives.

105. John C. Calhoun to William Clark and Auguste Chouteau, May 8, 1818, Chouteau Collections.

106. John C. Calhoun to William Clark, Apr. 22, 1818, in Carter, ed., *Territorial Papers,* XV, 384.

107. Treaty with Quapaws, Aug. 24, 1818, in *American State Papers, Indian Affairs,* II, 165–66.

108. Treaty with Peoria, Kaskaskia, Michigamea, Cahokia, and Tamaroa tribes, Sept. 25, 1818, in *ibid.,* 165–66.

109. William Clark to John C. Calhoun, Oct. 1818, in Carter, ed., *Territorial Papers,* XV, 454–55.

110. *Ibid.*

111. Thomas Hart Benton to Auguste Chouteau, Feb. 13, 1827, Chouteau Collections; Agreements and Treaties between the U.S. and Various Indian Tribes, 1831–38, Records of the U.S. Superintendency of Indian Affairs, I; William Clark to Superintendent of Indian Affairs, May 28 and July 22, 1830, Letterbook, Letters Sent, IV, William Clark Papers, Kansas State Historical Society.

112. See, for example, John C. Calhoun to William Clark, Feb. 10, 1820, in Carter, ed., *Territorial Papers,* XV, 586–87, in which Clark is instructed to consult with Chouteau on the matter of the removal of the Kickapoos to the Osage River.

113. *Missouri Gazette,* Nov. 13, 1818, and Mar. 17, 1819.

114. John C. Calhoun to Auguste Chouteau, Mar. 25, 1819, Chouteau Collections; Commissioners to John C. Calhoun, June 7, 1819, and Treaty with Kickapoos, July 30, 1819, in *American State Papers, Indian Affairs,* II, 196–97.

115. Indian Commissioners to John C. Calhoun, July 1820, and July 30, 1820,

Auguste Chouteau to John C. Calhoun, Aug. 29, 1820, John C. Calhoun to Auguste Chouteau and Benjamin Stephenson, Oct. 4, 1820, Chouteau Collections; William Clark to John C. Calhoun, Feb. 20, 1821, Clark Papers.

116. John C. Calhoun to Auguste Chouteau, Aug. 4, 1820, in Carter, ed., *Territorial Papers*, XV, 630.

BUSINESS AS USUAL

WITH MORE American newcomers crowding almost daily into St. Louis, the easygoing French village gradually began to take on the appearance of a bustling American town. Newly built brick and frame buildings, reflecting the American type of construction, occupied the once-vacant spaces separating the older French-style buildings, while in the background the deserted Spanish stone towers at the outskirts of the city stood as silent reminders of a bygone era. American modes of dress won wide acceptance, especially among the younger people, and along the busy streets and in the new business establishments, English increasingly replaced French as the principal language.[1]

Although the Chouteaus undoubtedly viewed these developments with a tinge of sadness, they showed no inclination to abandon the field to the "bustling, driving, and eager men of traffic from the Atlantic states"[2] now pouring into their community. Far from it: the experienced elder Chouteau managed to hold his own with the best of the sharp-trading Yankees. In fact, in the fields of fur-trading, banking, and real estate, Auguste remained virtually peerless in St. Louis, until advancing age gradually forced him to curtail his activities. Pierre, distracted by his official duties in the prime of life, never equaled his brother's business successes, but he accumulated enough assets during his lifetime to become one of the city's wealthiest residents.

Despite the uncertainties of the marketplace, both men engaged in the fur trade until after the close of the War of 1812. While profit margins declined over the years, the 27 percent average returns provided more than enough incentive to keep them involved.[3] Shortly before the American acquisition of Louisiana, Auguste and Pierre dissolved their long-standing partnership in the Osage trade.[4] Although the precise reasons for that decision are unknown, Pierre's mounting indebtedness to Auguste and to his other creditors may have prompted him to open a store in St. Louis to pursue the Indian trade independently. The agreement between the brothers to terminate their joint venture appears to have been amicable, since they remained on friendly terms and routinely transacted business with each other.[5]

Once he was on his own, Pierre lost little time in seeking the support he needed to expand his trading operations. True to form, he took advantage of every possible opportunity during his 1804 trip to Washington to advance his personal interests. Not only did he urge governmental leaders to grant him control over the trans-Mississippi fur trade, he also made overtures to several Philadelphia merchants about the possibility of establishing business connections. Taking his cue from the earlier agreement Auguste had negotiated with the Spanish government, giving him a monopoly of the Osage trade in return for his assistance in controlling that tribe, Pierre attempted to persuade U.S. officials that a similar arrangement would greatly enhance his ability to carry out his duties as Indian agent. Although the Americans took exception to his request, they hesitated to reject it outright for fear they might offend the influential merchant.[6] While awaiting governmental approval for his plan, Pierre turned to the eastern business community for financial backing. His pitch proved convincing enough to elicit at least cautious interest from several Philadelphia firms.[7] The grandiose scheme never materialized, but the cosmopolitan Frenchman was already learning to make his way among American politicians and businessmen.

While Pierre lobbied in the East for favorable treatment, Auguste kept busy hosting the newly arrived Americans in St. Louis. Yet even with his hectic social schedule and the inevitable uncertainty accompanying the change in governments, the senior Chouteau forged ahead with business as usual. Not long after he bade Lewis and Clark adieu as they departed on their journey to the Pacific, seven pirogues bearing furs from Regis Loisel's post on the upper Missouri arrived at his St. Louis warehouse.[8] Realizing that the resumption of hostilities between Great Britain and France the previous year had once again disrupted the fur markets, Chouteau pondered how to dispose of these latest shipments most profitably. Reports from two of his Montreal agents that international uncertainties had caused them to sell his furs locally at public auction rather than risk sending them to London made him hesitate. According to their accounts, not only had fur sales in Europe fallen off drastically, but a poor Canadian harvest had substantially diminished the local demand for buffalo robes. By late fall, Josiah Bleakley informed Chouteau from Montreal that the situation in Europe was so unstable that it was impossible to give any advice concerning furs. He feared that unreasonable credit demands from British firms and uncollected accounts from the previous year's trading would result in heavy losses for fur dealers.[9] The news from New Orleans was equally discouraging. The firm of Cavelier and Son reported difficulties in selling Auguste's shipment of skins from the Arkansas River, and if that were not bad enough, they also informed him that many of those skins had rotted inside their packs.[10]

Having become conditioned long ago to expect such temporary disappointments, Auguste pressed ahead with his trading operations despite the recurring discomfort caused by his chronic gout, which made even routine tasks a painful chore for him. Since traders and trappers in his employ operated out of both St. Louis and Michilimackinac, Chouteau found it necessary to devote many hours attending his far-flung ventures. George Gillespie, a well-known trader at Michilimackinac, assisted Auguste in outfitting his employees at that post, but the elder Chouteau still looked after the hiring and equipping of many of the traders who set out each year in late summer from St. Louis bound for the Indian country.[11] While returning to that city in September 1806, the Lewis and Clark expedition met two such Chouteau trading parties heading up the Missouri to establish camps at the Pawnee, Omaha, and Sioux villages.[12]

Although the volume of Auguste's fur shipments slowly declined in the years following the American takeover, he continued to ship sizable quantities of peltries to Canada and to New Orleans. He also had entered the American market, most probably utilizing the services of Kaskaskia merchant William Morrison. In 1803 Gillespie lamented that Chouteau had sold bear skins to the Americans instead of sending them to Canada.[13] In truth, Gillespie had no reason to fear any immediate loss of Chouteau's business. As in the past, the St. Louis merchant sent the major portion of his finer furs northward. The habits of nearly two decades were too deeply ingrained to be set aside with ease.[14] Besides, the change in governments provided no real incentive for Chouteau to redirect his trade to New Orleans or elsewhere. On the contrary, following the transfer of authority in the gulf port, Auguste experienced new difficulties in settling his accounts there, since no one would honor drafts he held on the Spanish treasury in payment for services and merchandise he had provided to the preceding government. Moreover, the New Orleans suppliers continued to lag behind their British counterparts in the quality and quantity of their Indian trade goods.[15]

Be that as it may, the Louisiana Purchase placed the long-established hegemony of the Canadian traders at Michilimackinac and the other northern posts in jeopardy. Despite the disappointing results of Spain's efforts to reduce British influence in the fur country west of the Mississippi, the Americans seemed determined to succeed where their predecessors had failed. Governor James Wilkinson's attempts to deny licenses to British traders, the opening of a U.S. trading factory at Michilimackinac in 1806, and John Jacob Astor's persistent efforts to enter the western marketplace all portended an uncertain future for Canadian fur merchants in the far West.

In a move to counter the growing American competition, a group of Michilimackinac-based merchants and traders formed the Michilimackinac Company in 1806. Seeking to retain control over as much as possible of the fur trade in their traditional strongholds in the Old Northwest and the region west of the Mississippi, the company's influential organizers affiliated themselves with the powerful North West Company.[16] Following the new firm's creation, its directors invited Auguste to join them. Their obvious desire for the St. Louis merchant's support testified to his standing within the Canadian business community. Bleakley informed Chouteau that they would be flattered if he chose to accept their invitation, but the northern fur dealer hastened to add that even if Auguste found it necessary to decline, he and his associates would still welcome his business.[17] But since he was eager to maintain his independence as a trader and equally determined not to give the Americans any cause to doubt his loyalty, Chouteau decided not to become a member of the Michilimackinac Company.

Chouteau turned down the overtures of the Michilimackinac traders, but he found it more difficult to resist the mounting pressures to expand his operations to the upper Missouri and beyond. Ever since Lewis and Clark had returned to St. Louis in 1806 with reports of streams teeming with beavers, the traders in the Mississippi River community seemed poised for a stampede into the distant Rockies. In the past the cautious Chouteaus had labeled all such ventures too risky for their participation, but when their arch-rival Manuel Lisa, in association with William Morrison and Pierre Menard, seized the initiative and headed up the Missouri with plans for exploiting the Rocky Mountain fur resources, the Chouteaus reconsidered their long-standing aversion to entering the northern trading zone.

As previously noted, Auguste Pierre Chouteau was the first family member to take up the challenge. Pierre had turned to his sons for assistance when federal officials openly questioned the propriety of his attempts to engage in private business while in government service. By assigning his boys to oversee his trading operations, Pierre hoped to silence his American critics. Consequently, while Auguste Pierre had taken charge of assembling the trading party that accompanied Pryor's unsuccessful mission to return Shahaka, his younger brother, Pierre Jr., had gone to the Osage villages to supervise the trade there. Auguste Pierre and Pierre Jr. went on to win fame as traders in their own right, but in 1807 they almost certainly were acting as agents for their father.[18]

Even Auguste Sr. joined the rush that year to capitalize upon the commercial possibilities in the far north. Before word of the Pryor expedition's debacle reached St. Louis, the patriarch of the Chouteau clan had entered the lists and given financial backing for an eighty-man party being organized by Ramsay Crooks in association with Robert McClellan. After encountering Indian resistance on the way upriver, Crooks and McClellan fell back to Council Bluffs, where they established a trading post which they operated for several years. McClellan, a veteran of General "Mad Anthony" Wayne's Indian campaigns, had turned to the fur trade following his arrival in St. Louis in 1805, while Crooks, a Scot who had immigrated to Canada, had come to St. Louis from Michilimackinac. In 1810 Crooks and McClellan joined John Jacob Astor's

Pacific Fur Company as partners, and both men participated in the ill-fated overland expedition to Astoria in 1811. Crooks, who subsequently married Auguste and Pierre's grand-niece Emilie Pratte, went on to become a key figure in the American Fur Company.[19]

Manuel Lisa's initial foray up the Missouri was financially more successful than either of the ventures under Chouteau sponsorship. Indeed, Pryor subsequently attempted, without real justification, to blame Lisa for his misfortunes at the hands of the angry Indians, and Crooks and McClellan, likewise, had little good to say about the Spanish trader in later years. Nonetheless, when Lisa returned to St. Louis in 1808 with enough beaver skins to discredit any would-be detractors, the Chouteaus fully appreciated the seriousness of his challenge. Characteristically, it was the more impulsive Pierre who made the first move. As was indicated earlier, he laid aside his past differences with Lisa and joined him and several other prominent local entrepreneurs to form the St. Louis Missouri Fur Company. In agreeing to pool their capital with long-time competitors, the Chouteaus assured themselves a continued place in the vanguard of the western fur trade.[20]

Although Auguste opted to allow his brother and his nephew Auguste Pierre to take the lead, he undoubtedly advised them throughout the lengthy negotiations during the winter of 1808–9 which culminated in the company's formation. The detailed provisions contained in the final articles of agreement approved in St. Louis on February 24, 1809, clearly mirrored the almost legendary Chouteau propensity for caution. Members of the company pledged themselves to share all expenses equally and not to engage in private trading apart from the company's operations. Major purchases required the approval of a majority of the firm's partners. Significantly, the articles of agreement granted Pierre full authority over the military expedition assigned to escort Chief Shahaka to his village in conformity with the terms of the company's controversial contract with the U.S. government. Moreover, in an additional article agreed to the following September, the partners empowered William Clark and Pierre Chouteau to sign and execute notes, bills, obligations, and disbursements for the company.[21]

Throughout the Missouri Fur Company's relatively brief history, Pierre Chouteau assumed an active role in managing its affairs. After seeing Shahaka safely home he returned to St. Louis, where he took charge of handling many routine operations. With Lisa compelled to spend most of his time in the field, Chouteau enjoyed a relatively free hand in St. Louis, which he no doubt used to his advantage. As the Missouri Company's principal supplier, he furnished it with nearly $40,000 in merchandise from his stocks, and more than likely he and his brother purchased many of the furs from the firm's members for resale.[22] Thanks to the profits from those transactions, Pierre may have fared better than most of his partners in the concern; but the persistent demands from his creditors suggest that if he reaped any immense windfall from the venture, he managed to keep it well hidden.[23]

The Missouri Fur Company never measured up to the expectations of its founders. Even with the 7,000-dollar governmental subsidy the firm received for conducting the Mandan chief up the Missouri, final returns to the investors proved to be meager. Losses sustained at the hands of hostile Blackfoot and Gros Ventre tribesmen and depressed fur prices caused by the unstable international situation contributed to the firm's disappointing financial showing. Efforts to revitalize company operations failed, and the owners finally agreed to dissolve the partnership in 1814.[24]

The times certainly had not been propitious for such an ambitious undertaking. Ever since the fighting had resumed in Europe in 1803, the fur markets had remained in a state of flux. From the remoteness of the American wilderness the Chouteaus followed the course of events in Europe with keen interest. Napoleon Bonaparte's exploits particularly intrigued Auguste, and during his 1806 trip to Washington, Pierre purchased for his brother a biography of Napoleon, accounts of various Napoleonic campaigns, and the seven-volume *Histoire des Gaulois et des Français en Italie*.[25] The inventory of Auguste's estate, prepared following his death in 1829, gives further evidence of his interest. Numerous paintings and engravings of Napoleon, his generals, and scenes depicting important events of the revolutionary and Napoleonic eras are included in the list.[26]

While the Chouteaus watched from afar, Bonaparte's advancing armies rolled over those of the Third Coalition, leaving only the British navy in the way of a total French victory. With the Napoleonic forces occupying important Prussian trading centers, prices again slumped downward, causing Auguste to sustain serious losses in his 1806 shipments to Europe.[27] Napoleon's decision to resort to commercial warfare in an attempt to ruin the nation of shopkeepers across the channel further impeded international trade. The maze of blockades and counter-blockades imposed by the French Continental System and the British Orders in Council caught neutral nations like the United States in the crossfire. The Jefferson administration's 1807 embargo, which banned all foreign trade in an effort to force the European powers to recognize the United States' neutral rights, dealt most American mercantile operations, including those of the Chouteaus, a further blow. The unpopular measure put commerce at a virtual standstill in all American ports.

Warnings from New Orleans merchants that "furs have no value at present" forced Chouteau to smuggle his shipments through Canadian outlets.[28] Although in most cases his agents appear to have eluded American authorities along the Canadian border, the collector at Niagara did seize eight boats belonging to the Michilimackinac Company on May 21, 1808, including two carrying merchandise consigned to Auguste. The authorities ultimately released the confiscated goods, but only after Chouteau and the other owners took their case to Washington at considerable personal expense.[29] Manuel Lisa encountered similar difficulties and informed Pierre in 1810 from Detroit that it was impossible to get even a needle past the embargo.[30] Fur shipments that did get through often went begging for buyers in Canada because of the troubled international situation. Noting the sad state of affairs in St. Louis in 1810, Charles Gratiot advised John Jacob Astor that the fur trade was totally annihilated.[31] Congressional attempts to lessen the embargo's negative economic impact brought no real improvement in the western river entrepot.

Shortly after the United States declared war on Great Britain in June 1812, British forces occupied the American fort at Michilimackinac and effectively closed that strategic post to traders from the United States. As if that were not bad enough, American soldiers confiscated 316 packs of deer and bear skins which had been consigned to St. Louis traders John Pierre Cabanné and Antoine Chenie, including fifty-seven packs belonging to Auguste Chouteau. The Americans sold the furs at auction, but it is not clear if Chouteau and the others managed to recover any of the proceeds from that sale. If they did, they still would have suffered a substantial loss after paying their legal costs. For the duration of the war, trade with Canada was impossible as the border remained closed.[32] Even attempts to correspond with Canadians by mail proved to be fruitless, as letters were returned undelivered to their senders.[33]

Despite the wartime dislocations which hampered all business activity in the Missouri Territory, Auguste continued buying and selling furs and marketing them through American outlets, albeit on a limited scale. In 1813, for example, he sent beaver skins to William Morrison, and during the two succeeding years he sold deer skins to his brother-in-law Charles Gratiot, who purchased them for Astor.[34] Gratiot, who was indebted to Astor, had renewed his efforts to bring the powerful American dealer into the St. Louis market, but, as they had a decade earlier, the Chouteaus and their associates again rejected his entry for fear that his immense capital would soon enable him to dominate the local trade. Although during the war they occasionally did ship him some deer skins through Gratiot, they had vetoed the latter's suggestion in 1811 that Astor be invited to invest in the faltering Missouri Fur Company.[35]

As the war continued, Gratiot informed the influential New York merchant that the conflict had greatly impeded the flow of furs into St. Louis. Whereas in normal years traders in that town could expect to receive as many as 1,000 packs of deer skins plus other skins and assorted fine furs, only 120 deer-skin packs arrived there in 1814. Gratiot blamed the poor showing on Indian unrest, severe shortages of trade goods, and difficulties in recruiting *engagés* to assist in transporting the goods to market.[36]

With the fur trade so severely depressed, Auguste attempted to offset his declining revenues by expanding his lead sales in New Orleans. The strong demand for lead between 1804 and 1815 made it a popular item of trade with Chouteau. It ranked second only to furs in importance among the various commodities that he regularly bought and sold. For many years miners, such as Julien Dubuque, had sent shipments of the malleable mineral from their diggings along the upper Mississippi to St. Louis. Dubuque was a regular Chouteau customer who since 1788 had operated with Indian assistance the so-called Spanish Mines, located on the Mississippi River 500 miles above St. Louis at a site just below present-day Dubuque, Iowa. In 1804 Auguste purchased a half-interest in the Dubuque mine for $10,848.60.[37] Already deeply in debt to Chouteau, Dubuque used the sale to cancel his obligations and to secure additional goods and supplies. Since he was also in the process of seeking the U.S. government's confirmation for his Spanish title to the mines, Dubuque undoubtedly looked upon his new partner as a powerful ally whose assistance would be invaluable in dealing with the American authorities. That judgment seemed to have been borne out when the Board of Land Commissioners voted to confirm that grant in 1806. Although that decision was later overturned and the matter remained under litigation for nearly a half-century before the claim was finally rejected, Dubuque did not live long enough to know any of that. Meanwhile, work at the mines continued. In 1810 Auguste sent his nephew Pierre Jr. to the site to initiate mining operations on his claim. Shortly before he arrived at the mines, Dubuque unexpectedly died. Pierre Jr., who was called Cadet as his father had been as a young man, took over operations at the Spanish Mines and directed them until 1812, when expanding Indian hostilities forced him to withdraw from the area.[38] In addition to the lead he secured from the upper Mississippi mines, Auguste also made frequent purchases from Jean Baptiste Vallé in Ste. Genevieve. Vallé's family had long worked the diggings at Mine La Motte, located at the headwaters of the St. François River, but, as was the case almost everywhere else, the wartime disorders soon disrupted mining operations there too. Late in 1812 Moses Austin, the territory's foremost mining entrepreneur, reported that labor shortages caused by the frequent militia call-ups and unusually severe weather conditions had temporarily brought lead mining to a standstill in the Missouri Territory.[39]

The temporary interdiction of normal lead supplies prompted a search for new and more convenient sources of that vital mineral. In 1813 a boatman returned to St. Louis claiming to have discovered a rich ore deposit on land belonging to Pierre Chouteau. The report created considerable excitement in the lead-hungry town, and Pierre, in an uncharacteristically expansive mood, promised the boatman a 1,200-dollar reward if the find proved as rich as it was believed to be. Pierre and his sons made a trip to inspect the site on Gravois Creek, a branch of the Osage River, and upon returning to St. Louis they signed a lease with the U.S. government authorizing them to operate mines on the 600-acre tract. The discovery must not have measured up to their initial expectations, however, inasmuch as the one-year lease was never renewed.[40] Auguste, of course, continued occasionally to deal in lead once mining operations in the region returned to normal.

When the War of 1812 finally ended, St. Louisans eagerly looked forward to a return of the pre-war prosperity. Governmental leaders in Washington were especially eager to see a reopening of the western fur trade now that the terms agreed to at Ghent had paved the way for ending Britain's lengthy domination of the northern trade routes. With an eye to supplanting the British operatives and expanding American trading activities into the far reaches of the Missouri, officials in the nation's capital once again turned to the Chouteaus for advice. In response to a request from the secretary of war, Auguste prepared a detailed report predicting a promising future for the Rocky Mountain fur trade, but he cautioned the Americans that it would take at least three years to set up contracts, to erect military fortifications, and to take the other steps necessary for initiating that traffic.[41] In transmitting Auguste's report to Washington, Governor Ninian Edwards advised the secretary that no one was more knowledgeable about Indian trade than Chouteau, who "had pursued it in this country for forty years with such success as to have amassed an immense fortune by it."[42]

In actual fact, aside from an enlargement in the size of the area the St. Louis traders visited, fur operations in that town had remained substantially unchanged since the early Spanish years. Even the American advent had failed to alter the time-honored frontier trading practices. Attempts to introduce innovations usually encountered stiff opposition from the established trading moguls. Such was the case with the U.S. government's efforts to establish government-owned trading factories west of the Mississippi. Although those factories were not numerous, were often poorly run, and were not particularly competitive with the more aggressive private trading posts in the region, they siphoned off enough furs to cause private traders to wage an intense campaign for their elimination. Auguste blamed the government factories for the decline in the fur trade and undoubtedly helped persuade Missouri's Senator Thomas Hart Benton to use his influence to secure their abolition. Responding to powerful lobbying from Astor in the East and the Chouteaus and their associates in the West, Congress did away with the factory system in 1822.

Although as Governor Edwards had noted, Auguste was universally acknowledged as the preeminent authority on the western fur trade, the elder Chouteau knew better than anyone that the time had arrived for him to step aside. On November 23, 1816, he announced in the columns of the *Missouri Gazette* his intention to close his mercantile establishment and to retire from the fur trade. Auguste asked his customers to conclude their business and settle their accounts with him no later than March 1, 1817.[43] However, after conducting business in St. Louis for nearly a half-century, the task of closing out his accounts proved to be a monumental undertaking which intermittently required his attention until the time of his death nearly thirteen years later.[44]

At about the same time Pierre also withdrew from active participation in the fur business. In stepping aside, Pierre turned his operation over to his sons, who along with Auguste's offspring now took up the challenge of keeping the Chouteau name in the front ranks of the North American fur trade. For Pierre the chore of settling accounts proved even more trying because of the substantial sums he still owed his suppliers.[45] In September 1817, however, he momentarily dropped everything else to join with other family members in welcoming home his eldest son, Auguste Pierre. Young Chouteau and his trading partner Jules de Mun had returned to St. Louis empty-handed and in rags after spending forty-eight days in a dreary Santa Fe prison cell charged with trading illegally in Spanish territory. All of St. Louis was abuzz as the two men recounted the details of their ordeal at the hands of their captors. Not only had the Spaniards kept them in chains during part of their incarceration, but they had also confiscated more than $30,000 worth of their property.[46]

Gradually, as the excitement abated and things got back to normal, members of the Chouteau family returned to the more mundane matters of their everyday business affairs. Even after they had closed their mercantile establishments, Auguste and Pierre retained an active interest in many other business and financial ventures in St. Louis. For example, Auguste continued to operate his gristmill, and in 1820 he had considerable difficulty locating suitable new millstones to replace the old ones worn out by many years of use.[47] His distillery continued to produce whiskey and various other alcoholic spirits as late as 1826, although his offer to sell several stills of different dimensions in 1820 suggests that he may have reduced the size of his operations as a consequence of the increased competition in St. Louis.[48]

Auguste also looked after numerous business and residential properties. The post-war economic boom in St. Louis afforded almost daily opportunities for real estate profits, and Chouteau was quick to capitalize on them. Prior to 1816 St. Louis had remained confined to the original three streets that Laclède had plotted, but the influx of newcomers prompted Auguste and John B. C. Lucas to open the first addition to the town on the hill immediately west of the original village in that year.[49] A persistent housing shortage in the city also worked to Chouteau's advantage. After informing his son Cerré that "cellars, haylofts, and all the small inns are full not only of people, but of merchandise," Auguste contracted with Philip Rocheblave to construct a row of brick structures on Main Street.[50] Following the completion of the Chouteau buildings, as they were commonly called, their owner leased them at rates which at least some considered too high.[51] As with any landlord, Auguste spent much time locating tenants for his property, collecting rents, and seeing to normal maintenance and repairs.[52]

Auguste also devoted considerable time in his later years to banking. After serving as the community's unofficial banker for many years, Chouteau had spearheaded a drive to establish a bank in St. Louis shortly after the outbreak of the War of 1812.[53] A chronic shortage of specie had long impeded the region's economic development, but the situation worsened drastically following the near-collapse of the international fur market. Charles Gratiot observed in 1810 that the depression of cash was so great that it threatened to embarrass some of the community's most respectable inhabitants.[54] Financial hard times and capital shortages showed themselves to be no respecters of nationality, so when the movement to charter a bank gained momentum in 1813, French and American businessmen alike turned to Auguste for assistance. Although the initial effort involved a cross section of the St. Louis business community, the opening sentence of the territorial legislature's enactment authorizing the incorporation of the Bank of St. Louis simply read, "Whereas Auguste Chouteau and others have by their petition presented to the legislature & prayed that a banking company may be incorporated. . . ."[55] Clearly, in this case one name was enough.

Despite such an auspicious beginning, the Bank of St. Louis did not actually get under way for another three years. Wartime economic conditions had made it impossible to secure enough subscriptions for the bank's stock at the outset, and by the time the necessary capital had been raised and the bank opened its doors for business on December 13, 1816, Chouteau had withdrawn his backing and formed a rival institution known as the Bank of Missouri. After concluding that many of the Bank of St. Louis's stockholders favored a freewheeling and highly speculative approach to banking, Auguste and some of his conservative associates decided to create a bank guided by financial policies more to their liking.[56] As Chouteau later explained to Secretary of the Treasury William H. Crawford, "The Bank of Missouri, unlike most other banking institutions, owes not its origins to any selfish or speculative purposes. Self-defense alone has given it birth, and the same principle has continued uniformly to govern its operations all along."[57]

Auguste initially purchased thirty 100-dollar shares of stock in the new bank, which was capitalized at $250,000. In the fall of 1816 the Bank of Missouri began conducting business in the basement of Auguste's mansion even before it had been granted a charter. Among those joining Chouteau in the new venture were Alexander McNair, John O'Fallon, Lilburn Boggs, John B. C. Lucas, Christian Wilt, Charles Gratiot, Bartholomew Berthold, Pierre Chouteau, Jr., Sylvestre Labbadie, John P. Cabanné, and Joseph Philipson. Supporters of the Bank of St. Louis waged an intense campaign in the territorial legislature to block Chouteau's efforts to secure a charter for a second bank, but their efforts failed as the still-influential Chouteaus carried the day. When William Neely, the president of the Legislative Council, resigned in protest, opponents of the Bank of Missouri engaged in some last-minute parliamentary maneuvering to keep the recently approved bank bill from reaching the governor's desk. Unwilling to be denied their victory, the bill's supporters snatched it from the feuding officers of the upper chamber and delivered it to territorial Governor William Clark, who promptly signed it into law. Later attempts to challenge the unorthodox fashion in which the bill had been handled failed, and Auguste emerged from the fray with his charter intact.[58]

With the elder Chouteau serving as the Bank of Missouri's president, other triumphs followed. In 1817 the U.S. government selected that institution over its rival, the Bank of St. Louis, to be the federal depository in the Missouri Territory. Under the arrangement which brought more than $1,088,333 into the bank's coffers during the years that it served in that capacity, the United States agreed to maintain a minimum deposit of $150,000 at all times. The federal monies provided a welcome boost to the Bank of Missouri.[59] A financial statement which appeared in the *Missouri Gazette* on November 6, 1818, showed the bank to be in good financial condition, with deposits totaling $312,900, and the following year it moved into its own quarters in a new building located at 6 North Main Street.[60] Unlike the strife-torn Bank of St. Louis, which went out of business in 1819, the Bank of Missouri weathered the initial phases of the Panic of 1819. In time, however, the severely depressed economic conditions placed the institution's future in jeopardy as deposits declined and public confidence in all banks waned.[61]

The strain caused by these developments also took their toll on the bank's elderly president, who cited advancing age and declining health as the reasons for his decision to resign his post early in 1821.[62] Six months later, the hard-pressed financial institution was forced to close its doors permanently.[63] Although most of the blame for the bank's failure can be attributed to the economic downturn, excessively large and poorly secured loans to the bank's directors, including a 6,400-dollar loan to Auguste backed only with his shares of bank stock as collateral, had further weakened the Bank of Missouri's financial position.[64] Undoubtedly the hard times had caused Chouteau and the others to solicit the loans for themselves. There certainly is no indication of any intent on the directors' part to defraud, but that cannot completely absolve them of responsibility for their unwise actions. After the bank's closing, Auguste joined with General William Clark, Bernard Pratte, John O'Fallon, and Robert Wash in serving as trustees to liquidate the bank's assets and to close its books.[65]

Following the bank's demise and his retirement from active involvement in public affairs, Auguste directed most of his remaining energies to the management of his real estate holdings. Because of the importance the typical frontier settler attached to land, most territorial residents stood somewhat in awe of the Chouteau brothers and their immense holdings. Through the years both men had acquired extensive tracts in St. Louis and the surrounding region, and Auguste, whose confirmed titles exceeded 60,000 arpents at the time of his death, enjoyed the honor of being the Missouri Territory's largest land-owner. The nearly universal preoccupation with land moved Timothy Flint, an itinerant frontier preacher, to observe, "I question if the people of Missouri generally thought there existed higher objects of envy, than Chouteau and a few other great land-holders of that class."[66]

The Chouteaus accumulated their vast acreages by design rather than by accident. Land acquisition was a lifetime proposition for both Auguste and Pierre. Even in the earliest days of St. Louis, when land had relatively little value, they showed interest in acquiring concessions from Spanish authorities and from Indians. In anticipation of rising land prices, they accelerated their land purchases at the time of the American acquisition of Louisiana. Yet because their landholdings were based upon Spanish concessions, the Chouteaus began urging the U.S. government to confirm the Spanish titles as soon as the first American officers arrived in St. Louis.[67]

The issue proved to be an especially difficult one for the Americans to resolve. Because some charged that certain Spanish officials had, immediately following the Louisiana Purchase, issued antedated patents confirming fraudulent grants to large tracts of land, U.S. officials hesitated to authorize blanket approval for the Spanish titles. Establishment of the Board of Land Commissioners to validate Spanish land patents failed to resolve the issue, and the debate over the land titles continued to rage long after Auguste and Pierre died.[68] During their lifetimes, however, both men remained in the forefront of the movement to persuade the American government to honor their claims. With so much at stake in the issue, the Chouteaus used their considerable influence whenever possible in St. Louis and in Washington. They organized meetings to protest governmental restrictions they considered too stringent and bombarded federal officials with petitions demanding changes in laws governing confirmation of land titles.[69] They also hired attorneys to represent them before the land commissioners and in the courts.[70]

Whenever possible they personally pressed their cases with influential territorial officials. For example, they persuaded Governor Harrison to accept inclusion of a proviso in the Sac and Fox treaty of 1804 designed to protect Auguste's recently purchased interest in the Dubuque mines. Four years later Governor Lewis rejected Pierre's efforts to gain the incorporation of a statement in the Osage treaty intended to uphold the validity of his 30,000-arpent concession from members of that tribe, but setbacks such as that failed to dissuade them from their campaign to secure approval for their titles.[71]

Over the years their persistence paid off as Congress gradually eased the guidelines for confirming the Spanish titles. An 1814 act for the "final adjustment of land titles in the State of Louisiana and the Territory of Missouri," which transferred authority for ruling on land claims from the Board of Commissioners to a recorder of land titles, permitted the confirmation of numerous titles previously declared invalid. Prior to its enactment, Auguste held twenty-four confirmed certificates entitling him to 9,000 acres and seven town lots in St. Louis and St. Charles, but thanks to the measure's more liberal provisions he gained approval for five more town lots and six additional tracts, raising his total confirmed holdings to 23,500 acres. At the same time Pierre's confirmed acreage went from 500 to more than 22,700.[72]

Even after this so-called final settlement, both men retained many additional still-unconfirmed Spanish land patents. In most instances they were for very large tracts. Undaunted, the Chouteaus continued to press their cause in the halls of Congress and in the courtroom in an effort to remove all remaining obstacles to final confirmation. A case in point would be the 30,000-arpent concession the Osages had granted Pierre in 1792. Spanish officials had approved the donation in 1799 without delineating any exact boundaries except to note that it was to be located on the Lamine River and to include the salt springs near the point where that stream joined the Missouri. Pierre made no attempt to define the property's limits more precisely until settlers began moving into the region prior to the War of 1812.[73]

In his belated efforts to locate the tract, he submitted two different sets of boundaries for the proposed tract as he attempted to insure inclusion of the most valuable lands in the region. Such uncertainties and maneuverings did little to strengthen his case with the land commissioners, who declined to confirm his title in 1811 and again in 1816. Failing for a second time to secure governmental confirmation, Pierre solicited assistance from William H. Ashley, a local entrepreneur whose recent appointment as register of preemption claims promised to make him a valuable ally. After acquiring a one-fourth interest in the tract in 1819, Ashley filed a new claim with yet another set of boundaries. Although the grant was not officially confirmed until 1836, Ashley, who was by then a renowned fur trader and a member of the U.S. Congress, had played a key role in securing final approval. For Pierre the triumph was completed in 1837, when he sold his interest in the tract to Ashley for $43,000.[74]

In his efforts to secure confirmation for the Chouteau tract, Ashley, as a member of the Private Land Claims Committee, had helped push through Congress in 1833 a law creating still another Board of Land Commissioners with new rules for determining the validity of unconfirmed land titles. Using those even more lenient guidelines, the commissioners approved several additional tracts belonging to Pierre and to Auguste's heirs, but the board continued to reject others.[75] Auguste's devisees then went to court to challenge the rulings that had gone against them. Their plea came before the U.S. Supreme Court for final resolution. In two opinions written by Chief Justice John Marshall, the court declared that Auguste had met the spirit of the legal requirements, thus upholding the family's claims to the tracts in question.[76] Although Pierre's 30,000-arpent claim had not been included in those suits, the judges' favorable ruling for the claimants had aided Ashley in securing congressional confirmation of the Lamine River tract the next year.[77]

Even when final approval had been gained, other obstacles sometimes had to be surmounted before the lands could be claimed. Because so many years had elapsed, the disputed lands had often been occupied, and in at least some instances conflicting titles to the same tracts had been confirmed previously. This confused legal tangle often necessitated additional litigation to determine the rightful claimant. In one such suit involving Pierre's claims to common lands in St. Charles, the Missouri Supreme Court refused to approve his petition to eject William Eckert from the disputed tract. In that case and in a few others, such as the one involving the Dubuque mines, the final decisions went against the Chouteaus, but these were generally the exceptions.[78]

The success with which they pursued their claims through the complex maze of legislative and judicial channels provided the ultimate confirmation of their adaptation to the American system of governance and justice. Through decades of political change and through years of enduring the fragile economic fortunes of a dangerous frontier, the Chouteaus had mastered not only the skills of the survivor, but they had developed an intuition about the marketplace which led them to be alternately aggressive and cautious. Usually this acquired reflex served them well. By their old age, they had become consummate practitioners of the art of American politics and business, capable of holding their own with the best of their hard-driving Yankee fellow countrymen.

NOTES

1. Washington Irving captured the city's cultural blend in his 1810 description of St. Louis: "Here were to be seen about the river banks, the hectoring, extravagant, bragging, boatmen of the Mississippi, with the gay, grimacing, singing, good-humored Canadian voyageurs. Vagrant Indians, of various tribes, loitered about the streets. Now and then, a stark Kentucky hunter, in leathren hunting-dress, with rifle on shoulder and knife in belt, strode along. Here and there were new brick houses and shops, just set up by bustling, driving, and eager men of traffic from the Atlantic States; while on the other hand, the old French mansions, with open casements, still retained the easy, indolent air of the original colonists; and now and then the scraping of a fiddle, a strain of an ancient French song, or the sound of billiard balls, showed that the happy Gallic turn for gayety and amusement still lingered about the place."

Washington Irvng, *Astoria;* reprinted in Herbert L. Kleinfield, ed., *The Complete Works of Washington Irving* (Boston, 1976), 93.

2. *Ibid.*

3. Stoddard, *Sketches,* 298.

4. Pierre Chouteau's account with his brother Auguste, Apr. 2, 1803, Chouteau Collections, Missouri Historical Society.

5. The destruction of Pierre's records in the 1805 fire that destroyed his home makes it impossible to reconstruct his business activities and the exact nature of his association with Auguste. According to Edward Rowse, Pierre had his own store in St. Louis in 1804. See Rowse, "Auguste and Pierre Chouteau," 72.

6. Albert Gallatin to Thomas Jefferson, Aug. 20, 1804, Jefferson Papers.

7. Pierre Chouteau to Samuel McKer, Nov. 19, 1804, and to M. Turascon, Nov. 22, 1804, Pierre Chouteau Letterbook, Missouri Historical Society.

8. Whitehouse's Journal, June 12, 1804, in Thwaites, ed., *Journals of Lewis and Clark,* VII, 35.

9. Atkin and Patterson to Auguste Chouteau, Apr. 3, 1804, and Josiah Bleakley to Auguste Chouteau, Sept. 22 and Oct. 27, 1804, Chouteau Collections.

10. Cavelier and Son to Auguste and Pierre Chouteau, Apr. 21, 1804, Chouteau Collections.

11. See, for examples, Notation of advances and equipment made to men of Auguste Chouteau by George Gillespie & Co., July 9, 1805, and Promissory note of Francis Ragotti and François Foucher to pay Auguste Chouteau for equipment for hunt and trade, Aug. 18, 1813, Chouteau Collections; Frederick Bates to Auguste Chouteau, Sept. 23, 1809, Billon Collection, Missouri Historical Society.

12. Thwaites, ed., *Journals of Lewis and Clark,* Sept. 12 and 14, 1806, V, 382, 384.

13. George Gillespie to Auguste Chouteau, July 16, 1803, Chouteau Collections.

14. See Accounts and statements of Auguste Chouteau with George Gillespie & Co., including interest calculations on peltries sent to London etc., Apr. 20, 1805– May 17, 1821, Chouteau Collections. In 1807 William Clark sent Secretary of War Dearborn a statement regarding the Indian trade which he procured from "Old Mr. Chouteau, who is better acquainted with the Trade advantages and Situation of this Country than any Merchant in it. From his statistical view, you will observe that much the greater portion of the rich furs and peltries are Carried to Canada, and most of it, immediately from the Indian Country." Clark to Dearborn, May 18, 1807, in Carter, ed., *Territorial Papers,* XIV, 124.

15. For example see Cavelier and Son to Auguste Chouteau, Apr. 21, 1804, Jan. 21, 1805, May 28, 1805, and May 13, 1806, Chouteau Collections.

16. Paul C. Phillips, *The Fur Trade* (Norman, Okla., 1961), II, 131–32.

17. Josiah Bleakley and T. Potheir to Auguste Chouteau, Jan. 7, 1807, and George Gillespie to Auguste Chouteau, Jan. 10, 1807, Chouteau Collections.

18. William Clark to Henry Dearborn, June 1, 1807, in Carter, ed., *Territorial Papers,* XIV, 126; List of licenses to trade with the Indians, Oct. 1, 1807, Louisiana Territory Papers, Missouri Historical Society. Their respective careers are ably summarized in Janet Lecompte's "Auguste Pierre Chouteau" and "Pierre Chouteau, Junior," both in LeRoy R. Hafen, ed., *The Mountain Men and the Fur Trade of the Far West* (Glendale, Calif., 1965–72), IX, 63–90, 90–123.

19. Harvey L. Carter, "Robert McClellan," in Hafen, ed., *Mountain Men and the Fur*

Trade, VIII, 224; Oglesby, *Manuel Lisa,* 32–33, 53–54; Porter, *John Jacob Astor,* 181–82, 202–5, 750.

20. Oglesby, *Manuel Lisa,* 51–53, 67–70, 99–100; Nathaniel Pryor to William Clark, Oct. 16, 1807, in Jackson, ed., *Letters of Lewis and Clark,* 432–33.

21. Articles of Agreement, Feb. 24, 1809, and Additional Articles, Sept. 20, 1809, Chouteau Collections.

22. Oglesby, *Manuel Lisa,* 147–48. See also Douglas-Nasatir, *Manuel Lisa,* 139.

23. For examples of the persistent demands of Pierre's creditors see M. Fortier and Son to Pierre Chouteau, May 27, 1805, and May 16, 1807, Cavelier and Son to Auguste Chouteau, Mar. 1, 1809, Nov. 1, 1810, Jan. 25, 1813, Dec. 26, 1813, May 27, 1816, Feb. 15, 1817, and Mar. 20, 1823, Bryan and Schlatter to Pierre Chouteau, Jr., Nov. 12, 1809, Bryan and Schlatter to Pierre Chouteau, Feb. 26 and Aug., 1811, and William Morrison to Pierre Chouteau, Mar. 13 and Oct. 29, 1811, Chouteau Collections.

24. Oglesby, *Manuel Lisa,* 97–98.

25. McDermott, "Auguste Chouteau," 10.

26. Inventory of Auguste Chouteau's estate, May 13, 1829, Chouteau Collections.

27. George Gillespie to Auguste Chouteau, Feb. 1, 1807, and May 18, 1808, Chouteau Collections.

28. Cavelier and Son to Joseph Robidoux, Feb. 20, 1809, and Cavelier and Son to Auguste Chouteau, Mar. 1, 1809, Chouteau Collections.

29. Statement of expenses, Dec. 31, 1809, Chouteau Collections.

30. Manuel Lisa to Pierre Chouteau, Feb. 14, 1810, Chouteau Collections. Also printed in Douglas-Nasatir, *Manuel Lisa,* 140–42.

31. Charles Gratiot to John Jacob Astor, June 14, 1810, Gratiot Letterbook, Missouri Historical Society.

32. Charles Gratiot to John Jacob Astor, Feb. 13, 1813, Gratiot Letterbook; Porter, *John Jacob Astor,* 275.

33. Cerré Panet to Auguste Chouteau, Mar. 12, 1815, Chouteau Collections.

34. William Morrison to Auguste Chouteau, July 7, 1813, Chouteau Collections; Charles Gratiot to John Jacob Astor, May 29, 1814, and Mar. 20, 1815, Gratiot Letterbook.

35. Barnhart, "The Letterbooks of Charles Gratiot," 130–32; Porter, *John Jacob Astor,* 274–78.

36. Charles Gratiot to John Jacob Astor, May 29, 1814, Gratiot Letterbook.

37. Documents relating to Julien Dubuque claims, Sept. 20, 1806, Chouteau Collections; and *American State Papers, Public Lands,* II, 381, and III, 607. See also Thomas Auge, "The Life and Times of Julien Dubuque," *The Palimpsest* 57 (Jan./Feb. 1976), 9–10. For examples of the continuing demand for lead see Cavelier and Son to Auguste Chouteau, Jan. 21, 1805, Mar. 1, 1809, Aug. 30, 1812, and May 12, 1815, Chouteau Collections.

38. Lecompte, "Pierre Chouteau, Jr.," 93–94; Agreement between Auguste Chouteau and Fergus Moorhead, Mar. 20, 1811, Chouteau Collections; Halvor Gordon Melom, "The Economic Growth of St. Louis, 1803–1846" (Ph.D. diss., University of Missouri, 1947), 381.

39. Auguste Chouteau to Baptiste Vallé, Feb. 18 and May 23, 1805, Apr. 20 and June 24, 1806, Aug. 26, 1809, and May 2, 1812, Chouteau Collections. Lead was an important commodity in the economy of the Missouri Territory. A statement in the

Missouri Gazette, Oct. 26, 1811, estimated that the territory would export 2,000,000 pounds of lead that year at a price of $5 per hundredweight. Austin's gloomy assessment the following year can be found in Moses Austin to James Bryan, Oct. 19 and Dec. 4, 1812, in Eugene C. Barker, ed., *The Austin Papers* (Washington, D.C., 1924), II, 218, 220.

40. John B. C. Lucas to Robert Lucas, Oct. 31, 1813, Lucas Collection, Missouri Historical Society; Lease of lead mines to Pierre and Auguste Pierre Chouteau, Sept. 25, 1813, Bates Papers, Missouri Historical Society; Marietta Jennings, *A Pioneer Merchant of St. Louis 1810–1820: The Business Career of Christian Wilt* (New York, 1939), 108. Under U.S. policy the federal government held all mineral lands in reserve, but in 1807 Congress authorized the leasing of mineral lands for terms not to exceed three years. Because of the controversial leasing system, the Chouteaus first had to obtain the federal government's permission before they could operate mines on the lands at Gravois Creek. Their lease called for them to give the U.S. government eight pounds of lead for every hundred pounds produced at the mine.

41. Auguste Chouteau's Report on the Fur Trade, 1815, in *American State Papers, Indian Affairs,* II, 66–67.

42. Ninian Edwards to the Secretary of War, Nov. 1815, in *ibid.,* 66.

43. *Missouri Gazette,* Nov. 23, 1816.

44. For selected examples of Auguste's efforts to settle his accounts see Cavelier and Son to Auguste Chouteau, Jan. 31, 1818, Auguste Chouteau to Baptiste Vallé, Apr. 17, 1818, François Menard to Auguste Chouteau, Feb. 24 and Apr. 4, 1823, Auguste Chouteau to Gabriel Paul, Oct. 12, 1823, J. V. Garnier to Auguste Chouteau, Sept. 1, 1825, Ramsay Crooks to Auguste Chouteau, Mar. 23, 1829, and Auguste Chouteau's personal account book, 1822–27, Chouteau Collections.

45. See, for example, Cavelier and Son to Auguste Chouteau, Feb. 15, 1817, Pierre Chouteau to John P. Cabanné, Oct. 28, 1817, and Cavelier Sr. to Auguste Chouteau, Mar. 20, 1823, Chouteau Collections.

46. *Missouri Gazette,* Sept. 13, 1817.

47. François Menard to Auguste Chouteau, Mar. 22 and June 6, 1820, Chouteau Collections.

48. *Missouri Gazette,* Mar. 8, 1820; David Diggs to Auguste Chouteau, Apr. 3, 1826, Chouteau Collections. The 1810 federal census listed twelve distilleries in operation in the district of St. Louis. See Melom, "Economic Growth of St. Louis," 407.

49. *Missouri Gazette,* May 18, 1816.

50. Auguste Chouteau to Cerré Chouteau, Jan. 8, 1818, and Report of James C. Laveille and James Fremin, Oct. 31, 1820, Chouteau Collections.

51. *Missouri Gazette,* Jan. 5, 1820; for examples of leases see William M. O'Hara & Co., Feb. 3, 1820, and Asa Wheeler, Dec. 1820, Chouteau Collections. In 1822 Ramsay Crooks reported, "Mr. Chouteau wants too much for his house and we may have to use the one where we had the packs but I think it is too small." Ramsay Crooks to Samuel Abbott, Nov. 30, 1822, Chouteau Collections.

52. Notices advertising Chouteau's rental property frequently appeared in the *Missouri Gazette,* and the Chouteau Collections contain numerous leases, rent receipts, and repair bills related to Chouteau's St. Louis properties.

53. The most comprehensive treatment of early Missouri banking can be found in Timothy Hubbard and Lewis E. Davids, *Banking in Mid-America: A History of Missouri's Banks* (Washington, D.C., 1969).

54. Charles Gratiot to John Jacob Astor, June 14, 1810, Gratiot Letterbooks.

55. Original Act to Incorporate the Stockholders to the Bank of St. Louis, Aug. 21, 1813, reprinted in Hubbard and Davids, *Banking in Mid-America*, 192.

56. *Ibid.*, 15–20.

57. Auguste Chouteau to William H. Crawford, Aug. 9, 1819, in *American State Papers, Finance*, III, 749.

58. *Missouri Gazette*, Sept. 14, 1816; Hubbard and Davids, *Banking in Mid-America*, 20–21.

59. Hubbard and Davids, *Banking in Mid-America*, 29–34; William H. Crawford to the Speaker of the House of Representatives, Feb. 15, 1822, in *American State Papers, Finance*, III, 720.

60. Hubbard and Davids, *Banking in Mid-America*, 34.

61. *Ibid.*, 34–39.

62. Directors of the Bank of Missouri to William H. Crawford, Feb. 2, 1821, in *American State Papers, Finance*, III, 752.

63. Louis Bompart to William H. Crawford, Aug. 17, 1821, in *ibid.*

64. Hubbard and Davids, *Banking in Mid-America*, 36–39; Notes of Auguste Chouteau for money due the Bank of Missouri, 1819–21, Chouteau Collections.

65. *Missouri Republican*, Aug. 14, 1822.

66. Timothy Flint, *Recollections of the Last Ten Years . . . in the Valley of the Mississippi* (Boston, 1826), 198–99.

67. The St. Louis Archives contain many land transactions involving Auguste and Pierre during 1803 and 1804. See also Chap. 5 above concerning their early effort to win confirmation for their land titles.

68. Lemont K. Richardson, "Private Land Claims in Missouri," *Missouri Historical Review* 50 (Jan., Apr., July 1956), 132–44, 271–86, 387–99; Foley, *History of Missouri*, 74–75, 83, 95–96, 100–102, 108–12, 140–43, 168–70.

69. For example see Petitions to Congress dated Feb. 1, 1806, Feb. 13, 1807, Jan. 2 and Dec. 18, 1808, and June 20, 1809, in Carter, ed., *Territorial Papers*, XIII, 425–29, and XIV, 98–99, 161–63, 245–46, 279–80.

70. John Edgar to Auguste Chouteau, Nov. 1, 1807, and Agreement between Auguste Chouteau and L. E. Lawless and G. F. Strother, May 24, 1826, Chouteau Collections.

71. William H. Harrison to Auguste Chouteau, Jan. 4, 1806, Lucas Collection.

72. Richardson, "Private Land Claims," 393–94.

73. Richard M. Clokey, *William H. Ashley: Enterprise and Politics in the Trans-Mississippi West* (Norman, Okla., 1980), 37–38.

74. *Ibid.*, 37–38, 247–48, 270–72.

75. *American State Papers, Public Lands*, V, 727, 728, 737, 828, 833–34.

76. *Chouteau et al.* vs. *United States* and *The Devisees of Auguste Chouteau* vs. *United States*, Feb. 21, 1835, reprinted in *American State Papers, Public Lands*, VII, 730–31. Marshall's favorable rulings are not particularly surprising in view of his own extensive involvement in land acquisition and speculation. See Irvin S. Rhodes, *The Papers of John Marshall: A Descriptive Calendar* (Norman, Okla., 1969), I, vii–viii.

77. Clokey, *William H. Ashley*, 248.

78. *Pierre Chouteau* vs. *William Eckert* (1841) and *Pierre Chouteau* vs. *William Christy* (1829), Early Missouri Supreme Court Records, Missouri State Archives, Jefferson City.

Chapter 10

FIRST CITIZENS OF ST. LOUIS

THE WORLD counted Auguste and Pierre Chouteau among the elite group of frontier patricians whose wealth and influence exceeded that of ordinary citizens. Persons of both high and low estate who had occasion to call upon them in their stately St. Louis mansions esteemed them as perfect hosts epitomizing Old World charm and New World hospitality. But those who took time to look beyond the outward symbols of success and charm also perceived that the lines of care etched in Auguste's rounded countenance and in Pierre's angular profile were witness to decades of hard work and anxiety. For along with their many triumphs and achievements, both men suffered the innumerable petty irritations that beset all persons, tasted the bitterness of defeat, and experienced the lasting pain of personal loss. Each understood that life is effort, a lesson they tried to pass on to their children. Although not all of their offspring grasped this vital truth, the large figure that the second-generation Chouteaus cut in the world suggests that most of them did.

Like others hewing out a life on the wilderness frontier, the Chouteaus were family men. Auguste and Pierre maintained lifelong close personal ties with one another, but the lines also extended in other directions to sons, daughters, grandchildren, nieces, nephews, and numerous relatives by marriage. None was more vital than the bond to their mother, Madame Marie Thérèse Bourgeois Chouteau. Long after her death in 1814, the brothers mourned her passing.[1] As they drew strength from that remarkable woman, they took pride in the nearly 100 grandchildren and great-grandchildren she left behind.[2] But like parents everywhere, the elder Chouteaus also suffered when one of their children proved profligate and disrespectful.

As men of property the Chouteaus had to endure major catastrophes like the fire that destroyed Pierre's home in 1805 and the conflagration that threatened Auguste's residence in 1818. Fortunately a band of helpful neighbors extinguished the latter blaze before its flames could consume the mementos of a lifetime.[3] Such tragedies were rare, but the minor annoyances common to most frontier landowners, including timber thefts, poaching, and trespassing, were more frequent. Disagreeable as those incidents might have been, the Chouteaus usually found it possible to remedy them informally with newspaper notices and increased surveillance.[4] But some of the conflicts arising in the

Chouteaus' careers were not so easily handled. Many times they felt constrained to resort to the courts of law to resolve thorny disputes. So frequently did Auguste and Pierre traffic in the courts as plaintiffs, defendants, and executors of estates that it seems surprising they found time for their demanding activities in commerce and public affairs.[5]

Important as their private interests were, however, the Chouteau brothers never ignored their public responsibilities. As the fathers of their city and as honored citizens of their territory, the two patriarchs continued to devote portions of their energies and their fortunes to the advancement of St. Louis and Missouri. Although Americans quickly outnumbered the older French inhabitants, the Chouteaus persisted in their efforts to maintain influence within their community.

The record of the first Chouteaus' personal lives is limited. Their papers provide only brief glimpses of the men behind the public images, but it is clear that both were devoted family men who sought to provide their children with the best possible educational opportunities. In 1800, while making arrangements to send his eldest son to Canada for schooling, Auguste summed up his feelings in a letter to his brother-in-law Pierre Louis Panet:

> The education of my children is the most important thing for a good father, since it concerns their happiness or unhappiness, and finding myself living in a country where it is impossible to get a good one for mine, I finally decided to separate myself from mine, and its particular purpose was stronger than paternal love. So, although reluctantly, I am separating. I must send him away from me, from a country where he can never conform himself to the usage of the world and good society and acquire such talents as would distinguish him in the world or at least make him the equal of all that is called good society.[6]

In 1802 Auguste Aristide Chouteau arrived in Montreal, where Panet, a prominent public official, arranged for his studies. The Canadian metropolis was a far different place from St. Louis, and the adjustment proved difficult for the nine-year-old lad. The boy's letter asking his father to send a bow and quiver of arrows, so that he could exercise, along with his deer antlers and moccasins ornamented with porcupine quills, showed the strong influence of Indian culture in his native village and perhaps suggested why the elder Chouteau thought it necessary to send his firstborn son so far from home to secure a proper education.[7]

Panet's first reports about the youngster's progress were encouraging, but as time elapsed the story soon changed, as Auguste ran away from school and roamed the streets. He once stole a pair of skates from a fellow student, and at least two schools expelled him because of his unruly conduct. In typical parental fashion, Auguste Sr. sought to place some of the blame on his son's teachers, but Panet cautioned him that the schoolmaster did not deserve to be reproached for the boy's misbehavior.[8]

The beleaguered Panets made every effort to help their wayward nephew. They took him into their own home, but the situation did not improve. After four years of working with young Auguste, Panet advised the boy's father that the youth would have to be sent back to St. Louis, since none of the good schools would any longer accept him. On the positive side, Panet observed that the boy was beginning to express himself rather well in English, but he hastened to add, "As for writing, as well as for French, you will find him very ignorant, due to his lack of application and absolutely determined distaste for study."[9] Panet's assessment is borne out by the unusually poor spelling in the few letters that Auguste Aristide wrote in later years. When he signed his marriage contract in 1810, he misspelled his own last name,[10] although perhaps that was simply a case of wedding-day jitters.

Through the years, Auguste's eldest boy frequently sought his father's assistance. In 1816 he informed his father that he was about to lose his horse because of an unpaid debt. In seeking his parents' help, the now-grown son asked them to forget all the bad things he had done.[11] But only a few months before Auguste Sr. died, Auguste Aristide was again seeking his father's advice concerning his "unfortunate situation."[12] The elder Chouteau's thoughts about his first son have not been preserved, but he apparently always stood ready to come to his assistance. The inventory of Auguste Sr.'s estate revealed that Auguste Aristide owed his father $7,015.[13]

Fortunately, Auguste Sr.'s other surviving children did rather well in their maturity. Gabriel Sylvestre, known to the family as Cerré, served in the War of 1812 and after that ascended the Missouri River to become a fur trader. In later years he returned to St. Louis to manage the Chouteau water mill.[14] Marie Thérèse Eulalie married Paris-educated René Paul. An officer in Napoleon's army, Paul was wounded while on board the French flagship at the battle of Trafalgar. After coming to St. Louis, Paul formed a business partnership with Bartholomew Berthold, and for many years served as surveyor in St. Louis.[15] Marie Louise married René Paul's brother Gabriel,[16] while Emilie Antoinette, called by one memoirist "a lady of much beauty and many accomplishments," wed U.S. Army Captain Thomas F. Smith, after abandoning her plans to become a nun.[17] Little is known of Edward, who apparently spent most of his life in St. Louis, but Henry Pierre, a St. Louis businessman who served for many years as county clerk and recorder, died tragically in a railroad accident when a bridge spanning the Gasconade River collapsed.[18]

There were, of course, many happy times for Auguste, who particularly relished private moments with his family. In 1791, for example, he informed a friend that the merry bustle of Christmas festivities had prevented him from answering his letter sooner.[19] Because most of the children remained in St. Louis, Auguste seldom had any reason to write them. Yet when young Cerré spent several years trading on the upper Missouri, his parents eagerly awaited any news from him. Auguste's letters to the young man combined parental affection with an occasional word of fatherly advice.[20]

Auguste Aristide's unhappy experience in Canada did not deter the senior Chouteau from seeking to provide his other children with the best available educational opportunities. He sent his second son Gabriel Sylvestre to the Catholic college at Bardstown, Kentucky. His daughter Emilie attended the Catholic girls' school which Mother Philippine Duchesne operated at nearby Florissant, while Henry and Edward enrolled at the St. Louis Academy opened by Father Francis Niel in 1818.[21] And since Chouteau wanted his children to be broadly educated and cultured individuals, he arranged for them to take piano and art lessons along with their regular studies.[22] Such a practice was unusual, because providing educational opportunities in frontier Missouri was a costly matter, quite beyond the reach of most St. Louis families. An account dated September 1821, for instance, indicates that Chouteau paid Father Niel $184.19 for tuition, board, books, and supplies.[23]

Like his brother, Pierre Chouteau sired a considerable family, and he was equally concerned with their education and general well-being. Pierre used his influence to win appointments to the U.S. Military Academy for his eldest son, Auguste Pierre, and for his nephew Charles Gratiot. Both men graduated from West Point in 1806, but the following year Auguste Pierre resigned from the service to enter the fur trade. Through the years he took part in numerous ventures, but the financial successes that came so easily to others in his illustrious family somehow eluded him. Although he may have lacked the Chouteau talent for making money, he did share his father's congenial personality and his affinity for the red man's culture, and those talents made him one of the best known and best loved, if not successful, Indian traders. In fact, he virtually abandoned St. Louis and passed most of his later years living and working with his Indian friends in present-day Oklahoma, where he died deeply in debt.[24]

By contrast, Pierre and Pelagie Chouteau's second son, Pierre Jr., became a very wealthy man and a prototype of the successful merchant-capitalist. Long active in the fur trade, Cadet formed a partnership with his brother-in-law, Bartholomew Berthold, and later secured control of John Jacob Astor's powerful American Fur Company. Eventually he branched out into other enterprises and acquired substantial holdings in railroads, iron, and real estate. Pierre Jr. spent most of his final years in New York and was a multimillionaire at the time of his death.[25]

Paul Liguest followed in his father's steps as an Indian trader and eventually became, as his father before him, U.S. agent to the Osage tribes. Pierre's only daughter, Pelagie, married Bartholomew Berthold, Pierre Jr.'s business partner.[26]

Pierre Sr. and his second wife, Brigitte, had five sons: François Gesseau,

Cyprien, Pharamond, Charles, and Frederick. Like his older half-brothers, François entered the fur trade. In 1821 he opened a trading post along the banks of the Missouri River on the site of present-day Kansas City, and thus became one of the founders of Missouri's second great city. Cyprien was also a fur trader and spent many years among the Indians. Little can be said of Pharamond, but he worked for several years at the trading post of his youngest brother, Frederick. Charles also entered the fur business and managed Frederick's store after Frederick had branched off from his early association with his elder brothers François and Cyprien.[27]

Like his brother, Pierre often acted to boost his childrens' chances in the world. Prior to Auguste Pierre's graduation from West Point, for example, Pierre tried to secure the young man a choice appointment by writing to Secretary of War Henry Dearborn and saying: "The interest which you then evinced for him is so precious to me and I regard it as so necessary to his advancement and his happiness and I beg you urgently to please maintain it."[28] Moreover, he saw to it that at least two of his other sons attended the St. Louis Academy.[29]

Pierre's fondness for his children continued throughout his life and was lavishly extended to them long after they had passed childhood. When business matters took Pierre Jr. and his wife, Emilie, to Philadelphia and New York in 1824, they left their young children under the care of Pierre Sr. and Brigitte. In a letter, the proud grandfather informed his son and daughter-in-law that their children rushed to have him kiss them and that young Charles, who was just beginning to talk, happily announced, "Good day grand papa," every time he encountered the elder Chouteau.[30] The patriarch's attachment to his family was equally evident at the time of Brigitte's death. Having learned of the sad event, Auguste Pierre wrote to his brother Pierre Jr. in St. Louis: ". . . as you say it is one of those blows from which Papa can hardly recover . . . it is up to you and Pelagie who are there to give him every care."[31]

Despite its size, the entire Chouteau clan was a close-knit family with strong social ties and business connections among not only brothers and sisters, but cousins, nieces, and nephews as well. Marriages further cemented the close bonds among Madame Chouteau's numerous descendants. Chouteaus, Labbadies, Gratiots, Papins, Prattes, Menards, Cerrés, Sarpys, Bertholds, Cabannés, and De Muns, among others, were linked by kinship as well as by commerce. Until her death in 1814, Marie Thérèse Chouteau, the grand matriarch, observed with pride the manifold accomplishments of her large and growing progeny, whom a later writer aptly labeled the "Royal Family of the Wilderness."[32]

The affairs of the expanding clan, as well as the far-flung business operations of the Chouteaus, occasioned, as previously indicated, a vast array of litigation. Auguste and Pierre directed many of their legal efforts toward the settlement of estates for relatives, friends, and business associates.[33] Probate cases frequently became so entangled that years passed before final judgments could be handed down. As executors, the Chouteau brothers found themselves repeatedly summoned to give testimony, to supervise land sales at auctions, and, as in the case of the estate of St. Paul Lacroix, even to petition for the arrest and confinement of debtors seeking to avoid payments due to the estate.[34] The case of Auguste Chouteau and Bernard Pratte, executors of the Sylvestre Labbadie estate, *versus* François LeSieur, the surviving partner of Joseph LeSieur and Company, dragged on interminably. Chouteau and Pratte filed the suit in 1807 in an attempt to recover $4,000 in damages. Yet despite numerous hearings and the collection of many depositions, as well as the generation of much ill will, it apparently remained unresolved as late as 1813, when the records break off.[35]

Besides their labors on behalf of the estates of a wide circle of associates, the Chouteaus came to court as plaintiffs or defendants in civil suits. As merchants with a variety of commercial interests, they regularly encountered difficulties in collecting debts, determining ownership of land and merchandise, and settling contractual disputes. Although the records contain a host of examples of the civil suits which involved the Chouteaus, none compares in interest with an unusual case brought against Pierre by a group of his slaves.

Claiming that as descendants of an Indian woman, Marie Scypion, they had been illegally enslaved, several of Pierre's slaves sued for their freedom. Despite Pierre's heated denials that the black slaves were part Indian, a Jefferson County jury ruled in their favor and ordered six of them freed in a case tried in Herculaneum on November 8, 1836. Pierre attempted to overturn the verdict on appeal, but the next year the Missouri Supreme Court upheld the lower court's decision.[36]

This remarkable struggle against one of the state's most powerful families had begun thirty years earlier, when the petitioners first attempted to press their cause in the territorial courts. Using court-appointed attorneys, they pursued their fight for freedom through the courts against seemingly insurmountable odds. Along the way they endured beatings at the hands of their unsympathetic master, endless delays in the courts, and numerous unfavorable rulings, which had to be set aside through a lengthy and complicated appeals process. Through it all they persevered with a dogged determination that in the end brought them victory. Although they failed to secure the monetary damages they had sought, their triumph was no less sweet. Perhaps the most surprising aspect of the entire episode was that Missouri's judicial system accorded them as much legal protection as it did. Pierre fought their efforts at every step, and when the courts finally forced him to give up these slaves, he was an old man who undoubtedly viewed the outcome as yet another sign of the changing times.[37]

As slaveowners, the Chouteaus held conventional views and counted slaves as an important part of their personal wealth. Slaves accounted for nearly one-third of St. Louis's total population in the days of the first Chouteaus, and it would have been extraordinary had the city's most distinguished family not owned some. Madame Chouteau, for instance, provided for the emancipation of one of her Indian slaves in her will, but ten blacks and mulattoes were sold at auction following her death.[38] Similarly, Auguste and Pierre owned slaves in proportion to their wealth, and no doubt used them for a variety of tasks.[39] It is quite likely that the slaves labored in the Chouteau milling and distillery operations, and on occasion the family probably farmed some of them out to other entrepreneurs for a fee.[40]

Pierre's claims that an irate female slave set fire to his house in 1805, Auguste's problems with a frequent runaway named Charles, and the celebrated case involving Marie Scypion's descendants all suggest that friction between master and slave was seldom far below the surface in the Chouteau households.[41] Although their treatment of slaves was no worse than most, they stood for the indefinite maintenance of the peculiar institution in Missouri and sided with the political forces sharing that view.[42] As city officials, Auguste and Pierre unfailingly supported stringent black codes to govern the activities of black bondsmen and bondswomen, but Auguste did, for reasons unknown, free at least one of his slaves.[43]

Slavery increasingly dominated political conversations in Missouri after the War of 1812. Although it did not emerge as the predominant political issue until the debate over Missouri's admission to the Union, slaveowners had been uneasy since 1804, when the territory had been placed under the administration of officials from the Indiana Territory, a region in which the Northwest Ordinance of 1787 prohibited slavery.

As much as the future of slavery concerned the Chouteaus and their associates, they worried even more about the consequences of the flood of new American settlers pouring into their territory following the war. In 1814 the territorial populace numbered only 25,000, but six years later it exceeded 65,000.[44] These dramatic figures highlighted the changing demographic character of post-war Missouri as Americans steadily increased their numerical superiority over the once-dominant French population. Realizing that the American electoral system would likely favor the champions of the ambitious and land-hungry newcomers at their expense, old-guard politicians like the Chouteaus struggled to prevent full implementation of democratic government in their territory even though the tide of history and immigration was against them. Consequently, their political activities in the post-war era did not change so much in character as in direction. They continued their familiar policy of attempting to influence important political leaders in a direct and personal way. But from the war years on, and especially after 1815, they found themselves more and more on the defensive as they tried to hold on to contested Spanish land claims, complained about government control of lead and saline lands, inveighed against government trading factories, and disputed the timeliness, if not the propriety, of democratic and representative government in the territory.

Defense remained a premier issue in territorial politics during the troubled years of frontier conflict. A succession of governors from James Wilkinson to Benjamin Howard had failed to create confidence in the national government's understanding of Upper Louisiana's problems or in its ability to defend the region's inhabitants. As a result, after 1808 pressure intensified to change the territory's status from first-class to second-class. Most territorial residents assumed that since the second-class status would give them a representative in Congress and would move them closer to actual statehood, federal authorities in Washington would pay closer attention to their problems following the shift.[45]

Although the Chouteaus favored improved defenses, they resisted the call for a change in territorial administration. They were comfortable with the 1805 arrangements placing Upper Louisiana under the control of a governor, a secretary, and three judges, all appointed by the president. Since second-class status would bring a popularly elected territorial house of representatives and would separate legislative and judicial authority at the local level, Auguste and Pierre recognized that inescapably the change in governmental forms would reduce their leverage in political decisions and favor the influence of the multiplying ranks of newcomers. Opponents of the move to second-class status argued that a popular assembly would be costly, would add to the tax burden, especially of property owners, and would increase the territorial governor's powers, but the deteriorating circumstances on the frontier in the last years before the war with Great Britain generated strong local sentiment for the proposed change.[46]

A bill, put before Congress in January 1810,[47] failed to pass in that session, but its backers indicated that they intended to renew their efforts at the next session. Moving in 1811 to mobilize forces in opposition to the proposed change, the Chouteaus joined some of St. Louis's leading citizens in petitioning Congress to retain the existing system, claiming that the territory's population was too diverse in character to make an elective assembly feasible.[48] Arguments that the advance in status would create turmoil and disorder might have seemed plausible to the St. Louis magnates, but they had little appeal for members of a popularly elected Congress representing citizens from many diverse states. In any case, with the hazards of war looming, Congress approved the creation of the Missouri Territory as a second-class territory in June 1812. Full statehood seemed only a short step away.[49]

Dismayed as they were by the drift of political matters, the Chouteau brothers did not abandon the field to their opponents. Adjustable as always, they maneuvered to hold office under the changing American governments in the territory.[50] As has already been demonstrated, both Auguste and Pierre served in important posts in Indian affairs and frontier defense. They also participated in the political struggles and won for themselves a variety of offices in both the territorial and city administrations. As early as 1804, Governor Harrison had appointed Auguste a judge of the court of common pleas for the St. Louis district and a justice of the peace as well.[51] Auguste lacked formal legal training, but given the nature of frontier litigation, it seems unlikely that anyone was more qualified to render fair and equitable decisions than someone of Auguste's character and experience. Contemporaries must have thought so, because Auguste secured reappointment to the court after the reorganization of the territory in 1805 and retained his seat until 1813.[52] Besides swearing in various local officials and presiding over the trial of many ordinary civil and petty criminal disputes, Chouteau occasionally heard cases involving influential persons in the territory.[53] For example, in 1808 Auguste served as associate justice in the case of George Drouillard, who was accused of killing a deserter from a trading party led by Manuel Lisa up the Missouri River.[54] Lisa had sent out Drouillard, a veteran of the Lewis and Clark expedition, with orders to bring back the deserter, Antoine Bissonette, dead or alive. In attempting to secure Bissonette's return, Drouillard inflicted a wound which subsequently caused his death. When the party came back to St. Louis, local authorities charged Drouillard with murder. After hearing the case, the jury recessed for fifteen minutes and returned with a not-guilty verdict. It is not clear whether Chouteau had any direct effect on the jury's decision, but it is certain that the trading community at large applauded the outcome as an underpropping for discipline and order on the wilderness expeditions.[55]

In 1813 Auguste stepped down from the court of common pleas even though his fellow justice Silas Bent, father of famed fur traders and businessmen Charles, William, George, and Robert, implored him to stay on to combat the influence of political rivals in the judicial system. In an attempt to persuade Chouteau to reconsider his decision to leave the court, Bent took note of the territory's changing political climate. "Your loss," he warned, "will be severely felt by the french people, for I am convinced that those americans who declare the most inveterate hatred to the french and manifest a disposition to govern law . . . will likely be appointed to office."[56] Actually Auguste removed himself from further consideration for the bench in order to accept a position that he hoped would offer him more leverage in public affairs. On March 13 the *Missouri Gazette* reported that President Madison had appointed Chouteau one of the members of the territorial Legislative Council as provided under the law which made Missouri a second-class territory. The Legislative Council served as an upper house to the popularly elected territorial Assembly, and Auguste's French constituents expected his membership in that body would put him in an even better position to protect their interests. Significantly, however, Chouteau was the only old French inhabitant to be named to the council, which not only limited his effectiveness as a legislator but demonstrated once more the ebbing of French influence. The point was not lost on Bent, who cautioned his French-speaking friend that he would be at a serious disadvantage in his new post on the council because "no interpreter can keep pace with the debates . . . and nothing but eloquence can sound against a majority in a popular assembly."[57]

Meanwhile, Pierre performed his duties as Indian agent and served one term as justice of the peace.[58] Both he and Auguste accepted municipal posts during these years despite their heavy schedule of federal and territorial obligations. In 1808, at a time when Pierre was at a low point in his relations with officials in Washington and when his duties as Indian agent had been considerably decreased, he stood for election to the Board of Trustees of the city of St. Louis along with Auguste. Both he and his brother succeeded at the polls, and the new board elected Auguste to be its first chairman.[59] In subsequent years the Chouteaus won reelection as trustees. In fact they served on six of the twelve boards chosen between 1810 and 1822.[60]

As officials of a growing and thriving town, the Chouteau brothers had to devote considerable time and attention to a variety of urban problems. They solved some in their typical direct way. For example, on the elementary issue of where to hold elections in St. Louis, the answer seemed obvious—at Auguste's house.[61] After all, everyone knew the location well, and the Chouteau mansions had served for years as unofficial community centers. Other problems could not be so conveniently resolved, however. Positions such as city collector had to be filled, fire-fighting brigades had to be organized, roads and bridges had to be maintained, and, since nineteenth-century frontier cities had distinctive problems, the trustees also had to deal with such matters as horses running in the streets, slave patrols, and gunpowder storage.[62] And as in all governments, the trustees also had to concern themselves with financial matters. Levying taxes is never a popular undertaking, and it is quite likely that the citizens of St. Louis roundly criticized Auguste and his fellow trustees for the municipal taxes they adopted in 1810.[63] Auguste's orders, as chairman of the board, for the city collector to seize the goods of some citizens who had failed to pay their taxes undoubtedly occasioned even greater unhappiness, but at the same time the town's residents must have been pleased to discover that the city treasury had a balance of over $130 when Auguste finished his term as chairman in 1811.[64]

Actually, the Chouteau brothers remained quite popular as city officials for many years, among at least some segments of St. Louis society. The voters reelected Pierre to the Board of Trustees in 1811, in 1820, and again in 1824.[65] During his stint on the board of 1820–21 he served as chairman, and like

Auguste before him, he left office with a healthy treasury balance.[66] By the time of statehood, town government in St. Louis had become increasingly complex. Pierre's accounts for the city showed collections for taxes on billiard tables, fines for transgressions of Sunday ordinances, and interest payments.[67] In the space of a lifetime the river city had advanced from a clearing in the wilderness to a surging city experiencing the complications and advantages of urban development.

Although able to win elections to the St. Louis Board of Trustees, both Auguste and Pierre failed in their bids to become mayor.[68] Running in 1823 and 1826 respectively, the patriarchs could not secure a majority in a city which had swollen to over 5,000 inhabitants, most of whom were Americans with little in common with the Chouteaus and their supporters. When the rapidly developing territory advanced to third-class status in 1816, even members of the Legislative Council had to be popularly elected. These changes forced the Chouteaus and their allies, commonly known as the "St. Louis junto," to resort to undisguised electioneering in order to contest the rising power of Missouri's new men.

Perhaps they were novices in the rough game of popular politics, but with decades of experience in the business of political infighting and in the critical enterprise of reading human nature, the Chouteaus proved to be effective contestants, even in the politics of retreat. In the disputed 1817 election, the junto succeeded in electing John Scott as the territory's delegate to Congress.[69] With Scott defending their interests in Washington, especially in the all-important matter of the Spanish land grants, and with their close ally William Clark in the territorial governor's chair, the pro-French forces managed to hold their own politically until Missouri became a state.

The Chouteaus maintained a fairly low profile during the great debate over Missouri's admission to the Union. Naturally they sided with the pro-slavery forces, and the people of St. Louis County did elect Pierre Jr. to the 1820 constitutional convention on a platform advocating the permanency of slavery in the state.[70] By then the family had become reconciled to statehood, and when word reached St. Louis that Congress had approved the Missouri Enabling Act on March 6, 1820, Pierre, as chairman of the Board of Trustees, ordered the city illuminated on March 30 as a sign of celebration.[71]

The returns from the new state's first gubernatorial election quickly tempered the Chouteau exuberance as the little junto's candidate, William Clark, suffered a defeat at the hands of Alexander McNair, who had deserted their ranks to join the opposition.[72] Following that setback the Chouteaus and their associates intensified their campaign to elect Thomas Hart Benton to the U.S. Senate. With David Barton seemingly assured of taking one of the seats, they focused their attention on the contest for the other senatorial seat. In that race Benton, a friend of the Chouteaus, faced opposition from several candidates, including John B. C. Lucas, a bitter enemy of the St. Louis clique. Since members of the state legislature chose the U.S. senators and since the outcome in the second contest remained uncertain, the little junto brought enormous pressure to bear on Marie Philippe Le Duc, who would cast a critical vote in the close election. It seems doubtful that Le Duc needed much convincing, but the Chouteaus and their allies took no less pleasure in Benton's election.[73] Although the voters of St. Louis County elected Pierre Sr. to the Missouri Senate in 1821, Benton's election represented the old guard's last great political victory, and even Benton soon parted company with them to join the surging popular forces.[74]

Missouri's changing political climate mirrored a broader national trend toward greater democracy that threatened to render the attitudes of people like the Chouteaus extinct. It was not surprising that members of the Chouteau family became staunch Whig supporters during the 1820s at the moment when Jacksonian democracy was in the ascendency. In 1824 they supported Henry Clay for the presidency, and despite his failure to gain the office, they invited the famous compromiser to visit their city in 1827.[75] Clay did not come, but the old clique remained steadfast in its advocacy of John Quincy Adams's administration. Auguste presided over a rally of the Friends of the Administration in November 1827 which received favorable comment from the *Missouri Republican,* but it was a sign of the times that the newspaper referred to Auguste as the "venerable . . . founder of our city."[76] As even their friends were beginning to suspect, the political impact of the city's founding fathers was becoming a thing of the past.

If the Chouteau political clout was retreating into history, the same cannot be said for their warrants in the commercial and social worlds. In almost every sphere of economic activity and public service, the Chouteau name continued to loom large in the affairs of St. Louis and the trans-Mississippi West. Because of Auguste's prominence in the St. Louis banking community, Secretary of War John C. Calhoun named him to the fairly thankless and unexalted post as U.S. pension agent for Missouri in 1818.[77] The task of disbursing pensions to veterans of the Revolution occasioned a great volume of correspondence and required the issuance of frequent reports, but the aging Chouteau held on until his declining health forced him to resign the position in 1821.[78] In other areas of civic responsibility, Auguste and Pierre could be relied upon to rally to the community's call for assistance even though both men retained many contending obligations. In 1817, to cite a case in point, Auguste agreed to serve on the first board of trustees of the St. Louis public schools, and the same year he supervised a public lottery designed to raise money to furnish the city with fire engines and other appropriate equipment.[79] In 1819 Pierre managed the cotillion parties for the city, and Auguste donated $11 to help pay for a public banquet.[80] On other occasions Auguste conducted an investigation into the condition of the city's streets and alleys, lobbied for the construction of an almshouse for the town's poor, and with John B. C. Lucas donated a tract of land for a new county courthouse and jail.[81]

Auguste also found time to participate in local agricultural and historical societies.[82] His active involvement in the affairs of the region from its earliest days made him an acknowledged authority and a valuable source of information on topics ranging from geography and history to Indians and land policy. When Theodore Hunt, the recorder of land titles for Missouri, attempted to compile a record of the ownership of land in St. Louis and its vicinity, he repeatedly turned to the elder Chouteau for testimony. Auguste appeared before the recorder on numerous occasions in 1825, and his sworn depositions, along with those of his brother, preserved in *Hunt's Minutes,* provide a synopsis not only of property transfers but of selected episodes in the city's early history. Likewise, Auguste's notes on the tribal boundaries of the western Indians constitute an important documentary source for that topic.[83]

It was fitting that the two men who had done so much to foster the development of St. Louis frequently presided over important public events and in so doing lent their prestige to the proceedings. Typical of such occasions was the commemoration of American independence celebrated in "Chouteau's Town" in 1810. At 3:00 P.M. on July 5, a large crowd assembled in Didier's Orchard and partook of a "sumptuous dinner." Auguste presided over the festivities, which featured a full-length portrait of General Washington along with a living eagle that periodically spread its wings to their full six-foot extent. After numerous toasts to various patriotic events and personalities, everyone joined in a rousing rendition of "Yankee Doodle."[84]

Any important visitor to St. Louis wanted, of course, to make the famous Chouteaus' acquaintance. A good example was Paul Wilhelm, Duke of Württemberg, who came to America in 1823. Paying a visit to Auguste's farm in Florissant, the duke found Chouteau to be a "kind host" and "a vivacious old man of seventy-three." Württemberg's only regret was that Chouteau had never published an account of his many adventures with the Indians. Auguste's recollections equally impressed the Duke of Saxe-Weimar-Eisenach, who called on him in 1826.[85]

But no visitor to early St. Louis provoked more excitement than the renowned Marquis de Lafayette, who came there in May of 1825. Currently between revolutions in France, Lafayette toured many cities in the United States in 1824–25. The eager citizens of St. Louis began preparing for his arrival as early as September 1824, when town leaders selected Auguste and Pierre to serve on a committee organized to make arrangements for the marquis's sojourn in the city.[86] By the time Lafayette arrived on board the *Natchez* in May, the people of St. Louis stood ready to give him a memorable reception.[87] Amid resounding cheers he stepped ashore, and Mayor Stephen Hempstead welcomed him to the city. After a short reply, the "Hero of Two Worlds" climbed into a carriage with Hempstead, Auguste Chouteau, and, for symbolic reasons, a now-unknown veteran of the American Revolution. Captain Archibald Gamble's horse troop escorted the carriage, pulled by four white horses, through the streets. The mounted unit formed a square on Main Street facing Colonel Chouteau's house, and, after it took its position near the carriage, a large crowd of citizens followed on foot. The carriage conveyed the party to Pierre's home, where arrangements had been made for the marquis to stay while in St. Louis. The city fathers hosted a reception for Lafayette there, and later in the evening they gave a "splendid ball."[88] Pierre eventually received $150 for the use of his house during the celebrated visit, and the committee received slightly more than $65 for wines and other expenses.[89] Even though the city council's decision to pay these expenses out of the public treasury provoked some critical comments, St. Louisans long remembered Lafayette's visit to their city, which appropriately the Chouteau brothers had helped make a success.[90]

Despite the dubious status of the union of Madame Chouteau and Laclède, the Chouteau family also contributed substantially to the establishment and well-being of the Roman Catholic Church in St. Louis. There is no evidence to suggest that the patriarchs were anything more than conventionally pious Catholics, but they took their obligations to the church as seriously as they did other civic responsibilities. Following the example of Laclède, who had assisted with efforts to erect a new church building for St. Louis in 1776, the Chouteaus remained members in good standing in the local parish. In 1792 Auguste was in the vanguard of a movement to secure Father Joseph Didier's appointment as the local priest and to supervise long-overdue repairs on the city's rapidly deteriorating original house of worship. When the Louisiana Purchase ended all forms of governmental aid, the Chouteaus renewed their efforts to secure qualified clergymen for the parish and to maintain adequate facilities for worship. While serving as first church warden in 1811, Pierre assumed responsibility for obtaining the services of an ordained priest. He finally arranged for Father Javine, the *curé* at Cahokia, to celebrate the sacraments in St. Louis at least once during Advent season.[91] In the boom times following the War of 1812, the availability of clergy was a less serious problem than the poor condition of the city's church building. Parishioners in a frontier city not known for its exceptional piety occasionally flagged in their zeal for keeping up the church, especially in the absence of a resident priest. Therefore, when Bishop William Louis DuBourg came to St. Louis in 1818, he lamented that his cathedral resembled a stable.[92] With his heart set upon building a brick church to replace the old structure, DuBourg launched a subscription drive to raise the funds. He collected over $4,000 in the campaign, in which the Chouteaus exhibited their usual generosity, at least when it came to community improvements, by contributing $650 among them.[93] When DuBourg called for a second subscription a short time later, the family undoubtedly responded with another contribution. The new building, constructed on the corner of Market and Second streets, opened for services on Christmas Day 1819 even though it remained unfinished.

The construction costs for the St. Louis cathedral exceeded expectations, however, and the various subscriptions failed to offset those expenses. So as members of the building committee, Auguste, Pierre, and their fellow merchant and family business associate Bernard Pratte agreed to assume personal responsibility for retiring the 4,500-dollar debt on the structure. The hard times following the Panic of 1819 placed the committee in an embarrassing position, though, when it appeared that the three men might have to pay the church's debt out of their own funds. In fact, in July of 1820 Auguste had to pay the commissioners $2,000 from his personal account.[94] The bishop of Louisiana regretted this development, but informed the commissioners that further collections from the diocese were out of the question for the time being.[95] Facing ruinous demands on their credit, the Chouteaus and their fellow commissioners finally sought reimbursement by appealing to the state legislature to pass an act requiring the sale of church property in St. Louis excluding the cathedral and cemetery lots.[96] The Missouri General Assembly obliged late in 1822, and by the following June the commissioners pressed the local priest, Father Francis Niel, who was also president of the St. Louis Academy, to comply with the new law. Niel questioned the constitutionality of the legislature's actions, but reluctantly agreed to offer the property for sale, with the intention of buying it himself and then turning it over to the commissioners.[97] In September Niel purchased the property at auction, and the following May he relinquished the land to the commissioners except for the plot on which the academy stood.[98] After holding the property for several years, the Chouteaus and Pratte sold it back to the diocese in 1828 for a little over $4,700.[99] The entire business evoked considerable controversy, but the fairest judgment in the matter came from Bishop Joseph Rosati, who wrote to the commissioners expressing his thanks for their troubles on behalf of the Church of St. Louis.[100] As Bishop Rosati noted, the men had sacrificed a great deal in seeing the project through and "should not be the victims of their devotion to the public good."[101]

Over the decades the Chouteau brothers had done many things to contribute to the public good. Undeniably they served their private interests, but they also maintained a sense of commitment to the public welfare throughout their long and useful lives. If their attitudes were patrician, and if they acted from a sense of *noblesse oblige,* that does not negate the value of their service to the community. In that regard, they were certainly the first citizens of St. Louis.

The infirmity which Auguste had acknowledged to Secretary of War Calhoun in 1821 finally brought the old trader's service to a close. He died on

February 24, 1829, at the age of eighty.[102] At the time of his brother's death Pierre was already a man of seventy-one, and there is little evidence available to fill in the two decades he survived Auguste. It does seem clear that he withdrew completely from active commercial pursuits and performed only ceremonial duties in public affairs. In all likelihood he devoted himself during his closing years to the family he held so dear. His death came on July 9, 1849, at the age of 91.[103]

Both brothers left considerable fortunes when they passed away, in real property if not in cash. Auguste's personal property was valued in excess of $100,000, and that did not include his substantial real estate holdings. Those assets included $82,000 in promissory notes, accounts, and mortgages, many of which admittedly were uncollectible, but only $32.12 in cash.[104] Auguste's landed property, on the other hand, totaled a little over 60,000 arpents, with another 10,000 arpents in unconfirmed titles. Along with his fine library of over 600 volumes, he also left fifty slaves valued at $12,250, forty-two pounds of silver, and a variety of personal items.[105] Perhaps it was inevitable that such a large estate would be the object of much disputation among that substantial and litigious family. In the event, various heirs brought claims and counterclaims to the courts, and the estate remained unsettled in 1839.[106] Auguste, who had a world of experience in these matters, would probably have smiled knowingly. Pierre's estate was valued at $79,000. Most of that sum was in notes and accounts due, many of which were also probably uncollectible. The remainder was in slaves and other personal possessions. By the time of his death he had disposed of most of the vast real estate tracts he once held.[107]

Auguste and Pierre Chouteau's importance in the early history of St. Louis and the trans-Mississippi West is self-evident. Not only did they help initiate the fur trade in the region, but they also made important contributions in merchandising, banking, and real estate, for they were first and last merchant-entrepreneurs.[108] Their trading experience with the Indians equipped them to carry out important functions as diplomats and governmental agents, and conversely, their effectiveness in Indian diplomacy was a measure of their abilities as fair and reliable traders. Indeed, the Chouteau experience provides a prime example of the flag following trade on the frontier.

The Chouteau brothers were not selfless men, however. It would be a false and shallow tribute to claim that they always placed the public good ahead of their individual interests. But at the same time, there is every reason to believe that they saw themselves as honest men who took the concept of honor seriously in all of their dealings with whites and Indians alike. As they knew the value of most things, they understood the worth of a good name. A few of their rivals and enemies questioned their motives, but the records contain a multitude of testimonials to the steadfastness and decency of their characters. In their time and place they were widely esteemed as exemplary figures.

The evidence also affirms their devotion as family men who took a loving interest in their wives and children. It seems clear that affection more than duty prompted their frequent exertions on behalf of their families. In a similar fashion, they took a paternal pride in the city and territory which they had so powerfully shaped, never shirking from the responsibilities and monetary demands which their positions required. Their frequent displays of civic virtue were not the product of some theoretical vision of the commonwealth, but the palpable evidence of their belief that public and commercial advancement were inseparable.

Although the Chouteau brothers had much in common and held similar views, they were two distinct individuals. Auguste was quieter, more calculating, and less emotional. A man of guarded speech, his letters were taut and to the point. Only occasionally in his family correspondence did he abandon the arid shield and allow expressions of internal warmth to surface. While affable and courteous in public, he seldom let down his guard. Since he spoke only French, he must have appeared even more remote to the Americans who encountered him in his maturity. The always calm and formal Auguste remains a man history can truly know only in a public sense.

No less shrewd than Auguste, Pierre was more extroverted in character. If the Indians respected and perhaps feared Auguste, Pierre captured their affections. They never tired of praising him and showering him with gifts, and he seems to have been far more the tribal brother to them than Auguste could ever have been. But this accommodating relationship with the tribes did not signify weakness. On the contrary, Pierre displayed a resolute firmness in his dealings with the tribes, and he frequently demonstrated physical courage under extremely dangerous circumstances. More than any other man, he deserves credit for holding the formidable Osage tribe loyal to the United States at a time of grave peril on the frontier.

Pierre may have been an emotional man, occasionally prone to outbursts of violence, but he was seldom foolish in his actions. Although he often considered the American government's treatment of him unfair, he knew how to keep his counsel and choose the better part. His ability to master himself contributed to the excellence of his character. In sum, it seems fair to say that the Chouteaus' commonality of purpose reinforced by their complementary character traits contributed immeasurably to their commercial and political success. They were, in short, a prodigious team.

The Chouteaus were genuinely faithful to the United States, but they did not believe that they should sacrifice their commercial advantages when the United States annexed Louisiana. They may have entertained briefly the notion that the American presence would be temporary, but they surely forgot such thoughts once the Americans made it clear that they were there to stay. After that, they contributed mightily to the American government's achievements on the frontier, although they may be fairly charged with stretching the limits that the Americans would place on the combination of public office with the pursuit of private gain. In part that may have been because of their experience under the Spanish regime, but it should be added that certain American officials with whom they were in close contact appeared to interpret the rules on this subject in a liberal fashion too.

A desire to prosper in the marketplace drove both Auguste and Pierre, and in that calling they succeeded far better than most. They did so, in part, because they were clever and aggressive but not foolhardy businessmen. Their accomplishments, however, cannot be detached from the opportunities available to them in a virgin territory. Their willingness to undertake great enterprises in a new land opened up the opportunities that enabled them to become the significant historical figures we now know. For in becoming the pioneers of St. Louis, for the unexceptional purpose of gaining their livelihoods, they equipped themselves for the broader roles in politics, civic life, and diplomacy that time and fortune presented to them. While it is tempting in retrospect to look back upon their lives as ordered and even inevitable, that, of course, was not the case. When Auguste stood on that limestone bluff overlooking the Mississippi as a young boy in 1764, he did not know and could not have known what the years and the river would bring.

More than two decades after Lafayette stepped off the *Natchez* at the St. Louis waterfront, the city's residents held another celebration which also lingered long in the memories of those who were there. Auguste had been dead almost twenty years when St. Louisans set aside February 15, 1847, as a special day to commemorate the founding of their community.[109] St. Louis was a far different place in 1847 than it had been in those early seasons when it was known as "Paincourt." With an economy diversified beyond the dreams of its first inhabitants, the once-small French village was by then an American urban phenomenon well on its way to becoming one of the continent's great metropolises. The old mud paths had given way to broad paved avenues, and the rough log cabins had become mansions with pillared porticoes. Its riverboats plied the great waters of the West, and its docks were loaded with goods from all over the globe. Even Auguste's famed mansion had been torn down in 1841 to make way for the construction of new places of business in the booming town.[110] But one vital link with the city's wilderness origins remained: Pierre Chouteau, eighty-eight years of age, was there to preside over the festivities.

The celebrants organized a lengthy parade to mark the occasion. Militia and fire companies, floats, and marching units galore joined in the procession through the streets of St. Louis. Near the beginning marchers carried an elegant satin banner stitched by the ladies of St. Louis in honor of the city's founder. Four mounted Indians in full ceremonial dress escorted an open carriage transporting Pierre, attended by his sons Pierre Jr. and Paul Liguest, and his nephew Gabriel. The decision to include the Indians was a fitting tribute to the man who had known their people best. At 4:00 P.M. that afternoon a crowd of 400 gathered in the state tobacco warehouse to honor the old man with a dinner. The assembled guests toasted Pierre and his father, Pierre de Laclède Liguest, the city's founder, now dead for almost seventy years. Following the toasts, Pierre rose to his feet and spoke simply of the early days, of the simplicity and honesty of those times, and of the love of justice he had shared with those men and women of long ago, but even on this special occasion the elderly patriarch could not bring himself to acknowledge publicly his true relationship to Laclède.[111] Significantly, Chouteau delivered his reminiscences in his native French tongue, for despite his many years as an American citizen he, like his brother, never mastered the English language.[112] A band's rendition of the "Laclède March," composed especially for the occasion, brought the memorable celebration to a close.[113]

What must Pierre's thoughts have been on that winter evening in 1847? Surely he held in his mind the picture of his father and that indomitable woman, his mother, Madame Chouteau. Undoubtedly he also recaptured the image of his departed half-brother, that other empire builder who had inaugurated the building of a city and a state while still in his boyhood. Perhaps too, after the tumult and the cheering had died away, other faces appeared to him: the long-dead Pelagie and Brigitte, Meriwether Lewis and James Wilkinson, Shahaka and White Hair, Zenon Trudeau and Manuel Pérez, Manuel Lisa and James Cheek, Thomas Jefferson, and the countenances of many a Labbadie, Gratiot, Papin, and other old friends. He may have mused over the long nights before the campfires of remote Osage villages, or summoned up visions of the untamed rivers of his youth upon which he and his *amis* had forged a commercial dynasty. And if he dreamed, he must have smiled at the memories of those candle-bright evenings so long past, when music filled the air in his or Auguste's St. Louis home and youthful feet tramped out the cadence on the dark, polished, and shining floors. In the gathering shadows he must have glimpsed the coming end to his full and complete life, but in the same moment perhaps his thoughts also carried him back to the frontier dawn of his pilgrimage, when the first Chouteaus were truly the barons of the river.

NOTES

1. In 1825 Auguste and Pierre erected an iron cross on their mother's tomb. Receipt dated July 10, 1825, Chouteau Collections, Missouri Historical Society.

2. *Missouri Gazette,* Nov. 19, 1814.

3. *Ibid.,* Apr. 24, 1818.

4. Chouteau notices against trespassers in *Missouri Gazette,* Oct. 3, 1811, Apr. 2, 1814, Oct. 14, 1815, Jan. 6, 1816, and June 16, 1819.

5. For a sample of the many cases involving the Chouteaus see Missouri Supreme Court Records, Boxes 5–27, Missouri State Archives, Jefferson City.

6. Auguste Chouteau to Pierre Louis Panet, May 10, 1800, Chouteau Collections.

7. Auguste A. Chouteau to Auguste Chouteau, Sr., Nov. 26, 1802, Chouteau Collections.

8. Pierre Louis Panet to Auguste Chouteau, May 9, 1803, May 18 and Dec. 7, 1804, and May 18, 1805, Chouteau Collections.

9. Pierre Louis Panet to Auguste Chouteau, Dec. 28, 1806, Chouteau Collections.

10. Marriage contract of Auguste A. Chouteau and Constance Sanguinet, June 8, 1810, and Auguste A. Chouteau to Auguste Chouteau, Sr., Apr. 3, 1816, Chouteau Collections.

11. Auguste A. Chouteau to Auguste Chouteau, Sr., Apr. 3, 1816, Chouteau Collections.

12. Auguste A. Chouteau to Auguste Chouteau, Sr., Aug. 19, 1828, Chouteau Collections.

13. Inventory of Auguste Chouteau's estate, May 13, 1829, Chouteau Collections.

14. Cunningham and Blythe, *Founding Family,* 7.

15. *Ibid.*

16. *Ibid.,* 7–8.

17. Darby, *Personal Recollections,* 276; *Missouri Republican,* Nov. 28, 1825; Mother Philippine Duchesne to Father Barat, Mar. 7, 1821, in Louise Callan, *Philippine Duchesne, Frontier Missionary of the Sacred Heart, 1769–1852* (Westminster, Md., 1957), 335, 351, 361, 766n23.

18. Cunningham and Blythe, *Founding Family,* 8.

19. Auguste Chouteau to Vallé, Dec. 26, 1791, Vallé Papers, Missouri Historical Society.

20. Auguste Chouteau to Cerré Chouteau, Mar. 6, 1816, Jan. 8, 1818, and Oct. 23, 1822, Chouteau Collections.

21. Frederick L. Billon, *Annals of St. Louis in Its Territorial Days, 1804–1821* (St. Louis, 1888), 166; Callan, *Mother Duchesne,* 335; Auguste Chouteau's receipt from Father Francis Niel, Sept. 1821, Chouteau Collections.

22. Receipts to Auguste Chouteau for piano lessons and copying music for son and daughter, 1818, and receipt from Father Francis Niel, Sept. 1821, Chouteau Collections.

23. *Ibid.*

24. Lecompte, "Auguste Pierre Chouteau," 63–90.

25. Lecompte, "Pierre Chouteau, Junior," 91–123.

26. Cunningham and Blythe, *Founding Family,* 61.

27. *Ibid.,* 62–63.

28. Pierre Chouteau to Henry Dearborn, Apr. 12, 1806, Pierre Chouteau Letterbook, Missouri Historical Society.

29. Father Francis Niel to Pierre Chouteau, July 22, 1820, Chouteau Collections.

30. Pierre Chouteau, Sr., to Pierre Chouteau, Jr., Sept. 21, 1821, and Dec. 14, 1824, Chouteau Collections.

31. Auguste P. Chouteau to Pierre Chouteau, Jr., July 7, 1829, Chouteau Collections.

32. John Francis McDermott's Introduction in Cunningham and Blythe, *Founding Family,* iii–vi.

33. For example, Auguste and Pierre were joint administrators of their mother's estate, which was not finally settled until 1825, some eleven years after her death. *Missouri Republican,* July 18, 1825. Pierre also administered the estate of Françoise Brazeaux Charleville in 1826, having to supervise the sale of certain lots to pay off the debts of the estate. *Missouri Republican,* July 20 and Nov. 16, 1826. Among other estates the Chouteaus administered were those of Joseph Hortiz, Pelagie Labbadie, Joseph Robidoux, and Julien Dubuque.

34. As administrator of the Lacroix estate, Auguste took legal action to have Baptiste Janot Provost detained in the St. Charles county prison for the latter's failure to settle his accounts with the estate. *Missouri Gazette,* Mar. 29, 1817, and Dec. 11, 1818.

35. Missouri Supreme Court Records, Box 8.

36. *Marguerite et al.* vs. *Pierre Chouteau.* All records, depositions, and other papers pertaining to this case are located in Files 273 and 274, Jefferson County Circuit Clerk's Office, Hillsborough, Mo.

37. The contesting slaves first sued for their freedom in a St. Louis territorial court in 1806. A succession of trials and appeals followed. During the course of the lengthy legal battle the case was transferred on a change of venue to St. Charles County and once again to Jefferson County, where the final decision was rendered. At various times eighteen of Marie Scypion's descendants were parties in the litigation, but several had died before the court freed them. The slaves involved had originally belonged to Joseph Tayon, grandfather and guardian of Pierre's first wife, Pelagie Kiersereau.

38. Will of Marie Thérèse Bourgeois Chouteau, Jan. 13, 1813, photocopy in Chouteau Collections; *Missouri Gazette,* Sept. 10, 1814.

39. The 1830 U.S. Census indicates that Auguste's widow owned thirty-seven slaves, Pierre Sr. owned fifteen, Pierre Jr. owned twenty-four, and Auguste Pierre owned eleven. U.S. Census of 1830, Missouri, St. Louis Township, Schedule of Whole Number of Persons within the District, No. 4, 361, National Archives.

40. Melom shows that unskilled slaves were rented for as little as $18 per month. Melom, "Economic Development of St. Louis," 292.

41. See correspondence regarding Charles between Auguste and François Menard, July 8, 1820, Mar. 5, 1821, and May 19, 1822, Chouteau Collections. Although Auguste Chouteau denied having had any such conversation, Madame Marie Louise Chauvin testified in court that he once confided to her that when some of his slaves had been disobedient and claimed their liberty, "he had them whipt, being tied to four sticks and they had talked no more about their Liberty." Notes from 1806 trial in Lucas Collection, Missouri Historical Society.

42. When he stood for election as a delegate to the 1820 constitutional convention, Pierre Jr., for example, was listed as a candidate committed to "the eternal importation of slaves." *Missouri Gazette,* May 3, 1820.

43. *Ibid.,* Dec. 28, 1809, and Mar. 14, 1811; Certificate of manumission of slave François, Sept. 26, 1826, Chouteau Collections.

44. Foley, *History of Missouri,* 166.

45. Foley, "Territorial Politics in Frontier Missouri," 111–12, 146–58.

46. These objections were initially put forth by Joseph Charless, editor of the *Missouri Gazette,* in 1809. *Missouri Gazette,* Jan. 25, 1809.

47. A Bill for the Government of Louisiana Territory, Jan. 22, 1810, in Carter, ed., *Territorial Papers,* XIV, 362–64.

48. Petition to Congress by Inhabitants of St. Louis, Nov. 9, 1811, in *ibid.,* 486. Signers of the petition included Auguste and Pierre Chouteau, Bernard Pratte, Marie Philippe Le Duc, Charles Gratiot, and Antoine Soulard.

49. William E. Foley, "The American Territorial System: Missouri's Experience," *Missouri Historical Review* 65 (July 1971), 419–21.

50. See Ronald L. F. Davis, "Community and Conflict in Pioneer Saint Louis, Missouri," *Western Historical Quarterly* 10 (July 1979), 337–55.

51. Commission to Augustine Chouteau, St. Louis District, to Office of Judge of Court of Common Pleas, Oct. 1, 1804, Governors Papers, Missouri Historical Society.

52. Silas Bent to Auguste Chouteau, Feb. 21, 1813, Chouteau Collections.

53. James A. Wilkinson to Auguste Chouteau, July 17, 1806, Chouteau Collections; Objections of plaintiff's attorney in *Manuel Lisa* vs. *James Berry,* Mar. 12, 1808, Lisa Papers, Missouri Historical Society.

54. *Missouri Gazette,* Oct. 12, 1808.

55. Oglesby, *Manuel Lisa,* 3–6.

56. Silas Bent to Auguste Chouteau, Feb. 21, 1813, Chouteau Collections.

57. *Ibid.; Missouri Gazette,* Mar. 13, 1813.

58. Rowse, "Auguste and Pierre Chouteau," 254.

59. *Missouri Gazette,* July 26, 1808; Minutes of Board of Trustees, Aug. 10, 1808, photocopy in St. Louis History Papers, Missouri Historical Society.

60. Davis, "Community and Conflict," 343.

61. *Missouri Gazette,* Nov. 16, 1809. Pierre's house was used in 1812 for meetings of the territorial House of Representatives and later for the Legislative Council, until they decided his $3-per-day fee was too high. See *Missouri Gazette,* Dec. 5, 1812, and Dec. 16, 1815.

62. *Louisiana Gazette,* Jan. 11 and 18, Feb. 15, and Mar. 15, 1810; *Missouri Gazette,* Jan. 3, 1821; Bill for translation of ordinances by the Board of Trustees paid to Joseph V. Garnier, Apr. 5, 1810, St. Louis History Papers; Fragment of Minutes of St. Louis Board of Trustees, May 5, 1821, Western Historical Manuscripts Collection, University of Missouri, Columbia.

63. *Louisiana Gazette,* Mar. 15, 1810.

64. Order of Auguste Chouteau, chairman of Board of Trustees, to seize the goods of Peter Smith and Isaac Molton, July 31, 1810, Chouteau Collections; *Missouri Gazette,* Jan. 4, 1812.

65. Announcement of Pierre Chouteau's election as a trustee of St. Louis, Jan. 4, 1811, and Certificate of Pierre Chouteau's election to St. Louis Board of Trustees, Dec. 5, 1820, Chouteau Collections; *Missouri Republican,* Apr. 12, 1824.

66. *Missouri Gazette,* Jan. 3 and Feb. 7, 1821.

67. Statement of Monies Received and Expended for the Corporation of the Town of St. Louis, *Missouri Gazette,* Feb. 7, 1821.

68. *Missouri Republican,* Mar. 26, 1823, and Mar. 30, 1826; Davis, "Community and Conflict," 346–47, 349.

69. Foley, *History of Missouri,* 198–202.

70. *Missouri Gazette,* May 3, 1820.

71. Frederick Arthur Culmer, *A New History of Missouri* (Mexico, Mo., 1938), 160.

72. Jerome O. Steffen, *William Clark: Jeffersonian Man on the Frontier* (Norman, Okla., 1977), 124–28.

73. Darby, *Personal Recollections,* 30–31. For a corrective to Darby's account see also Perry G. McCandless, *A History of Missouri, 1820–1860* (Columbia, Mo., 1972), 15–18.

74. Pierre was elected in a special election to fill a vacancy created by Bernard Pratte's resignation. He served only that term, and although little is known about his activities in the Senate, it seems doubtful that he exercised much influence. A case in point would be the legislature's decision shortly after he took office to locate the permanent state capital in Jefferson City. Chouteau had been deeply involved with Angus L. Langham in efforts to locate the capital at Cote Sans Dessein, where he claimed large tracts of land. Indeed the uncertainties surrounding Chouteau's land titles may have contributed to the decision in favor of Jefferson City. *Missouri Gazette,* Oct. 31, 1821. Numerous documents pertaining to Chouteau's association with Langham in the Cote Sans Dessein affair are contained in the Abiel Leonard Collection, Western Historical Manuscripts Collection, University of Missouri. A brief discussion of the debate over the capital site can be found in McCandless, *History of Missouri,* 21–22. Likewise, McCandless also provides a careful analysis of Benton's decision to disassociate himself politically from the St. Louis junto. See McCandless, *History of Missouri,* 18, 67–91.

75. *Missouri Republican,* Aug. 30, 1827.

76. *Ibid.,* Nov. 29, 1827.

77. John C. Calhoun to Auguste Chouteau, July 16, 1818, Chouteau Collections.

78. Auguste Chouteau to John C. Calhoun, Jan. 25, 1821, in W. Edwin Hemphill, ed., *The Papers of John C. Calhoun* (Columbia, S.C., 1963–), V, 571.

79. Act of the Missouri General Assembly incorporating the board of trustees of the St. Louis public schools, in Carter, ed., *Territorial Papers,* XV, 546–47; *Missouri Gazette,* Mar. 8, 1817.

80. *Missouri Gazette,* Dec. 8, 1819; Receipt to Auguste Chouteau for his part in a public dinner on June 19, 1819, Chouteau Collections.

81. *Missouri Republican,* May 14 and July 16, 1823; Petition to the state legislature for an appropriation to build an almshouse, St. Louis History Papers; Documents concerning the selection of a site for the St. Louis courthouse, Aug. 25, 1823, photostatic copy in Bernard F. Dickman Papers, Western Historical Manuscripts Collection, University of Missouri.

82. Rowse, "Auguste and Pierre Chouteau," 266–67.

83. Selected portions of Auguste's testimony in *Hunt's Minutes* have been reprinted in McDermott, *Early Histories,* 89–97. See also Foreman, ed., "Notes of Auguste Chouteau on the Boundaries of Various Indian Nations," 119–40.

84. *Missouri Gazette,* July 14, 1819.

85. Savoie Lottinville, ed., *Paul Wilhelm, Duke of Württemberg: Travels in North America, 1822–1824,* tr. W. Robert Nitske (Norman, Okla., 1973), 180, 206–7; McDermott, "Auguste Chouteau," 12–13.

86. *Missouri Republican,* Sept. 20, 1824.

87. *Ibid.,* May 2, 1825.

88. For accounts of Lafayette's visit see *ibid.;* Darby, *Personal Recollections,* 12, 57–61.

89. *Missouri Republican,* Mar. 2, 1826.

90. *Ibid.*

91. Citizens of St. Louis to the Baron de Carondelet, July 16, 1792, and Jacques Clamorgan and Auguste Chouteau to Carondelet, 1792, Archivo General de Indias, Papeles de Cuba, leg. 215A, photostatic copies in John Francis McDermott Mississippi Valley Research Collection, Lovejoy Library, Southern Illinois University at Edwardsville; Brother Urbain to Pierre Chouteau, June 18, 1811, and Father Javine to Pierre Chouteau, Dec. 2, 1811, Chouteau Collections.

92. John Rothensteiner, *History of the Archdiocese of St. Louis* (St. Louis, 1928), I, 271.

93. *Ibid.,* 272. Auguste contributed $400, Pierre $200, and Auguste Pierre $50.

94. Auguste Chouteau Check to Commissioners of the Church, July 22, 1820, Chouteau Collections.

95. L. Guillame, bishop of Louisiana, to Auguste and Pierre Chouteau and others, May 7, 1822, Chouteau Collections.

96. Rothensteiner, *History of the Archdiocese,* I, 274.

97. Father Niel to Auguste Chouteau, Pierre Chouteau, and Bernard Pratte, June 19, 1823, Chouteau Collections.

98. *Missouri Republican,* Aug. 13, 1823; Rothensteiner, *History of the Archdiocese,* I, 275.

99. Rothensteiner, *History of the Archdiocese,* I, 275.

100. Joseph Rosati to Bernard Pratte, Auguste Chouteau, and Pierre Chouteau, Mar. 23, 1828, Chouteau Collections.

101. *Ibid.*

102. *Missouri Republican,* Feb. 24, 1829.

103. *Ibid.,* July 10, 1849.

104. Inventory of Auguste Chouteau's estate, 1830, Chouteau Collections.

105. *Ibid.;* McDermott, *Private Libraries,* 129.

106. Darby, *Personal Recollections,* 276–77; *Pauls* vs. *Chouteaus and Smith,* Sept. 8, 1838, St. Charles Circuit Court Records, St. Charles, Mo.; *Chouteau, Smith and Wife, Chouteau and Chouteau* vs. *Paul et al.,* 1833, 3 *Missouri Reports,* 260.

107. Rowse, "Auguste and Pierre Chouteau," 265–66.

108. Lewis Atherton's studies of the frontier merchant-traders provide excellent insights regarding their important roles in the development of the American West. See Atherton, *The Frontier Merchant in Mid-America,* rev. ed. (Columbia, Mo., 1971) and "The Santa Fe Trader as Mercantile Capitalist," *Missouri Historical Review* 77 (Oct. 1982), 1–12.

109. *Report of the Celebration of the Anniversary of the Founding of St. Louis, February 15, 1847* (St. Louis, 1847).

110. A brief campaign to save Auguste Chouteau's historic mansion from destruction in 1841 failed, but it did inspire the following plea from an early preservationist:

THE CHOUTEAU HOUSE
BY M. C. FIELD

Touch not a stone! An early pioneer
Of Christian sway founded his dwelling here,
Almost alone.

Touch not a stone! Let the Great West command
A hoary relic of the early land;
That after generations may not say,
"All went for gold in our forefather's day,
And of our infancy we nothing own."

Touch not a stone!

Touch not a stone! Let the old pile decay,
A relic of the time now pass'd away.
Ye heirs, who own
Lordly endowment of the ancient hall,
Till the last rafter crumbles from the wall,
And each old tree around the dwelling rots,
Yield not your heritage for "building-lots."
Hold the old ruin for itself alone;
Touch not a stone!

Built by a foremost Western pioneer,
It stood upon Saint Louis bluff, to cheer
New settlers on.
Now o'er it tow'r majestic spire and dome,
And lowly seems the forest trader's home;
All out of fashion, like a time-struck man,
Last of his age, his kindred and his clan,
Lingering still, a stranger and alone;—
Touch not a stone!

Spare the old house! The ancient mansion spare,
For ages still to front the market square;—
That may be shown,
How those old walls of good St. Louis rock,
In native strength, shall bear against the shock
Of centuries! There shall the curious see,
When like a fable shall our story be,
How the Star City of the West has grown!
Touch not a stone!

The poem was reprinted in Richard Edwards and Menra Hopewell, *The Great West and Her Commercial Metropolis* (St. Louis, 1860), 534–35.

111. *Report of the Celebration of the Anniversary of the Founding of St. Louis;* Mc-Dermott, "Pierre Laclède and the Chouteaus," 279–83.

112. In 1826 Mayor William Carr Lane commented that "Major Chouteau understands very little English and I very little French, and it is therefore not at all surprising that we should misunderstand one another." Quoted in Davis, "Community and Conflict," 349.

113. *Report of the Celebration of the Anniversary of the Founding of St. Louis.*

CHOUTEAU GENEALOGY

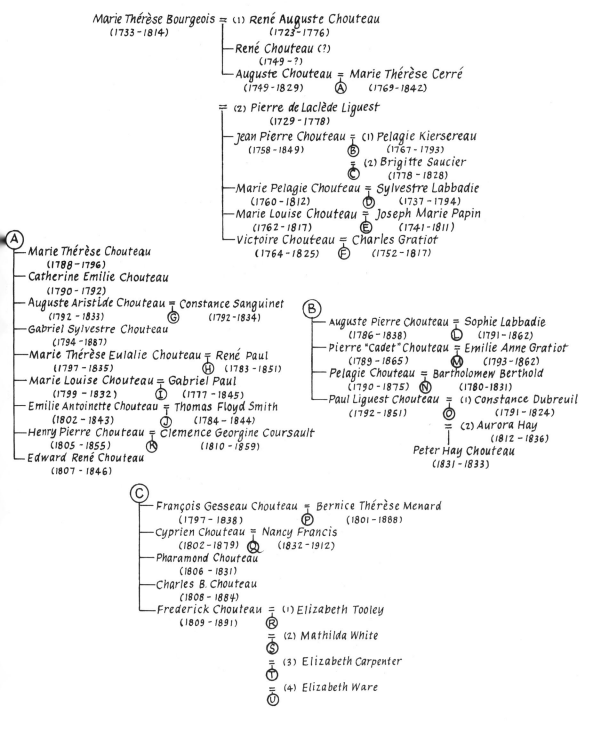

Marie Thérèse Bourgeois = (1) René Auguste Chouteau
(1733 – 1814)   (1723 – 1776)

  René Chouteau (?)
   (1749 – ?)

  Auguste Chouteau = Marie Thérèse Cerré
   (1749 – 1829)   (A)   (1769 – 1842)

= (2) Pierre de Laclède Liguest
      (1729 – 1778)

  Jean Pierre Chouteau = (1) Pelagie Kiersereau
   (1758 – 1849)   (B)   (1767 – 1793)
                    = (2) Brigitte Saucier
                     (C)   (1778 – 1828)

  Marie Pelagie Chouteau = Sylvestre Labbadie
   (1760 – 1812)   (D)   (1737 – 1794)

  Marie Louise Chouteau = Joseph Marie Papin
   (1762 – 1817)   (E)   (1741 – 1811)

  Victoire Chouteau = Charles Gratiot
   (1764 – 1825)   (F)   (1752 – 1817)

(A)
  Marie Thérèse Chouteau
   (1788 – 1796)
  Catherine Emilie Chouteau
   (1790 – 1792)
  Auguste Aristide Chouteau = Constance Sanguinet
   (1792 – 1833)   (G)   (1792 – 1834)
  Gabriel Sylvestre Chouteau
   (1794 – 1887)
  Marie Thérèse Eulalie Chouteau = René Paul
   (1797 – 1835)   (H)   (1783 – 1851)
  Marie Louise Chouteau = Gabriel Paul
   (1799 – 1832)   (I)   (1777 – 1845)
  Emilie Antoinette Chouteau = Thomas Floyd Smith
   (1802 – 1843)   (J)   (1784 – 1844)
  Henry Pierre Chouteau = Clemence Georgine Coursault
   (1805 – 1855)   (K)   (1810 – 1859)
  Edward René Chouteau
   (1807 – 1846)

(B)
  Auguste Pierre Chouteau = Sophie Labbadie
   (1786 – 1838)   (L)   (1791 – 1862)
  Pierre "Cadet" Chouteau = Emilie Anne Gratiot
   (1789 – 1865)   (M)   (1793 – 1862)
  Pelagie Chouteau = Bartholomew Berthold
   (1790 – 1875)   (N)   (1780 – 1831)
  Paul Liguest Chouteau = (1) Constance Dubreuil
   (1792 – 1851)   (O)   (1791 – 1824)
                    = (2) Aurora Hay
                       (1812 – 1836)
         Peter Hay Chouteau
          (1831 – 1833)

(C)
  François Gesseau Chouteau = Bernice Thérèse Menard
   (1797 – 1838)   (P)   (1801 – 1888)
  Cyprien Chouteau = Nancy Francis
   (1802 – 1879)   (Q)   (1832 – 1912)
  Pharamond Chouteau
   (1806 – 1831)
  Charles B. Chouteau
   (1808 – 1884)
  Frederick Chouteau = (1) Elizabeth Tooley
   (1809 – 1891)   (R)
                    = (2) Mathilda White
                     (S)
                    = (3) Elizabeth Carpenter
                     (T)
                    = (4) Elizabeth Ware
                     (U)

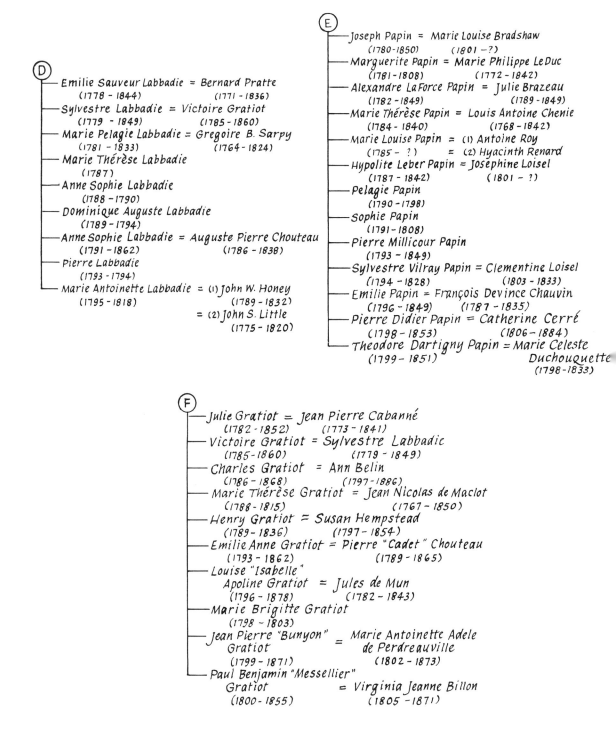

Ⓓ
Emilie Sauveur Labbadie = Bernard Pratte
(1778 – 1844)   (1771 – 1836)
Sylvestre Labbadie = Victoire Gratiot
(1779 – 1849)   (1785 – 1860)
Marie Pelagie Labbadie = Gregoire B. Sarpy
(1781 – 1833)   (1764 – 1824)
Marie Thérèse Labbadie
(1787)
Anne Sophie Labbadie
(1788 – 1790)
Dominique Auguste Labbadie
(1789 – 1794)
Anne Sophie Labbadie = Auguste Pierre Chouteau
(1791 – 1862)   (1786 – 1838)
Pierre Labbadie
(1793 – 1794)
Marie Antoinette Labbadie = (1) John W. Honey
(1795 – 1818)   (1789 – 1832)
= (2) John S. Little
(1775 – 1820)

Ⓔ
Joseph Papin = Marie Louise Bradshaw
(1780 – 1850)   (1801 – ?)
Marguerite Papin = Marie Philippe LeDuc
(1781 – 1808)   (1772 – 1842)
Alexandre LaForce Papin = Julie Brazeau
(1782 – 1849)   (1789 – 1849)
Marie Thérèse Papin = Louis Antoine Chenie
(1784 – 1840)   (1768 – 1842)
Marie Louise Papin = (1) Antoine Roy
(1785 – ?)   = (2) Hyacinth Renard
Hypolite Leber Papin = Joséphine Loisel
(1787 – 1842)   (1801 – ?)
Pelagie Papin
(1790 – 1798)
Sophie Papin
(1791 – 1808)
Pierre Millicour Papin
(1793 – 1849)
Sylvestre Vilray Papin = Clementine Loisel
(1794 – 1828)   (1803 – 1833)
Emilie Papin = François Devince Chauvin
(1796 – 1849)   (1787 – 1835)
Pierre Didier Papin = Catherine Cerré
(1798 – 1853)   (1806 – 1884)
Theodore Dartigny Papin = Marie Celeste
(1799 – 1851)   Duchouquette
(1798 – 1833)

Ⓕ
Julie Gratiot = Jean Pierre Cabanné
(1782 – 1852)   (1773 – 1841)
Victoire Gratiot = Sylvestre Labbadie
(1785 – 1860)   (1779 – 1849)
Charles Gratiot = Ann Belin
(1786 – 1868)   (1797 – 1886)
Marie Thérèse Gratiot = Jean Nicolas de Maclot
(1788 – 1815)   (1767 – 1850)
Henry Gratiot = Susan Hempstead
(1789 – 1836)   (1797 – 1854)
Emilie Anne Gratiot = Pierre "Cadet" Chouteau
(1793 – 1862)   (1789 – 1865)
Louise "Isabelle"
Apoline Gratiot = Jules de Mun
(1796 – 1878)   (1782 – 1843)
Marie Brigitte Gratiot
(1798 – 1803)
Jean Pierre "Bunyon" = Marie Antoinette Adele
Gratiot   de Perdreauville
(1799 – 1871)   (1802 – 1873)
Paul Benjamin "Messellier"
Gratiot   = Virginia Jeanne Billon
(1800 – 1855)   (1805 – 1871)

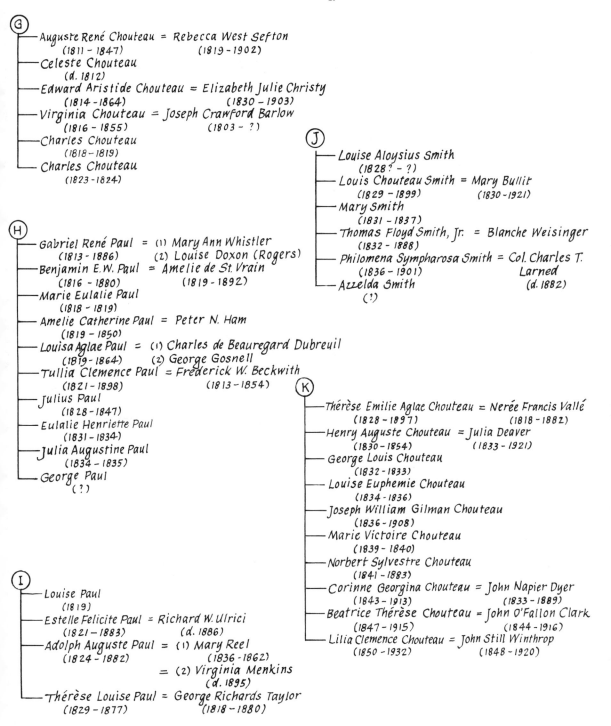

G

Auguste René Chouteau = Rebecca West Sefton
   (1811 – 1847)   *(1819 –1902)*

Celeste Chouteau
   (d. 1812)

Edward Aristide Chouteau = Elizabeth Julie Christy
   (1814 -1864)   *(1830 -1903)*

Virginia Chouteau = Joseph Crawford Barlow
   (1816 - 1855)   *(1803 - ?)*

Charles Chouteau
   (1818 –1819)

Charles Chouteau
   (1823 -1824)

J

Louise Aloysius Smith
   (1828? - ?)

Louis Chouteau Smith = Mary Bullit
   (1829 - 1899)   *(1830 -1921)*

Mary Smith
   (1831 - 1837)

Thomas Floyd Smith, Jr. = Blanche Weisinger
   (1832 - 1888)

Philomena Sympharosa Smith = Col. Charles T.
   (1836 - 1901)   Larned

Azzelda Smith   *(d. 1882)*
   (?)

H

Gabriel René Paul = (1) Mary Ann Whistler
   (1813 - 1886)   (2) Louise Doxon (Rogers)

Benjamin E.W. Paul = Amelie de St. Vrain
   (1816 - 1880)   *(1819 -1892)*

Marie Eulalie Paul
   (1818 - 1819)

Amelie Catherine Paul = Peter N. Ham
   (1819 - 1850)

Louisa Aglae Paul = (1) Charles de Beauregard Dubreuil
   (1819-1864)   (2) George Gosnell

Tullia Clemence Paul = Frederick W. Beckwith
   (1821 -1898)   *(1813 -1854)*

Julius Paul
   (1828 -1847)

Eulalie Henriette Paul
   (1831 -1834)

Julia Augustine Paul
   (1834 - 1835)

George Paul
   (?)

K

Thérèse Emilie Aglae Chouteau = Nerée Francis Vallé
   (1828 - 1897)   *(1818 -1882)*

Henry Auguste Chouteau = Julia Deaver
   (1830- 1854)   *(1833 - 1921)*

George Louis Chouteau
   (1832 -1833)

Louise Euphemie Chouteau
   (1834 -1836)

Joseph William Gilman Chouteau
   (1836 -1908)

Marie Victoire Chouteau
   (1839 - 1840)

Norbert Sylvestre Chouteau
   (1841 -1883)

Corinne Georgina Chouteau = John Napier Dyer
   (1843 - 1913)   *(1833 -1889)*

Beatrice Thérèse Chouteau = John O'Fallon Clark
   (1847 - 1915)   *(1844 -1916)*

Lilia Clemence Chouteau = John Still Winthrop
   (1850 -1932)   *(1848 -1920)*

I

Louise Paul
   (1819)

Estelle Felicite Paul = Richard W. Ulrici
   (1821–1883)   *(d. 1886)*

Adolph Auguste Paul = (1) Mary Reel
   (1824 -1882)   *(1836 -1862)*

         = (2) Virginia Menkins
           (d. 1895)

Thérèse Louise Paul = George Richards Taylor
   (1829 -1877)   *(1818 -1880)*

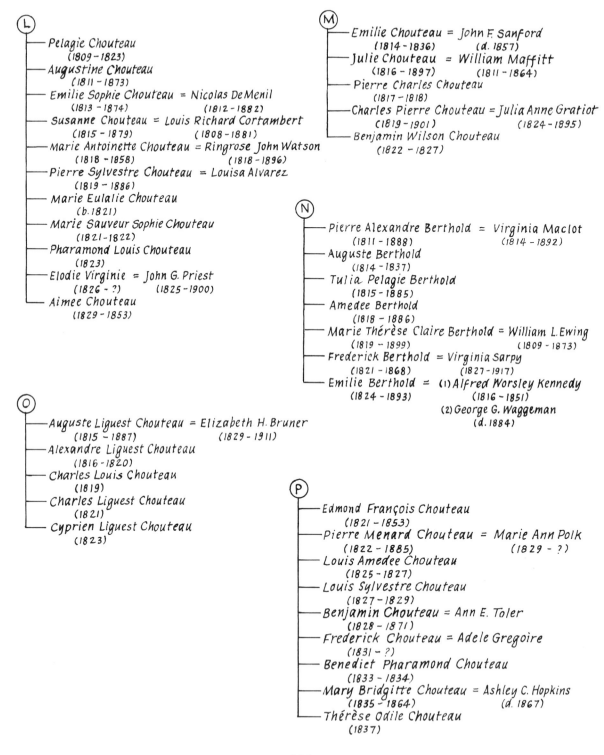

Ⓛ

— Pelagie Chouteau
 (1809 – 1823)
— Augustine Chouteau
 (1811 – 1873)
— Emilie Sophie Chouteau = Nicolas DeMenil
 (1813 – 1874)   (1812 – 1882)
— Susanne Chouteau = Louis Richard Cortambert
 (1815 – 1879)   (1808 – 1881)
— Marie Antoinette Chouteau = Ringrose John Watson
 (1818 – 1858)   (1818 – 1896)
— Pierre Sylvestre Chouteau = Louisa Alvarez
 (1819 – 1886)
— Marie Eulalie Chouteau
 (b. 1821)
— Marie Sauveur Sophie Chouteau
 (1821 – 1822)
— Pharamond Louis Chouteau
 (1823)
— Elodie Virginie = John G. Priest
 (1826 – ?)   (1825 – 1900)
— Aimee Chouteau
 (1829 – 1853)

Ⓜ

— Emilie Chouteau = John F. Sanford
 (1814 – 1836)   (d. 1857)
— Julie Chouteau = William Maffitt
 (1816 – 1897)   (1811 – 1864)
— Pierre Charles Chouteau
 (1817 – 1818)
— Charles Pierre Chouteau = Julia Anne Gratiot
 (1819 – 1901)   (1824 – 1895)
— Benjamin Wilson Chouteau
 (1822 – 1827)

Ⓝ

— Pierre Alexandre Berthold = Virginia Maclot
 (1811 – 1888)   (1814 – 1892)
— Auguste Berthold
 (1814 – 1837)
— Tulia Pelagie Berthold
 (1815 – 1885)
— Amedee Berthold
 (1818 – 1886)
— Marie Thérèse Claire Berthold = William L. Ewing
 (1819 – 1899)   (1809 – 1873)
— Frederick Berthold = Virginia Sarpy
 (1821 – 1868)   (1827 – 1917)
— Emilie Berthold = (1) Alfred Worsley Kennedy
 (1824 – 1893)   (1816 – 1851)
                       (2) George G. Waggeman
                           (d. 1884)

Ⓞ

— Auguste Liguest Chouteau = Elizabeth H. Bruner
 (1815 – 1887)   (1829 – 1911)
— Alexandre Liguest Chouteau
 (1816 – 1820)
— Charles Louis Chouteau
 (1819)
— Charles Liguest Chouteau
 (1821)
— Cyprien Liguest Chouteau
 (1823)

Ⓟ

— Edmond François Chouteau
 (1821 – 1853)
— Pierre Menard Chouteau = Marie Ann Polk
 (1822 – 1885)   (1829 – ?)
— Louis Amedee Chouteau
 (1825 – 1827)
— Louis Sylvestre Chouteau
 (1827 – 1829)
— Benjamin Chouteau = Ann E. Toler
 (1828 – 1871)
— Frederick Chouteau = Adele Gregoire
 (1831 – ?)
— Benedict Pharamond Chouteau
 (1833 – 1834)
— Mary Bridgitte Chouteau = Ashley C. Hopkins
 (1835 – 1864)   (d. 1867)
— Thérèse Odile Chouteau
 (1837)

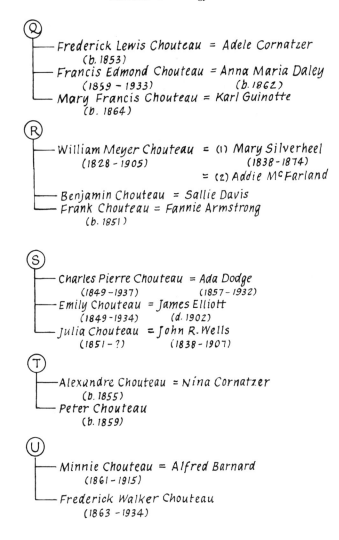

(Q)

— Frederick Lewis Chouteau = Adele Cornatzer
  (b. 1853)
— Francis Edmond Chouteau = Anna Maria Daley
  (1859 – 1933)   (b. 1862)
— Mary Francis Chouteau = Karl Guinotte
  (b. 1864)

(R)

— William Meyer Chouteau = (1) Mary Silverheel
  (1828 – 1905)   (1838 – 1874)
                          = (2) Addie McFarland
— Benjamin Chouteau = Sallie Davis
— Frank Chouteau = Fannie Armstrong
  (b. 1851)

(S)

— Charles Pierre Chouteau = Ada Dodge
  (1849 – 1937)   (1857 – 1932)
— Emily Chouteau = James Elliott
  (1849 – 1934)   (d. 1902)
— Julia Chouteau = John R. Wells
  (1851 – ?)   (1838 – 1907)

(T)

— Alexandre Chouteau = Nina Cornatzer
  (b. 1855)
— Peter Chouteau
  (b. 1859)

(U)

— Minnie Chouteau = Alfred Barnard
  (1861 – 1915)
— Frederick Walker Chouteau
  (1863 – 1934)

The authors are indebted to Cunningham and Blythe, *Founding Family of St. Louis* (1977) for much of the information contained in this genealogy.

BIBLIOGRAPHY

I. ARCHIVAL MATERIAL

Jefferson County Circuit Court Records. Hillsboro, Mo.

Kansas State Historical Society. Topeka, Kans.

    William Clark Papers

Library of Congress. Washington, D.C.

    Jefferson, Thomas, Papers

    Monroe, James, Papers

Lovejoy Library, Southern Illinois University at Edwardsville. Edwardsville, Ill.

    John Francis McDermott Mississippi Valley Research Collection

Missouri Historical Society. St. Louis, Mo.

Bates Papers

Billon, Frederic, Collection

Bissell, Daniel, Papers

Census Papers

Chouteau, Pierre, Letterbook

Chouteau Collections

Clamorgan Papers

Clark Family Papers

Delassus Collection

Fur Trade Papers

Governors Papers

Gratiot, Charles, Letterbook

Gratiot, Charles, Papers

Indian Papers

Jefferson, Thomas, Papers

Laclède, Pierre, Collection

Lewis, Meriwether, Papers

Lisa, Manuel, Papers

Louisiana Territory Papers

Lucas Collection

St. Louis Archives

St. Louis History Collection

Ste. Genevieve Papers

Sibley, George, Papers

Stoddard, Amos, Papers

Vallé Papers

Vasquez Papers

Wilkinson, James, Papers

Wilt, Christian, Letterbook

Missouri State Archives. Jefferson City, Mo.

    Early Missouri Supreme Court Records

National Archives. Washington, D.C.

    Census of 1830, Missouri

    Records of the Bureau of Indian Affairs

        Letters Sent by the Secretary of War relating to Indian Affairs, Record Group 75

    Records of the War Department

        Index to Military Service, War of 1812, M602

        Letters Received by the Secretary of War, Record Group 107

        Letters Sent by the Secretary of War, Record Group 107

St. Charles County Circuit Court Records. St. Charles, Mo.

State Historical Society of Missouri. Columbia, Mo.
  Ste. Genevieve Archives, microfilm copy.
University of Virginia Archives. Charlottesville, Va.
  Folder 7605.
Western Historical Manuscripts Collection. University of Missouri, Columbia, Mo.
  Dickman, Bernard F., Papers
  Fragment of Minutes of St. Louis Board of Trustees, May 5, 1821
  Leonard, Abiel, Collection

II. GOVERNMENT DOCUMENTS

American State Papers: Indian Affairs, Public Lands, Finance, Miscellaneous. 38 vols.
  Washington, D.C.: Gales & Seaton, 1832–61.
Annals of the Congress of the United States, 1789–1824. 42 vols. Washington, D.C.:
  Gales & Seaton, 1834–36.
Carter, Clarence E., ed. *The Territorial Papers of the United States,* vol. VII, *Indiana,*
  1800–1810 (1939); vol. XIII, *Louisiana-Missouri, 1803–1806* (1948); vol. XIV,
  Louisiana-Missouri, 1806–1814 (1949); vol. XV, *Louisiana-Missouri, 1815–1821*
  (1954). Washington, D.C.: Government Printing Office, 1934–62.
Hunt, Theodore, comp. *Testimony before the Recorder of Land Titles.* St. Louis, 1825.
Representation and Petition of the Representatives Elected by the Freemen of the Territory of
  Louisiana. Washington, D.C., 1805.

III. NEWSPAPERS AND PERIODICALS

North American Review
St. Louis *Louisiana Gazette*
St. Louis *Missouri Gazette*
St. Louis *Missouri Republican*
Washington, D.C., *National Intelligencer*

IV. BOOKS

Abel, Annie Heloise, ed. *Tabeau's Narrative of Loisel's Expedition to the Upper Missouri.*
  Norman: University of Oklahoma Press, 1939.
Alvord, Clarence W. *The Illinois Country.* Springfield: Illinois State Historical Library,
  1920.
———, ed. *Kaskaskia Records, 1778–1790.* Springfield: Illinois State Historical Library, 1909.
Alvord, Clarence W., and Clarence E. Carter. *The Critical Period, 1763–1765.* Springfield: Illinois State Historical Library, 1915.

————. *The New Regime, 1765–1767*. Springfield: Illinois State Historical Library, 1915.

————. *Trade and Politics, 1767–1769*. Springfield: Illinois State Historical Library, 1921.

Ammon, Harry. *James Monroe: The Quest for National Identity*. New York: McGraw-Hill, 1971.

Atherton, Lewis. *The Frontier Merchant in Mid-America*. Rev. ed. Columbia, Mo.: University of Missouri Press, 1971.

————. *The Cattle Kings*. Bloomington: Indiana University Press, 1961.

Baird, W. David. *The Osage People*. Phoenix, Ariz.: Indian Tribal Series, 1972.

Barker, Eugene C., ed. *The Austin Papers*. 2 vols. *Annual Report of the American Historical Association for the Year 1919*. Washington, D.C.: Government Printing Office, 1924.

Berkhofer, Robert F., Jr. *The White Man's Indian: Images of the American Indian from Columbus to the Present*. New York: Alfred A. Knopf, 1978.

Billon, Frederic L. *Annals of St. Louis in Its Early Days under the French and Spanish Dominations, 1764–1804*. St. Louis, 1886.

————. *Annals of St. Louis in Its Territorial Days, 1804–1821*. St. Louis, 1888.

Callan, Louise. *Philippine Duchesne, Frontier Missionary of the Sacred Heart, 1769–1852*. Westminster, Md.: Newman Press, 1957.

Clark, John G. *New Orleans, 1718–1812: An Economic History*. Baton Rouge: Louisiana State University Press, 1970.

Cleaves, Freeman. *Old Tippecanoe*. New York: Charles Scribner's Sons, 1939.

Clokey, Richard M. *William H. Ashley: Enterprise and Politics in the Trans-Mississippi West*. Norman: University of Oklahoma Press, 1980.

Culmer, Frederick Arthur. *A New History of Missouri*. Mexico, Mo.: McIntyre Publishing Co., 1938.

Cunningham, Mary B., and Jeanne C. Blythe. *The Founding Family of St. Louis*. St. Louis: Midwest Technical Publications, 1977.

Darby, John. *Personal Recollections of Many Prominent People Whom I Have Known*. St. Louis, 1880.

Davidson, G. C. *The Northwest Company*. Berkeley: University of California Publications in History, 1918.

De Menil, Alexander. *Madame Chouteau Vindicated*. St. Louis: William Harvey Nirner Co., 1921.

Dillon, Richard. *Meriwether Lewis: A Biography*. New York: Coward-McCann, 1965.

Douglas, Walter B. *Manuel Lisa*. With hitherto unpublished material annotated and edited by Abraham P. Nasatir. New York: Argosy-Antiquarian Ltd., 1964.

Edwards, Richard, and Menra Hopewell. *The Great West and Her Commercial Metropolis*. St. Louis, 1860.

Esarey, Logan, ed. *Governors' Messages and Letters: Messages and Letters of William Henry Harrison*. Indianapolis: Indiana History Commission, 1922.

Flint, Timothy. *Recollections of the Last Ten Years Passed in Occasional Residences and Journeyings in the Valley of the Mississippi*. Boston: Cummings, Hilliard, and Co., 1826.

Foley, William E. *A History of Missouri, 1673–1820.* Columbia: University of Missouri Press, 1971.

Foreman, Grant. *Indians and Pioneers: The Story of the American Southwest before 1830.* Rev. ed. Norman: University of Oklahoma Press, 1936.

Goodspeed, Weston Arthur. *The Province and the States.* 7 vols. Madison, Wis.: Western Historical Association, 1904.

Green, Everts B., and Clarence W. Alvord, eds. *The Governors' Letterbooks, 1818–1834.* Springfield: Illinois State Historical Library, 1909.

Hafen, LeRoy R., ed. *The Mountain Men and the Fur Trade of the Far West.* 10 vols. Glendale, Calif.: Arthur H. Clark, 1965–72.

Hagan, William T. *The Sac and Fox Indians.* Norman: University of Oklahoma Press, 1958.

Hammond, George P., ed. *New Spain and the Anglo-American West.* 2 vols. Lancaster, Pa.: Lancaster Press, 1932.

Hemphill, W. Edwin, ed. *The Papers of John C. Calhoun.* 13 vols. Columbia: University of South Carolina Press, 1963–.

Horsman, Reginald W. *Expansion and American Indian Policy, 1783–1812.* East Lansing: Michigan State University Press, 1967.

Houck, Louis. *A History of Missouri from Earliest Explorations and Settlements until the Admission of the State into the Union.* 3 vols. Chicago: R. R. Donnelley & Sons, 1908.

———, ed. *The Spanish Regime in Missouri.* 2 vols. Chicago: R. R. Donnelley & Sons, 1909.

Hubbard, Timothy, and Lewis E. Davids, *Banking in Mid-America: A History of Missouri's Banks.* Washington: Public Affairs Press, 1969.

Innis, Harold A. *The Fur Trade in Canada.* Rev. ed. New Haven: Yale University Press, 1962.

Irving, Washington. *Astoria.* 1836; reprinted in Herbert L. Kleinfield, ed., *The Complete Works of Washington Irving.* Boston: Twayne, 1976.

Jackson, Donald. *Thomas Jefferson and the Stony Mountains: Exploring the West from Monticello.* Urbana: University of Illinois Press, 1981.

———, ed. *The Journals of Zebulon Montgomery Pike with Letters and Related Documents.* 2 vols. Norman: University of Oklahoma Press, 1966.

———, ed. *Letters of the Lewis and Clark Expedition with Related Documents, 1783–1854.* Urbana: University of Illinois Press, 1962.

James, Edward. *Account of an Expedition from Pittsburgh to the Rocky Mountains Performed in the Years 1819 and '20 . . . under the Command of Stephen H. Long. . . .* 2 vols. Philadelphia: H. C. Carey and I. Lea, 1823.

James, Thomas. *Three Years among the Indians and Mexicans.* Waterloo, Ill., 1846; reprint (Milo M. Quaife, ed.), New York: Citadel Press, 1966.

Jennings, Marietta. *A Pioneer Merchant of St. Louis 1810–1820: The Business Career of Christian Wilt.* New York: Columbia University Press, 1939.

Jones, Charles T., Jr. *George Champlin Sibley: The Prairie Puritan, 1782–1863.* Independence, Mo.: Jackson County Historical Society, 1970.

Jordan, H. Glenn, and Thomas M. Holm, eds. *Indian Leaders: Oklahoma's First Statesmen.* Oklahoma City: Oklahoma Historical Society, 1979.

Josephy, Alvin M., Jr. *The Nez Perce Indians and the Opening of the Northwest.* New Haven: Yale University Press, 1965.

Kinnaird, Lawrence, ed. *Spain in the Mississippi Valley, 1765–1794.* 3 vols. *Annual Report of the American Historical Association for the Year 1945.* Washington, D.C.: Government Printing Office, 1946.

LaFlesche, Francis. *Rite of the Chiefs. Thirty-sixth Annual Report of the Bureau of American Ethnology.* Washington, D.C.: Government Printing Office, 1921.

Lamar, Howard R. *The Trader on the American Frontier: Myth's Victim.* College Station: Texas A & M University Press, 1977.

Lottinville, Savoie, ed. *Paul Wilhelm, Duke of Württemberg: Travels in North America, 1822–1824,* tr. W. Robert Nitske. Norman: University of Oklahoma Press, 1973.

———, ed. *Thomas Nuttall's A Journal of Travels into the Arkansas Territory during the Year 1819.* Norman: University of Oklahoma Press, 1980.

Lyon, E. Wilson. *Louisiana in French Diplomacy, 1759–1804.* Norman: University of Oklahoma Press, 1934.

McCandless, Perry G. *A History of Missouri, 1820–1860.* Columbia: University of Missouri Press, 1972.

McDermott, John Francis. *A Glossary of Mississippi Valley French.* St. Louis: Washington University Studies no. 12, 1941.

———. *Private Libraries in Creole St. Louis.* Baltimore: John Hopkins University Press, 1938.

———, ed. *The Early Histories of St. Louis.* St. Louis: St. Louis Historical Documents Foundation, 1952.

———, ed. *The French in the Mississippi Valley.* Urbana: University of Illinois Press, 1965.

———, ed. *Frenchmen and French Ways in the Mississippi Valley.* Urbana: University of Illinois Press, 1969.

———, ed. *The Spanish in the Mississippi Valley, 1762–1804.* Urbana: University of Illinois Press, 1974.

Malone, Dumas. *Jefferson and His Time.* 6 vols. Boston: Little, Brown, 1948–81.

———, ed. *Dictionary of American Biography.* 44 vols. New York: Charles Scribner's Sons, 1933.

Marshall, Thomas M., ed. *The Life and Papers of Frederick Bates.* 2 vols. St. Louis: Missouri Historical Society, 1926.

Mathews, John Joseph. *The Osages: Children of the Middle Waters.* Norman: University of Oklahoma Press, 1961.

Moore, John Preston. *Revolt in Louisiana: The Spanish Occupation, 1766–1770.* Baton Rouge: Louisiana State University Press, 1976.

Musick, James B. *St. Louis as a Fortified Town.* St. Louis: Press of R. F. Miller, 1941.

Nasatir, Abraham P. *Before Lewis and Clark: Documents Illustrating the History of Missouri, 1785–1804.* 2 vols. St. Louis: St. Louis Historical Documents Foundation, 1952.

———. *Borderlands in Retreat.* Albuquerque: University of New Mexico Press, 1976.

———. *Spanish War Vessels on the Mississippi, 1792–1796.* New Haven: Yale University Press, 1968.

Oglesby, Richard E. *Manuel Lisa and the Opening of the Missouri Fur Trade.* Norman: University of Oklahoma Press, 1963.

Phillips, Paul C. *The Fur Trade.* 2 vols. Norman: University of Oklahoma Press, 1961.

Porter, Kenneth Wiggins. *John Jacob Astor: Business Man.* Reprint ed. 2 vols. New York: Russell & Russell, 1966.

Primm, James Neal. *Lion of the Valley: St. Louis, Missouri.* Boulder, Colo.: Pruett Publishing Co., 1981.

Prucha, Francis Paul. *American Indian Policy in the Formative Years: The Indian Trade and Intercourse Acts, 1790–1834.* Cambridge: Harvard University Press, 1962.

————. *The Sword of the Republic: The United States Army on the Frontier, 1783–1846.* New York: Macmillan, 1969.

Report of the Celebration of the Anniversary of the Founding of St. Louis. St. Louis: [printed by the editors of the *Missouri Republican*], 1847.

Rhodes, Irwin S. *The Papers of John Marshall: A Descriptive Calendar.* 2 vols. Norman: University of Oklahoma Press, 1969.

Rothensteiner, John. *History of the Archdiocese of St. Louis.* 2 vols. St. Louis, 1928.

Saum, Lewis O. *The Fur Trader and the Indian.* Seattle: University of Washington Press, 1965.

Scharf, J. Thomas. *History of St. Louis City and County, from Its Earliest Periods to the Present Day.* 2 vols. Philadelphia: Louis H. Everts & Co., 1883.

Sheehan, Bernard W. *Seeds of Extinction: Jeffersonian Philanthropy and the American Indian.* Chapel Hill: University of North Carolina Press, 1973.

Smith, William H., ed. *The St. Clair Papers: Life and Public Services of Arthur St. Clair.* 2 vols. Cincinnati: Robert Clarke & Co., 1882.

Steffen, Jerome O. *Comparative Frontiers: A Proposal for Studying the American West.* Norman: University of Oklahoma Press, 1980.

————. *William Clark: Jeffersonian Man on the Frontier.* Norman: University of Oklahoma Press, 1977.

Stevens, Wayne E. *The Northwest Fur Trade, 1763–1800.* Urbana: University of Illinois Studies in Social Sciences, 1928.

Stoddard, Amos. *Sketches, Historical and Descriptive of Louisiana.* Philadelphia: Mathew Carey, 1812.

Terrell, John Upton. *Zebulon Pike: The Life and Times of an Adventurer.* New York: Weybright and Talley, 1968.

Thwaites, Rueben Gold, ed. *Original Journals of the Lewis and Clark Expedition, 1804–1806.* 7 vols. New York: Dodd, Mead & Co., 1904–5.

Wade, Richard C. *The Urban Frontier.* Paperback ed. Chicago: University of Chicago Press, 1964.

V. ARTICLES

Atherton, Lewis. "The Santa Fe Trader as Mercantile Capitalist." *Missouri Historical Review* 77 (Oct. 1982), 1–12.

Auge, Thomas. "The Life and Times of Julien Dubuque." *The Palimpsest* 57 (Jan./Feb. 1976).

Carter, Clarence E. "The Burr-Wilkinson Intrigue in St. Louis." *Missouri Historical Society Bulletin* 10 (July 1954).

Davis, Ronald L. F. "Community and Conflict in Pioneer Saint Louis, Missouri." *Western Historical Quarterly* 10 (July 1979).

Douglas, Walter B. "Jean Gabriel Cerré—a Sketch." In 1903 *Transactions of the Illinois State Historical Society,* Springfield, Ill. (1904).

Ewers, John C. "'Chiefs from the Missouri and Mississippi' and Peale's Silhouettes of 1806." *Smithsonian Journal of History* 1 (1966).

Fisher, Robert L. "The Treaties of Portage des Sioux." *Mississippi Valley Historical Review* 19 (Mar. 1933).

Foley, William E. "The American Territorial System: Missouri's Experience." *Missouri Historical Review* 65 (July 1971).

———. "James A. Wilkinson: Territorial Governor." *Missouri Historical Society Bulletin* 25 (Oct. 1968).

Foley, William E., and Charles David Rice. "The Return of the Mandan Chief." *Montana, the Magazine of Western History* 29 (July 1979).

———. "Visiting the President: An Exercise in Jeffersonian Indian Diplomacy." *American West* 16 (Nov./Dec. 1979).

Foreman, Grant, ed. "Notes of Auguste Chouteau on the Boundaries of Various Indian Nations." *Glimpses of the Past* (Missouri Historical Society) 7 (Oct.–Dec. 1940).

"Founding of the First Chouteau Trading Post in Oklahoma at Salina, Mayes County." *Chronicles of Oklahoma* 24 (Winter 1946–47).

Fox, John Sharpless, ed. "Narrative of . . . Jean Baptiste Perrault." *Historical Collections and Researches Made by the Michigan Pioneer and Historical Society* 37 (1910).

Goodwin, Cardinal. "A Larger View of the Yellowstone Expedition, 1819–1820." *Mississippi Valley Historical Review* 4 (Dec. 1917).

Gregg, Kate L. "Building of the First American Fort West of the Mississippi." *Missouri Historical Review* 30 (July 1936).

———. "The History of Fort Osage." *Missouri Historical Review* 34 (July 1940).

———. "The War of 1812 on the Missouri Frontier." *Missouri Historical Review* 33 (Oct. 1938, Jan. and Apr. 1939).

Hagan, William T. "The Sauk and Fox Treaty of 1804." *Missouri Historical Review* 51 (Oct. 1956).

Hall, F. R. "Genêt's Western Intrigue, 1793–1794." *Journal of the Illinois State Historical Society* 21 (1928).

"Index to Spanish Judicial Records of Louisiana." *Louisiana Historical Quarterly* 8 (Apr. 1925) and 11 (July 1928).

Isern, Thomas D., ed. "Exploration and Diplomacy: George Champlin Sibley's Report to William Clark, 1811." *Missouri Historical Review* 73 (Oct. 1978).

Liljegren, Ernest R. "Jacobinism in Spanish Louisiana, 1792–1797." *Louisiana Historical Quarterly* 22 (Jan. 1939).

Loos, John L. "William Clark's Part in the Preparation of the Lewis and Clark Expedition." *Missouri Historical Society Bulletin* 10 (July 1954).

McDermott, John Francis. "The Battle of St. Louis, 26 May 1780." *Missouri Historical Society Bulletin* 36 (Apr. 1980).

———. "The Exclusive Trade Privileges of Maxent, Laclède and Company." *Missouri Historical Review* 29 (July 1935).

———. "Laclède and the Chouteaus: Fantasies and Facts." Unpublished manuscript in McDermott Mississippi Valley Research Collection.

———. "Paincourt and Poverty." *Mid-America* 5 (Apr. 1934).

———. "Pierre Laclède and the Chouteaus." *Missouri Historical Society Bulletin* 21 (July 1965).

"Minutes of the Meeting of the Board of Directors of the Oklahoma Historical Society, Oct. 23, 1944." *Chronicles of Oklahoma* 22 (Winter 1944–45).

Morris, Wayne. "Auguste Pierre Chouteau, Merchant Prince at the Three Forks of the Arkansas." *Chronicles of Oklahoma* 48 (Summer 1970).

———. "Traders and Factories on the Arkansas Frontier, 1805–1822." *Arkansas Historical Quarterly* 28 (Spring 1969).

Nasatir, Abraham P. "The Anglo-Spanish Frontier in the Illinois Country during the American Revolution, 1779–1783." *Journal of the Illinois State Historical Society* 21 (Oct. 1928).

———. "The Anglo-Spanish Frontier on the Upper Mississippi, 1786–1796." *Iowa Journal of History and Politics* 29 (Apr. 1931).

———. "Ducharme's Invasion of Missouri: An Incident in the Anglo-Spanish Rivalry for the Indian Trade of Upper Louisiana." *Missouri Historical Review* 24 (Oct. 1930).

———. "The Formation of the Missouri Company." *Missouri Historical Review* 25 (Oct. 1939).

———. "Jacques Clamorgan, Colonial Promoter of the Northern Border of New Spain." *New Mexico Historical Review* 17 (Apr. 1942).

"Oath of Allegiance to Spain, November 19, 1769." *Louisiana Historical Quarterly* 4 (Apr. 1921).

Phelps, Dawson A. "The Tragic Death of Meriwether Lewis." *William and Mary Quarterly,* 3rd ser. 13 (July 1956).

Richardson, Lemont K. "Private Land Claims in Missouri." *Missouri Historical Review* 50 (Jan., Apr., July 1956).

Rickey, Don, Jr. "The British-Indian Attack on St. Louis, May 26, 1780." *Missouri Historical Review* 55 (Oct. 1960).

VI. THESES AND DISSERTATIONS

Barnhart, Warren Lynn. "The Letterbooks of Charles Gratiot, Fur Trader: The Nomadic Years, 1769–1797." Ph.D. diss., St. Louis University, 1971.

Burns, Charles F. "Auguste and Pierre Chouteau, Fur Trading Magnates." M.A. thesis, Washington University, St. Louis, 1932.

Foley, William E. "Territorial Politics in Frontier Missouri, 1804–1820." Ph.D. diss., University of Missouri, 1967.

Holt, Glen E. "The Shaping of St. Louis, 1763–1860." Ph.D. diss., University of Chicago, 1975.

Melom, Halvor Gordon. "The Economic Growth of St. Louis, 1803–1846." Ph.D. diss., University of Missouri, 1947.

Nasatir, Abraham P. "The Chouteaus and the Indian Trade of the West." M.A. thesis, University of California, Berkeley, 1922.

———. "Indian Trade and Diplomacy in the Spanish Illinois, 1763–1792." Ph.D. diss., University of California, Berkeley, 1926.

Rowse, Edward F. "Auguste and Pierre Chouteau." Ph.D. diss., Washington University, St. Louis, 1936.

Tevebaugh, John L. "Merchant on the Western Frontier: William Morrison of Kaskaskia, 1790–1837." Ph.D. diss., University of Illinois, 1962.

INDEX

The following abbreviations are used: AC—Auguste Chouteau,
PC—Pierre Chouteau; PLL—Pierre de Laclède Liguest

A NOTE ON THE AUTHORS

WILLIAM E. FOLEY was born in Kansas City, Mo., and received his Ph.D. from the University of Missouri in 1967. He has been a member of the history department of Central Missouri State University since 1966, and in 1980 received a Distinguished Faculty Award from the university's College of Arts and Sciences. He was also co-recipient, with C. David Rice, of two writing awards: in 1978 from the State Historical Society of Missouri, and in 1979 from the Montana Historical Society. His previous publications include *A History of Missouri, 1673–1820* (1971) and, with Perry McCandless, *Missouri: Then and Now* (1976).

C. DAVID RICE was born in Atlanta, Ga., and received his Ph.D. from Emory University in 1973. He has been a member of the history department of Central Missouri State University since 1973, and in 1981 received a Faculty Achievement Award from its College of Arts and Sciences. He is the author of a number of journal articles on the subject of western history. This is his first book.

Huthiel Cabanne